3000 800014 05435
St. Louis Community College

E V

WITHDRAWN

 St. Louis Community College

Forest Park
Florissant Valley
Meramec

Instructional Resources
St. Louis, Miss

D1071911

Assessment in Higher Education

Assessment in Higher Education

Second Edition

JOHN HEYWOOD
Trinity College, The University of Dublin

JOHN WILEY & SONS

Chichester · New York · Brisbane · Toronto · Singapore

Copyright © 1977, 1989 by John Wiley & Sons Ltd.

All rights reserved.

No part of this book may be reproduced by any means,
or transmitted, or translated into a machine language
without the written permission of the publisher

Library of Congress Cataloging-in-Publication Data:

Heywood, John, 1930–
    Assessment in higher education / John Heywood.—2nd ed.
        p.   cm.
    ISBN 0 471 92032 0
    1. Universities and colleges—Examinations.   2. College teaching—Evaluation.
    3. Education, Higher—Evaluation. 4. Education, Higher—Aims and objectives
    I. Title.
    LB2366.H49   1988
    378′.166—dc19   88-14423
                                                                                 CIP

British Library Cataloguing in Publication Data:

Heywood, John, 1930–
    Assessment in higher education.—2nd ed.
    1. Higher education institutions. Students. Academic achievement.
    Assessment.   I. Title
    378′.1664

    ISBN 0 471 92032 0

Filmset by Bath Typesetting Ltd, Bath, Avon
Printed and Bound in Great Britain by Anchor Press Ltd, Tiptree, Essex

For
Pauline

Contents

scripts—Question design and the design of essay examinations—Question spotting: perceptions of assessment and performance—Student perceptions of essay writing—Feedback—Short-answer questions—Open-book examinations—The timing of examinations: prior notice (seen) questions

Preface

When the first edition of this book was published in 1977, while the problems of testing and assessment in respect of reliability and validity were well understood, assessment of students remained an afterthought of the educational process. It was felt that tests and examinations had a backwash effect on student learning, but exactly how that effect could be used to enhance it was little investigated. My purpose in the first edition was to explore the relationship between assessment, instruction and learning, and that continues to be the purpose of this edition.

I argued that assessment had to be seen as an integral part of the learning process. The objectives of assessment, learning and instruction were the same. Thus the instructional procedure used by a teacher in higher education had to be selected so as to achieve the objectives of instruction, and at the same time the assessment techniques had also to be a valid test of those same objectives. The consequences of this view for class and course design were profound, for the time required for the completion of the units of instruction and their assessment determined what could be accomplished in a course. In consequence, the task of selecting a few significant aims and objectives was of great importance in the design of assessment and instruction. This task, which, following E. J. Furst, I called 'screening', depended on the teacher in higher education evolving an epistemological basis for his work together with a defensible theory of learning as a foundation for the attainment of those aims and objectives thought to be significant. The many sources of aims and objectives were discussed and the activity of instruction and assessment design was shown to be complex. In the closing chapters it was argued that there was an obligation on teachers to evaluate their teaching and that the model of illuminative evaluation provided a way forward.

Much has happened since then. A great deal has been written on forms of assessment other than written tests, on anxiety and tension resulting from testing and instruction, objectives, teaching and learning styles, and the ways in which examinations and tests influence learning, which all has a bearing on the activity of screening. Nevertheless, this work has been done by a small band of individuals and not on an institution-wide basis.

At the same time, the managers of higher education are calling for institutional approaches to the problems of teaching and learning. In Britain the recommendations of a committee of the Committee of Vice-Chancellors and Principals chaired by Professor P. A. Reynolds on external examining have been acted on. These call for the assessment of staff (appraisal), the assessment of teachers by students (student evaluation), and the review of departments. In at least one university ideas gained from the accreditation techniques used in the United States have been seriously considered.

The effectiveness with which such judgements can be made depends on the willingness of institutions and the individuals within them to be clear about the 'significant' aims and objectives which they wish to obtain. Thus the model of assessment discussed in this book is also that for institutional evaluation.

In the first edition it was argued that no single technique of assessment could be expected to evaluate even a few significant objectives. For this reason, a multiple-objective approach to teaching and learning had to be taken to the design of the curriculum, its assessment and instruction. This point is made in the recent report of the Governors of the United States on the assessment of quality in higher education. They believe that the assessment of institutions of higher education and the individuals within them should be multi-strategy in approach.

Ultimately the success of this newfound movement in assessment and teaching in higher education will depend on the seriousness with which institutions take the remit and the ways they find to encourage teachers not only to be good research workers but good researchers of their own classroom practice. For this, the teachers themselves will need to become practised in the reflective thinking about the art of their teaching or, as it is commonly called today, self-assessment. This book is intended to provide a basis for practice and reflection on assessment in higher education.

Acknowledgements

I am especially grateful to Dr Georgine Loacker of Alverno College, Milwaukee, for her continuing support of my work over the years. I am also grateful to the President of Alverno and her colleagues for the welcome which they extended to my wife and myself when we visited the College. Their introductions led to encouragement and help from Dr Russel Edgerton, President of the American Association for Higher Education and his colleagues. Dr Clifford Adelman of the Office of Educational Research and Improvement, US Department of Education, provided a continuous flow of 'fugitive literature' as well as introductions to other persons working in the field.

My friends Dr James Freeman of the University of Manchester and Dr Seamus McGuinness of the University of Dublin, who helped me through the first edition, once again came to my support. I am grateful to them for their many helpful suggestions, as I am also to the publishers' unknown referee.

Finally, I would like to thank the University of Dublin, Trinity College, for the grant which enabled me to visit the United States and the Dean of the Faculty of Arts, Dr Patrick Kelly, for all his help.

CHAPTER 1

Assessment in Higher Education: An Introduction

ATTENDING TO ASSESSMENT IN HIGHER EDUCATION: AN HISTORICAL NOTE

When I wrote the first edition of this book in 1977 the title of the opening chapter was inspired by a weekly satire on British television called *Not so much a Programme, More a Way of Life*, for that is what I believed examinations and testing in higher education to be. There was very little interest in Britain in examinations, yet, because they grade individuals, they were and are probably the most important activity in education. Thus in order to create interest in the problem of assessment I began with the following statement, which was typical of the situation at that time:

> 'Senate approved the syllabus for our new degree course at its last meeting. X will act as Director of Studies and co-ordinate the timetable for the new degree (Head of Department, April 1986).
>
> Please let me have your questions for the Part 1 examination (of the new degree course) by the end of next week at the latest (Director of Studies, February 1987).
>
> Hell, I'd forgotten all about the exam. Let's see what I set in this course in the other degree programme last year ... (Teacher, February 1987).

And the Director of Studies will probably get his questions. The students will be sensible enough to look up the questions set by the lecturer in previous examinations in similar courses, and with a bit more luck, few will fail. Examinations are the great afterthought of the educational process. Most new courses are set up without one thought being given to the methods of examining. The examination is remembered as a necessary evil when the Course Director asks for the annual set of questions and subsequently gets the teacher to vet the printer's proofs of the examination paper. Some teachers use examinations as their objectives (Wiseman, 1961), and some go so far as to give the students the answers in thinly disguised formats. It might be argued in the absence of an understanding of their purposes that this is a step forward, since there is at least a semblance of a relationship between assessment and teaching. Just occasionally someone breaks away from set patterns and involves him- or herself in the additional hard graft which worthwhile innovations in assessment seem to demand.'

Had I substituted 'testing' for 'examinations' I believe that the same or similar paragraph would have been true of the United States. Instead of 'essay' examinations at the end of the year the example would have been informed by the stereotype of multiple-choice tests and quizzes. These were (and generally are still) not common in Britain. There is a great hostility to objective testing, despite its widespread and successful use in medicine, science and technology. It is for this reason that Chapter 12 on objective tests is relatively long in that the arguments for objective tests are set out in detail and recent developments in their analysis described. They are likely to be increasingly used as computer-assisted instruction develops.

At the time that I wrote the first edition the use of the term 'assessment' was relatively novel in Britain. I had wanted to use the phrase 'control of learning' in the title of the book for the reason that I held (and continue to hold) that, if we are to improve learning, we will have to improve the methods of testing and learning we use. They will have to become intimately related. Unfortunately, a book of that title was published just after I had completed the manuscript. For this reason, I used the term 'assessment', which I did not define except by implication.

Until the 1960s the term 'assessment', when used in Britain, applied to the assessment of school pupils for special units which catered for children with special social and psychological needs. Its usage in this way derived from the pioneer of intelligence testing, Alfred Binet, who, in his work in Paris, was concerned with the assessment of mentally retarded children. However, during the 1950s various universities and colleges in higher education (or, more correctly, various individuals in higher education) reacted against the single terminal examination at the end of the year. They felt that it was an inadequate measure of a student's performance, which they believed should be assessed on several occasions during the student's academic career. They called assessment of this type 'continuous'. It was not perceived to be formal, formative assessment (see Chapter 4). Later, in 1969, a major conference sponsored jointly by the Association of University Teachers and the Committee of Vice-Chancellors and Principals of the universities was called 'The Assessment of Academic Performance' (CVCP, 1969). Given this interest in assessment in Britain, I felt that the title was self-explanatory, although some critics did not.

If it was self-explanatory, then it certainly is not now. A study of American literature shows that assessment has a variety of meanings, so it is necessary to examine these in order to resight the parameters of this study. Unfortunately, that is not the only problem of terminology, for, what do we mean by higher education?

When I first chose the title of this book it related in Britain to universities and a limited number of institutions in the public sector called polytechnics, which were able to offer degrees recognized by the State. This is a very limited definition when compared with the definition given to higher education in the United States. These differences often give rise to misleading comparisons between the American and English systems of education.

Its use in that way in Britain arose from the fact that, until 1987, the sector which coped with technician, craftsman and operative qualifications which was financed by the State through Local Education Authorities (LEAs) was called the 'Further Education' sector. Within that sector courses were defined as non-advanced and advanced (DES, 1987b). The advanced courses embraced higher-level technician studies as well as degree-level programmes validated by an officially approved validating authority called the Council for National Academic Awards (CNAA).

Thus when the Society for Research into Higher Education was founded in 1965 it embraced only research done in universities and those parts of the state (public) sector which undertook degree programmes. The activities of the Society reflected the interests of its members, a small body of researchers and university administrators who had been encouraged by the research undertaken for the Robbins Committee on Higher Education (Robbins, 1963) as well as the recommendations of the Hale (1964) and Brynmor-Jones (1964) committees on university teaching methods.

At the same time, appointments were made to posts in higher education *per se*. Most of them were short-period fellowships which undertook research in the areas of residence, methods of teaching, and university examinations. Cox (1967) (whose paper has been much quoted) and this writer were the two appointees in the area of examinations. Nationally, there was very much more interest in teaching methods than examinations, and it is significant that those who made the appointments thought that research on examinations should be conducted independently of the curriculum and teaching. It is a view that continues to be widely held. The picture with which this chapter opened was intended to illustrate this divorce. A primary purpose of this book is therefore to demonstrate that the design of assessment procedures cannot be carried out independently of either the design of instruction or that of the curriculum.

Although there was little interest in research on examinations in comparison with teaching methods and policy, the Society was involved in the publication of two issues of *Universities Quarterly*, which concentrated on topics related to assessment. In the first (published in 1967), in addition to the paper by Cox, another article questioned the twenty assumptions about examinations listed in Table 1 (Oppenheim *et al.*, 1967). They wrote:

'Empirical testing is possible for most of these assumptions, but it will take a long time if it is done at all. In the meantime, the rationality of the examination system could surely be enhanced if universities were to decide which of these assumptions, here made explicit, they wish to maintain and which to abandon'.

Twenty years later despite many innovations, the position was much the same, with the exception that universities worldwide were being forced to explicitly state their views on assessment. Similarly, the belief expressed by Ager and Weltman (1967) in the same issue 'that a variety of techniques should be used in the university examinations, such techniques being chosen according to the functions that the examination performs' is now generally accepted. Whereas in the past the concern was with the reliability of examinations, interest has now begun to focus on validity and the design of valid measures, especially in the area of professional competency. The meaning of the terms 'validity' and 'reliability' was the subject of scrutiny (Hammersley, 1987). Assessment centre techniques, developed for the selection of managers in industry and commerce, illustrates the new approach to validity in the design of assessment instruments, as do the competency-based approaches to learning used in medicine (Freeman and Byrne, 1976).

Table 1. Twenty assumptions underlying the use of university examinations listed and discussed by Oppenheim *et al.* (1967). (Reproduced by kind permission of the Editor of *Universities Quarterly*)

1. The assumption that university examinations can include some so-called imponderables such as 'quality of mind', 'independent critical thinking', 'breadth', etc. in their assessment.
2. The assumption that 'quality' of academic performance is rateable on a single continuum from first-class honours to failure.
3. Whereas many courses include a good deal of practical work, and a few approach some type of apprenticeship training scheme or sandwich course, we usually pay less attention to those aspects of the course when examining.
4. To some extent it is assumed that examination performance is a mock–real life performance.
5. The assumption that each examinee should have individual responsibility for his own performance; we do not expect collaboration or teamwork, no matter how common this may be in real life performance.
6. The assumption that a student who fails has only himself to blame, for not working hard enough, or for being stupid, or in some other way.
7. The assumption that the proper place for examinations is at the end of certain courses—not later or sooner.
8. The assumption that university teachers should also be university examiners and university selectors.
9. The assumptions about the impartiality of examination.
10. The assumption that the university should have the sole authority to examine at this level.
11. The assumption that the use of external examiners prevents bias.
12. The assumption that forced regurgitation of knowledge under stress is predictive of future performance.
13. Assumptions concerning mental growth and development and the acquisition of an 'educated mind' influence the type and timing of exams.
14. The assumption that pressure is required.
15. The assumption that anxiety is necessary.
16. The assumption that examination results should be distributed in a certain way.
17. We are forced to make, and then retract, all kinds of assumptions about the comparability of degrees from university to university and from country to country.
18. The assumption of the need for uniformity in undergraduate exams: all students in a given year group must pass the same examination paper, and we do not allow examinations to be tailored to individual needs.
19. The assumption that 'learning is to be valued for its own sake' and not merely as a preparation for career and financial gain.
20. The assumption that the outside world wants the results of university examinations or takes much notice of them.

A second symposium published in 1971 dealt with the problem of 'wastage', as it is known in Britain or 'drop-out' in the United States. Apart from a review of research on wastage (Heywood, 1971a), several of the papers were much concerned with the pool of ability in schools which, it was claimed, was not being utilized (for example, E. H. Cox).

These papers showed that wastage could not be understood simply as a function of ability. There were many psychological and social factors which could contribute to performance. For example, some students were found to be temperamentally unsuited to the terminal written examinations which characterized the British system at that time. Others might, for a variety of reasons have chosen the wrong course and given the virtual impossibility of being able to change courses the student was left with no alternative but to leave higher education.

The impact of college life on performance is, as the causal models in Chapter 2 show, complex. Apart from the internal structure of the institution the influences of the sub-system of higher education in which it operates and the system of education more generally are profound. The understanding of and the meanings given to performance are functions of the sub-system observed and depend in no small way on the policies made in respect of participation in the system.

However, having observed the failure of prescriptive approaches to policy problem-solving which treated the sub-educational systems separately, Martin Trow (1974) and this writer in a later report to the Council of Europe advocated open-system studies of the educational system as a whole (see note 2 of Chapter 2).

Policy making should be influenced by a thorough understanding of the social mechanisms at work. For example a highly selective system of higher education will cause the curriculum in secondary (high) schools to be geared toward the entry requirements of higher education. In its turn the system of higher education will both influence and be influenced by the educational requirements of jobs and more particularly the professions. A discernible 'curriculum drift' in which low status institutions emulated high status institutions (e.g. Ivy League and Oxbridge) was noted in both the UK and the US in the sixties and seventies. One outcome in selective systems of higher education is pressure on students in their second-level studies which may cause some of them to experience difficulties with learning. Thus student performance in higher education cannot be isolated from a student's past experience of education and particularly as it caused that student to prepare for his or her future (Figure 1). For this reason, the mechanisms of selection into higher education and their dependence on second-level education are of considerable importance not only to policy makers but to the institution, for they inform teachers' views of what should be studied in higher education and how it should be taught. This applies equally to choice of institution and subject in higher education (Kealy and Rockel, 1987). By implication, as will be demonstrated in the paragraphs on selection which follow, there can be no absolute definition of higher education related to content, since what can be taught not only relates to

6

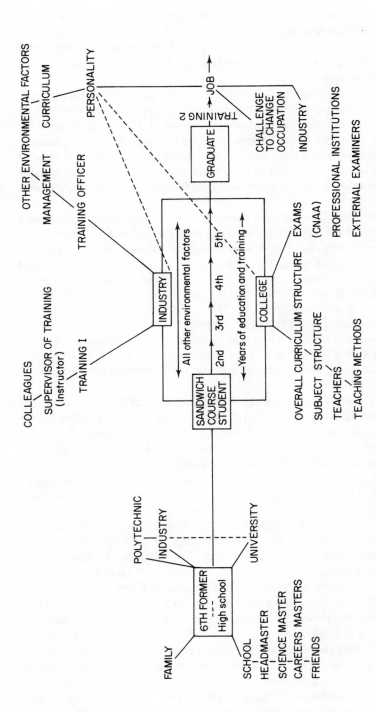

Figure 1. A descriptive model of a subsystem of higher education which shows the forces acting on a sandwich (co-operative) course student in a College of Advanced Technology or polytechnic in Britain. (See Chapter 2 for a discussion of this figure.) (From Heywood, J. (1974c). *New Patterns of Courses and New Degree Courses*, Strasbourg: Council of Europe)

the aims of education as perceived in a particular culture but also to the level attained at input to the system.

SELECTION FOR HIGHER EDUCATION AND THE SYSTEM OF EDUCATION

The institutions which, when grouped together comprise the higher education sector vary from one country to another. However, as access to a system increases, more comparability is discernible between the systems of different countries. Within the English-speaking world it is possible to contrast the relatively open-access system of the United States with the binary systems operating in Australia, Britain and Ireland.[1] At one extreme all post-compulsory education is higher education: at the other, only the universities offer such education. In a few short paragraphs it is not possible to consider in any detail the problems involved in comparing the educational system of one country with another. The focus here will be on the system of grading and some of its implications.

The structure of two school systems in relation to degree studies is shown in Figure 2. Within these systems there are important differences between the age at which pupils transfer from primary to secondary school and the compulsory age of leaving school to further study for examinations leading to admission to university. In one system, the Irish, the period of second-level education is five years and in the other, the English, it is seven.

In both countries the curriculum is largely determined from the top down and not from the bottom up. That is, the requirements for higher education govern the subjects which high-achieving students take in their second-level education. In Ireland, admission to higher education is controlled by a points system. The Leaving Certificate examination may be taken at two levels— higher and ordinary. Each subject in each level is graded and each grade carries a certain number of points, the highest number being awarded for a grade A at the higher level. The points are summed for the purposes of admission to the institutions of higher education. The number of points required is governed by the number of places available in particular departments in particular institutions and their departments (subject faculties). Entry into some subjects will require a very large number of points (for example, medicine), where the number of students is strictly regulated. Some subject areas may specify high points in particular subjects—for example, in mathematics and modern languages. Others may require additional tests (for example, music and art) where skill in these subjects is demonstrated by a practical exposition or a portfolio of products.

Generally speaking, a student will pursue at least six subjects in the Leaving Certificate, of which a minimum of four are likely to be studied at the higher level if entry to university is required. The system is very similar to the Scottish system, which is of this same broad entry type. With one or two exceptions, a student will have pursued studies in these same subjects in the three-year junior cycle, and have obtained a pass in them at the Intermediate Certificate level.

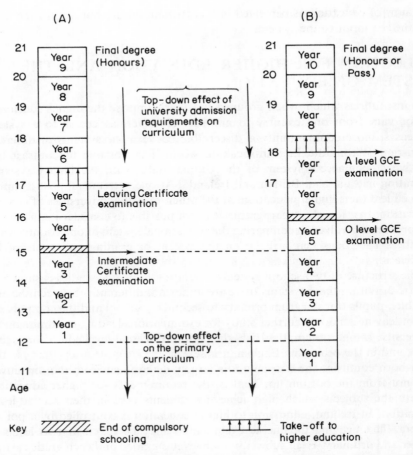

Figure 2. Simplified model of two systems of education ((A) = Ireland, (B) = England) showing location of public examinations and effect of university admission requirements on school curricula

This broad entry requirement to the institutions of higher education in Ireland is in contrast to that in England, which is highly selective. Here, the subject departments (faculties, schools) make quite specific demands on the student. For example, a student will be required to pass in three subjects (in the Advanced level of the General Certificate of Education (GCE A level)) which are closely related to the subject he or she wishes to take at university. The grades required in each subject will be specified. There is no such thing as a liberal arts degree, in which the student takes a wide range of subjects while accumulating credits en route. The student sets out to study one or two subjects to honours level, and the results of his or her examination are published as a single grade. The same is true of the Irish universities. There is, however, one difference, and that is that many students take two subjects (variously known as 'double honours', 'double or joint major', or in the University of Dublin, 'two-subject moderatorship'), whereas in England the majority take a single subject. The argument against the two-subject pattern is simply that students find that the lecturers in specific subjects make the same demands on them as they do on students taking the single subject to honours level. This makes it difficult for them to obtain a first-class honours. The problem is intensified by the fact that the results from the two subjects are combined into one grade. A first-class performance in one subject with a lower performance in the other is not reported as such, even though the result of the latter modifies the former, to the detriment of the student. Most students believe that their chances of a good grade are better in a single-subject course.

Within such a course all the topics studied relate to that subject. These courses are therefore a professional preparation where the students obtain the knowledge and skills thought to be essential to performance as, say, a geographer or a historian. This is not to say that a geographer will not learn statistics or a physicist mathematics. In the case of the latter the course requirement for mathematics will be relatively large: the same is true of engineering.

It is the studies which lead up to these courses that are of prime interest, for not only do they govern the take-off level in higher education (more especially in science and the modern languages) but they also exert an influence on the subjects taken by students throughout the school curriculum, for what has to be achieved in school is determined by the take-off level. Because the approaches and standards achieved in the second level curriculum in these two models differ, the take-off levels are also different. Studies in Australia, where the states do not operate a common system of examining, have shown that each system influences the school curriculum in a different way. How the effects of selection on the curriculum can be minimized has been the subject of a major study by McGaw (1984).

Because the age when children may leave school differs by one year (15 and 16 respectively) the standards of knowledge obtaining in the longer cycle must necessarily be higher than those in the shorter one among the comparable groups of high-achieving students. Therefore a Leaving Certificate pass at the lower level is not much different to a reasonable grade in the GCE at the Ordinary level (GCE O level). However, the Leaving Certificate is designed to test a much wider range of achievement than that of the GCE Ordinary level, and this is obtained by means of the two levels with the same certificate examination. In England a separate examination is used for this purpose, called the Certificate of Secondary Education (CSE) (until 1988). This examination was originally designed as a terminal examination for those who left school at 15. In 1988 the O level and CSE were combined into a single examination for the 16 year-old group, to be called the General Certificate of Secondary Education (GCSE).

These examinations are set by independent examining boards. Those concerned with the GCE have their origins in the universities, who established them to set their examinations for matriculation, that is, for entry into university. These, together with the CSE boards, have joined together in association to provide the new GCSE examination. It will be seen that there are some similarities with the work of the College Entrance Examination Board, the Educational Testing Service (ETS) and the American College Testing Program in the United States. However, there is no equivalent to the Scholastic Aptitude Test, the similar test from ACT or the Australian Scholastic Aptitude Test, which are designed to be independent of the teaching in the school curriculum and to assess general abilities in key skill areas. The College Board's tests in specific subjects are often similar in style to the examinations set in the Ordinary and Advanced levels of the GCE and the Leaving Certificate Examination in Ireland.

All students in British and Irish universities have to be matriculated. In England, separate matriculation examinations are no longer set, and the GCE is used for this purpose. In recent years universities have developed regulations for mature matriculation which allow older students to enter university without qualifications. Interviews are used and special note is taken of the candidate's experience. For the majority of applicants who are school leavers the *minimum* requirement for matriculation is three passes at the Advanced and one at the Ordinary level, or two passes at the Advanced and three at the Ordinary level. However, this is an entirely theoretical minimum, for, in practice, in many subjects the number of applicants exceeds that of places. Because of the pecking order between institutions, there is, as in the United States, an admissions market: institutions vie with each other to get high-grade students and the latter compete for places in the universities of their choice. In both Britain and Ireland admissions are handled by central offices established for this purpose.

The Oxbridge (and US Ivy League) universities are criticized by some academics, because they cream off the more able students and also take more students from the public (fee-paying) schools like Eton and Winchester. There has been (and remains) a considerable alignment between socio-economic class, intelligence, school and higher education institution attended (DES, 1987a).

Each year there is a well-published scramble for places. Popularity and ease of entry ratings are given in the national newspapers, as are the results of students' final examinations, all of which serve to illustrate the importance of grades. Because of this competition, no student would apply with only one O level of the GCE: most intent on university would have taken between eight and ten. Their subject choice will be balanced in the direction of the studies which they wish to take in the sixth form.

It is argued that the top-down approach creates early specialization but, given that most students will take a relatively large number of O level subjects, it is difficult to defend this view when they can be equated with the Leaving Certificate examinations in other countries, if the evaluation of the Leaving Certificate in Ireland by Madaus and MacNamara (1970) is anything to go by. (*NB*: This report is disputed by the Inspectorate who set the examinations.) Even so, a new level has been introduced into the English system called the 'As' level. This is intended to cause a broadening of the sixth-form curriculum and to be equivalent to half an A level taken over two years. Two As levels will be equivalent to one A level. Some authorities have suggested that a more fundamental reform is required, such as the introduction of the International Baccalaureate (Saul, 1987).

When they enter the fifth and sixth years of study their specialism in three or four subjects means that these subjects can be studied in considerable depth. Thus the A level examination of the GCE will be equivalent to the examinations taken at the end of the first-year (and sometimes second-year) university study in many other countries. It is for this reason that the English system is so efficient and attractive to politicians to maintain. The take-off level is high and the students already have experience of the 'standards' of university education, even if they are not adjusted to the freedom which goes with university study or the distance from their personal lives at which university staff operate when compared with their teachers in school. Although the drop-out rates vary considerably between the subjects they average out at around 11% at the end of the first year and at no more than 2% in finals, and these are among the lowest drop-out rates in the world (Heywood, 1971a).

The debate about the relative merits of broad and narrow based entry examinations to university in England and Wales is far from over. In June 1988 the Secretary of State for Education rejected the findings of committee established to examine the senior cycle of secondary education which recommended that five rather than three subjects should be the norm (Higginson, 1988). Theoretically it should be possible to test the validity of this thesis. In 1987 regulations of the European Economic Community made it possible for students from Ireland to attend university in England. Because of the much lower costs for study in the UK which these regulations entailed some 1000 students from the Republic were accepted for courses of study in Northern Ireland and England. There exists, therefore, a group of students with broad based entry qualifications who can be compared with students in the same courses whose entry qualifications would be regarded as narrow.

Because of their significance in the educational system, the A level examinations, like the Scholastic Aptitude Test in the United States have been the subject of much research. There has, for example, been continuing interest in the relation between performance in them and in university final examinations (Heywood, 1971a; Petch, 1961). The Examination Boards have established their own research units and have given much attention to the comparability between subjects as examined by the different boards. They have also made developments in assessment techniques including multiple-strategy approaches. Because of the standards obtained, they may be treated as examinations in higher education. For this reason, several of them are described in this book.

Not every student will take eight or more O levels. Some may taken only one or two together with other subjects in the CSE. It is expected that around 60% of the age group will take the new GCSE.

Apart from the universities and polytechnics the system of education in

England presents a confusing picture to the outsider. In the past, students in grammar schools stayed on at school for sixth-form studies and those in the secondary modern schools generally left these institutions at the age of 15. They could go on for full- or part-time study in general education or vocational courses in institutions called technical colleges, which belonged to the further education sector. They are now called Colleges of Further Education, and some are embraced within institutions of higher education. Many of the courses which they offer would be regarded as higher-education programmes in the United States and the higher-technician courses would be equivalent to US engineering technology degrees. Technician courses are validated by the Business and Technician Education Council (BTEC), which has introduced new approaches to assessment and course design (BTEC, 1986).

When the school system was reorganized so that most of the State schools became comprehensive (high schools), some new institutions were created. These were called sixth-form colleges. In some respects, these colleges, and the curriculum in them, corresponds with the Community Colleges in the United States.[2]

This description is oversimplified. Comparisons are difficult, but it is clear that much of what is done in assessment in the further education sector outside the universities and polytechnics is relevant to the general problem of assessment in systems of higher education, where there is relatively open access. A broad rather than a narrow definition of higher education is therefore taken in this book.

MEANINGS OF ASSESSMENT, EVALUATION AND APPRAISAL IN HIGHER EDUCATION

Much more attention seems to be paid to assessment and its many forms in the United States than in Britain. In a recent review of assessment and its meaning in higher education in the United States, Hartle (1986) said that the term 'assessment' has many meanings (uses), of which six are commonly deployed in the United States. He suggested that in the United States the most common meaning of assessment refers to State-mandated requirements to evaluate academic programmes for quality, and gives as examples of indicators of quality the use of testing for counselling and placement, admission into other areas of higher education and the use of licensing examinations, as, for example, in teaching and nursing.

Linked to this objective for assessment is the view of some State legislators that institutions should be rewarded for the performances of their students against established criteria which relate to learning in general education in a major field of study and satisfaction with experience of education obtained. At the University of Tennessee the Performance Funding Program of the State of Tennessee has allowed departments to relate learning to curriculum offerings in order for them to benefit from the university's budgetary process (Ewell, 1984, 1986).

For about half of the academic programs, nationally standardized tests are used. However, forty-five departmental faculties have developed their own examinations for their majors. These are of the comprehensive type described in Chapter 13. Banta and Schneider (1988), who have evaluated this development, report that while the initial motivation to undertake test development was the promise of a financial supplement faculty soon formulated their own rationale for proceeding with the task. They report that the process of test development in many cases produced benefits for faculty and students which were independent of student performance on the test.

In Australia, Britain, Ireland and Norway binary systems are in operation. The universities, by virtue of the Royal Charters which they possess, set their own examinations and award degrees on the basis of the marks obtained in those examinations. External examiners are used to judge that the standards as between institutions and the subjects offered are comparable (see Chapter 2). In general, only those students who obtain high grades in these examinations can obtain grants for full-time study in masters' and doctoral programmes.

In Britain it is mandatory on the local education authorities to pay the course fees of anyone accepted by the universities as an undergraduate. This also applies to applicants resident in the other countries of the European Economic Community. A means-tested system of grants for board and lodging applies to all students. The system is expensive for a government, and the provision of funding and the structures described in the previous section have to be seen in this light. The different institutions are assessed for their cost-effectiveness, although the term 'assessment' will not be used in this way in this book.

In the State or public sector those institutions which award degrees (Colleges of Advanced Education in Australia and polytechnics in Britain) are subject to validation by an external agency whose degree they obtain. In Britain this agency is the Council for National Academic Awards, which has a Royal Charter for this purpose. In Ireland, a similar agency, the National Council for Education Awards, validates degree and technician qualifications. The procedures for validation which entail the approval of staff, facilities and syllabuses set standards within which the teaching for a degree can take place. The examinations and assessments during and at the end of the course are set by the teachers and checked by external examiners in the same way as by the universities. Assessment is sometimes used to embrace the term 'validation'. A distinction may be made between *propter-hoc* and *post-hoc* validation. In the former the validation or accreditation is based on facilities and personnel, and is often used by institutions to obtain more money from the local authorities from which they obtain their finance. It predicts that quality will be maintained if all these parameters meet specified requirements. *Post-hoc* validation simply asks if the objectives set out in the course description were obtained. It does not assume that certain grade levels are required by personnel or that certain facilities are needed for quality to be maintained.

Validation, concludes Church (1988), not only symbolizes institutional status but is a system which ensures that people think seriously and consistently about the design, operation and effects of their teaching. In this respect it is the technique which professionals in higher education must use if they are to be self-accountable (Heywood, 1983). It is a necessary condition for maintaining and controlling quality but not a sufficient one (Church, 1988; Shattock, 1986).

In parallel with these institutions of higher education in Britain, are a number of licensing authorities who also have to be satisfied that their requirements are met. These include the General Medical and Dental Councils, the Council of Engineering, Councils for the various paramedical professions, Accountancy, etc. Apart from the General Medical and Dental Councils, these organizations had more influence on the public sector than on the universities. Increasingly, however, the universities have had to adjust their programmes to meet the requirements of these institutions, and the same would seem to be true of developments in the United States.[3] These activities correspond to accreditation in the United States, and the terms 'assessment', 'accreditation' and 'validation' are often used to describe the same thing.

Hartle draws attention to the fact that post-secondary testing in the United States has risen in popularity because 'legislators' have begun applying the same logic to higher education: if we can define core abilities for high-school students as a way of focusing attention on the central elements of an education, why cannot we do the same for college students? In Britain and Ireland much consideration is being given to the promotion of a common-core or national curriculum which all children must experience in school. However, the universities continue to offer subject programmes, and general education as such is the curriculum in a subject or subjects. This is in contrast to the liberal education programmes available in the United States, where not only does a different definition of education pertain but it is possible to discuss the aims of education *per se*, independently of any linkage with particular subject specialisms. Any discussion of assessment fails if it is not linked to the general aims of education as perceived by the institutions and the society in which it functions.

Some testing in the United States attempts to measure the 'value-added' dimension of a curriculum by the pre- and post-testing of students to assess gains in their general education and skill development. The University of Missouri has, since 1974, used a variety of modes to make such assessments (Ewell, 1984). These have included standardized tests for freshman and sophomore students, examinations like the Graduate Record Examination Subjects Test,[4] the License Examinations used for certain occupations, and attitudinal surveys of students and alumni.

Some colleges in the United States use standardized tests to examine either general or specialized knowledge. The College Outcomes Measures Project of the American College Testing Program is used to assess general knowledge and skills against problems which adults are likely to encounter.[5] Some 250 institutions use this instrument, which covers functioning in social institutions, using science and technology, and using arts to test skills in communication, problem-solving and the clarification of values.

There is no equivalent to these programmes in England. One of the few nondimensional tests for which there is no syllabus requirement is the 'General Studies' Advanced level GCE examination of the Joint Matriculation Board. This attempts to assess knowledge, comprehension, and analysis across a spectrum of general education areas, including modern languages.

There is a much greater degree of homogeneity and conformity between the examinations of universities in Britain whereas the diversity in US institutions means that organizations selecting students for work or further study may want (and often use) standardized methods of achievement, such as the Graduate Record Examination, mentioned above.

However, this examination has been criticized on a number of grounds. In the subject area the tests of content do not always reflect the work done in departments. Investigations have shown that the distribution of the items reflects a 'core' around which there are many variations, and these variations are often determined by factors such as the size of the department and the resources available to it (Devore and McPeek, 1985; Oltman, 1982). Since it is used from year to year it is relatively inflexible (Brown, 1970). Although this approach seems to be in contrast to that used in England, where the examinations reflect what the teachers do, there is nevertheless a high level of conformity within subjects and their approaches to assessment. In electrical engineering, for example, Carter and Lee (1974) have shown that first-year courses concentrate on a relatively limited range of knowledge which could easily be tested by a common bank of objective questions (items). The department would draw the items appropriate to its course. Such an arrangement would give some idea of comparability between the different departments in the universities. In the United States the Federal Department of Education, in response to a report on *Indicators of Education Status and Trends* (NCES, 1985), is sponsoring investigations which will develop summative measures which, it is hoped, will show what students learn in each of the major disciplines throughout colleges in the United States.[6]

'Assessment' is also used to describe the measurement of student attitudes and values, for it is assumed that the experience of higher education will cultivate all those things which Newman wrote about in *The Idea of a University*, such as open-mindedness, tolerance and self-esteem. There seem to be no equivalents in other countries to the American Council on Education/Cooperative Institutional Research Program, which undertakes such research (CCHE, 1973). These matters are left to individual research workers with an interest in this sphere.

While it is commonly accepted that students should evaluate their teachers (see below) it is not widely acceptable to institutions that they should be appraised by students. Yet evaluations do take place, and, given the views that institutions have of their role and the influence of grading structures on the attainment of their goals, such studies are of considerable importance. Mitchell (1986), for example, using his Inventory of Higher Education and Life Values, has shown that life values are related to higher education, and he suggests that higher education institutions have the potential to influence those values which give definition to the character and fruitfulness of life itself. In any event, the goals of an institution necessarily influence departmental and individual teacher objectives. In Britain distinctions are made between assessment objectives and general objectives. It is important to know if the pursuit of assessment objectives interferes with the attainment of the general goals of higher education, a matter which is considered in Chapters 2 and 3. An institution, it seems, which is not committed to an aims and objectives approach is less likely to achieve significant aims, and in such circumstances the 'objectives approach' can become trivialized. Much of this book is concerned with the selection of significant objectives with which to guide student learning (Chapters 5–9).

As has been inferred, the term 'evaluation' may be used to describe activities at a variety of levels of institutional behaviour. At one level it is the totality of that process which determines the effectiveness of a system or institution in achieving its goals. Such evaluations may include student schedules of the type mentioned above. At the other end of the institutional spectrum evaluation is that process which analyses the factors that influence the attainment of goals in a particular course.

Evaluation has broad objectives, and generally takes into account factors which are beyond the control of the teacher and the course-assessment procedure. For example, in our study of *Science for Arts Students*, Montagu-Pollock and I were concerned with the extent to which the instructional procedures we introduced were attained. Our approach was to evaluate the objectives of learning and assessment, and not to look at the institutional factors which effected the long-term development of the course and thus student attitudes towards the programme. We considered that our problem was to motivate the students, whatever difficulties the institution put in our path (Heywood and Montagu-Pollock, 1976).

Nevertheless, institutional perceptions of how its goals may be achieved are often at variance with the effects of the structures which institutions put in place. The same is true of society and the structures it creates for higher education. Both affect the way in which students pursue grades as well as the particular grades they seek. They also influence the behaviour of teachers in the classroom. It is for this reason that Chapters 2 and 3 are concerned with systems of higher education and the educational structures which influence social, student and teacher attitudes toward grading and thus to assessment.

ASSESSMENT BY STUDENTS OF TEACHER PERFORMANCE

Assessment by students of teacher performance are commonly called 'student evaluations', and generally relate to questionnaires issued to students to judge the course they have attended. Such schedules have been used for many years in the United States (Flood Page, 1974) and many attempts have been made to assess their value. Even so, it seems that students do not believe that much attention is paid to their evaluations (Marlin, 1987)! American schedules have been used successfully in Australia (Marsh, 1981).

In the future they will be used in Britain as one of the components of staff appraisal, and some experiments have already been carried out (Nisbet, 1986). Many staff already issue their own evaluation forms or make use of published schedules (Gibbs and Haigh, 1984). Since this type of assessment will not be considered in detail elsewhere in this book, some comments on the use of such schedules is appropriate. The real danger of such schedules is that if they attend to the acting performance of teachers they will neglect the learning effectiveness of what is done for students. Staff may then concentrate on their role as performers rather than as managers of learning. It is a recurring theme of this book that the objectives of assessment are also the objectives of learning. We create assessment procedures in order to condition learning. Yet it is the periodic assessment of learning which should lead to instructional improvement (Centra, 1980). Too often institutions create structures which impede learning as several examples in the chapters which follow show.

I do not mean to imply in the foregoing that an evaluation should leave course objectives unchanged. In professional courses, for example, the issue of relevance to subsequent career is of considerable importance as has been shown in the theory–practice debates in such areas as medicine, engineering and teaching (Lomax, 1985).

It follows that student questionnaires should be designed to judge whether on face validity grounds the objectives of the course have been achieved. It also follows that since courses are supposed to influence learning that the entering characteristics of the students need to be known and for this reason it may be advisable to obtain pre-course information as well as post-course data as we did in our *Science for Arts Students* evaluation (Heywood and Montagu-Pollock, 1976). These were concerned with the broad understanding that the students had of course goals and not the specific knowledge that they had at entry. Related to this is the view of R. R. Renner, G. Greenwood and C. Scholt (1986) who from the assumption that responsible behaviour rather than excellent behaviour should be assessed have developed a two part instrument which uses students to monitor acceptable employee behaviour in teaching settings to satisfy management needs, while at the same time providing qualitative information on instructor performance. As L. R. B. Elton (1984) remarks, the assessment of teaching and teachers are similar activities which have different aims. Both are feasible if the criterion of good teaching as the central objective is abandoned. Both have to allow for an active role in the person being assessed and that is with the management of learning.

Appraisal is another term which is increasingly used. Student evaluations may contribute to teacher appraisal. J. D. Wilson describes appraisal as a post-hoc process in which a person's past performance is evaluated. It may or may not be used to set new objectives for future performance. The latter describes more general use of performance appraisal in industry. Appraisal takes into account the whole of the teacher's role and therefore includes administration and research. The only aspect of the teacher's role with which this book is concerned is with the teacher as manager of learning and therefore as a designer of assessment. Many studies support the view that successful appraisal or evaluation depends on the use of many instruments (e.g. student question-naires; examination of course materials; observation—either live or video; and in certain circumstances peer group evaluation) (Anderson, 1983; Bare, 1980; Feletti, 1982; Marsh, 1982). What is important in all evaluations whether they are of the system, the institution or the teacher is that mechanisms should be built into them so that any changes suggested by an evaluation can be implemented and in their turn evaluated.

To summarize and to quote Hartle (1986) 'What assessment appears to have become in higher education is a catch-all phrase that refers to a wide range of efforts to improve educational quality.... Nonetheless, upgrading the edu-cational quality of higher education—often in the name of assessment—will be of growing interest of state policy makers and an increasingly important challenge to educators in the next decade'.

The recent report of the Governors (NGA, 1986) and the University Grants Committee's judgements on academic departments (Shattock, 1986) indicate that this is the case. As Marchese (1985), Vice-President of the American Association for Higher Education, quoted: 'It's coming at us like a runaway train'.

THE IDEA OF MULTIPLE-OBJECTIVE AND MULTIPLE-STRATEGY ASSESSMENT

In the first edition of this book I used the term 'multiple-objective assessment' to describe a set of subtests within a subject, each of which was designed to focus on and test a specific and important criterion. I argued that the engineering science examination described in the case studies in Chapter 13 was a multiple-objective one. Since then I have described these key areas as 'focusing objectives'. They focus on a key activity and test for the key skills within that activity (Heywood, 1984). In this book I shall also use the term 'domain objective'. My colleagues preferred the term 'multiple strategy' and used it in the book which described our work (Carter et al., 1986). In the United States the term 'multiple-strategy' has been used by the collective body of State governors to describe their approach to assessment in higher education.

Their task force on college quality focused on how colleges and universities could demonstrate that student learning occurs. For this reason, the organizing concept of their study was 'assessment'. They also investigated how data on student outcomes could be used to assess the effectiveness of academic programs, curricula and institutions. In their report published in 1986 they said that they had learnt that 'rigorous, systematic assessment programs help colleges and universities focus attention on, and enable them to demonstrate that they are accomplishing, their institutional missions' (NGA, 1986).

The task force recommended that a systematic multiple-strategy approach to assessment be adopted by each college, and it seems clear that they intend it to embrace the totality of the educational experience. For example, what effect does residence have on student performance? How well are the aims of general education achieved? Such questions go well beyond the objectives of the subject-teacher in the classroom:

> Assessment of undergraduate learning and college quality needs, at minimum, to include data about student skills, abilities and cognitive learning: substantive knowledge of individual students at various points in their undergraduate career: instructional approaches used by faculty; and educational curricula. Because the nature of undergraduate education requires many skills and cognitive abilities be acquired and developed, colleges and universities should use a number of assessment approaches and techniques... An assessment program that uses multiple measures of student learning will more accurately and fairly depict a student's knowledge and abilities, regardless of background or status. Instead of limiting education access, assessment may actually provide incentives to ensure that unprepared students receive proper counseling, placement and academic assistance needed to perform in college and to graduate in a reasonable amount of time (NGA, 1986).

The governors and many other authorities (Adelman, 1986; NIE, 1984) have illustrated their views of what could be achieved by reference to work at Alverno College, North-East Missouri State University and the University of Tennessee at Knoxville (Loacker et al., 1986; Ewell, 1986) In Chapter 13 the work at Alverno College will be described with two other case studies which illustrate approaches to multiple-strategy assessment at the level of student learning. As the President of Harvard's discussion infers of Alverno, good ideas are likely to be taken over by prestigious institutions and modified (Bok, 1986).

Although the governors admit that colleges and universities collect a very large amount of data about students they argue that it is not systematized. Moreover, they quote a 1986 survey by the American Council on Education, who found that 64% of the respondents were not clear what to evaluate, 58% lacked faculty support and 57% thought that there were no good evaluation instruments (El-Khawas, 1986). The percentages would be much higher in the rest of the higher education world faced with the same proposals. In 1987 and 1988 the assessment debate pervaded the whole of the higher education scene in the United States.

It is unlikely that the various participants in this debate will agree to standardize the meaning of 'assessment', for the perceptual starting points of a State governor, a university president or vice-chancellor, and a teacher in higher education are very different. Nevertheless, it is clear that the ultimate responsibility for improvement in quality lies with the teachers and their students. Just as teachers have an obligation to their students, so students have an obligation to their learning. Thus assessments should be designed to enhance and not impede learning. There is sufficient evidence to show that, even when assessment enhances learning, its effects are extremely limited. In its Latin origins, as Loacker points out, assessment means 'to sit beside'. Thus assessment is a judgemental process for the purpose of improving student performance. Assessments and, in particular, written terminal examinations are too often appraisals about which the student receives no feedback. While this is widely recognized and although much more attention is paid to the assessment of coursework, little has been done to remedy this defect. Unfortunately, these new structures seldom derived from a fundamental appraisal of student capability and learning.

There is undoubtedly a need for a theory of assessment, and the first edition of this book was an attempt to provide such a theoretical framework. The evidence reviewed in this new edition continues to support the view that a systems approach to the design of assessment is required. The case studies are included in Chapter 13 to demonstrate the validity of this argument. A fourth case study on the teaching of arts to science students will be found in the last chapter of the first edition.

It is clear that, if the objectives of assessment are to be achieved and feedback introduced, instructional procedures will have to be designed to meet the objectives of assessment. Assessment is therefore an integral part of curriculum and instructional design, not an afterthought, as is so often the case. It is of significance that, in the survey reported by El-Khawas (1986), the largest area of agreement in baccalaureate colleges was for linking assessment to instructional improvement, and this is a major theme of this book.

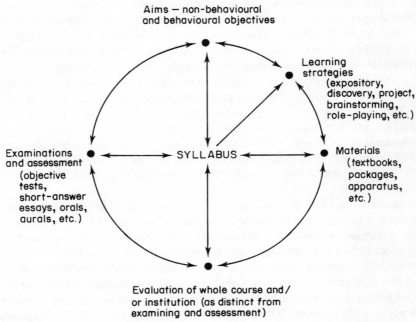

Figure 3. A model of the assessment–curriculum–instruction process

One model which illustrates these themes is shown in Figure 3, which shows the essential characteristics of the instruction–learning–assessment cycle. The fundamental proposition is whether the focus is the design of the curriculum, an assessment procedure, or even the evaluation of an institution—the starting point is the same, i.e. the understanding and expression of what we are trying to do. Today that would be summarized in a statement of aims and objectives.

For each objective which has to be obtained there will be a method of testing which is likely to be more appropriate than others. An objective is more likely to be obtained when the instructional strategies (including materials) are designed to obtain that objective. This is not to deny that all learning has a major collateral component (Hogan, 1980), or that there are many unintended and expressive outcomes to any learning experience (Eisner, 1979). It is to argue that in all learning there must be a focus which necessarily implies an objectives approach, since all learning requires organization, structure and meaning. Thus the understanding of 'learning', which is the centre goal of any education, necessarily contributes to the objectives just as it does to the selection of strategies to obtain those objectives (see Chapters 7–9).

It follows from this approach that the syllabus is the sum of the activities designed to meet the objectives thought to be essential. In the sense that we only learn that which is confirmed, the feedback or communication lines in the model are lines of learning.

Since everyone teaches according to his own philosophy whether he knows it or not, it is incumbent, says Sherrin and Long (1972), 'that each of us recognize and formalize our personal philosophy because, whether we know it or not, that is the way we relate to students, and that is the way they communicate with us'. Sherrin and Long argue that if an educator does not know his own philosophy he cannot be expected to understand the philosophy, career goals, attitudes and views of the curriculum of his or her students:

If we want Clyde to learn what we must teach him, we must
— be able to rationally communicate to him our reasons for choosing certain instructional goals and objectives;
— consider Clyde's goals and objectives as we search for our optimum instructional system;
— be able to convince Clyde that it is important to learn certain behaviours, attitudes and skills which will become his 'professional characteristics' as he interacts with society in the practice of his profession;
— be able to understand the value of the subject we offer for the fulfilment of Clyde's purposes, our purposes and the purposes of society.

A systematic approach to assessment has therefore to take into account the characteristics of the students, and Figure 4 is a rearrangement of Figure 3 focused on the instructional as opposed to the curriculum-assessment process.

In the view of Sherrin and Long, while an understanding of our basic philosophy is essential if we are to be able to communicate with students, it is equally necessary for us to have a theory of education, for through the aid of theory we translate our philosophies into practice in the classroom. Moreover, it is educational theory which considers the question of the relative importance of the knowledge, skills and attitudes which we wish to teach. However, in answering these questions we also need a theory of learning, for, as Furst (1958) was bold enough to write: 'Every instructor and every college should formulate and use a defensible theory of learning.' The derivation of objectives ('screening', as Furst calls this process) not only involves us in an understanding of our philosophical position but in the formulation of a defensible theory of learning.

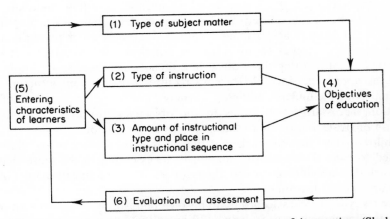

Figure 4. Theoretical generalization about the nature of instruction (Shulman's (1970) generalization of Cronbach's view of the nature of instruction). Item (6) has been added by this writer. Examples of the variables given by Shulman: (1) content of subject defined in task terms; (2) expository–discovery (degree of guidance), inductive–deductive; (3) number of minutes or hours of instruction, position in sequence of instructional types; (4) products, processes, attitudes, self-perception; (5) prior knowledge, aptitude, cognitive style, values; (6) knowledge, comprehension, problem-solving skills, etc.

From the above it will be seen that the processes of curriculum, lecture design and assessment are the same. Moreover, it is a complex activity. While it is convenient to begin with aims and objectives, any discussion of these must, at one and the same time, consider the learning experiences (strategies) necessary to bring the students from where they are (entering characteristics) to where they should be (objective): the most appropriate mode of assessment and the essential knowledge required. This approach to curriculum design and assessment places the syllabus as the final outcome of the procedure. This is not to argue that knowledge is unimportant, it is to place knowledge in the perspective of the essential concepts and principles necessary for understanding and autonomous learning. It creates the essential balance between product and process. This approach poses two fundamental questions for the teacher:

(1) What concepts and principles are essential for the development of the skills necessary to obtain the objectives?

(2) What knowledge (concepts and principles) is essential for our understanding of a subject within the general context of our culture (i.e. values and beliefs)?

To summarize:

(1) Curriculum design, assessment and evaluation begin at the same point. That is the understanding and expression of what it is we are trying to do.
(2) For each general objective there will be an appropriate method of testing.
(3) Specific learning strategies will be required if the objectives are to be successfully obtained.
(4) The combination of all these elements may lead to a substantial reorganization of the syllabus.

An integrated approach of this kind demands a considerable change on the part of the teacher to the planning and implementation of assessment. It is unlikely to be accomplished unless it is shown to be linked with those notional aims to which teachers in higher education are emotionally attached.

There is no escape from the fact that the way institutions interpret the general aims of education and the structures which they create to achieve their goals substantially influences the behaviour of their staff and the performance of their students. Teachers, students or the institution are not free of pressures from government and the organizational structure of society.

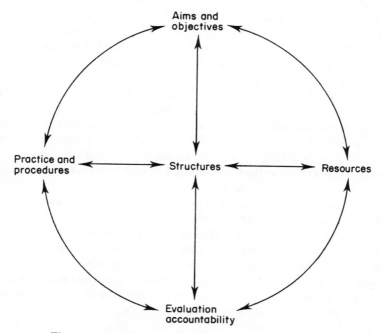

Figure 5. A model of the institutional evaluation process

In the sense that all institutions are learning systems, the model of evaluation is similar. It, too, must begin with a definition of institutional objectives. The outcome of the practice to bring these about will be the structures of the institution which should be responsive to the changing demands on and within the institution as they are reflected in its aims and objectives (Figure 5). Thus any understanding of assessment and student performance must take into account societal and institutional influences. It is with these and the student search for grades that Chapters 2 and 3 are concerned.

Notes

1. Binary system: the term arises from the historical development of education in those countries in which vocational studies were supported by local education authorities and academic studies in the universities. The former are called public or state sector colleges; the universities are regarded as independent even though they receive a large part of their finance from the State. In Ireland the universities and polytechnics (called National Institutes of Higher Education) are financed via a higher education authority.

   In England until 1988 the universities were financed by the Universities Grants Committee and the polytechnics by LEAs. The Education Reform Bill (20 November 1987) took polytechnics and other colleges of higher education away from the LEAs and provided for direct funding by the Department of Education and Science, the funds to be administered by the Polytechnics and Colleges Funding Council. The University Grants Committee was replaced by a Universities Funding Council. Advanced Courses are defined as those of a standard higher than A level. These are defined as higher education. Further education is defined to cover all other provision for those who have left school.

   I have argued elsewhere that a binary system is a stage which some countries have to negotiate en route to a unitary system of higher education. Given that the two funding agencies have broadly similar functions and that there is a population decline, it might be expected that a unitary system will emerge in Britain during the next 20 years.

2. A useful introduction to the Community Colleges is to be found in *Status of Testing Practices at Two-Year Post Secondary Institutions* (1985), ACT and American Association of Community and Junior Colleges, Iowa: ACT.

3. See Harris I. B. (1987). *Communicating Educational Reform through Persuasive Discourse: A Double Edged Sword*, Denver Conference on Assessment in Higher Education of the American Association for Higher Education. Among others, he draws attention to the following reports:

   American Association of Colleges of Teacher Education (1985). *A Call for Change in Teacher Education. Report of the National Commission for Excellence in Teacher Education, Washington, DC: AACTE.*

   American Dental Association (1983). *Strategic Plan, Report of the American*

Dental Association's Special Commission on the Future of Dentistry, Chicago: American Dental Association.

American Nurses' Association (1980). *Nursing: a Social Policy Statement— Report of the Task Force on the Nature and Scope of Nursing Practice and Characteristics of Specialization in Nursing*, Kansas City, Missouri: American Nurses' Association.

4. The Graduate Record Examination. Two types of tests are offered: (1) General Test; (2) Subject Test (in 17 disciplines).

(1) The General Test gives separate scores for general verbal, quantitative and analytical abilities, and it consists of seven 30-minute sections of testing time. The verbal measure (two 30-minute sections) comprises four types of questions: antonyms, analogies, sentence completions and reading comprehension sets.

The quantitative measure (two 30-minute sections) deploys three types of questions. There are three discrete quantitative questions and data interpretation questions: to test basic mathematical skills, understanding of mathematical concepts and ability to reason quantitatively and solve problems in a quantitative setting. The analytical measure (two 30-minute sections) employs two types of questions—analytical reasoning and logical reasoning. The final section (30 minutes) is not used in scoring the test. The items are used as pre-tests for future tests.

(2) The Subject Tests are each of 2 hours and 50 minutes in length, and are intended to deal with materials which students would have encountered in their major field of undergraduate study. Details are contained in *Guide to the Use of the Graduate Record Examinations Program* (1986–7), Graduate Record Examinations CN 6000, Princeton, NJ 08541–6000, USA. The GRE Board publishes a free *Information Bulletin* which contains a free practice test as well as practice tests in the subject areas for which payment is required. The GRE is a much-researched examination. (See also Conrad, L., Trismen, D. and Miller R. (eds) (1977). *Technical Manual*, Graduate Record Examinations, Princeton, NJ: Educational Testing Service.

5. College Outcome Measures Program (COMP), the American College Testing Program, PO Box 168, Iowa City, Iowa 52243, USA, is designed to measure the outcomes of college education which are related to the knowledge and skills required to function in society. This testing is organized along two dimensions:

I. *Process*—communication, solving problems, clarifying values.
II. *Content*—functioning within Social Institutions, Using Science and Technology, Using the Arts.

There are three primary test instruments:

(1) *The Composite Examination:* This comprises 15 simulation exercises

based on stimulus materials from contemporary adult society. The intention is to test applications of knowledge and skills to issues commonly confronted by adults. The candidates respond to the stimulus materials with short written answers, oral responses which are taped and multiple-choice items. These take 4 hours.

(2) *The Objective Test:* a 2-hour test also using 15 simulation activities.

(3) *The Activity Inventory:* a $1\frac{1}{2}$-hour test designed to assess out-of-college activities plausible for both young and mature adults. It uses self-report and multiple-choice format.

See COMP Research Reports.

Defining and Measuring General Education and Knowledge Skills. Increasing Student Competence and Persistence.

6. Private communication from Dr Clifford Adelman.

CHAPTER 2

En Route to a Degree

INTRODUCTION

The grade achievements of students depend not only on their abilities but also on their personal dispositions (drives, emotions, interests) and the pressures in their socio-educational systems which impede or enhance their learning. This chapter is concerned with the influences on, and the response to, these pressures by students as they pursue their grades.

Students may be regarded as role players in the subsystem of higher education. Descriptive models of this new subsystem show that it is overlapped by numerous other role sets that, directly or indirectly, influence student behaviour. Significant among these are the students' school and family subsystems and those subsystems in higher education and life which impede the students' expectations. Some influences on the pathway of student achievement and motivation are illustrated by a descriptive model of the student on a sandwich (co-operative) course (see Figure 1 in Chapter 1).

Descriptive models such as these can be quantified, and much work has been done on causal models in the United States, particularly in respect of student persistence in higher education. Both the descriptive and the causal models show that the grades obtained by students are in part a function of the institutional and societal 'press' on the internal dispositions available to the student for learning.

These pressures arise from the expectations that society has of higher education and the way in which society differentially organizes itself in response to its value system. Thus society expects higher education to act as a filter, in which students are selected and sorted into the variety of life's paths. One consequence of this in Britain is that status and level of professional qualification have become intimately linked. Competition in working life has been pushed back into higher education and schooling. The routes selected in these systems, deliberately or by default, become important, since it is most difficult to change from one route to another once the student has begun his or her educational career. Educational structures can impede public policy, for a public policy which is to create a flexible workforce may find itself hampered by rigid structures imposed on education by the same society which that public policy represents.

Admissions policies and the test procedures associated with them reflect the internal structure of the institutions of higher education. The more selective they are, the greater their influence on secondary education. In the United States, where the pressures on high school are less, the Grade-Point-Average of high-school students has been found to be as good as any other predictor. Nevertheless, there is evidence of pressure on students to improve their scholastic aptitude test performance through extra training in mathematics

At the other end of the university career all sorts of contradictions are to be found among employers in the way they use subjects and grades to select personnel. They are not found to speak with one voice in either the United States or Britain.

When all is said and done, little attention is paid by anyone in the system to the ideal purpose of grading—that is, for the promotion of learning. How students cope with grading and then with the structures of higher education remains a matter of the utmost significance for all those concerned with the life of students at college and university.

It is widely appreciated that the pursuit of grades is not a simple matter. Not all learning is goal-directed: a variety of influences work on the learner to produce the final result. While I suspect that most academics in higher education believe this to be the case, their behaviour at times towards their students would lead me to think otherwise. In this and Chapters 3 and 4 the concern is with influences on learning and development, particularly as they relate to the search for grades. How the social and education systems interact in the process of selection is the subject of this chapter, which begins with a brief description of systems approaches to the analysis of such problems. It is concluded that in the immediate future grading at all levels will continue to be of considerable importance for students, more especially for those seeking careers for which specialist knowledge is required.

SYSTEMS APPROACHES TO THE STUDY OF THE IMPACT OF COLLEGE ON THE STUDENT PURSUIT OF GRADES

Descriptive Systems

The purpose of this section is more to remind the reader of the complexity of the environment in which students have to pursue their studies than to evaluate the efforts which have been made to quantify system models.

Figure 1 in Chapter 1 is taken from the report of an investigation which I conducted between 1961 and 1963 into the structure and functioning of sandwich courses, [Heywood, 1969].[1] These were four-year programmes for the training of engineers and technologists similar to co-operative courses in the United States. Most engineering students, who at that time formed the majority of sandwich-course students, were sponsored by firms (industry-based students), while most of those in the other technologies had to find their industrial places (college-based students).

At that time in Britain sandwich courses were primarily provided by ten Colleges of Advanced Technology (CATs). These awarded a Diploma in Technology which was accredited by a National Council for Technological Awards, the forerunner of the Council for National Academic Awards mentioned in Chapter 1. The sponsors of the enquiry were concerned with, among other things, the supply of students from the schools, the in-course arrangements, and the support of industry. The Dip. Tech., as the qualification was called, was intended to be the equivalent of an engineering or applied science degree but oriented towards industrial application or manufacturing. In order to meet the research brief, information had to be obtained from pupils in schools and schoolteachers about the reasons why pupils chose (or did not choose) to enter technological courses in these colleges. They were faced with a variety of choice, but more especially with the universities which had higher status and with whom the CATs were in competition. They were also faced with the decision to be sponsored by an industrial organization or to go it alone with the help of the department. Within the colleges the students and the staff had also to supply information, since a major remit was to establish if there was any preferred arrangement for the spacing (length of time) of the periods in industry and college. Some 21 different arrangements were in operation. Was there a particular structure which would provide the most effective integration of education and training? The sponsors wanted to see if it would be possible to open the colleges all the year round. There would be two 6-month sessions. The industrial place taken by student A would be filled by student B when student A returned to college. That would have meant an increase in the number of industrial places, for which reason it was important to see if industrialists were satisfied with the courses and if, in addition, they would increase this number.

A major problem relating to the supply of students was that the award obtained was called a diploma, not a degree, and as such was believed to have lower status than a degree, which made recruitment difficult. The colleges felt that students might (unjustly) perceive the quality of their work to be less than that of universities. This view was confirmed by the studies made of school pupils (Heywood, *et al.*, 1966). Not surprisingly, the perception of college quality has been found to influence student choice of institution in the United States (Kealy and Rockel, 1987). It was important therefore to establish if the diploma was equivalent to a degree (which was assumed to be the case). For this reason, it was also necessary to obtain the views of university teachers, external examiners, professional institutions and all those concerned with the development and validation of the syllabuses and examinations.

The most important focus was on the students and their experience. One simple example illustrates the problem of the environment. Industry-based students had their course paid for by the employers: in their industrial periods they received a wage. The question was, did these students transfer their work habits to their approach to study in college? Did they expect to be taught from 9 to 5 because this was what their employers would expect? If they did, would it affect (1) their approach to learning and (2) their satisfaction with the course?

These investigations used inventories designed to establish disposition and fact. Today we would use a battery of instruments to try to understand the situation, and, in particular, instruments such as personality and study habit inventories, as happened in later studies of students on sandwich courses (Smithers, 1976).

This study was unique in that it tried to evaluate a subsystem of higher education in Britain. Its procedures arose from the belief that policy planning situations could only be made if the system was understood. As it was, the usual approach was to undertake prescriptive planning[2] based on beliefs about the supply and demand for places in higher education.

An interesting feature of this particular investigation was that the aims of the Diploma in Technology and the Colleges of Advanced Technology were well defined in public documents. It cannot be said that they were achieved. They did not increase the supply of technologists into the system because there was no real shortage. Many of those they produced wanted to go into Research and Development in preference to manufacturing. In many respects their courses emulated those in the universities.[3] History will probably show that the major effect of these institutions and their courses was to hasten the change-over from an essentially part-time system of education for technologists to one which was full-time. The ten colleges became universities, and it is significant to the issue of prescriptive versus systems planning that in the cuts in higher education in the 1980s several of them suffered very badly, in spite of the fact that they were oriented towards technology and industry. However, that is another story of the relative prestige of institutions in the British system. (For a recent review of sandwich–co-operative education in Britain see Daniels, 1980.)

Causal Models

In the United States there have been attempts to quantify such models using a form of critical path planning. In contrast to those in Figure 1, the arrows in causal models follow one direction. They indicate quantities in a direction from a variable to the variable(s) which they affect. (For this reason they are called causal models and causal variables.) Causal models have been used, for example, to show the socio-economic process of achievement and the effect of peer influences on ambition. Various classes of model have been developed. There are those in which the direction of flow is assumed to be one-way (recursive) and others which are two-way (non-recursive) (Wolfe, 1985).

Of particular interest to the problem of grading in higher education are the models illustrated in Figure 6, developed by Ernest Pascarella to assess the effects of different college environments on student learning and cognition (Pascarella, 1985). It will be seen that they contain elements similar to those in Figure 1. In Figure 1 the lines are, to some extent, vector quantities in the sense that those factors on the perimeter of the model are predicated to have less influence on the path of motivation of the student than those near the path. Pascarella's model relates more to the central system, which is directly representative of the immediate college environment.

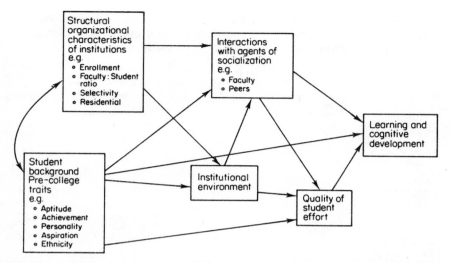

Figure 6. A general causal model for assessing the effects of differential college environments on student learning and cognitive development. (From Pascarella, E. T. (1985). Influences on learning and cognitive development. In Smart, J. C. (ed.), *Higher Education: Handbook of Theory and Research*, Vol. 1, New York: Agathon Press. Reproduced by kind permission of Dr E. T. Pascarella)

Subsequently he and Terenzini have applied this to a theory of withdrawal proposed by Tinto. The model in its application to withdrawal is shown without the quantities in Figure 7. Tinto's (1986) theory explained withdrawal as a function of the degree of integration into the social and academic systems of the college that the students had. This means that withdrawal studies have to take into account family background, individual attributes and pre-college schooling as well as a variety of commitments in college. In respect of the direct causes of persistence Pascarella and Terenzini were able to show that the influences of academic and social integration were about equal, whereas those of goal commitment and institutional commitment were not. They argued that the historical background characteristics did not have significant direct effects. Such effects that they had were transmitted through social and academic integration or through subsequent commitments to the institution and the pursuit of their own goals. An Australian study has cast some doubt on the applicability of Tinto's model to the outcomes of tertiary education other than withdrawal. Non-intellective factors were not found to be valid predictors of academic progress. None of the potential predictors could differentiate between failure and withdrawal outcomes (Watkins, 1982). Hilton (1982), in the United States, also obtained similar findings from among 21 000 students. The only important factors determining persistence were found to be good college examination marks and having been in a college preparatory course in high school.

The importance of these models is that, although the ideas have been around for many years (as, for example, in Bey's social theory of intellectual development, see p. 94) they show factors which are important to individuals, and while they may not apply in one situation they may in another.

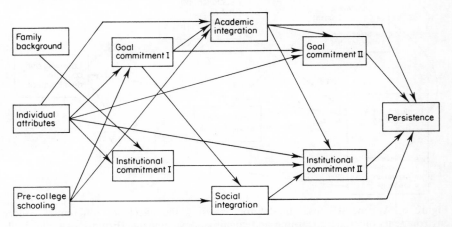

Figure 7. A causal model for the evaluation of factors influencing drop-out. (Simplified from Pascarella, E. T. and Terenzini, P. T. (1983). Predicting voluntary freshman year persistence withdrawal behaviour in a residential university. A path analytic validation of Tinto's model. *Journal of Educational Psychology*, **75**, 221; reproduced by kind permission of Dr E. T. Pascarella. The numerical values attributed to each path have been omitted: note the significance given to commitment)

In England, Stevens at Sunderland Polytechnic developed a similar theory about withdrawal from the polytechnics which throws some light on the problem, since it takes into account the fact that discontinuities are often not foreseeable (private communication). The major problem with causal models lies in their construction. If they are not adequately formulated then, says Duncan (1975), they will be of little use to research in higher education. It seems that this entails the selection of a principal focus. In the model in Figure 1 this focus is the central horizontal line which was defined as the path of motivation of the student. It illustrates that factors intrinsic and extrinsic to the student have a bearing on the attainment of grades. Models which can show the relative intensity of the factors in the student press are likely to have much to offer both policy makers and teachers. At the same time, once the model is described there are various principles which can be applied to our understanding of the situation without resorting to quantitative data, and more especially as they relate to the understanding of social phenomena. Common to all of these models is that they interrelate those dimensions of the system which educationalists call 'process' and 'product'.

Clearly, grade achievement is the outcome of a complex interaction between the environment in which the student learns his or her internal dispositions. Thus the grade obtained is in part a function of the institutional and societal press on the internal dispositions available to the student for learning.

It is with such issues that this chapter and several other sections are concerned.

SOCIETY, EDUCATION AND GRADES

Educational systems and the subsystems which contribute to the outcomes are open ones, even though in certain dimensions (for example, modes of teaching) they have a remarkable capacity to conserve and persist. The perceptions that students have of the wider society are important factors in the subjects which they take and the grades they pursue. In all education systems the top-down effect is at work, but, because its derivation is in the value systems functioning in the wider society, direct note is taken by school students of what happens in society and in the educational system.

Judgements are made about future prospects in relation to educational needs, and for those sections of the community which rely on educational merit for their progress grades these will have considerable meaning. A market is created, the operation of which is such as to result in a differential prestige among institutions (Seneca and Taussig, 1987).

In turn, a society expects the education system to do the selection, sorting out and categorization of individuals necessary for that society to function. This selection operates through the grades obtained in the particular subjects taken, and opens both narrow and wide doors to career paths. There are groups at either end of the spectrum of wealth for whom no advantage is to be gained from participation in education. In Western society it is still possible for persons without a complete education to get to the top as innovators. Witness some of the successful pop-stars, or innovators like Clive Sinclair and entrepreneurs like Alan Sugar in the world of pocket calculators and microcomputers.

However, for the mass of individuals in the middle, education is essential if they are to become relatively successful, and for many a route is selected which will give them professional standing. Because some do well and some fail, the system 'cools out' individuals into different routes as a partial function of their merit as measured by academics (Clarke, 1960). The hidden curriculum contributes greatly to the perceptions that students obtain of themselves, and while grades are of supreme importance all kinds of other factors help them to assess their potential. Given that the educational process is as much about the development of the power of self-assessment (perception) as about the pursuit of grades, then the evaluation of the quality of educational systems is as much about the totality of the environment which contributes to cognitive functioning as about the classroom and tests.

Nevertheless, the overt means by which society carries out the selecting and sorting function is by the tests which it uses to grade students either within or in parallel with the institution, as, for example, the tests leading to the Grade-Point-Average and the Graduate Record Examination in the United States or the civil service examinations taken after graduation in Britain (Friedman and Williams, 1982).

Since tests are taken for entry into colleges during and at the end of a course they are the major hurdles which students have to overcome, whether they live in West Germany, Japan, Britain or the United States. Similar problems are to be found in all four countries, although their expression is a function of the culture in which the particular system is embedded (Rohlen, 1983; Heywood, 1989).

GRADES, PROFESSIONALISM AND THE SYSTEM OF EDUCATION

In Britain, because of the curriculum offered by the universities in the nineteenth century there grew up a group of professional institutions who provided examinations which would admit those who passed into membership of the particular institution whose examinations were taken. These institutions often acquired a Royal Charter which 'sanctified' their qualifications. Initially, the technical colleges offered study for the examinations of these institutions in the evening and then during the day. The majority of engineers were qualified by part-time study until the end of the 1950s. The engineering institutions have maintained their educational functions to this day, although they now exercise them through a Council of Engineering. Other areas which have had qualifying institutions are chemistry and physics, although the majority of chemists and physicists graduated via the universities. Thus the status of the professional institutions became intimately related to level of qualification. The ability to relate occupation and profession and education in this way led to a number of other groups (semi- or subprofessions) seeking professional recognition to seek status in this way, and by the mid-1960s the further education sector in Britain catered for a large number. Not that in these institutions there has been no conflict between the desire of the professional body to control entry and monitor standards, and that of the lecturers to design their courses, although in the case of physiotherapy this reconciliation seems to have been accomplished with relative ease (Brook and Parry, 1985). In these developments a number of 'approved' institutions were supported by the actions of government which at that time had decided to make most of these courses, full-time or sandwich (co-operative). Marshall (1963) wrote of these developments that groups seeking professional status adopt

> recognized courses of training in a specialized technique, a means of testing efficiency in that technique, the admission of those duly qualified into an association, the building up of the prestige of the association as against non-members, the imposition of certain standards of honourable dealing and the rudiments of a code of ethics. The foundation of the whole structure is the specialized technique that has made possible the spread of these organizations.

The acquisition of specialized knowledge and status became the technique for gaining prestige. Low-status institutions emulate the high-status ones, and while the internal mechanisms may be arranged at one time to prevent movement up the hierarchy and at another allow such movement unless the culture changes its value system, the positions of prestige remain the same.

In a system like the British, where the chasing of some professional qualifications begins at 16, the effect on individuals is that they get locked into a subsystem within the system. If the age of school-leaving is extended (and that would seem to be the case in Britain) it is likely to cause even greater competition within the school system and to lock more people into preordained career routes. Marshall, it seems, correctly forecast the way things would go when he suggested that as the length of time in the education system lengthens, the competition which occurred in working life would be transferred to the school system. The effects of the ladder to subprofessionalism are such as to limit career opportunities to those which society regards as possible for a given slot. The parameters of the slot are defined by the education and examination structure:

> ...these new semi-professions are really subordinate grades placed in the hierarchy of modern business organizations. The educational ladder leads into them but there is no ladder leading out. The grade above is entered by a different road, starting at a different level of the educational system.

The consequences of this situation for mobility and thus for secondary education are profound, for, as Marshall pointed out:

> Social structure, in so far as it reflects occupational structure, is frozen as soon as it emerges from the fluid preparatory stage of schooling. Mobility between generations is increased, but mobility during the working life of one generation is diminished... the chance to move comes early, during school days. Once it has been missed and a career has been started at a non-professional level the whole system of formal qualifications makes movement at a later stage well nigh impossible... That appears to be the direction in which things are moving today, towards the transfer of individual competitiveness from the economic to the educational world, from the office and workshop to the school and university.

Given that government policy is to create a workforce which is more adaptable, this structure would seem to reinforce the opposite, and to reduce mobility. Nevertheless, the beginnings of flexibility are to be found in a credit transfer scheme which has been introduced by the Council for National Academic Awards. Polytechnics have formed consortia so that students can take appropriate modules in different institutions in the London area. The students have to collect 360 points. One year's full-time academic study is equal to 120 points. Newspapers have been attracted to the fact that industrial organizations see this structure as a means of broadening in-company training. Much attention has been given to the MBA developed for a major national retailing organization by Oxford Polytechnic (The Independent, May 11th 1988. *Credit Boom Widens Access to Degrees*). There is also considerable interest in the provision of suitable courses for adults (Smithers, 1986; Roderick and Bilham, 1982), as there is in the United States (Long, 1983)

To appreciate the difference between the American and British systems it is necessary to understand that the British one begins at 16 which is the age at which pupils may leave school. The effect of recent developments in Britain to relate secondary education more towards industry (business) will be to lengthen the period of formal education until the age of 18 for average and below-average students, but it will not postpone the training which leads into low-grade technician and other careers for which a specialized technique is required. The only way to achieve this would be to open school education for everyone, so that high school would become the norm, as it is in the United States. Such postponement would, it seems, transfer professional goal-seeking to higher education as we have defined it here. This has happened in the United States, for, to quote Fincher (1986):

> Many four-year colleges are seen as pre-professional colleges in which the value of the programs is attested by the number of graduates entering graduate or professional school. The content and substance of their undergraduate courses is seen as more in tune with professional entrance requirements than with the traditional values of liberal education. Similar arguments are heard concerning general education and the significance of the value of undergraduate degrees that do not result in career placement.[4]

In both nations there is a search for excellence. Numerous reports have appeared on this problem in the United States, and as we saw in Chapter 1, they are having an effect on policy (Davies and Slevin, 1983; HEA, 1984; Morgan and Mitchell, 1985). In both countries there is a demand to increase the standards of high school education and one way to attain this is seen to be a core curriculum. Among the reasons for this state of affairs in America which, given the previous discussion, are of interest are that:

1. The increasing variety of students in attendance has tended to push schools toward differentiated curricula as a way of interesting and holding these students in school.
2. America's effort to expand educational opportunity over the past century can be viewed as the purchase of democratic access at the price of longer years of school.
3. Selectivity in education has not been eliminated but only delayed until college or beyond.
4. The notion of a high-level academically oriented curriculum is a radical idea because it takes seriously the goal of a fully educated citizen—not just a long-schooled one.[5]

As in the United States, British policy has been informed by the economic imperative, even though the links between education and the economy are far from understood. These views have been reinforced by particular interpretations of the success of Japanese high schools, because Japanese education is held to be one of the causes of that country's success. However, there is another interpretation, and that is that the problem lies in the culture of which education is a prime support. The trouble is that public policies are often contradictory. While seeking to accomplish certain goals, they contrive to serve its defeat on the other. Thus in the 1980s in Britain, while demanding that technological education should be informed by industry, the same universities which had close links with industry had their grants cut while the more influential in the establishment retained their shares in the annual allocation. As we have seen, the British structures of education and the assessments associated with them may well impede rather than enhance later life flexibility. In any event, changes in structures in any system of higher education will have a profound effect on admissions and the use of tests in admission procedures, and, as we have seen, it is in this respect that school education and tests have significance for higher education.

ADMISSIONS POLICIES

The difference between admissions policies in England and the United States is startling. In England, grades have always been important for entry into the universities. Every entrant to a university will be initially competent in the area of their future study or potentially able for study in subjects not taken at school, such as philosophy. There is virtually no problem of literacy and numeracy. Most students are likely to have studied English and Mathematics to GCE O level and would have little difficulty with the American Scholastic Aptitude Test (SAT). Remedial courses do not have to be supplied in these areas as they are in very many American colleges.

Throughout the last 20 years there have been variations in the grades acceptable which have been a function of enrolment numbers. This particularly has been the case in science. The available data do not suggest any great change in standards. Nevertheless, the reduction in funding has limited places, and grade levels change as a function of the number of places available. Policy in Britain has been to maintain a low staff–student ratio (of the order 10:1). Experience of the Irish system with ratios in the range 16–28:1 suggests that similar standards can be maintained, although different approaches to assessment and teaching might improve the quality of the output.[6] The overall entry to these universities is at a lower level (see Figure 2 in Chapter 1). It seems that the British system could take in more students if it were to have a similarly broad curriculum at entry and take more tutorial care of them during their first year.

The system may be drifting in this direction with the introduction of As levels, while the American system might go towards to something like the International Baccalaureate (Fox 1985). While there is much agreement in Britain that university courses are inflexible in that they do not allow students to change their options, there is little will to take the issue seriously. If anything, the opposite is true for the University of Keele, which, set up on the Newman ideal, has been actively discriminated against by the funding agencies. Its foundation year was one which gave students the chance to change their minds, and many did, usually in a direction away from science. They then followed a normal university course for another three years (Iliffe, 1968). General education as an ideal is not understood in Britain.

As in Britain, admission requirements in the United States inform the high-school system. Bartlett Geamatti writes that:

> The high schools in this country are always at the mercy of the colleges. The colleges change their requirements and their admissions criteria, and the high schools, by which I mean public and private parochial schools, are constantly trying to catch up with what the colleges are thinking.[7]

This works its way through to the SAT. Eisner makes the interesting point that, whether true or not, students believe that more work in mathematics will lead to higher scores on the SAT, and because of this they fail to enrol on courses that genuinely suit their interests and attitudes. Many schools have created specific courses to help students to acquire good scores with these tests (Eisner, 1979).

The Committee on Ability Testing in the United States reported that colleges vary in their admissions decisions. Initial applications are sorted into three categories:

(1) Presumptive–admit: those who have strong academic endowments;
(2) Hold: not so outstanding academically but who have some special qualification indicated in the application form or letters of commendation;
(3) Presumptive–deny: weak credentials.

Many institutions use cut-off scores on the high school GPA and SAT. The Committee reported that precise information on the use of test scores in admissions procedures was not available. However, the available evidence is that the high-school GPA is given more weight than test scores, and that it is a better predictor than either the ACT or SAT scores (Wigdor and Garner, 1982). It seems that the best predictor is a combination of the test scores and GPA (Skager, 1982; Stice, 1979).

It is interesting to note the experience of England in this respect. In the mid-1960s the Committee of Vice-Chancellors and Principals designed an equivalent to the SAT, called the Test of Academic Aptitude. It was hoped that it might be a better predictor than the A level GCE, but this was not found to be the case (Choppin, 1973). It seems that this is because the A level is in the subject that the students are going to learn in college. The additional knowledge which students have gives college teachers a different starting point at entry. Given the broader curriculum in American colleges, it is perhaps surprising that general tests of academic aptitude do not produce a better correlation than GPA. Another surprising feature of correlation studies in England is that the General Studies A level examination of the Joint Matriculation Board was found to be a relatively good predictor of academic performance in universities.

Although the American colleges are not very selective when compared with other countries it is surprising that the concern for excellence seems to have caused colleges and universities to raise their admissions requirements at a time of stable and (for some) declining enrolments. An interesting argument against the raising of standards in this way is that high-ability students in high schools which, for one reason or another do not respond to the new demands, will be penalized.

In England objections to the A level GCE examination are that it does not predict performance in university finals. By this is meant grade-level of honours. What it does, as we saw, is make a reasonable prediction that a person who has these examinations has a substantial chance of passing finals at some grade-level or another (see, for example, Wilson, 1981; Crum and Parikh, 1983). The experience of universities was that those with two A levels stood much less chance of passing than those with three. It was also found in the 1960s that, in technology, those who entered sandwich courses from part-time studies while in industry did better than those who had two A levels, and nearly as well as those with three. One interpretation of these facts was that while the so-called national certificate student had the advantage of a knowledge of engineering he lacked the academic approach of A level (Heywood, 1971a).

Another criticism of GCE A level is, as we saw above, that by setting the level too high, students are excluded from university who, with an alternative approach to sixth-form studies, would succeed in higher education. The experience of the two universities in Dublin might be cited in favour of this view. However, the most common criticism of these examinations, as we have also seen, is that they restrict the range of study undertaken by students in their school education.

A general criticism of the selection process in Britain is that it takes very little account of other variables which might be important (for example, interests and personality). The same criticism has been made of tests in the United States, against which it has been argued that measures of these kinds of attributes have not been shown to improve the prediction of academic performance. In Britain some universities, particularly Oxbridge, do place some store on the interview. Others use interviews as a means of 'selling' their institutions. Yet, as we have seen from some studies (Hilton, 1982; Watkins, 1982), it does not seem as though much is to be gained from such tests. However, Crum and Parikh (1983) found at one university in England that variables like application, reliability and intelligence had a dominant role in determining degree performance. The problem would seem to be to increase confidence in school reports.

Tests scores become important as their role in the admissions process increases. In Britain admission depends on the grades obtained at A level, and these relate to the prestige of the institution and the characteristics of the pool of applicants available to the institution. At the output end of the system it is the significance which grades have for employers which is of importance to the student.

THE MEANING THAT GRADES HAVE FOR EMPLOYERS

In Britain it has been shown that technicians require management skills rather more than high-level mathematics, yet colleges concerned with the training of technicians continue to emphasize higher levels in science studies than is necessary for the jobs which have to be done (Clements and Roberts, 1980). By contrast, it is only recently that the University Grants Committee has funded a number of universities to run four-year courses to embrace manufacturing and production. It is also of note that Oxford and Cambridge were among the eight universities initially selected for this task. It is equally significant that industry in the past has recruited its manufacturing personnel from the shopfloor (Youngman et al., 1977). So the effects of this development on industrial development will be of considerable importance to future historians of higher education. What is of interest here is the fact that, when far-reaching changes are seen to relate to social control, the high-prestige institutions begin to exert their influence. In this context it will be interesting to see if the curriculum-drift phenomenon does, in fact, produce the engineers who will change industry or if, because of differential selection, the persons who could change industry enter the civil service or the world of high finance, and dictate industrial and social needs without an understanding either of industrial practice or the contribution which industry makes to society. A general education ought to take such things into account, and in this respect the development of programmes in electronics, information technology, and craft, design and technology in the public (private) schools in Britain might be interpreted as a take-over bid for subjects thought to be important. A specialist subject-oriented curriculum cannot do this, and, in any case, changes in the financing of British universities to make them more responsive to the needs of industry will not achieve this goal, for three reasons. The first is the reward system. If the rewards are greater elsewhere, students will not pursue careers in industry. The second is that there is no basis in the argument that there is a shortage of technologists (see note 1). Finally, and most significant of all, is the fact that in the United States and Britain industry and commerce are apparently happy with the system as it is. The organizations and individuals which are said to be representative of industry are not.

The persistence of these attitudes is strong in Britain. Two surveys, spaced by 20 years, came to roughly the same conclusions (see note 1). The most recent, by Roizen and Jepson (1985), concluded as follows:

(1) Employers do not speak with a single voice.
(2) Employers do not generalize their conclusions.
(3) Employers show a decidely pragmatic approach to educational issues. The continued reliance on GCE A levels in selecting individuals is likely to be a source of considerable grief to educators who, for many years, have tried to broaden perspectives on learning and promote acceptance of the value of other kinds of knowledge and skills. The majority of employers acknowledge the importance of other forms of knowledge and non-academic

qualities while at the same time relying on A levels because these are the simplest measure for setting a base line for the recruitment process. As resources of recruitment decline, simplicity in the process of recruitment appears to be even more important.

(4) Employers make few specific proposals themselves except that levels of numeracy should be improved.

(5) University graduates are generally preferred to those from the public sector colleges.

(6) Employers generally advocate more contact between higher education and industry.

(7) Many employers value work experience immediately after graduation (graduate apprenticeship) or by sandwich (co-operative) or work during the vacations.

(8) Most employers are relatively satisfied with the higher education system as it operates.

(9) Almost all employers are currently able to meet their manpower recruitment needs using one strategy or another.

The findings of my 1962 survey are almost identical. Although larger, it was confined to technologists (Heywood, 1969). The 1980s study covered the spectrum of graduate employment in Britain. We found that employers would disregard qualifications if a person could do the job they wanted to be done. We also found that the persons often cited as representative of industry were sometimes isolated within their organizations. Often in senior positions they did not recruit graduates or work out the companies' demands for different kinds of graduate. Even at that level, certain rules of thumb were used relating to the subject-matter of the degree (for example, accountancy, arts, engineering science) and the status of the institution in which it was obtained (for example, Oxbridge, provincial university, technology college).

A characteristic of the beliefs about graduates at that time was that the firsts and two–ones were thought to be more suited for research, whereas the thirds were considered more practical. This idea was shared by many industrialists, and they acted on such beliefs. There is some reason to think that this led to self-fulfilling behaviour on the part of graduates. Those receiving the higher grades believed in their capability to do research and wanted to become research workers. Those in the lower grades thought they were practical or followed careers in sales or marketing. The same seemed to be true of the graduates from low- and high-status universities. Those from Oxbridge believed that they were being trained to be the managers of industry. Those from the Colleges of Advanced Technology said that they were the engineers who would do the practical work. In their turn, those students thought that they were more practical. There is now much evidence to show that such attitudes are culturally determined.

The situation would appear to be very similar in the United States. There, numerous enquiries have focused on the specific relationships between grades and subsequent career performance. These seem to indicate that employers do not believe that there is a significant relationship between GPA and subsequent employment. This applies as much to medicine as to any other professional study. I found the same to be true of the graduates from the Diploma in Technology courses which I investigated (Heywood et al., 1968: see also Altricher, 1982; Anisef, 1982; Oxenham, 1984).

At the same time, it is a paradox that a large number of well-known companies in the United States continue to regard the Grade-Point-Average as very important. Milton, Pollio and Eison, reporting in 1986 on their National Grade Study, say that in the majority of companies grades are of moderate to crucial importance in obtaining the first job. When they asked companies to say if they had studied the relationship between GPA and career performance the majority said they had not. Industry and commerce, it seems, take a naive view of the value of a grade and the qualities with which it is associated. Industry takes what colleges and universities have to offer without too much comment.

Content is important for some professions as, for example, engineering, law and medicine, and the universities have undoubtedly responded to the demands created by the new knowledge. However, these demands have been in response to what they themselves do, without much attention to what people in jobs outside the universities actually do.

As in the United States, the most important function of grades in Britain is to provide information about students to academia, commerce, industry and the public sector. Milton et al. argue that this is in conflict with the ideal purpose of grading—that of promoting learning. They argue that business could help the attainment of this goal if it was to stop emphasizing the Grade-Point-Average and simply accept that a student has graduated. Their argument is based on the poor relationship between grades and subsequent achievements in life. An alternative view is that tests which examine strategic skills will be assessing skills likely to be used at work, whatever it is.

However the problem is approached, grades are of importance to students, and the most important function they have in our society as they combine with the structure of the curriculum is the differential reward of opportunity for performance by those groups of the population for whom college and university education matters.

How students cope with grading and thus with the structures of higher education remains a matter of the utmost significance for all those concerned with the life of students at college and university, although what is success for one student is not necessarily so for another.

Notes

1. During the same period two other studies were done which looked at the experience of sandwich course students in one institution (Jahoda, 1964; Marris, 1964). One of them (Marris) compared their experience with that of students in universities.

2. Trow (1974) defines the differences between prescriptive and systems planning thus:

> Prescriptive planning, the kind that is most commonly practised by the governing agencies and ministries in advanced societies, aims to spell out in detail the size and shape of the system of higher education over the next several decades, and the content and forms of instruction; in brief, what will be taught, to whom, to how many and in what kind of institution, at what expense? Prescriptive planning necessarily rests on analysis of secular trends (and only some of those). Typically, it bases itself on estimates and projections of the demand for higher education, both in the population at large and by the economy, and the resources available to higher education marked by diversity and flexibility. It would not aim to specify in detail what those institutions of higher education will look like or how and what they will teach, to whom. The difference in these modes of 'planning' is between planning the specific size, shape and content of an educational system, and planning the structure or form of a system of higher education which is best able to respond to the combination of secular trends and unforeseen developments. . .
>
> Growth itself stimulates prescriptive planning: the more higher education grows, the more money is needed for it, the more interest there is in it among larger parts of the population, the greater demand there is for tight control over its shape and costs. The growing demand for 'accountability' of higher education, for its ability to demonstrate its efficiency in the achievement of mandated and budgeted goals, inevitably translates itself into tighter controls and prescriptive planning. But this control can only be exercised rationally in terms of available knowledge based on foreseeable trends and projections.

The fundamental questions which Trow asked were:

(1) Is increasing control over the forms and functions of higher education by central public agencies or authorities an inevitable concomitant of expansion and increased costs?

(2) Is the (increasing) role of public authorities presently a force working against diversity in higher education in their functions and standards, their modes of governance, their forms of instruction, their sources of support and their relations to other institutions of society?

(3) If so, are these 'standardizing' tendencies inherent in central governmental control, or is it possible for central governing and financing agencies to function in ways that sustain and increase the diversity in higher education? If so, what governing and funding structures would have that effect and what principles of operation would govern their activities? How can efforts to support diversity be sustained against political pressures in almost all advanced societies? See also Heywood (1974c).

3. Wherever there is competition between institutions, as in Britain, Japan and the United States, most of them at the bottom of the pile want to emulate those at the top. There are exceptions, like Alverno College, which have something quite different to sell. Among the effects of curriculum drift are:

(1) A reduction in the amount of institutional diversity (Hodgkinson, 1971). Davies (1986) calls it entropy. When left to themselves, colleges will become increasingly alike.

(2) It is difficult to introduce new programmes or new methods of grading and assessment (McConnell, 1962).

(3) Low-status colleges attract staff from high-status ones who may introduce curricula that are inappropriate to local conditions (Riesman and Jencks, 1962).

(4) Conflicting ideologies are created. In Britain, for example, Collier (1982) describes the conflict between the economic renewal ideology and the academic one. While the government finances technological education, there is, at the same time, a strong core in society which gives the highest status to 'Oxbridge' ideas. The power of such institutions is such as to suppress any fundamental discussion of the aims of education. The well-established disciplines maintain their ascendancy.

(5) Even within subjects which are supposed to be cultural, like English Literature, students are likely to find them dominated by the specialized technique of the profession which teaches the subject (see Riesman and Jencks, 1962).

4. For example, there is evidence of the use of electives in the United States as a means of pursuing further study in the major field of interest. The loosening of curricular requirements was also thought to be because of the need to satisfy demands for relevance (Blackburn *et al.*, 1976).

5. Quoted by Morgan, A. W. and Mitchell, B. (1983), from Resnick, L. B. and Resnick, D. P. (1982) *Standards, Curriculum and Performance: A Historical and Comparative Perspective. A Report to the National Commission on Excellence in Higher Education* (item 3 has been adapted from the quotation).

6. My department in the University of Dublin has a student–staff ratio of 28:1. We have external examiners for our postgraduate secondary teacher training course who tell us that our products are similar to those produced in England. The standards obtained can be judged from my two books written specially for these courses (Heywood, 1982, 1984).

7. Barry, P. (1982). Interview: a talk with A. Bartlett Giamatti. *College Board Review*, No. 123, 2–7. There is some evidence to suggest that the more selective admissions procedures are in the United States, the higher the quality of academic programme (for example, Braxton, J. M. and Nordvall, R. C. 1985). Selective Liberal Arts Colleges: higher quality as well as higher prestige? *Journal of Higher Education*, **56** (5), 538–54; Skager, R. On the use and importance of tests of ability in admission to post-secondary education, pp. 286–314 in Wigdor and Garner (1982). See also Stice, J. E. (1979a). Grades and test scores, do they predict adult achievement? *Engineering Education*, **69** (5), 390–93.

CHAPTER 3

Grades and Grading

INTRODUCTION

Chapter 1 began with a list of assumptions commonly made about tests and examinations which are seldom discussed. By implication, a function of this book is to examine these premises. Despite the fact that universities are apparently expected to achieve many aims, they only formally measure certain aspects of the academic performance of students. Nevertheless, examinations pervade the whole domain of university life, and these should be both reliable and valid. This chapter is primarily concerned with the issue of reliability.

Various systems of grading and scoring are described. That grades are not absolute has been demonstrated on many occasions during the last 80 years. The consequences of this unreliability for the final grades which students receive are discussed and its implications for the scaling (standardization) of marks and for grade intervals are considered.

Variations in the distribution of honours between the subjects of the curriculum (differential grading) have caused much concern in Britain and the United States. A statistical method used to overcome this problem by one university in the United States is described. This technique is very similar to techniques used by the examination boards in England to evaluate the relative standards of the subject which they test.

The problem of grade inflation and deflation in the United States is considered. One investigation suggests that graders in higher education adapt to the ability levels of the students they teach.

Because institutions seek comparability between the subjects they test, work by the public examining authorities on the comparability of examinations used for selection to higher education is of considerable interest. Of all the techniques discussed cross-moderation has been shown to be the one with the most potential.

Cross-moderation has some similarity with the system of external examining in use in Britain and in which there is now interest in the United States. Until recently there has been little research into the effectiveness of external examiner systems. Such as there has been suggests that there has been much confusion about the role. The recently published code of practice by the Committee of Vice-Chancellors should eliminate this problem. However, it cannot solve problems of the 'departmental' press. Given that external assessors are the only source of information about standards, comparability exercises of the kind undertaken by the school examining boards by university teachers could be extremely rewarding. One approach might be to develop grade criteria in each subject along the lines of those being developed for secondary examinations in Britain. In this respect many ideas are to be found in the multiple-strategy approaches of testing developed for school examinations in Britain and in competency-based assessment in medicine and the liberal arts (for example those at Alverno College), which are described in Chapter 13. Chapters 5–9 are concerned with the different kinds of objectives which might be tested in higher education and their derivation.

THE PERVASIVE INFLUENCE OF EXAMINATIONS AND TESTS

We have seen in the previous chapters that grades are important, for all sorts of reasons. They are particularly important as criteria for admission to higher education, and this applies in every situation, even those like the American one, which has relatively open access. They may determine the college to which one goes, and they may determine within colleges the subject one enters. It has been estimated that in an academic year in the United States between 72 million and 108 million final marks will be awarded.

Throughout the Western world grading is a massive exercise which occupies academics for substantial periods of their time. In these circumstances it is surprising that it does not occupy them in much more debate about its value than is apparently the case. Indeed, many teachers never seriously question those assumptions made about examinations listed in Table 1. In one way or another most of these are questioned in the sections of this book and are found to be of doubtful validity.

Perhaps it is even more surprising that politicians have not investigated its cost effectiveness. Yet, as I indicated previously, it is a subject which is avoided unless someone creates a stir, and occasionally this happens, as was the case in the United States in 1986 and 1987.

The major argument seems to have begun with the student unrest in the late 1960s, which affected the United States as well as Europe. In Britain the students did have a temporary influence on universities. Almost all of them instituted assessment committees: many held teach-ins on assessment. Formidable among the students was Tom Fawthrop, who refused to accept his degree and led a sit-in at the University of Hull. The pamphlet which he wrote on the subject took on board two issues which he interrelated (Fawthrop, 1968). These were simply that examinations were a constraint on education, but by education he meant something larger than the subject-specialisms which are the *modus vivendi* of the British system. Given the continuing debate about the liberal education and the goals of American higher education, his criticisms remain pertinent today. Among other things, he wrote:

> From the educational viewpoint examinations are a supreme form of alienation in the modern world. This is also relevant to the teaching sphere, in which the

genuine aims of the tutor are periodically subverted by the exigencies of the system, which emphasize that his first obligation is to get them through the examination at all costs rather than to stimulate a relevant contribution to the advancement of learning. One might well ask what does a society profit if it gains a whole world of degrees and yet loses its own educational soul? In a world of ignorance what can we give in exchange for true knowledge—a million scraps of paper certifying student degree status?

and concerning his own recommendations:

Doubtless administrators will cry in horror at the thought of such a flexible amorphous system, but neither the production of degrees nor the administration of the system is the proper end of education, but the development of the student's personality with particular reference to intellectual capacity.

Had Fawthrop read Katz and Sanford (1962) in *The American College* he would undoubtedly have quoted them in support of his thesis, for they argued that:

Our universities, in spite of the seeming objectivity of their curricular orientation, seem in fact committed to one particular and quite subjectivistic position: the value premise of the dominance of the intellectualist; and this in turn is tied to the implicit personality theory which views personality as primarily intellectualist in nature. 'Intellectualist' may be distinguished from 'intellectual' if the former term is taken to denote an emphasis on the manipulation of conceptual symbols in more or less detachment from the needs of outer and inner reality. Making this distinction helps to clarify the claim of some recent defenders of the traditional view that they find no abundance of intellectuality, but there is an abundance of intellectualism, and this may be one of the causes of intellectual apathy. Some students, of course, find that there are high regards for conceptual agility as such. For, in our society, as well as in others, examinations of increasing severity serve as an objective way of selecting people for positions of leadership and occupational superiority.

Despite the fact that Universities are apparently expected to achieve many aims, they only formally measure certain aspects of the academic performance of students. Thus examinations pervade the whole domain of university life and influence student approaches to learning. It is therefore of the utmost importance that tests and examinations should be both reliable and valid. That is, they should be seen to be fair.

DIFFERENTIAL GRADING BETWEEN SUBJECTS

In Britain the National Union of Students (1968) was very concerned with the effects of reliability and validity on grading. The grade of a final degree in Britain and Ireland is, as we saw in the Chapter 2, an important mechanism of selection into a career. A teacher who is a graduate with an honours degree gets paid more than one with a pass. In Ireland the certificate which enables a graduate to teach after a one-year course of teaching is graded into pass and honours in order to meet the salary requirements of the Department of Education, and this procedure also applies to the Master in Education degree. Generally speaking, only those with high honours can get into the higher grades of the civil service or obtain grants to enter graduate school. The level obtained in a degree is therefore of considerable importance and it became a matter of great concern to the National Union of Students, when it found the data listed in Table 2.

Table 2.

(A) Distribution of first-class honours awards among students graduating in 1962 in Britain (National Union of Students (1967), *Report on Wastage*, London):

Percentage of awards in each subject

Social Studies	3
History	4
Theology	5
Philosophy	5
English	5
Modern Language	7
Geology	9
Classics	12
Physics	12
Chemistry	12
Mathematics	14

(B) Terminology used to describe honours degrees in Britain with an example of a mark scale:

Class I ('First')	Above 70%
Class II.1 ('Two–One')	Above 60%
Class II.2 ('Two–Two')	Above 50%
Class III ('Third')	Above 40%

The terminology is universal but the grade levels differ between universities. Some universities also include a 'Pass' level. Not all the subjects will have to be passed at the same level as the grade awarded. Below the Third or Pass will be a level at which a student may compensate a mark in one subject. In the case of this scale it is 35%. For example, a candidate may have passed in six subjects and failed one. The rules may allow him or her to pass if the mark obtained is between 35% and 40%. The rules vary between universities and subjects.

This table shows that the number of first-class honours awarded in any year varies considerably between the subjects. Moreover, it is a persistent trend. It is evidently easier to get a first in the sciences than in the arts, although when we enquire further we find that the drop-outs from the sciences are more numerous than those from the 'arts'. So an 'arts' student is more likely to get a degree than a science one. This raises many questions. For example, does Table 2 imply that arts subjects are more difficult than science subjects.

In respect of this kind of issue the Stanford University curriculum study has shown the value of longitudinal studies of course transcripts, in this case between 1965 and 1980. The study shows that the popular view in the US that grading in the humanities is "easy" while grading in engineering is "tough" is not held. Little difference was found in mean grades among the natural sciences, social sciences, and humanities when class size differences are taken into account (Boli, Katchadourian and Mahoney, 1988). Related to this is the idea that the difficulty of courses taken by students influences long term grades through the short term grades obtained in these courses (Schurr, Ellen and Ruble, 1987).

Criticisms of both honours and general grading systems were also made in the United States at the time of the student revolt. One outcome was the introduction of pass/fail systems, although honours programmes are not *per se* the norm as they are in Britain (Wittich, 1972). Although these systems seemed to have a rapid growth they never caused any significant change in the system of grading. The purpose of these courses was to encourage students to take a broad range of courses without impediment to their Grade-Point-Average. At the California Institute of Technology students in the first courses of that kind undertook the reading which it was hoped they would do. However, by the third year, the improvements in learning which had been noticed in the first year had declined (Milton *et al.*, 1986). Such systems have not been of great interest to students despite the fact that at the time the Muscatine Committee (1968) reported that half of the students in their survey wanted more pass/fail grading.

In the United States, as in Britain, two grading systems run alongside each other. The first are the grades which the subject teachers or subject examiners (who are very often the same people) give. The second arises from the numerical collation of these results into the final award or Grade-Point-Average. In most American universities a five-letter scale is used, where A = 4.00 and F = 0.00, to arrive at the GPA, the result of which is presented in the form 3.75, 2.8, etc. Whereas the teacher scale is coarse scale, the GPA is a fine grade one of 400 points. Teacher scales range from 2 (pass/fail) to 13 points (at A, A−, B+, B, B−, etc.).

In Britain many teachers in the humanities use a letter grade and sometimes the Greek alphabet is used. Scientists use number grades. A conversion takes place at some stage to arrive either at a number which can be added into another mark to give a percentage (as when papers are sectionalized between subjects) or a percentage to give a grade. A single marker scoring a 3-hour paper requiring answers to five questions will probably mark each question out of 20. A 3-hour paper demanding three questions may have each question marked out of 33. There are many variations in practice. Some markers prefer fine scales and others coarse ones. There are very few attempts to justify practices statistically. For example, when two markers assess the same paper it is assumed that they score to the same mean and standard deviation.

Marking and grading practices differ between the public examinations in Britain and, in E. R. Whiteley's opinion, cause a great deal of unnecessary confusion. In examinations like GCE A level (for example, two 3-hour papers and coursework) the marks are brought together and may be as many as 200. Certain grade levels are recommended and the examining board computes the rest of the grade levels (see below).

In the United States the credit requirements of universities and colleges have not encouraged breadth of study. Students' extra-major credit distributions have been found to be much less than they might have been, while their extra-major specialization has often been greater than it need be. (Boyer and Ahlgren, 1987). Milton and his colleagues report that 53% of all institutions allow students to take one pass/fail course per term. In a complete undergraduate career about 25% of all institutions allow a total of four pass/fail courses.

Problems similar to those experienced in the United States arise in Britain and elsewhere when accumulating points from repeats. For example, in the Secondary Education Teachers Diploma awarded by my institution a repeat candidate cannot get more than a 'pass' grade unless the repeat is for medical reasons. In the United States by contrast, a large number of institutions replace the original grade with the new one, which is usually higher. Some use an averaging method in which the original grade and the new one are averaged. More universities are likely to replace grades than are colleges and vice versa. When grades are transferred from one institution to another the majority do not report that revised grades have been included in the cumulative GPA (Milton et al., 1986).

I have no doubt that academics will advance perfectly good explanations and have logical reasons for the decisions they make. Indeed, I have sat through hours of interminable debate on such matters. The question in the end is 'What does a B mean?', and this is exceptionally difficult to answer. Consider the question 'Does a B from institution Z mean the same thing as a B from institution X?' The answer is quite simply that we have no means of knowing. In England and Ireland the difference is between departments. Academics will knowingly say, 'Ah, but a II.1 from department Y is not as good as a II.1 from department X'. Such statements are made in spite of the fact that the external examiner system is supposed to protect and ensure that the standards as observed by them in the examination scripts are comparable. Even in this regard employers in the United States who might be expected to want something better ask for the cumulative GPA, or, as Milton et al. (1986) report, seek a higher level of honours than the job might justify in Britain. An important outcome of the national grade study in the United States has been to demonstrate that the views which teachers and students have of grades and grading not only differ between the two groups (this is to be expected) but among themselves. It is, the authors say, 'shattering to have a student who received a B in a course become depressed because to that student the grade B meant failure as a person'. Similar stories can be related about students in Britain, but the system does not regard this as of any great consequence. Perhaps the more compelling comment in Milton et al.'s report is this:

> At Southern Oregon State College, for example, students sought redress in the courts (*McBeth, P. E. W.* versus *M. Elliot*, 1978), because two faculty members,

joined by the President and Registrar, refused to obey the order to change grades issued by the school's duly authorized grievance committee. Such is the power of grades and of those who bestow them. The letters A, B, C, D, F must symbolically signify omnipotence to their wielders. Apparently the power of authority of disciplinary knowledge possessed by a faculty member is insufficiently gratifying.

So are grades absolute? Do they have absolute meanings?

GRADING: ABSOLUTE OR RELATIVE?

If grades are absolute, then they are only so in the eyes of the beholders, the teachers and the students, for it has been understood since 1908 (Meyer, 1908) in the United States and 1935 in Britain that the marks of examiners are highly variable. Starch and Elliott (1912, 1913a, b) showed that the marking of test papers in English, History and Mathematics was highly variable when they were marking against a 100-point scale. Not only were different marks recorded for the same candidate when scored by two different teachers, but even the same teacher accredited different marks to the same candidate when that teacher re-marked that paper.

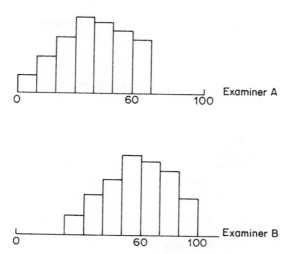

Figure 8. Hypothetical distributions of marks for the same group of students in the same subject due to different examiners

In Britain Hartog and Rhodes (1935) obtained similar results for Chemistry, English, French, History and Latin examinations. They concluded that the marks of examiners were unreliable. Reliability (or consistency, as S. Wiseman preferred to call it) is the measure of the extent to which a test or examination gives consistent results with repeated applications. This is the reliability of a test in time. It has been generally understood that a test will not be valid, (i.e. assess the objectives for which it was designed), unless it is reliable although this axiom has been questioned in recent years. Both reliability and validity are generally determined by correlational analyses. No wonder that public examinations like the ACT, GCE, and SAT have been subject to many rigorous reliability studies. Hartog and Rhodes (1935, 1936) not only drew attention to the lack of correlation between two examiners marking the same papers but to the fact that they were likely to produce two different distributions. This point is illustrated in Figure 8.

Consider the problem of a candidate at a borderline (Figure 9). Using the British notation, two examples are given. These are at the 60% level which divides two classes and at the level of compensation, 35%. One marker might give candidate A 59 and another marker 61; similarly, candidate B might be given 34 by one marker and 36 by another. Which are the correct marks? There is no answer to that question. Now consider candidate C at the 50% level, who is a candidate for our secondary teachers' diploma. If that student gets 51 he or she has an additional annual salary increment throughout his or her teaching career; if 49 is awarded, this increment is lost.

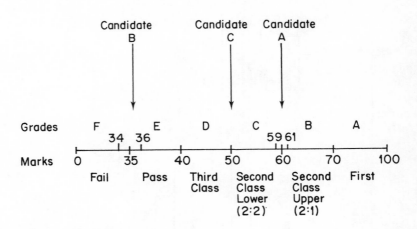

Figure 9. Example of a grading scale for an examination with total marks of 100 to show the problem faced by courts of examiners at the borderlines.

The problem of justice is accentuated by the fact that it is reasonable to hypothesize that, a month or so later, these examiners might reverse their marks. It is for this reason that the notion of continuous assessment, in which a series of marks is collected over the period of an academic year, might prove, when averaged, to be a more accurate assessment of the candidate than a single mark.

Error is inherent in any type of test, be it essay, objective or, for that matter, oral. The three main types of error are 'time error' due to short time changes in the candidate's performance, marker errors due to inconsistencies in marking and discrepancies in marking, and paper-content errors which are demonstrated by differences between the results of supposedly different papers.

One of the problems in the interpretation of reliability data is that analysts tend to concentrate on the disagreements between examiners rather than the extent of agreement. Vernon (1965) was impressed by the latter when he evaluated Hartog and Rhodes' study, for they showed that important public examinations at matriculation and university honours level were marked consistently. For example, the median disagreement between any two examiners was not more than 3%. He felt that this figure probably represented the standard error of the mark, but accepted that some marks might be very much greater. He went on to say:

> Nevertheless, this study deserves to be taken very seriously, since it indicates that many less thorough examinations are deplorably unreliable; that in the absence of a scheme of instructions drawn up and applied by experienced examiners much worse discrepancies may arise; that when the average and dispersion marks are not standardized, gross differences may appear in the proportions of credits, passes and fails, etc., which are awarded and that even a percentage error may take all the difference between a pass and a fail, or a first and a second class.

His remarks are supported by the fact that very high reliabilities have been found between markers in GCE and CSE examinations (Murphy, 1982; Willmot and Nuttall, 1975). However, markers in these receive considerable guidance, which university markers do not. Recent investigations of university marking suggest that Vernon was somewhat sanguine. For example, in a study of the relationship between 'off the cuff' predictions of performance and actual scores Wilson (1986) found that the magnitude of error in forecasting was somewhat larger than the economics teachers might have expected. He said it seemed that some teachers accepted uncritically those outcomes which were expected but searched for 'reasons' to explain those which were not. It is a view which my observations of courts of examiners leads me to support. Another study of marking in electrical engineering papers where scoring might be expected to be reasonably consistent also casts doubt on the validity of Vernon's conclusion (McVey, 1976a,b).

Statistically a *standard error* may be computed which depends on the reliability and the standard deviation of the marks. It is this computation that is of particular value to examiners, for it demonstrates the range within which an assigned mark exists. A score is expressed as the score plus or minus the standard error. The *standard error* of a 100-item multiple-choice test is 5. So a candidate with a score of 59 should really have his or her score stated as 59 ± 7. That is to express the fact that the true score could be anywhere in the range of 52–66. As the test becomes longer, the proportion of error gets smaller. We might confidently predict that the standard error of an essay test will be even more, since the reliability of essays is much lower than that of objective tests.

McVey (1976a), of the Department of Electrical and Electronic Engineering at the University of Surrey, involved his colleagues in the determination of the standard error of their papers. He asked his colleagues to design two papers instead of the usual one which the students would sit. Each of the papers was to be of the same standard and to cover the same area of syllabus. They were vetted by the committee which looked at all the papers set in the examination. The two papers were set to the same group of candidates in place of those which they usually sat at intervals of between one and four days. The scripts of each pair were marked by the examiners. Eleven pairs and 578 scripts were marked over a period of three years. Of the differences in marks obtained between the examiners, 52% were 10 marks or less, 18% exceeded 20 marks, and 5% exceeded 30. He found the standard error to be 7.64 marks, which, he thought, given the limitations of the experiment, was too optimistic.

In a subsequent experiment he tried to distinguish between marker error and error due to the content of the paper (McVey, 1987b). The two are interrelated, and paper error must contribute to marker error, especially in circumstances where ambiguous questions are set. In essay or problem-solving papers where the number of questions to be answered is small, the content of the syllabus which is likely to be covered may be small compared with what had to be studied by the student. Therefore a student who has 'spotted' (predicted) the questions on a paper may be at an advantage compared with one who has not. McVey attempted to isolate paper-content error from marker error, and concluded that paper error is greater than marker error. He relied on paid student volunteers to take the two examinations which were necessary because of the need to remove marker error. James (1977), in a later replication of this experiment, was able to administrate the examinations as a normal part of a course. He obtained results similar to those of McVey. Both inquiries suffered from the defect of a small sample, and much more work needs to be done on this aspect of reliability. Nevertheless, those essay questions which I have designed and subsequently judged to be poor have seriously affected my marking.

Wilmut (quoted by Cresswell, 1986a) found that one of the main reasons for disagreement between examiners about marking was that they made random but straightforward mistakes, such as misreading graphs, overlooking points in answers, etc. This was certainly the experience of the moderators of engineering science at A level (Carter *et al.*, 1986) (see Chapter 11).

It is clear that marks are not absolute and that the design of questions and their marking needs to be rigorous. We cannot afford to be sanguine about our marking; neither can we afford to treat the setting of papers with indifference. For this reason, problems in essay writing and essay marking are considered again in Chapter 10.

The potential for error in examinations has implications for the way in which marks are combined from different examination papers to arrive at a single score. It also has implications within a single examination for the number of grade intervals which are used. Since the former relates to the responsibility of examiners and the latter to examining authorities, issues relating to the combination of examiners marks are considered first. There is necessarily some repetition of the previous argument, since both problems arise from the relative unreliability of examinations.

THE PERCEPTIONS OF EXAMINERS AND THE COMBINATION OF THEIR MARKS

We have seen that the marks of examiners for the same set of answers can vary, and that the shapes of mark distributions between examiners are also subject to considerable variation. It also seems that the behaviour of examiners tends to persist in time. That is, a person who tends to mark low will tend to do so in subsequent examinations, while one who tends to mark high will always mark high. Teachers in their role as examiners tend to adopt certain dispositions toward marking which arise from their beliefs about the purposes of examinations which define their frames of reference.

Thorndike and Hagen (1977) described three such frames of reference. They called them Perfection, Peer and Potential, and they relate to the standard against which a grade is given, i.e. 'absolute norm', 'relative performance' and 'change in performance during the term'. One American study (Geisinger, 1980) has shown that instructors using peer or perfection models tend to give lower grades than teachers who use a potential for growth model (I tend to use a peer model). Another study showed that students rated the grades as valuable if they were awarded on the basis of mastery as potential (Eizler, 1983). In the terminal examinations used in Britain student views would not matter, but they certainly do in coursework (see below). Frames of reference such as these partially account for the different mark distributions found among instructors marking the same papers.

Thus between different examiners in the same faculty (subject) there may be considerable differences in their mark distributions, and, to be fair to students, action needs to be taken to correct these misalignments which are due to variability in the marking of the papers and not to differences in either the qualities (objectives) tested or the individual performance of the students.

The significance of this issue may perhaps be best brought home by consideration of the marks on a school report of the kind issued by many British schools, for we would expect to do no less for our students in higher education than is done for our children in secondary school. The argument applies equally to the compilation of the Grade-Point-Average.

Suppose now that all the teachers who teach a particular class produce different distributions: then any summation of these marks will be unfair to the students. The unfairness of school reports is immediately apparent, for a mark of 60 by teacher A is an excellent one, whereas from teacher B it is only a little above average, if it is assumed that the subjects are of equal difficulty and the students had the same range of abilities and similar motivation to the tasks.

Marks on a report are comparatively meaningless without additional information, for which reason some schools also give the average mark of the class in each subject (Table 3)—not that this is entirely helpful. However, it is entirely wrong to add the marks of different distributions to arrive at a result for the distribution of one subject; this can reorder the ranking of distributions which are approximately the same, as Table 4 shows. In all cases in this rather extreme example the candidates obtain the same marks in subjects A and B. However, in Table 4(a) the range of marks for subject C is 40–60 with a spread of 20, whereas in Table 4(b) subject C is marked in such a way that it is given a spread of 60 with a range of 20–80. A more striking example is shown in Table 4(b), where a fifth subject is introduced in which the examiner spreads his marks over the smaller range 40–60 while preserving the rank order in Table 4(c). The pupils all obtain the same score. It is important to remember that changes in the average mark do not alter the ranking; it is the combination of marks which lie within different dispersions.

Table 3. An example of a school report

	Exam mark (%)	Average mark for group
Religious Knowledge	53	51
English Language	66	63
History	56	46
Geography	65	62
French	73	58
Mathematics	63	64
Science	77	58
Art	50	58
Music	75	
Physical Education	Fair	

Place in form: 6th
No. of pupils: 35

It is because of situations of this kind that some teachers advocate a technique which standardizes marks in that they are all brought to the same mean and standard deviation while at the same time preserving each marker's distinctions between his or her scores.

We do this with the assessments for our diploma course for graduates intending to become secondary school teachers (11–18 years). The justification for this procedure with our diploma examination has been described in detail by Cameron (1984) elsewhere. As a general finding, our written examinations are always marked more severely than the coursework, which constitues a considerable component of the final mark. Whereas each written examination is scored by a single marker, the coursework is scored by several. Nevertheless, the mean scores are consistent. Within each year and within each form of assessment there is considerable deviation between the marks of the examiners.

The coursework is set in the methodology of the subjects which the student intends to teach (for example, methods of teaching history). There are nine subject areas, each assessed by a different teacher. In one year the highest subject average was 71.5 (SD = 1.6) and the lowest 58.4 (SD = 7.6). This meant that only the very highest in the second subject could approach the lowest of the first. Such a poor comparative performance is hardly likely in practice. While we obtain considerable marker consistency from year to year, we experience considerable marker variability, and for this reason we scale or standardize our marks (Ebel, 1965).

Table 4. Hypothetical example of rank-orders arising from different distributions of marks

(a)

Student	Subjects A	B	C	Total	Rank Order
1	58	62	40	160	1
2	68	42	45	155	2
3	60	40	50	150	3
4	31	59	55	145	4
5	48	32	60	140	5

(b)

1	58	62	20	140	5
2	68	42	35	145	4
3	60	40	50	150	3
4	31	59	65	155	2
5	48	32	80	160	1

(c)

Student	A	B	Subjects C	D	E	Total
1	58	62	20	40	70	250
2	68	42	35	25	60	250
3	60	40	50	40	60	250
4	31	59	65	35	60	250
5	48	32	80	60	30	250

One of the difficulties with this procedure is that we are only one of a few departments which scale. It is university practice that students should know their grade but not their marks in individual subjects. Unfortunately, if the raw marks are converted to honours grades the results could be misleading. A student may find that he or she has a number of honours but is only awarded a pass. In order to tell students about their coursework we use a letter-grade system. We also publish and explain the procedure in use not only because we operate differently to other departments in the university but because it is part of the education of intending teachers.

Table 5. Examples of grade criteria in mathematics for the GCSE examination in England and Wales (*The National Criteria, Mathematics*, Secondary Examinations Council, 1985). (Reproduced by permission of the Controller of Her Brittanic Majesty's Stationery Office.) *NB*: These are preceded by statement of objectives and two lists of content. The numbers in the first column relate to the assessment objectives in their lists. Grade F relates to List 1 and Grade C to Lists 1 and 2

Assessment objective	Grade F examples	Grade C examples
3.3	Extract information from simple timetables. Tabulate numerical data to find the frequency of given scores. Draw a bar chart. Plot given points. Read a travel graph.	Construct a pie chart from simple data. Plot the graph of a linear function.
3.4	Add, subtract and multiply integers. Add and subtract money and simple fractions without a calculator. Calculate a simple percentage of a given sum of money.	Apply the four rules of number to integers and vulgar and decimal fractions without a calculator. Calculate percentage change.
3.5	Perform the four rules on positive integers and decimal fractions (one operation only). Convert a fraction to a decimal.	Perform calculations involving several operations, including negative numbers.
3.6	Measure length, weight and capacity using metric units. Understand relationships between mm, cm, m, km; g, kg.	Use area and volume units.
3.7	Perform a money calculation with a calculator and express the answer to the nearest penny.	Give a reasonable approximation to a calculator calculation involving the four rules.
3.8	Draw a triangle given three sides. Measure a given angle.	Use a scale drawing to solve a two-dimensional problem.
3.9	Continue a straightforward pattern or number sequence.	Recognize, and in simple cases formulate, rules for generating a pattern or sequence.
3.10	Use simple formulae, e.g. gross wage = wage per hour × number of hours worked, and use of $A = 1 \times b$ to find the area of a rectangle.	Solve simple linear equations. Transform simple formulae. Substitute numbers in a formula and evaluate the remaining term.
3.11	Recognize and name simple plane figures and common solid shapes. Find the perimeter and area of a rectangle. Find the volume of a cuboid.	Calculate the length of the third side of a right-angled triangle. Find the angle in a right-angled triangle, given two sides.
	In schemes of assessment where the objective is applicable:	
3.17	Carry out a simple survey; obtain straightforward results from the information obtained.	Investigate and describe the relationship between the surface area and volume of a selection of solid shapes.

One advantage of a system of scaling is that where students can choose between subjects they do not have to worry about the presumed severity of a particular examiner. They can take a course which is perceived to be interesting but tough without worrying about the assessor's severity, in the knowledge that the marks will be related to those of the other examiners. In New South Wales and Victoria (Australia) estimates of general achievement are used for purposes of university entry. Estimates of general achievement are obtained from the average result that each student obtained in all the other subjects studied. The marks in each subject are adjusted by scaling their distribution to that of the estimates of general achievement of the students taking the subject. In New South Wales scaling is introduced for students taking different amounts (levels) of a subject (McGaw, 1984).

The objections to scaling, as I and others (Isaacs and Imrie, 1980) have said, arise when examinations are so structured as to assess different qualities. For example, in non-native language study verbal fluency and literacy understanding are different qualities. Students may perform substantially better in the latter than in the former. Scaling may then be an unjustifiable smoothing. However, as the case for scaling disappears, so does that for a single mark. It is for this reason that there has been so much interest in profiling (see Chapters 6 and 11). An intermediate step between single-mark representations and profiles is the grade criterion in which the marks are related to well-defined criteria. This approach is being developed for the new GCSE examination for 16-year-olds in England. Each subject is now required to describe the award grades in terms of assessment objectives. The examples of the performances required for grades C and F for mathematics are shown in Table 5. In these days of regular student appeals Pulich's (1983) point that the more teachers mark to criterion grades, the less likely there are to be appeals is worth noting. It might also enhance learning. Gerhardt (1976) has designed a criterion schedule for this purpose which relates questions to subcategories similar to but broader than those in the *Taxonomy of Educational Objectives* (Bloom, 1956).

DIFFERENTIAL SUBJECT PERFORMANCE: THE PROBLEM OF COMPARABILITY

Unfortunately, scaling will not resolve the differences in marks which arise between subjects. In respect of Table 2 the National Union of Students pointed out that there were substantial differences in the percentage of first-class honours degrees awarded between arts and science subjects. It found it difficult to believe that this was due to the fact that students in arts subjects were of poorer quality. To illustrate their point, Figure 10 shows the distribution of marks between four subjects in the first-year examinations of a university. The last subject is mathematics. It is, of course, possible that in mathematics, where marking is fairly objective, this is a real distribution which is showing two different quality groups. At the same time, it is reasonable to suppose that each subject assesses something different to the other.

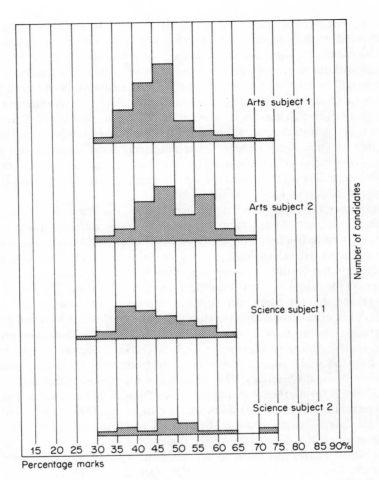

Figure 10. Distribution of marks in two arts and two science subjects in an institution of higher education

As we have seen, one of the problems is the perception that the markers have of the purposes of marking and the methods of scoring to achieve those ends. These vary between the subjects. For example, in the humanities many teachers use a 13 or so point letter scale (using either Roman or Greek letters), whereas in the sciences teachers use numbers. A conversion is required from numbers to letters in the United States (Thomas, 1984). I have seen one attempt to get teachers in the humanities to use numbers and to try to mark to the normal curve, but when they arrived at their marks the distributions came out as in the past. It seems that in their memories there was always that student who did so well—the superfirst—who never somehow appears again. Vernon (1965) put it another way: those teachers who claim this year to have had exceptional students seem, strangely enough, to have them every year. The opposite would seem to be true of teachers in some subject areas. It has probably as much to do with the disposition of teachers as with their subjects, and these dispositions may be related to the subjects they teach.

The problem has been particularly severe in the United States arising from grade deflation and grade inflation. Milton *et al.* (1986) in their discussions of this problem suggested a theory, subsequently tested, which throws further light on examiner behaviour. Between 1950 and 1965 grade deflation occurred. While the average SAT scores slightly increased, the GPA on leaving higher education slightly decreased. Higher-ability students found it more difficult to get grades. However, from around 1965 there was substantial grade inflation. The SAT scores on entry declined substantially while the GPA increases as a mirror of the decline. Milton *et al.* (1986) explain these changes as a function of the view which society has of grades during a particular period.

However, our concern is not with this aspect of the argument but with the proposition that, as grades vary from time to time, different performances are required from faculty and students. Following Goldman and Hewitt (1975, 1976), Milton and his colleagues used Helson's (1964) adaptation level theory to argue that teachers necessarily adapt to changing circumstances. Milton *et al.* argue that if college grades are considered as an adaptation level phenomenon, then the graders' standard for a given grade category will depend on the ability level of the students he or she teaches and has taught. For this type of analysis, grade inflation can be defined as the use of constant grade distribution in the face of lowered student ability levels, and grade deflation as the use of constant grade distribution in the face of raised ones. Similar arguments apply to subjects, and lead to the view that, while some fields may not have intrinsically lower standards, students having lower SAT scores seek out those fields if they are seen to give easy grading. In contrast, high-ability students gravitate toward the hard grading classes. In their study Milton and his colleagues found that students with high adaptation levels had higher GPAs even when SAT or ACT scores were taken into account, which implies that for some students a Grade C is probably no less valued than a grade A by others.

There is striking support for this theory from the University of Utah. De Nevers (1984) describes how the engineering department in that university became aware of the problem through complaints from business recruiters. They asked why engineering students had an average GPA of 2.8 compared with other students with average GPAs of 3.5 or more. Students below 3.5 were considered failures. Worse still, the students complained that, to earn their grade, they had to do much more work than their friends in other colleges with whom they had been at high school. When the engineers came to examine the problem they found that there was evidence in the colleges of the university of grade inflation. Moreover, this had an effect on the number of *summa cum laude* awards offered.

They plotted the correlation of average ACT score with average grade given in all junior- and senior-level classes for 1976–82 and showed evidence of grade inflation (Figure 11). For example, the average grade given in education was

3.7. About 70% of the class were given A's and 30% B's. In Nursing and Fine Art a similar situation pertained. In contrast, the engineers were at 2.8. Comparison with ACT scores for the period showed that the best grades were not going to the best students, for there was a significant negative correlation. The least talented, as measured by ACT, were going to the high-level grading colleges while those with high ACT scores were going to low-level ones. In 1976 a graduate with a GPA of 3.5 obtained *magna cum laude* and 3.1–3.49 *cum laude*. Thirty per cent of nursing graduates obtained *magna cum laude* whereas only 19% of the engineers were similarly rewarded. The engineers averaged 3.1 points higher on the ACT than the nurses. As a result of these findings, the university recorded a new measure called the honours point scale.

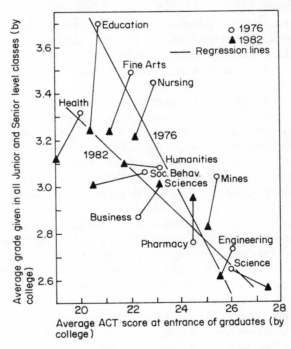

Figure 11. Relation between average grade given in upper-division classes and ACT score at entrance of graduates, by college, University of Utah, 1976 and 1982. The 1976 regression has $R^2 = 0.64$, $P = 0.0006$; the 1982 regression has $R^2 = 0.75$, $P = 0.0006$. The 1976 grades are the sum of autumn quarter grades in 1974 and 1975. The 1982 grades are for all of the academic year 1981–2. (Reproduced from N. de Nevers (1984). An engineering solution to grade inflation. *Engineering Education*, April, pp. 661–663.) (Reproduced by kind permission of the Editors of *Engineering Education*)

This has the effect of determining the number of honours awarded by reference to the average score of the class. A student must score above that average. If a student's grade is equal to the class average then his or her honours point is 3, independent of the grade. If a student receives A (GPA = 4) in a class where the class average is 3.5 then the student's honours point score is 3.5. If, however, the average for the class is 2.5 then the student will receive 4.5 honours points. *Magna cum laude* is awarded to those who are in the top 10% of the honours points and *cum laude* is awarded to those in the band 10–25%. The formula for this is:

Honours point score = student's grade (0–4) − Class average grade (0–4) + 3

As a result of the application of the formula the percentage of those graduating *magna cum laude* in nursing fell from 30% in 1976 to 0.8% in 1982. It is also clear that the academically able as measured by ACT now get the better grades.

This is no reason to suppose that the same does not happen in other parts of the world in departments where subjects are starved of students. For example, in England a very sophisticated network of information, published and unpublished, is available to school students about the grade requirements of departments, and it can fuel expectations. No studies of the kind undertaken at Utah have been published. However, there is a great deal of pressure on the nine GCE examining boards to maintain 'standards' not only among the subjects which they examine but between the same subjects offered by the same boards. That is, that a grade B in subject X should be equal to a grade B in subject Y, and that a grade B in History in board M should be equal to a grade B in History in board N.

The boards have carried out innumerable inquiries in both these areas. In regard to intersubject comparisons of the standards of subjects within a board the Joint Matriculation Board has completed investigations of GCE O and A levels which used techniques similar to those used by de Nevers (Forrest and Smith, 1972; Forrest *et al.* 1970). At O level the criterion used was not GPA at college but a standardized test for numerical and verbal skills. The average total reference test score of candidates in each subject sample was compared with the average GCE grade of the same candidates in that subject. From a regression analysis the relative leniency or severity of subjects was determined. However, as the authors of this investigation pointed out, no reference test can take into account the influence on examination results of factors such as the length of the course pursued by the candidates, the quality of teaching, and the motivation of the students. For this reason, they investigated an alternative technique for comparing standards and found it to give similar results. This method compared the average grades for all candidates offering a pair of subjects, so that the performance of a group of candidates in one subject is compared with their performance in another. The number of pairs of subjects may be extended, and if one subject is made common to each pair, the performance of candidates in the common or basic subject can be compared with their performance in the others. This approach does not require a reference test (Forrest and Smith, 1972).

Of greater interest are the comparability studies between subjects offered by the different boards (Forrest and Shoesmith, 1985). Such investigations are fraught with difficulty, because, apart from the fact that Subject X offered by board M might not have the same syllabus content as Subject X offered by board N, there are differences in the procedures used to rank-order candidates, and to draw the lines at the grade intervals. Therefore comparability on the basis of pass rates in the examinations from the different boards provides little useful evidence about relative standards. In any case, more candidates may be passed by one board than another because they deserve to pass. Reference tests provide no better judgements because certain assumptions which might be resolved statistically have to be made concerning the issues highlighted by the test results. For example, the results allow for no differences in calibre among the candidates, that is, apart from those shown by the test. Investigations using reference tests were made, as were those of several thousand candidates taking the same subjects in two boards.

In general, these studies highlighted difficulties rather than differences. Useful as they were, the boards finally came down on the side of cross-moderation as the technique to be developed. Most of the studies since 1977 have been of this type, in which experienced examiners from the different boards came together to mark each others' scripts. The reasons for this are worth repeating:

> Experience ... has revealed many of the limitations of comparability studies which use other methodologies: human judgement has at least the potential to form the basis of a more robust and practicable methodology.
>
> Cross-moderation methodology is particularly attractive, for it involves the very people who influence most of the critical decisions which are made after each examination: their experiences of reading and discussing scripts of different provenances are in their minds when those decisions are taken. In contrast, it has proved surprisingly difficult to design research studies which will result in conclusions of a quantitative kind capable of being readily translated into action at grading meetings.

It is very clear from the reports that, however crude these studies may be judged, a great deal of experience is obtained by the boards and their examiners about examining.

GRADING PRACTICES AND PROBLEMS OF SELECTION

Although the problem of comparability between subjects has been much discussed in Britain, the idea that there are other systems for the reporting of marks, or that the number of intervals in the awarding profile may be different, has been little considered except where the GCE A level examination is concerned. Yet it is clear from experience in the United States and Canada that the number of intervals is not sacrosanct.

In Canada the universities have anything between three to 12 passing grades (Ratzlaff, 1980; Taylor, 1977). In the United states the common practice is to relate a course grade which may be as few as two and as many as 12 points for a particular course to a fine grade (300 points) for the overall cumulative GPA for all courses. It has not always been thus, and Milton *et al.*'s analysis of why this has been the case is salutary.

It seems that, in the 300 years for which records exist, there have been short (1–4), nine-point, 13-point and 20-point scales. At Yale in 1783 there was a class called 'perjores' which derived its name from an English class of 'unmentionables' (The British now use the term 'unclassified' in their public examinations.) Written tests were introduced at Yale in 1930. The universities of Dartmouth and Georgia had external examining committees in the eighteenth century and the sessions were open to the public. This was something different to the British external examiner, since the persons brought in from outside also conducted the examination. Its parallel is with the ACT, SAT, and GCE examinations, which are set independently of the internal tests in the college.

Perhaps one of the most interesting ideas came from Professor Meyer (1908), at the University of Missouri. Arising from the fact that a professor had dared to fail a whole course, Meyer investigated grading practices and found chaos. He suggested a ranking scheme which seems to have underpinned the A–B–C–D–F system then beginning to make itself felt. He recommended the following rank order:

TDP			
	3%	Excellent	A
	22%	Superior	B
	50%	Medium	C
	22%	Inferior	D
	3%	Failure	F

Here we see the normal curve at work.

Distributions of this kind can have a powerful influence on results, particularly in systems which are highly selective, such as that operating in Britain. When the English initiated GCE A level in 1951 they agreed the norms shown in Table 6. These were intended to be regarded as no more than rough indicators. It will be seen that the shape of the distribution curve affects the distinctions made between candidates when the grade intervals are drawn (Figure 12).

An important consideration which relates to the standard error of marks is the narrowness of the B–C and C–D intervals. A person whose actual score is D could have had a true score in the C interval; the same might be true of a candidate in the C interval in respect of the B one. This can have profound consequences for candidates who are seeking admission to universities and require a C or B in that subject. The width of the intervals has therefore been the subject of much debate and statistical investigation in England. Two views have emerged. The first is that the intervals in a grading system should reflect the underlying reliability of the mark scale. Since there is an error this is best accommodated by a limited number of grades. The opposite view is based on the belief that if there are few grades there is a loss of information about the candidate.

Table 6. Recommended grade distributions against percentage of entry in the General Certificate of Education. (Source: Ministry of Education (1960)

Grade	Percentage of entry	Cumulative percentages
A	10	10
B	15	25
C	10	35
D	15	50
E	20	70
Ordinary level		
Pass	20	90
Fail	10	100

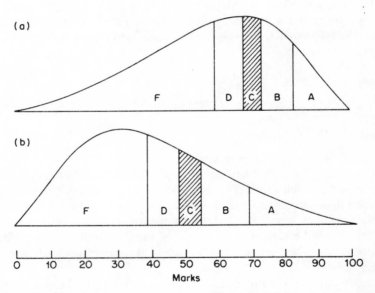

Figure 12. An illustration of the effects of the type of distribution on the marks (grades) of candidates to show that a given grade has different meanings in different distributions. (Adapted from Forrest, G. M. and Whittaker, R. J. (1983). *Problems of the GCE Advanced Level Grading Scheme*, Manchester: Joint Matriculation Board. In the original diagrams it was related to the percentage mark scheme shown in Table 6 and included E, O and F grades)

In a system of equal intervals the candidate stands less chance of moving outside the desired intervals when his number is small than when it is large. This point has been well illustrated by Cresswell (1986a) (Figure 13), who argues that those who use examinations as selection mechanisms are able to make finer distinctions between candidates if there are more divisions; and this

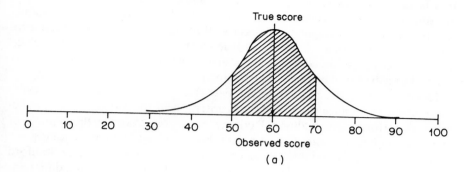

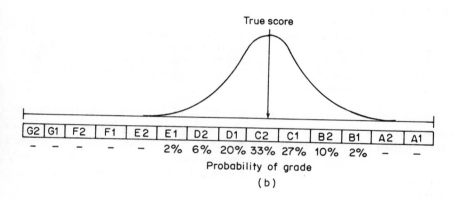

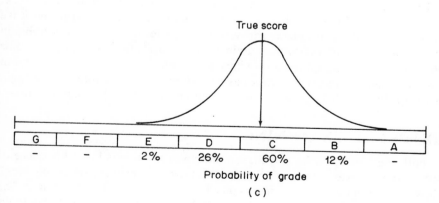

Figure 13. The effects of grade intervals on true score and grading. (Slightly adapted from J. Cresswell with his permission.) (a) For a candidate with a true score of 60 marks how likely it is that he will actually obtain any particular mark; (b) for a candidate with a true score of 60 marks how likely it is that he will actually obtain any particular one of a large number of intervals; (c) for a candidate with a true score of 60 marks how likely it is that he will actually obtain any particular one of a small number of intervals

may be necessary in selection procedures if there are more applicants than there are jobs or places at college. When broad bands are used some additional selection mechanism might be necessary. With large intervals a greater proportion of candidates are likely to get true scores. However, those scores which are incorrect are subject to very large errors, whereas the errors are greatly reduced in a system which uses narrow intervals.

Those who take the broad-interval view (Please, 1971; Mitchelmore, 1981) might argue that, since the broad-band criteria lead to relatively poor predictions of performance, additional criteria from, for example the reports of school principals, and interviews are desirable, provided that coherence is given to such a system and that it is competently done. In the United States, Stanford University makes a particular point of the value of variety in admissions procedures, including interviews, even though it is more costly. Their Dean of Admissions, Hargaden (1982) wrote:

> Contrary to popular myth, test scores and grades, in and of themselves, while not insignificant, are nevertheless secondary. In short, an applicant with a high level of achievement in a first rate academic program and only modest test scores fares better in our process than a student with high test scores and high grades but only a modest academic program.

One argument in favour of a large number of intervals is the motivational effect. It may be far easier for a student to perceive an advance over a small interval than over a large one. It has been demonstrated that the distance between B− and C+ is perceived by students psychologically to be much larger than between any other pair of adjacent categories (Stancato and Eizler, 1983).

The inescapable conclusion is that the best approach is not to use intervals at all but to quote the mark obtained together with the standard error and leave the selectors with the problem. This view is supported by the contention that in the initial stages of marking examiners are simply not able to make fine distinctions. The alternative, as we have seen, is to move toward some kind of criterion grading, and, although it has its own problems (Chapter 11), it might be of considerable help in the external examining and the validation of courses.

EXTERNAL EXAMINING

In both the United States and the Commonwealth there is long experience of some kind of external examining. In the former it extends over 300 years. However, the models in use differ considerably from the British model.[1] The best known, at Swarthmore College, has been in operation since the 1930s (Jones, 1933; Milton and Edgerley, 1976). Its purpose was to certificate the one-third of undergraduates seeking honours. In their junior year the students undertake a plan of study and negotiate a series of seminars. The external examiners set and mark terminal examinations in the field of the seminars. It is this method of examining which is used in GCE A level except that the three or four examiners who set and have responsibility for the marking of the papers have a number of assistants who help them to score the several thousand papers in each subject.

In both countries there is considerable interest in external examining. In the United States Fong (1987), who reviewed arguments for and against external examining, drew attention to a project begun in 1986 which involved eighteen institutions both large and small, in the evaluation of the work of external examiners in a variety of educational settings. Most of these institutions were to assess their students by a combination of written comprehensive and oral examinations. Some would use a thesis as a substitute for the written paper. The sponsors hope that a number of models will emerge which institutions could consider as an option in the search for appropriate means of assessing student learning and programme quality. (The project was sponsored by the Association of American Colleges.)

In Britain the Committee of Vice-Chancellors and Principals drew up the code of practice shown in Table 7. A report published in 1987 under the same title showed that this had had a considerable influence on university practice. At the time they declared that the purposes of the external examiner system are to ensure, first and most important, that degrees awarded in similar subjects are comparable in standard in all universities in Britain (while accepting that there will be variations in content); and second, that the assessment system is fair and is fairly operated in the classification of students.

Table 7. Code of practice for the external examiner system for first degree and taught Masters' courses. Extract from *Academic Standards in Universities* (1986). Report of a committee chaired by Professor P. A. Reynolds, Committee of Vice-Chancellors and Principals, London. (Reproduced by kind permission of the Committee of Vice-Chancellors and Principals)

Purposes and functions

1. It is neither possible nor desirable to establish a uniform external examiner system across all institutions and applicable to all subjects. Some of the points in the code will not be applicable to some universities or to some subjects because of variations, for example, in the structure of degree programmes (single honours, joint honours, modular) and in student numbers. But exceptions and reservations have deliberately been omitted in the interest of a clear statement of widely-applicable guidelines.

2. The purposes of the external examiner system are to ensure, first and most important, that degrees awarded in similar subjects are comparable in standard in different universities in the United Kingdom, though their content does of course vary; and, secondly, that the assessment system is fair and is fairly operated in the classification of students.

3. In order to achieve these purposes external examiners need to be able:
    (a) to participate in assessment processes for the award of degrees;
    (b) to arbitrate or adjudicate on problem cases;
    (c) to comment and give advice on course content, balance and structure, on degree schemes, and on assessment processes.*

70

4. External examiners are responsible to the Senate or other body which authorises the award of degrees.
5. No university degree should be awarded without participation in the examining process by at least one examiner external to the university institution who should be a full member of the relevant board of examiners.
6. External examiners concerned with courses validated by the university in associated institutions should be external both to the university and to the institution concerned. The procedures outlined in the code should normally apply similarly to the examining process in the university and in the associated institutions.
7. Each external examiner on appointment should be sent a written statement about the place of the relevant degree examination in the university's system of education in that subject, and on the organisation and phasing of the relevant curriculum, together with information about the role and functions of external examiners as seen by the university and by the particular faculty and department.

Selection, appointment and period of service
8. Departments are natural sources of recommendations for the appointment of particular persons as external examiners but scrutiny by the appointing body should have regard to the following:
   (a) only persons of seniority and experience who are able to command authority should be appointed;
   (b) in order to have sufficient time for the proper performance of their functions, individuals should normally be expected not to hold more than two external examinerships at first degree level;
   (c) an external examiner should not be appointed from a department in an institution where a member of the inviting university department is serving as an examiner; exceptions may however occasionally be unavoidable in the case of subjects taught in only a very small number of institutions;
   (d) former members of staff should not be invited to become external examiners before a lapse of at least three years or sufficient time for students taught by that member of staff to have passed through the system, whichever is the longer.
9. The number of external examiners for any particular degree programme should be sufficient to cover the full range of studies. More than one external examiner may be needed where there is a large number of students or where the degree programme covers a wide range.
10. There should be a formal limit to the period of service. This might be three or four years, sometimes with the possibility of limited extension.
11. External examiners from outside the higher education system, for example, from industry or the professions, are appropriate in certain circumstances.

Participation in assessment procedures
12. External examiners should see the syllabuses of courses on which the examinations are set.
13. An external examiner, as a full member of the relevant board of examiners, should have the right to be present at all examiners' meetings at which significant decisions are to be taken in regard to the specialisms with which he has been concerned (including the setting of papers) and should be required to be present at all final examiners' meetings in the subject(s) in which he has been involved. If an external examiner exceptionally cannot attend a meeting where his presence is formally required, he should be available for consultation by telephone.
14. All draft degree examination papers should be sent to an external examiner for approval. In appropriate cases external examiners may be expected to set some

questions or complete papers. In some subjects it may be essential for model answers to be prepared and scrutinised.

15.   An external examiner has the right to see all degree examination scripts. In those cases where it is agreed that the inviting department should make a selection of scripts to be sent to an external examiner, the principles for such selection should be agreed in advance.

16.   The guiding principle for any selection of scripts is that external examiners should have enough evidence to determine that internal marking and classification are of an appropriate standard and are consistent. External examiners should see a sample of scripts from the top, the middle and the bottom of the range. They should normally be sent all scripts of borderline candidates. They should also see all scripts assessed internally as first class or as failures.

17.   Where a *viva voce* examination is held for a proportion, but only a proportion, of the candidates, the principles for the selection of candidates should be agreed with an external examiner. Such an examination should normally be conducted by an external examiner who may be assisted by one or more internal examiners.

18.   An external examiner should have the right to see any work that contributes to the assessment and the degree classification. In some cases it may be agreed that the department should make a selection of such work to be sent to the external examiner, the principles for such selection being agreed in advance.

19.   The views of an external examiner must be particularly influential in the case of disagreement on the mark to be awarded for a particular unit of assessment, or on the final classification to be derived from the array of marks of a particular candidate at the examiners' meeting. The signature of an external examiner must be appended to the final list of degree results as evidence that he accepts the classification.

20.   External examiners should be encouraged to comment on the assessment process and the schemes for marking and classification. In some subjects participation in the devising of such schemes is essential. External examiners may often be able to give valuable advice to internal examiners, especially the inexperienced, either direct or through the head of department.

Discussion of course structure and degree schemes

21.   Departments and external examiners should use the opportunity afforded by the visits of external examiners to discuss the structure and content of the course and of the degree programme, and the assessment procedures. Any comments or suggestions made by the external examiners should be discussed by the department and an explicit decision made about whether or not to introduce changes.

Reports

22.   External examiners should make written annual reports as well as a written report at the end of their period of office. They should be free to make any comments they wish, including observations on teaching and course structure and content. Such observations are of particular importance in the final written report. A copy of the report made by an external examiner at the conclusion of his term of office might be copied to the incoming external examiner after the examinations at the end of his first year.

23.   Reports should be sent to the Vice-Chancellor, whose responsibility it is to see that they are considered and action taken by the Senate or other appropriate body.

---

* A course refers to a unit of teaching and study forming an examinable component of a degree programme.

All the work on reliability would suggest that this is a tall order. It would also require that the external examiner had the power to change teaching if it did not mean that the judgement of an examination script is the only one which has to be made.

However, the code of conduct is likely to have some beneficial effects in standardizing procedures and clarifying the role of the external examiner. The research I had done on external examiners of the Diploma in Technology showed that there was much role confusion and a variety of practice (Heywood, 1969). Piper (1985) has shown that this is still the case. In his substantive study of external examining in Britain he found that half the external examiners in his sample saw all the scripts rather than a sample but that only two-thirds of the respondents thought that the calibration of scores between institutions was a prominent duty.

In this respect another study by Creswell (1986b) of the borderline procedures used by the GCE boards is of considerable importance. These boards review the scripts of candidates at the borderline who have just failed with a view to raising these grades if possible. The inverse (of reviewing those just above the grade line in order to modify their marks) is not practised. In our Diploma the external examiner is given the scripts in the regions above and below where we think the grade lines ought to be drawn. Both activities involve examiners in re-marking or, at the very least, obtaining a substantive impression of the script. Cresswell points out that there will be a criterion error introduced into the re-marking if the independent assessors do not mark to the same criteria. Given that this is the case, both examiners should mark to the same criteria, and all the scripts, not just a sample, should be made available to external examiners if consistency is to be maintained.

Piper has also highlighted differences between the attitudes to external examining in the university and public (CNAA) sectors. Of interest is the fact that all CNAA external examiners produced written reports whereas only a quarter of the university external examiners completed such reports (see also Lawton, 1986). It is also evident, as Nightingale (1984) has indicated, that there is a similar lack of criteria in regard to the assessment and external examining of higher degrees which the code of practice covers.

One effect of the code might be to reduce the organizational 'press' of the department on the lone external examiner. They may also create common expectations about what is and what is not possible in the way of adjustments in teaching, curriculum and assessment as opposed to the adjustment of marks for internal consistency and external comparability. With only three two-day visits over three years it could be argued that little change is possible, given the strong internal influence of peers within the discipline (O'Neill, 1983) from which the external assessor is asked to stand apart.

It is in this sense that the validating committees of professional organizations, accrediting agencies and bodies like the CNAA may have a more powerful influence on change (Church, 1983). They have more power and in a sense are more truly assessors. Yet they act on a *post-hoc* basis, for they predict what will happen if certain resources (man and materials) are available to the students who will pursue a certain syllabus (Heywood, 1981b). They do not make ongoing studies of student learning against student outcomes, which is what the external assessor is asked to do. My findings concerning the committees of the National Council for Technological Awards were that they were inhibitive of innovation, and that this was a significant fact in the curriculum drift in the colleges of advanced technology to emulate the universities (Heywood, 1969).

All this leads to the view that if teaching and learning are to be improved, the role of the external examiner needs to be enhanced to take into account the instructional process and curriculum by which the goals are reached. In this respect those who have external examiner systems in the Commonwealth have much to learn from the experience of Alverno College, where the external assessors from business and academia have to attend a series of training sessions designed to orient them towards the college's purposes and assessment techniques (Mentkowski and Doherty, 1983). The purpose of external examining should be rather less about reliability, the solutions to which are rather strictly limited, and rather more about the validity of the whole process.

Given the diversity of American institutions and the desire to retain that diversity, it is not surprising that the advantages which Fong (1987) sees for external examining are at a deep level of involvement. He writes:

> Instructors have two goals for their classes. First, they want to invest a class with knowledge and skills that will enable each student to be competent in the subject of study. Second, they seek to maximize the abilities of individual students. Effectively, instructors seek a floor to student achievement, the pass/fail line, and above that to distinguish whether degrees of achievement are excellent, good, or merely satisfactory. Instruction in the classroom is guided by both criterion and selection-referenced considerations. Unlike commercial examinations, external examiners, themselves most frequently instructors at other institutions, are experienced in balancing these two goals in evaluation. An external's sense of what constitutes adequacy and excellence may differ from the host faculty's but the discussion and negotiation of these standards is precisely where the perspective of the outsider becomes invaluable.

The National Grade Survey in the United States concluded from its study of the attitudes of teachers and students in higher education, employers and parents, that above all, those surveyed wanted grades to be a communication device which served the cause of teaching and learning. The authors of the study argued that grades influenced educational practice in ways that were detrimental to learning. It is not without significance that in the United States, students' anticipated grades have been found to be positively related to their evaluation of their teachers (Feldman, 1976). They argued that because the numerical value of GPA meant different things to different people it should be abolished. Too many people jump to conclusions on seeing the GPA and do not look beyond it to establish a student's learning accomplishments. It is not, they argue, arithmetically proper to go from a relatively undifferentiated metric

(ABCDF) to a much more differentiated matrix. (In the British examinations the direction is the inverse, that is, from a percentage to a grade.)

At the level of subject (classroom) grading Milton and his colleagues think that is such a context-dependent phenomenon, subject to so many factors, that its exactness is in doubt. To overcome this problem they argue that the US system should move to a less differentiated one in which the objective is learning and mastery rather than ranking (and, by implication, selection). They also argued for a credit/no credit system with an honours grade available to the select few. To accommodate such a system faculty members would have to state what the acceptable level of knowledge was and when a student would not be certified as failing to command the relevant course content, all of which has implications for the role of the external examiner.

As things stand in Britain, the external examiners are the only real source of information about comparability, yet they never meet as a group in this role. Studies by them similar to those conducted by the school matriculation boards could be rewarding. A more instant approach would be to perceive the situation in the terms described by Fong above and to require departments to write criteria in ways similar to those expected in secondary education (see Table 5). This is what is done at Alverno College (see Chapter 13).

In any case, in the United States and the Commonwealth the demands for accountability, the trends in the curriculum, and the introduction of multi-strategy assessment are likely to have a considerable influence on the role of the teacher and thus on that of external examiners. Evaluation as a continuous activity advised by external examiners will demand new approaches to the design of assessment and instruction. The more they become integrated, the more the objectives of assessment will depend on an understanding of the factors which enhance and impede learning.

It is my view that the departmental 'press' is such that external examiners adapt to the circumstances in which they find themselves. Given that they are the only source of information about comparability, exercises of the kind undertaken by the GCE examining boards, among themselves, might be immensely rewarding.

Allowing for the problem of the criterion error referred to above, one approach might be for teachers in higher education to develop criteria for each of the grades awarded, as is being done in Britain at school level by the Secondary Examinations Council. Packages have been developed to help teachers to undertake such tasks (Baumgart, 1984; Cryer, 1986; Nathenson and Henderson, 1981). An alternative and radical approach is to criterion reference without differential grading, as is done at Alverno College in Milwaukee (Chapter 13). In any event, tests which are designed to meet precise objectives (multiple-strategy testing) are likely to be much more valid than those which assume that a range of objectives are tested without being designed for this purpose. Chapters 6–9 are concerned with types of and derivation of criteria. Chapter 13 describes various approaches to multiple-strategy testing.

Note

There is some confusion about the role of university teachers in the assessment of their students as between the United States and Britain. For example, in a recent informative paper on developments in the United States, Harris (1986) writes that 'unlike British or European Institutions, our certification of student achievement is done by the same teacher who teaches the student'. This is not quite true: exactly the same applies to universities and polytechnics in Britain.

I, as a university teacher, am appointed to teach a subject. The syllabus for that subject will appear in two or three lines in a handbook. Depending on the overall examination structure (which is more often than not determined by all the members of the subject department), I will be called upon to write an examination paper for the students to take at the end of the year. Alternatively, I may have to set coursework essays or a project. What these components are and what the questions will be in the examination is essentially my problem, with the proviso that the proposed papers and assessments are sent to an external examiner for his or her judgements of their appropriateness. I can choose to ignore the external examiner's comments when they are returned. After the papers are taken, I mark them and all or a sample are sent to the external examiner, who attends a meeting of all the examiners, when the marks are confirmed. The external examiner may, and sometimes does, suggest syllabus changes. All this accounts for the satire with which I began Chapter 1. While the tendency is to accept the advice of the external assessor, his or her remarks can be ignored. The external examiner is able to interview students, particularly those at borderlines.

CHAPTER 4

Temperament and Testing

INTRODUCTION

As we saw in Chapter 2, the motivation of a student to learn for grades can be influenced by a variety of factors, including those related to the psychological, sociological, economic and organizational domains of human experience. Theories of departure and persistence have to embrace all these aspects. The focal line of Figure 1 (Chapter 1) illustrated the factors influencing student motivation to get their final grades. Looked at from another perspective, the figure shows two aspects of the educational process which can be regarded as 'gifts'. On the one hand, there is the institutional 'press' and on the other, the student dynamics. Following management theory, we can look at what the institution brings to the student and what the student brings to the institution. The management task is to match these two to the benefit of both. In this chapter the concern is with what the student brings to the institution and, in particular with dysfunctional factors associated with his or her psychological disposition.

Many things can intervene en route to grades. Although students have long-term goals they also have short-term ones which are not necessarily in the same direction as their long-term goals and, as such, they are dysfunctional if they do not reinforce the long-term goals. The process might be regarded as a race in which a number of hurdles have to be overcome. Some of these hurdles are placed there by the institution, some may be forces external to the student, and some are erected internally by the student. In this chapter the concern is primarily with aspects of temperament as they relate to the assessment hurdles erected by the institution. In this respect it is necessary to distinguish between course anxiety and test anxiety. Research on test anxiety reveals that while it is a weak predictor of academic performance there is, it seems, a relation between type of test item set and anxiety (high/low) type. In some circumstances students perform better under stress. Other temperament types also appear to be better served by different test types and teaching situations. Clinical evaluations of students in difficulty also lead to the view that courses are best designed to include a variety of assessment techniques. Clinicians warn that variety is not a panacea of success, and may bring with it different kinds of stress. Too much in some courses may lead to confusion and be inhibitive of learning.

Despite contradictions between some of the researchers, they all lead to the view that course and assessment design will have to be undertaken with much more care than in the past. For many teachers and departments this will require a substantial change in attitudes to teaching and the workload created. Teachers are, *ipso facto*, expected by many students to undertake what is in effect a counselling role. Knowledge of the work done in the area of anxiety and temperament is a reminder that there are no simple solutions: for student behaviour, like worker behaviour, is complex. As teacher roles in higher education change so the counselling role is likely to become more formalized.

TEST ANXIETY

Investigations of test anxiety are difficult to carry out. Although there have been one or two attempts to study the conduct of undergraduates during a test, the majority of studies have relied on self-report inventories. Such items are often of the form:

While I may (or may not be nervous before taking an exam, once I start, I seem to forget to be nervous	I always forget	I am always nervous during an exam
When I am poorly prepared for an exam or test, I get upset, and do less well than even my restricted knowledge should allow	This never happens to me	This practically always happens to me
The more important the examination, the less well I seem to do	Always	Never

These items are taken from Alpert and Haber's (1960) inventory. The idea behind such inventories is to distinguish between students who have a low test anxiety and those who have a high test one. Does one group perform better in examinations than another? Can their performance be related to temperament?

One study made of students during their test required them to respond to questions immediately after the test paper had been read for the first time, halfway through the test, and about 10 minutes before completion. The purpose was to assess their 'internal dialogues' from ratings which they gave to a checklist of 18 positive and 19 negative thoughts. Another scale was used to rate their subjective states, i.e. totally calm to anxious and panicked.

The results were consistent with other studies. The low test anxiety students had more positive than negative thoughts than the high test anxiety ones. It was also shown that the 'dialogues' became more negative as the level of anxiety increased (Galassi *et al.*, 1981). In this experiment the low test anxiety students achieved higher test grades and experienced fewer bodily sensations which could be associated with arousal. They also predicted that they would have a successful performance, and felt that if the test was fair they would do well. Because of these feelings they were able to concentrate on the task at hand.

Physiological responses to test anxiety have been investigated many times (Hollandsworth *et al.*, 1979; Holroyd and Appel, 1980). One interesting finding which relates to the above-mentioned study was that the students with low test anxiety did not respond to low levels of physiological arousal. They were moderately to highly aroused during testing but this, they said, facilitated their performance. Spielberger (1966), whose studies are among the most often reported, found that although high anxiety had no effect on the performance of low-ability students it tended to facilitate the performance of the very brightest students in the middle of the range.

From the counselling perspective these findings are of some interest. They suggest that rather than train anxious types to relax they should persuade them to redirect the internal energies which they use up in test anxiety in directions which would help them facilitate their performance. This implies that the counsellors should explore with such students problems which they might have in learning (see Chapter 9).

An attempt at stress management training in a medical school taught the students in six $1\frac{1}{2}$-hour sessions over three weeks self-relaxation skills, schedule planning, priority setting, leisure-time planning, and cognitive modification techniques. In comparison with a control group, the experimental group showed improvement on a variety of measures that included knowledge about stress, self-support inventory scores (assessing stressing symptoms and life style), personal ratings of stressful situations, and their daily activity schedule (Kelly, 1982). Techniques for managing stress among engineering students have also been suggested by Pinsky and Wiegel (1983) of Iowa State University.

It seems that the type of items used in tests as well as the skills they portend to evaluate relate to anxiety. Spielberger (1966), for example, also found that high-anxiety students obtained superior test scores on a learning recall test when relatively few errors of recall were possible. In contrast, low-anxiety subjects obtained superior test scores when relatively more errors in recall were possible. Among his other findings were that low-anxiety students performed better than high-anxiety ones. Four times as many high-anxiety students failed as those of low anxiety. Perhaps the most important finding from the point of view of learning was that in learning concepts (see Chapter 7) high-anxiety/high-intelligence students perform better than low-anxiety/high intelligence ones. At the same time, high-anxiety/low-intelligence students performed less well than low-anxiety/low-ability subjects.

The performance of high test-anxiety students shows just how difficult the problem of test structure is. Early results from the Test Anxiety Inventory showed that this group of students performs best when it is not threatened with evaluation and faced with a difficult or challenging task.

At first sight, it might be assumed that assessment of a project would be an excellent substitute for a test for this group of students. It should stimulate interest and at the same time provide a challenge. It might also remove the threat from the situation. Unfortunately, in other studies it has been shown that this type of student does badly on essay and short-answer questions, whereas they do well on multiple-choice ones. This suggests that they might have difficulty with projects, an inference which is supported by the fact that the students from whom these data were obtained did badly in a take-home examination. The explanation offered by the investigators for this performance was based on an information-processing model of cognitive activity. In this model information is encoded, stored, organized and retrieved as required. A test demands the retrieval of information, and if a student's knowledge is inadequate because of problems in the encoding and retrieval of information, then he or she will not be able to perform well in an examination. The students in this study reported problems in learning material throughout the course, difficulties in picking out points in reading assignments, and generally in encoding information at a superficial level (Benjamin *et al.*, 1981). That this might be the case with regard to project work is indirectly supported by work on projects in engineering reported in Chapter 11.

Without this understanding there can be no interest, and if there was interest it may well have been deflated by the difficulty level of the task. The initial task for a counsellor assisting students in this situation would be to try to establish if there was both interest and aptitude on which further understanding could be developed. It may be that training in study skills could help. Hidden within the findings of this study is the idea that tests should be designed to focus on study skills. For example, comprehension tests could be designed to help students to focus on the essential points in an article (see Chapters 9 and 13). Other questions could be designed to elucidate concepts, the understanding of which is so often an impediment to learning.

Barger (1982) gave increased information to students about the questions likely to be set. In one format used in his classes in the University of Nebraska a previous test was issued with the information that the same content would be tested but by different questions. Another format gave the students the opportunity to be tested in the same course during two consecutive sessions. The findings suggested that while increased information reduced anxiety it did not necessarily improve higher test performance. In Britain essay-question spotting by students (see Chapter 10) can have disastrous consequences if there is no specific advice. Szafran (1981) reported that test anxiety was reduced among sociology students at the University of Nebraska when they were given as a study guide a pool of questions from which the actual test was to be taken several days before the test.

Teachers and counsellors are often in contact with students whom they think are anxious. One assumption which they may make is that high- and low-test anxiety students are simply two ends of a continuum. It seems they are not. Wine (1982), who analysed many studies of test anxiety, showed that the two groups differed from each other qualitatively. Some of the dimensions which characterize the two groups are shown in Table 8.

Table 8. Some characteristics of low and high test anxiety persons (from Wine, 1982)

	Low test anxiety	High test anxiety
1.	Concerns are relevant to the situation and appropriate actions are taken	Worry about the assessment to be given by the assessors and have fears of a negative assessment
2.	Focuses on the problem in hand	Focus on the self
3.	Task-oriented	Task-avoidant
4.	Believe they are actors who have to respond to the situation in which they find themselves	Believe they are observers who respond to stable personal dispositions
5.	Have behavioural, problem-solving cognitions	Have static cognitions
6.	Are active in nature	Are inactive and their behaviour is constrained
7.	Believe that they are able to perform the actions necessary to achieve the desired consequences	Do not believe they are self-efficacious and in consequence do not believe they can perform the actions necessary to achieve the desired consequences
8.	Have cognitions which they can vary from situation to situation	Have cognitions which are global, stereotyped and restricted in range
9.	Direct their physiological arousal as an energy with which to meet the demands of the test	Feel physiological arousal as distress with which they become preoccupied
10.	Use imagery—i.e. mentally rehearse problem-solving strategies	Use visual imagery to view themselves from the perspective of an assessor who is evaluating them negatively

Wine was also among a number of authorities to point out that the assumption made in earlier studies that test anxiety was simply a state of emotional arousal was without foundation. As we have seen, the cognitions are involved, and without their involvement it would not be possible to train for a redirection of energy; all that would be possible would be training in relaxation. It is clear from her evaluations that students should be able to be helped to redirect their energies. Briefly, she concluded that the person with high test anxiety was likely to respond to evaluative testing conditions with ruminative self-worry. During examinations such persons oscillate between worrying about their worries and the task in hand. She called this the direction–attention hypothesis, which she believed to be closely related to the dimension of worry–emotionality proposed by Morris and Liebert (1969). Wine concluded from all the evidence that:

(1) Highly test-anxious individuals tend to be generally self-preoccupied but negatively so. When asked to describe themselves with pencil and paper measures they do so in terms of self-devaluation.

(2) When testees are evaluated during their tasks more non-relevant thoughts are reported by those with high test anxiety than those with low.

(3) High test anxiety individuals are more likely to attribute responsibility to themselves for task failure and to set themselves low levels of aspiration when the test performance does not differ.

There are similarities between Wine's approach and the school of learning theorists centred on Entwistle in Edinburgh and Marton in Sweden (Marton *et al.*, 1984). They postulated that learners follow deep and surface approaches to learning (see Chapter 8). Marton reported that what mattered in the experimental situation he used with students was their experience of that situation. If they felt threatened and anxious they adopted a surface approach, whereas if they were relaxed and interested and not anxious they adopted a deep approach to the task. Interest and the promotion of interest through the test task may therefore have considerable implications for the level of test anxiety induced.

In general, it is found that females score more highly on measures of test anxiety than males, although the correlations with Grade-Point-Average are relatively small (Christenson, 1979). Fortunately, perhaps, and just to add to the complexity, Grade-Point-Average has been found to be significantly negatively correlated with scores on the test anxiety instruments mentioned above, and this relates also to course grades and aptitude tests.

While test anxiety is only a weak predictor of academic performance, it has been found that desensitization from anxiety coupled with training in study skills can improve academic performance (see below). Research on coping skills has not produced definitive results, although one study suggested that defence mechanisms may have a debilitating effect in that while they may reduce anxiety they may also distort the situation by diverting the student's attention away from the task at hand (Gur and Sackheim, 1979).

American studies indicate that intelligence and motivation are the most important factors in test performance, but motivation is a complex concept, and it is discussed later in this chapter and elsewhere. It is a reminder that some students, particularly high-achieving ones, like competition. There is some evidence to suggest that test anxiety may have most influence on students in the middle range of ability. Taking all this research together, what attitudes should the teacher take?

There are, it seems, specific things which can be done with tests. Because we shall always be faced with complex groups of students the least we can do is to ensure limited variety in the test procedures which students take. This applies generally to curricular strategies. For example, at the University of Newcastle in Australia it was decided that, rather than adopt medical or psychological treatment for students who were unable to cope, curricular strategies, assessment procedures, marking, feedback and timing should be changed. This had the effect of increasing student satisfaction toward the course (Feletti and Neame, 1981). Another Australian study showed that in medical examinations student levels of anxiety are not stable and predictable from one examination to another, which implies that examination anxiety is not necessarily a consistent response to a specific and recurring situation (Kidson and Hornblow, 1982). It also confirms the view that training (counselling) may be possible, and therefore the lesson overall would seem to be as significant for the counselling role as it is for the course designer. The problem of coursework and its assessment and anxiety due to course structure are considered again in later sections of this chapter.

Recently Nevo and Sfez (1985) have attempted to design a questionnaire which will help test designers to take into account examinees' feelings and attitudes towards tests. The Examinee's Feedback Questionnaire was used with a national examination for university entrance in Israel, which consisted of five multiple-choice tests (general knowledge, figural reasoning, mathematical reasoning, analytical thinking and English). The questionnaire was completed immediately after the examination. The results, while not bias free, have led to changes in the administration of examinations. One effect of this evaluation questionnaire was to make examinees feel that someone cares. Such questionnaires can reduce post-examination stress. The questionnaire is included at the end of this chapter with the permission of the authors.

Given the limitations of psychological instruments, it is not surprising that other approaches to temperament should reveal other dimensions. A good example of this is the work of Furneaux (1962), who investigated introversion/extroversion and neuroticism among students of engineering in Britain.

TEMPERAMENT AND PERFORMANCE

Measures of introversion/extroversion and neuroticism were obtained from a small sample of mechanical engineering students (high-achievers) from a prestigious university in Britain. The grades from the examinations which these students took within the normal procedures of the university were averaged into a single grade. The students were not given the grades in individual subjects. In only one of the examination papers was the style of questioning different to that of the others, and that was in engineering drawing. The investigation sought to answer the question: were those who were tense, excitable and highly strung likely to perform better than those who were phlegmatic, relaxed and apparently well-adjusted? Or, to put it another way, does the level of neuroticism influence performance?

It might be predicted that extroverts would not do so well as introverts, for, apart from nothing else, introverts tend to be bookish and academic studies have as their goal the development of bookish traits. Introverts work hard to be reliable and accurate, but in the extreme they take so much time at the task that they might do badly in examinations. In contrast, extroverts might do an examination quickly, but this is likely to be at the expense of reliability.

Furneaux categorized the students into four groups: stable–extroverts, neurotic–extroverts, stable–introverts and neurotic–introverts. The group most likely to fail university examinations were found to be the stable–extroverts followed by (but at some distance numerically) the neurotic–extroverts. In this particular study the neurotic–introverts did best.

Another simple test was administered to these students to measure intellectual speed, and it was found that among the stable–extroverts those who were slowest tended to obtain low examination marks. In most American studies of test anxiety a negative relationship has been found with intelligence, but it has been suggested that this could have been due to the particular tests used, since under the pressure of time their stress-inducing effects might contaminate the outcomes.

Furneaux explained the performance of the students in his sample in terms of the Yerkes–Dodson principle, which was derived from studies of the behaviour of rats. It was shown that rats who were hungry would make their way through a maze to find food more quickly than when they were replete. However, it was also found that if the drive which the rats exhibited reached too high a level, performance would decline. There is an optimal drive level for each task to be performed. Above this, performance falls off. The Yerkes–Dodson principle states that the optimal drive level is high for simple tasks but is reduced as the complexity of the task is increased. This means that high drive can soon go over the optimum level for complex tasks.

Given that people who easily enter into states of high drive are likely to obtain high neuroticism scores, then, Furneaux argued, it is this group which is likely to obtain high examination scores. Similarly, persons who have an extroverted disposition who at the same time have a low drive level will do badly in examinations. If these tendencies are related to the intellectual qualities of the examinees then an introvert with high drive will be able to compensate for relatively poor intellectual qualities whereas, in contrast, good intellectual qualities may compensate for extroversion and low drive.

Furneaux found that the more neurotic students did badly in the engineering drawing paper. Those who were stable did better. This, he argued, was because the task was so complex that optimum drive occurred at a low level. He found that the most common cause of failure was poor-quality drawing, which was of a kind that might be due to disturbing influences. Discussion with the examiner led him to the view that supra-optimal drive might have occurred, because there was some evidence of excessive sweating, lack of co-ordination, and faulty judgement.

There are lessons for teachers in this study. These are that teachers should be clear that the most appropriate objectives for a course are sought and that the examination is designed to obtain those objectives. Moreover, those objectives should take into account the temperament of the students. Furneaux showed that when the examination in engineering drawing changed, so did performance—for the better. The grade which had depended on the quality of the drawing presented was changed to respond to assessment of the ability to interpret and convey information using graphical methods. It is likely (although we are not told) that the students were more interested in this than they were in perfectionist drawing. Moreover, the skills performance required would correspond more to the skill requirements of the written examination. It was also observed that the students in the less stable groups improved their performance.

Table 9. Aptitude interaction studies. Example of the instruments used by Jackson (1985)

Course-assessment procedures used
Essay: 150 words of continuous prose following the traditional synoptic model; postulated skills of library research, study and materials organization, task orientation and motivation.
Analytic report: 1000 words of detailed comparative analysis involving two research papers in child development to identify key theoretical and methodological issues; postulated skills of thematic discrimination, systematic logical analysis, critical detachment, precision and specificity.
Child study: 2000 words of interpretive discussion based on structured observation of a young child in naturalistic circumstances; postulated skills of task organization, interpersonal sensitivity, observational detachment, data selection, data classification and theoretical integration.
Tutorial participation: Cumulative weekly assessment in small group tutorial sessions focused on set reading and lecture content distributed in advance; postulated skills of rational analysis, investigatory discussion and debate requiring self-confidence associated with orderly week-by-week time scheduling.

Aptitude predictors used in research on undergraduate academic performance
(a) *Autonomous–heteronomous*: confident, self-sufficient, resourceful versus hesitant, uncertain dependent. (Derived from Rutkowski, K., and G. Domino (1975). Interrelationship of Study skills and personality variables in college students. *Journal of Educational Psychology*, **67**, 784–9.)
(b) *Rigid–complex*: neat precise, well organized versus untidy disorderly. (Derived from Imam, A. (1974). Rigidity–flexibility and incidental learning. *Pakistan Journal of Psychology*, **7**, 3–17.)
(c) *Anxious–stable*: emotionally labile, chronically tense versus emotionally controlled, relaxed. (Derived from Dowaliby, F. J., and H. Schumer (1973). Teacher centred versus student centred. Mode of classroom instruction as related to manifest anxiety. *Journal of Educational Psychology*, **64**, 125–32.)
(d) *Introvert–extrovert*: shy unsociable versus outgoing sociable. (See study in text by W. D. Furneaux.)
(e) *Radical–conservative*: politically left wing or left inclined versus right wing. (Derived from Eysenck, H. J. (1970). *The Structure of Human Psychology*, London: Methuen.)
(f) *Syllabus bound–syllabus free*: narrowly constrained by scheduled coursework versus wide-ranging expansive. (Derived from Parlett, M. (1970). The syllabus bound student. In L. Hudson (ed.), *The Ecology of Human Intelligence*. Harmondsworth: Penguin.)

Since Furneaux published his research there has been continuing interest in the relationship between individual differences and learning which, as Fincher (1985) says, leads to the general but not very hopeful principle that some students can learn some subjects better under some teachers than they can learn others under other teachers. One might substitute instructional strategies for teachers. However, Aptitude Treatment Interaction research, as studies of this kind are now called (Cronbach and Snow, 1977; Gagne and Dick, 1983), does give considerable support to those who argue for multiple-strategy assessment as well as to those who argue for profiles. For example, Jackson (1985) of James Cook University in North Queensland, whose instruments are listed in Table 9, was led to argue from his results that since academic achievement is shown to be a dependent variable, gross totals such as degree grades and Grade-Point-Averages have doubtful validity. This is because they necessarily combine a range of different performances. The value of studies such as these is illustrated by the work of Freeman and Byrne described in Chapter 13.

Clearly, the factors which influence examination performance are many and the interrelation between them complex. Even though test anxiety and temperament are only weak predictors of performance. Many students across the range of ability do suffer considerably during their university studies, as the results of clinical research show.

EXAMINATION STRAIN (TESTING AND MENTAL HEALTH)

It is well known that tests can create anxiety days before (and well before the run-up to) an examination. In a situation where performance depends on a terminal examination this can be very serious for the student. Student health services have acquired specialist skills in dealing with this problem. Malleson (1965), who founded the Society for Research into Higher Education, wrote that 10% of the students at University College, London, where he was the physician, reported strain symptoms before their final examinations. He described three conditions of the pre-examinations strain.

(1) *Pre-examination strain*: 'There are two types: those that are overworking and getting overly anxious and hyper excitable, and those that are heavy and torpid, who cannot get down to study and who feel numbed and discouraged. For these examination cases, in contra-distinction to the cases of primary study difficulty, drug treatment and strong supportive therapy over the critical period of the examination are of the greatest value. The time factors, let alone the pressures of anxiety, forbid any thorough psychotherapeutic approach.'

(2) *Examination panic*: 'These are the cases of students who start their paper, but get increasingly anxious or exhausted and finally leave the examination room. Sometimes they are overcome by headaches or by migraine, but for the most part it is just an increasing and finally overwhelming feeling of nervousness, tension and despair, with an incapacity to remember things they previously knew. The great majority of these students have already suffered from a long period of mounting pre-examination strain with anxiety, though as a rule, have not come for treatment. Since one sees these cases very much at the last moment (they are very often hustled over to the student health centre), there is not a great deal that one can do. A few, however, do respond to very fine surrogative handling—not to say bullying, giving a cup of tea and two menthyl pentonyl capsules, then accompanying them back to the examination room, or obtaining permission for them to carry on with invigilation in the student health centre itself, is sometimes useful. Sometimes it is not.'

(3) *True examination phobia*: 'This is a comparatively rare, but interesting condition; the student is often an efficient student, and basically a healthy chap, measured by ordinary social and personal standards, but has an intensive irrational fear of examinations of a kind that can only be called phobic: it compares truly to the way that people have phobias about heights, cats or spiders. Sometimes these poor people are so terrified by the examination that they cannot get up the steps of the examination hall but turn and flee as they come in sight of the building. The management of these cases has been discussed elsewhere, but they are very difficult to help.'

One of the interesting problems which the physician faces is the problem of delay. Does the physician advise the student to take the examination at a later date or not? Such evidence as there is suggests that where poor students are concerned they may not be helped by a delay. It has also been suggested that students who fail, regardless of intellectual aptitude, become hostile as a result.

It is not surprising, therefore, to find that clinicians should recommend variety in assessment and this to include some coursework assessment. This view receives further support from other work which Malleson did on the emotional needs of students. He suggested that these would change during the students' educational career. In England he thought that tutors might observe among some students in their second year the following syndromes:

(1)	Obsessional slowing with ritual	Never gets started on his studying while making enormous preparations.
(2)	Poor study habits with general disorganization	More hysterical personality. Work is never organized efficiently. Written work is untidy.
(3)	Retention and recall difficulties	Hard worker who is never able to retain the material he has studied.
(4)	Product difficulties	Fear of being criticized prevents students from writing essays, preparing theses, etc.

Another pioneer of British student health, A. Ryle, listed three types of students who get themselves into difficulty (Ryle and Lungi, 1968):

(1) Psychiatrically disturbed, academically adequate students with good performance test scores and high N (neuroticism) scores on the Eysenck Personality Inventory.
(2) Psychiatrically disturbed, academically failing students who tend to do well on performance test scores except for a stress/gain measure which is significantly low.
(3) Psychiatrically well, academically failing students who tend to do badly on performance tests but show high stress gain; they tend to be stable extroverts.

Group (1) students appear to be disorganized by stress, while group (3) ones need to be put under pressure in order to make use of their capacities to the full. The former require security and treatment.

There is a resemblance between these findings and those of Furneaux. It would seem that such students might benefit from a tutorial approach to their teaching provided that the tutors could distinguish between and understand the needs of the two groups.

Ramsden (1984), as a result of his studies of the way in which students approached learning, using an entirely different methodology concluded that, because of the wide variety of styles of learning found among students and because of the empirical links between interest, approach and outcome, a mix of learning tasks and some choice over subject matter is desirable. Research on learning, it seems, confirms the findings of medical research. However, Ryle (1969) who was one of the first to draw attention to the effect of the examining system on students, said that any alternative system is likely to produce its own crop of casualties and its own varieties of stress. The solution, he said, seems to be to introduce a far greater flexibility and variety into the methods of testing used, so that individuals handicapped under one set of conditions have the opportunity to show their powers in a different testing situation. One cannot make an individual selection of students simply in terms of those who will succeed in one particular form of examination: each university must therefore endeavour to provide for students of widely differing temperaments the opportunity to give the best possible account of themselves. In practice, this could be achieved by relying upon a range of assessments for each subject being examined. Some weight could be given to coursework, without necessarily going as far as the American system of course credits. Formal examinations during and at the end of the course could include project work, dissertation and extended essays to a greater extent, so that memory and speed would be less crucial to success than they are in the present standard 3-hour feats of memory, endurance, and (to be generous) synthetic thinking ability. However, even the fairest method of assessment will still produce stress, because students have a human desire to do well and a human fear of failure. Medical evidence, therefore, supports the concept of multiple-strategy assessment.

COURSEWORK, MOTIVATION AND STRESS

The implications of this view for the total design of programmes are considerable. That it can be done is suggested by the work in the medical school at the University of Newcastle, New South Wales (Feletti and Neame, 1981). Nowadays most higher education courses in Britain include an element of coursework and in some it may be as much as 50% (Cox, 1985). Unfortunately, the potential demonstrated at Newcastle has not been realized. It has not been a panacea, as Ryle warned. Such evidence as there is suggests that it has been introduced without much thought being given to first principles. As Table 10 shows, there are many differences in approach. The data in this table are based on what was happening in one university in 1968, and are rather alarming.

88

Table 10. Some types of coursework in use in the U.K.

(a) *Cumulative assessment*

A proportion of the mark in a three (or four) year course is arrived at from scores achieved during the first and second years. The proportion of marks allowed for the first year is usually smaller than that for the second, e.g.

First year	12% = 100% of year
Second year	24% = 100% of year
Third year	64% = 100% of year

100% of total

The marks may be achieved by combinations of coursework assessment and examinations, or examinations alone. For purposes of certification they could be equated to 100%.

(b) *Diagnostic coursework*

An early assessment of student performance to determine those in difficulty and the nature of the difficulties.

(c) *Informal coursework assessment*

Most tutors make a judgement about the qualities of their students while a course is in progress. Such judgements are often used to moderate the marks given to candidates at the final meeting of examiners with the external assessor. Students are not informed about such procedures.

(d) *Formal coursework assessment*

The characteristics of such systems are that the students know how coursework will contribute to their final mark. There are several systems (the terminology is my own).

  (i) Fixed percentage schemes: In such schemes coursework is formally assessed and contributes a fixed percentage of the total degree mark. In the United States the proportion of marks awarded for continuous assessment seems to remain constant as between subjects. In England some universities operating such procedures do not impose such restrictions on departments. The proportions awarded depend on the value ascribed by individual departments to coursework assessment.

 (ii) Positive moderation schemes: these are schemes in which coursework is formally assessed but the result is only used to raise a candidate's final mark.

(iii) Formal requirement schemes: are those which require satisfactory performance in coursework before a person can either obtain a final degree or sit final examinations.

The scheme adopted depends very much on department (or faculty) objectives in initiating coursework assessment procedures. Broadly speaking, there are two categories which might usefully be described as supplementary and complementary in terms of the information sought by the examiners about a candidate:

  (i) In schemes which provide supplementary information the examiners hold that the coursework assessment is measuring the same abilities (qualities) as the written examination. It is therefore a check on the written examination and, as such, is used as a means of moderating the final mark.

 (ii) Coursework assessment which provides complementary information to the examination is thought to measure different qualities to those measured in written papers.

Apart from the fact that students often did not know what was expected of them, they were often overloaded with exercises from different tutors. During the next ten years a systematic study was made of the effects of coursework on students taking engineering science at GCE A level by the examiners. Both teacher and student attitudes were tested. These studies led to considerable reductions in the workload (Carter *et al.*, 1986) (see Chapters 11 and 13). It is a matter of observation that staff tend to overload students. Perhaps it is because sometimes coursework exercises can be exciting both for the tutor as well as the student, and I stand guilty on this point. The penalty which is often paid is an increase in staff preparation and in formal tutorial work.

Perhaps the best example I can give relates to my colleague Carpenter's study cited below. A student came up to me and said, 'Do you realize that you have asked me to produce a critical review of a book, give this in seminar and write it up for less than a per cent?' It was one of the biggest shocks of my educational experience! Even so, he had done much more than was expected. This seems to have happened elsewhere (Hartley and Branthwaite, 1976). Students are very unclear about what is expected of them and in consequence tend to do too much. Hounsell (1985) reported a study in Queensland by Roe which also demonstrates this point. Anderson (1962) confirmed this finding when he showed that those first-year students who believed their entry to the second year to be limited, worked alone, and had relatively more passes in the examinations than those who did not have this belief.

The motivational aspect of weighting is illustrated in a study by Carpenter (1975), who related it to the relative weighting of the coursework and examination components. In his study the class was divided into two groups. One group obtained their final grade by means of a combination of coursework and terminal examination marks and another obtained their mark entirely from coursework assessment. Carpenter found a high correlation between coursework marks when each contributed 50% of the mark. It could be that there is a cut-off point in some subjects when the ratio of marks is such that the written examination does not cause hard work, and this is a problem which bothers teachers. Carpenter wrote that a modest (33%) loading of the coursework fails to provide a strong stimulus in a class having low self-motivation and high preoccupation with other, possibly more major, subjects. However, this may not be the case if a variety of assessment procedures is used. For example, Starr (1968) assessed a group of 111 graduates in a teacher-training course on various pieces of coursework including two long essays and a diary at Queens University, Belfast. He found that the average intercorrelation between nine different methods of scoring was high (0.83). Those methods of assessment which were similar (for example, examinations) gave the highest correlations, as might be expected. Carpenter noted that there was a considerable enhancement in motivation but that the penalty was a substantial increase in staff preparation and informal tutorial work (Chalmers and Stark, 1968).

In an attempt to redesign a programme of undergraduate medical education at the University of Newcastle, New South Wales, formative assessment for frequent informal diagnostic feedback to the student, together with summative assessment, was introduced. The purpose was to move to an open system of assessment in which the marking was open to student scrutiny. In contrast to

Carpenter's findings, Leeder *et al.* (1979) found that an increase in satisfaction with summative assessment was not matched in respect of the formative assessments. They therefore set out to try to make the formative assessment more truly reflect the expectations of the defined objectives of the course. More significantly, they argued that the assessment of student progress and achievement can support or weaken the educational goals of an institution (see Lam's study below) which supports the views expressed in Chapters 1–3.

Lublin (1980), in a study of student abilities, had the students estimate in advance marks which they would expect to get in their third-year written reports and examinations. He found that the number of discrepancies between the predicted and obtained marks was small. Lublin concluded that students should be given fewer assessments whose marks are counted and more for use in learning diagnosis. Teachers at the Open University have also demonstrated the value of non-assessed assignments (Prescott and Jarvis, 1978).

If students become encumbered by activities similar to those which they take in examinations, assessment can become a drudge, and Hounsell has found this to be the case. In these circumstances coursework will inhibit rather than enhance learning. A national study in Britain by Ramsden and Entwistle (1981) confirms this view.

The problem of plagiarism of coursework has been little discussed, although hearsay evidence suggests that in order to meet time schedules students copy books when they are overloaded. It is a well-known problem in the United States (Hawley, 1984), and defeats the purposes of coursework.

Inspection of the literature suggests that much could have been learnt from the experience of secondary schools in England (Heywood, 1977; Hoste and Bloomfield, 1975; Smith, 1976). Newspaper reports in 1988 of the implementation of coursework in the GCSE examinations suggest that the school sector did not learn either. The high ideals for coursework in colleges in Britain have not been obtained, and this includes the goal of effective feedback. The explanation of this would seem to be that academics in Britain have seen coursework assessment as a simple extension of the terminal examination. In so doing, they have allowed themselves to become bemused by the same myths which have dominated their attitudes to terminal examinations. The need for the substantial enquiry for which Hounsell called is evident.

That the structure of a course as a whole produces different kinds of stress has also been established in the adult setting by Lam (1978), among others.

COURSE ANXIETY

As a result of an exploratory study among a small sample of adults attending professional courses in education Lam was led to distinguish between three types of anxiety which related to course structure, the interpersonal process, and the evaluation outcomes. The same types of anxiety have been found to be true of our in-service courses for teachers, whether they are evaluated for diplomas or not. Lam found that the predominant anxiety was course set-up.

Those whose expectations differed significantly from those of their instructors experienced the most anxiety. This finding has its analogy with the experience of management training, for those who had expectations different to those of the trainers were likely to be those least satisfied with the course. It is normal practice in management courses to try to reconcile these different perceptions and to tailor some of the course to try to meet the perceived needs of students. In this way, the managers become partially involved in course planning (Fitzgibbon and Heywood, 1986). There is no reason why undergraduates should not have some involvement in the planning of their courses. In this way, realistic objectives might be agreed.

With regard to anxiety arising from evaluation outcomes, Lam wrote:

> Emergent factors for reduced anxiety about evaluation outcomes include good reading materials, classmate sociability, occupation, and satisfaction with the instructors. The importance of formal feedback about learners' performance in the course in relation to reduced anxiety about evaluative endurance in the second period of the learning process, and its disappearance at the last period of the learning process seem to suggest that once adults are assured of their ability to perform well, their self confidence is re-established. It was also found that this did not require continued encouragement from the instructor in the last critical stage of learning. On the other hand, the perceived understanding of the course content through assigned reading materials, and the perceived acceptance by fellow learners were vital in reducing anxiety about evaluative outcomes. In line with the previous observation, this seems to suggest that the sources of adult self-confidence in performance had shifted from the formal assessment to their own perceived abilities and rapport with classmates.

The whole process indicates the need for clarity of objectives, and this applies where a large amount of work is required over a long period of time. Objectives which are perceived to be realistic will ease tension and enhance learning. These findings indicate that once adults are assured of their ability to perform well they become confident, and this surely applies to young students. They also indicate the importance of viewing coursework not as an adjunct in assessment but as part of the total assessment–instruction plan. They also suggest that there is some relationship with goal attainment, a finding which has driven the work of Jan Wankowski in Britain over a long period of time.

THE SHORT- AND LONG-TERM GOALS OF STUDENTS AND ACHIEVEMENT

Towards the end of the 1960s Wankowski (1969, 1973) investigated the dynamics of success and failure among students of the University of Birmingham. In addition to an inventory (Eysenck's) designed to measure neuroticism, he asked students questions about their long- and short-term goals in relation to:

(1) *Short-range goals*: name your vocational objectives, including plans for using your degree qualification.

(2) *Reasons for entering university*: state your two most important reasons for coming to university.

(3) *Long-range goals*: what are your most strongly anticipated goals within the next ten years?

He found that male high-achievers with clear goals tended toward stability, as did female high-achievers with less clear goals. On the introversion/extroversion dimension, however, he also found that male high-achievers with less clear goals tended rather towards introversion and the low achievers with less clear goals toward extroversion. He was led to the view that his study supported other investigations which had concluded that goal orientation might be associated with personality dimensions.

His view of the dynamics of success is shown in Figure 14. Wankowski offered the opinion that the 'problem of wastage is largely the problem of teaching'. Since then he has continued to develop this theme and, together with Raaheim, has looked at the problem of learning—how to learn, and the procedures which underpin such activities.

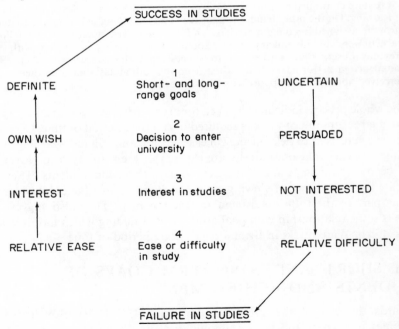

Factors on the right tend to pull towards failure

Figure 14. Wankowski's view of the dynamics of success and failure

Related to this work is a study by Brown and Daines (1981) who from interviews with a random sample of 130 university lecturers at Nottingham, sought to identify those elements of explaining thought to be valuable and those thought to be learnable. They came to the conclusion that a lecturer's views on explaining may arise from the lecturer's experience of studying a subject at undergraduate level. This finding serves to support the case for the training of university teachers.

Using the *Omnibus Personality Inventory* Elton and Rose (1966) found a significant difference between engineering students on the dimension of intellectual disposition. Strangely, an absence of high intellectual interests was found among the persisters. These results led them to suggest that the faculty might consider a second experimental programme with the objective of developing new avenues of professional competence for the 25% who withdraw. In another report they argued that student-leaving is a result of maladjustment and directed hostility.

Following on from Becker *et al.*'s (1968) study of student life which had shown that students develop different perspectives to their work as a function of their perceptions of grading, Milton *et al.* (1986) began their ten-year study to assess student attitudes and beliefs about grades. Like Wankowski, the parameters were goal oriented. In this case it was hypothesized that within colleges there were two groups of students who could be defined as learning- and grade-oriented. The former would view the classroom as a place in which the information gained was valuable both personally and professionally; the latter would think of college as a place which graded and tested them and had to be suffered as a necessary evil.

After a substantial pilot study an instrument was devised which would produce data against a fourfold typology of student orientations. These were:

(1) A group of students with both high learning and high grade orientations (High LO/High GO);
(2) A group of students with high learning but low grade orientations (High LO/Low GO);
(3) A group of students with low learning but high grade orientations (Low LO/High GO);
(4) A group of students with low learning and low grade orientations (Low LO/Low GO).

It was administered to many college and university students along with the Alpert and Haber anxiety scale, the Brown and Holtzman study habit inventory, the Sixteen Personality Factor Questionnaire, the Levenson IPC Scales, and the Myers–Briggs type indicator.

Of these groups, the Low LO/Low GO were the most difficult to identify. They were found to be high in tension, frustration and introversion, but reported levels in the middle range of test anxiety and average skills. The students whose college teachers would be likely to consider ideal were in the High LO/Low GO group. Capable of abstract reasoning, they showed self-motivation, inner-directedness and interest in intellectual matters. They acknowledged responsibility for their own actions in determining success and failure, and employed the most effective study methods. Anxiety facilitates their performance. They are in contrast to the High LO/High GO students, who had the highest level of debilitating test anxiety and the lowest scores on abstract reasoning. They were rather extrovert with a tough-minded approach to ideas and situations. Finally, the Low LO/High GO are distinguished by their personality traits, which included a strong desire to do the right thing and to act in conventional ways. They reported the lowest levels of facilitating test anxiety, and showed a consistent pattern of low scores on study habits and academic attitude dimensions.

Although Milton *et al.* found that they could distinguish students in all four categories, some features of their analysis are surprising. Taken as composite groups, learning- and grade-oriented students had similar perceptions of many of the purposes of grades. Two areas where they differed were those concerned with cheating and dropping classes. Grade-oriented students are likely to cheat and drop courses if they think that they are going to get poor grades. This lack of difference between the groups puzzled the investigators, and led them to suggest that the patterns measured by their instrument represented the different approaches which students adopt to help them with their learning in classroom situations. High GO students, they argued,

> find themselves in an uncertain world—the world of higher education—and look to external supports to evaluate how well or poorly they are doing. They are uncertain young people, and powerful others, such as parents, teachers, and future employers, as well as public symbols such as grades, all provide a structure within which these students can at least find some comfort and possibly some satisfaction.
>
> We feel that a student may be grade oriented not because he or she necessarily wants to be, but because such an orientation is a plausible and situationally effective way of dealing with the traditional classroom environment as well as with early post college endeavours. In many instances an instructor's classroom policies and procedures make such an orientation seem both logical and reasonable for the student.

It follows, they argued, that this group of students should have teachers who are not grade-oriented but emphasize and look for learning. They need not only to be given help with study skills but to search out answers to the question, 'Why study?' which will take them beyond 'getting a job' to the meaning that education has for them.

As long ago as 1961 Christian Bey had suggested that students could be distinguished by their dispositions to academic life, of which he identified three—the academic, the intellectual and the social. Academics worked hard to obtain good records; intellectuals strove to broaden their understanding and increase their power of reflection, while socials wanted, among other things, to be respected, liked and admired or loved by people. In Britain, Elizabeth Taylor (Gibbs *et al.* 1984) investigated student orientations at Surrey University, and concluded that there were four main types. She called them vocational, academic, personal, and social. The difference between the US and British typologies might be expected, for in Britain all courses are, as we have seen, to some extent vocational or professional. She was led as a result of her interviews to suggest that the first three types could each be divided into two subcategories defined by interest. Intrinsic interest categorized a student who is interested in the course for its own sake, whereas extrinsic interest characterized a student who was pursuing the course as a means to an end. In Taylor's classification the intrinsically academically oriented person follows intellectual interests, whereas the extrinsically academically oriented one is concerned with academic progress and grades. An intrinsic student with a personal orientation is concerned with broadening or self-improvement, whereas the extrinsically motivated person in this category would look for compensation or proof of capability. In a similar study of Open University students she did not find a social orientation. This is not surprising, since adult students taking a part-time degree are likely to be highly motivated. These orientations have been related both to methods of study and the concerns which the students have for the instructional and assessment procedures used.

A weakness of the Milton study is that it does not relate the student profiles to performance. We might predict, in keeping with previous studies of motivation, that the correlations between groups and performance will be relatively low except for the Low LO/Low GO group, which, it seems, is the most problematic.

These studies with their different orientations toward college life provide explanations of behaviour which might account for student behaviour that lecturers often dismiss as low motivation or, for that matter, low ability. An understanding of these orientations is of considerable importance if lecturers are to improve the overall effectiveness of their courses as well as the advice they give students. However, such studies do not account for the wide variety of situations which affect students daily, some of which substantially deflect them from their studies. While these orientations may represent dominant types, I have observed that persons who from a relatively young age have persisted with intellectual activities can, during their college career, suddenly find the social life so rewarding that it completely disrupts their studies. The severe conflict of goals which occurs is not necessarily recognized immediately by them, as they rationalize their model of normality to justify their conflicting circumstances.

In the preceding sections the tendency has been to look at extremes from the perspective of the teacher who has to help students. It has not meant to imply (and this point has been made on several occasions) that learning is best done under 'no-stress' conditions. Students, and indeed people in general, need to be stretched if they are to go beyond where they are (Dember, 1965), for which reason the tasks which they are set need to force them to make the small jump which is necessary for them to learn. Learning is an 'energetic' exercise which invovles stress, tension and anxiety, and this point needs to be remembered in any debate on matching teaching to learning styles (Grasha, 1984). It was a point which is relevant to the problem of cognitive dissonance (see p. 182).

Research on motivation in education leads us to the same conclusions as research on incentives and their effect on people at work. For example, Daniel and McIntosh (1972) wrote:

> In terms of understanding worker's [student's] behaviour and attitudes, the critical question is often not the one so frequently posed of what are people [students] really interested, or most interested in, or whether they are more interested in job [study] satisfaction and intrinsic rewards, but rather when are they interested in intrinsic rewards and when are they interested in extrinsic rewards.

The position in respect of students in higher education would seem to be similar, as my substitutions in brackets illustrate.

In these circumstances is it possible to have a satisfactory model of the learner and, if it is, what are its implications for assessment, teaching and learning? Once again, a parallel is to be found in the studies of organization and management theory. 'Man,' argued Schein (1965), is complex and likely to 'differ from his neighbour in the patterns of his complexity', Inevitably, learners are no different, for man and learner are the same thing and learning is essential to motivation, be it at work or in college. A picture of the complex learner emerges thus:

(1) The learner is complex. He or she is highly variable and has many motives, some of which are more important than others. The order of importance is likely to change from time to time with changing circumstances. Since his or her motive patterns are complex, the response to incentives will also change with circumstances.

(2) The learner is capable of learning new motives through his or her curriculum and institutional experiences. The psychological contract he or she makes with teachers and the institution is the result of a complex interaction between perceived needs and learning and institutional experiences.

(3) The learner's motives in different institutions or different subsystems of the same institution may be different; the student who is alienated in the formal structure may find fulfilment of his or her social and self-actualization needs in the student union or other parts of the extramural system or outside the system altogether. If the curriculum structure is complex in respect of perceived needs or apparent abilities, some parts of the curriculum may engage some motives while others engage other motives.

(4) The learner can become productively involved with the curriculum and institution on the basis of many different kinds of motive. His or her ultimate satisfaction in the institution depends only in part on the nature of the motivation. The nature of the task to be performed, the abilities and experience of the learner and the nature of teachers and administrators in the institution all interact to produce a certain pattern of work and feelings.

(5) The learner can respond to many different kinds of learning strategy depending on his or her own motives and abilities and the nature of the

task. There is no one correct learning strategy which will work for all learners at all times.

IMPLICATIONS FOR ASSESSMENT, COURSE STRUCTURE AND THE ROLE OF THE TEACHER

Understanding anxiety is important to instructors for two reasons. First, it provides a basis for helping students who seek advice. It tells us that helping students to relax may not be the best way to help them overcome the difficulty. It also reminds us that relaxation and coping are not the same thing. Second, it shows that variety in technique, i.e. type of test item and type of skill sought, is important. At the same time, clinicial studies have shown that variety (but not excessive variety) can produce a system of examining which is fair.

In England the experience of the introduction of coursework has been somewhat chaotic and, as predicted by Ryle, of systems designed without imagination. It is likely to have brought with it its own crop of stress-producing agents. This seems to have happened because coursework was introduced as an extension of examining, and the impact of examinations on learning has never been appreciated.

The work on persistence and withdrawal shows that, while students pursue long-term goals, they have to overcome many hurdles en route which may deflect them quite seriously from their studies.

Several studies support McKeachie's (1983) view that anxious students have difficulties in the initial learning phase. He found that they were reluctant to try something new, such as a specially designed learning-how-to-learn course. Emotionally, they cannot chance something that they know would work better. To overcome this problem, learning-how-to-learn courses should first, develop confidence in techniques that emphasize meanings and, second, instill an ability to apply the technique.

As a tutor I found that students who had received notice from their teachers that they were in difficulty did not attend courses laid on to help them whereas bright ones did. It is a not-uncommon finding that successful students face study problems, especially during the first year of their course (Wieneke, 1979).

Some problems arise from the expectations which students have of what constitutes 'thinking' in the written context of college assessment, and the fact that their teachers seem to believe that the students know what is required when they do not (see Chapter 10).

The process of higher education can be regarded as an obstacle race in which some of the hurdles are erected by the institution, others by the environment from which the student comes as well as the changing environment in which they live. Sometimes the institution can help; at other times there is little it can do. Mostly, however, institutions do less than they could to facilitate student learning, and this is because they have never seriously faced these issues. In the future institutional evaluations will have to take them into account.

The studies referred to above show clearly that remedial action should be

98

taken within the context of the whole course. That is, we have to take a causal view. It is not sufficient to begin with the student on day 1 without reference to the transition which he or she experiences in coming from home and school to university that requires new friendships and new dispositions to general behaviour. It has long been understood that the transition between primary and secondary schools is an important phase in a child's life. It is a discontinuity which is inevitable and which Derricott (1985) believes should be planned. The transition between school and college is equally important, as the experience of the problems of first-year students shows (McKeachie, 1983; Pinsky and Weigel, 1983; Wieneke, 1979). In the United States it has been demonstrated that students are not as academically prepared for college as they were some years ago. Remedial education in English and Mathematics is widespread.

For this reason, a core curriculum has many advocates. There is a view that colleges and universities could do more to forge links between teaching quality and education quality through school/college co-operative ventures. In Britain much has been done in sixth forms to foster study skills. For the most part, however, the problem is left to the enthusiasts, for university teachers are not required to have any training for teaching. This means that the problem is not seen as one which recurs. Students become ready at different times to participate in activities for which they believe they need help. Although it has never been tested formally, I am sure that it is safe to suggest that the lack of interest in these problems in England and Ireland is in no small measure due to the fact that most students are successful. Since 1985 the Newcastle upon Tyne Polytechnic and the University of South Carolina have run annual conferences in England on the problems of first-year tuition.

It is not understood that a great deal more could be achieved with students than is currently the case. However, for many teachers in higher education this would entail different methods of teaching and assessment and the relinquishment of some cherished ideals. In short, it would mean a change in the formal role of the teacher to embrace curriculum design and evaluation on the one hand, and student adviser to the extent of counselling on the other. If students are to be helped to learn-how-to-learn then the courses they attend and the tests they take should be designed to help them learn, and this is not an easy thing to achieve. If the subject tutor rather than the personal one is the person to whom they come with their personal problems then there is an obligation on teachers to acquire the basic counselling skills which will help them in these face-to-face situations.

I appreciate that very many teachers try to accomplish these tasks, but they are done informally, and not as part of the institutional mission. It is too easy to say there is a student counsellor or a student health service. Such services only cater for the few. In any case, the problem runs deep and relates to institutional and course structures—i.e. the general academic press.

Figure 15 shows a model which can be used by an institution in the British system to check its arrangements for assessment in relation to the process which students experience of higher education. Its intention is to illustrate how variety in assessment can be made purposeful in terms of the process of learning in higher education.

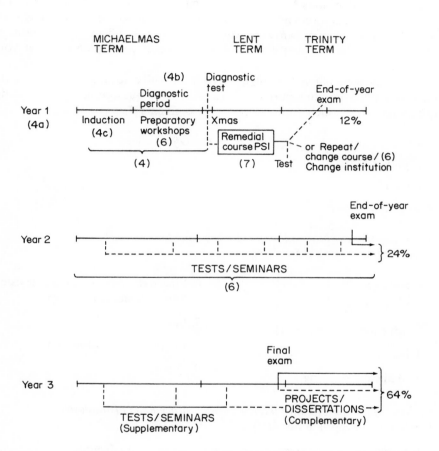

Figure 15. A model to illustrate some of the interrelationships between coursework assessment and examinations which can be made in the English system of examining

Note

The Examinees' Feedback Questionnaire by Janet Sfez and Baruch Nevo of the University of Haifa is reproduced below with their kind permission (see *Assessment in Higher Education*, **10**, (3), 236–49, 1987). Professor Nevo has completed a report in 1987: *The Practical and Theoretical Value of Examinees' Feedback Questionnaires (EFeQ)*.

National Institute for Testing and Evaluation

EXAMINEES FEEDBACK QUESTIONNAIRE—R

The following questions refer to the examination you have just completed. The purpose of this questionnaire is to obtain your evaluation of and comments on the test. Although your answers will not in any way affect your chances of acceptance to the University, we will be grateful if you would consider your responses seriously.

You may feel that not enough room is provided to answer many of the questions fully. For this purpose there is an open question at the end of the questionnaire in which you may add any comments that you wish.

Sex   *For Office Use*

  1 Male

  2 Female

Age (in years)

Which department have you applied to as your first choice?
(Circle the appropriate number)

  1 Social Sciences

  2 Natural Sciences, Mathematics

  3 Education, Social Work

  4 Humanities

  5 Medicine, Nursing

  6 Fine Arts, Art History, Television, Film, Music, Musicology

  7 Law

  8 Engineering, Technology

  9 Other:

1. How would you evaluate the registration procedures of the test?
(Circle the appropriate number)

  5 Registration procedures were simple, explicit and efficient.
  4 Registration procedures were more than satisfactory.
  3 Registration procedures were satisfactory.
  2 Registration procedures were somewhat complicated.
  1 Registration procedures were complicated and tiring.

2. How would you evaluate the Psychometric Entrance Examination Information Booklet?
(Circle the appropriate number)

  5 The booklet was very clear and explicit and proved very helpful in understanding the test.

4 The booklet was explicit and of some assistance in understanding the test.
3 The booklet was satisfactory
2 The booklet did not really help in understanding the test.
1 The booklet was unsatisfactory and even confusing.

3. Did you take any specific measures to prepare yourself for the test?
(Circle numbers from 6 to 1 according to the following definitions. Note: In this question you are allowed to mark more than one possibility)

6 I did not prepare at all for this test.
5 I studied the standard booklet carefully.
4 I tried to do some practice exercises and discussed the test with friends.
3 I reviewed one or more preparation books.
2 I took one or more special courses in preparation for the test.
1 I prepared myself in a different way. Detail:

4. How would you advise a friend to prepare for the psychometric examination?
(Circle the appropriate number. Note: in this question you are allowed to mark more than one possibility)

6 Do not prepare at all for the test.
5 Read the standard booklet carefully.
4 Do some practice questions, and discuss the text with friends.
3 Review one of the preparation books.
2 Take a special course in preparation for the test.
1 Prepare yourself in a different way. Detail:

5. Which tests did you prepare for in advance, and to what extent?
(Write numbers from 5 to 1 in the boxes below the name of each of the tests according to the following definitions.)

5 I prepared for this test very intensively.
4 I prepared for this test intensively.
3 I did some preparation for this test.
2 I did almost no preparation for this test.
1 I did not prepare for this test at all.

General Information	Figural Reasoning	Mathematical Reasoning	Analytical Thinking	English	The Entire Psychometric Examination
☐	☐	☐	☐	☐	☐

6. How would you rate the test instructions? Were they clear and explicit?
(Write numbers from 5 to 1 according to the following definitions.)

5 The test directions were very explicit and I knew exactly what to do.
4 The directions were sufficiently clear and I knew quite well what I was expected to do.
3 The directions were more or less clear and I knew approximately what to do.
2 The directions were not sufficiently clear and I did not know exactly what to do.
1 The directions were unclear and I was confused about what I was expected to do.

General Information	Figural Reasoning	Mathematical Reasoning	Analytical Thinking	English	The Entire Psychometric Examination
☐	☐	☐	☐	☐	☐

7. *How would you evaluate the answer sheet?*

5 Very convenient to use.
4 Convenient to use.
3 Fairly convenient to use.
2 Not convenient to use.
1 Not convenient at all to use.

8. *To what extent do you think these tests are really suitable for assessment of scholastic aptitude and student selection?*
(Write numbers from 5 to 1 below the name of each test according to the following definitions)

5 I find this test to be a very appropriate method of student selection.
4 I find this test to be quite a suitable method of student selection.
3 I find this test to be a moderately suitable method of student selection.
2 I find this test to be not quite suitable as a method for student selection.
1 I find this test to be a completely unsuitable method of student selection.

General Information	Figural Reasoning	Mathematical Reasoning	Analytical Thinking	English	The Entire Psychometric Examination
☐	☐	☐	☐	☐	☐

9. *How would you estimate the extent of your success on each of the test you have just finished?*
(Write numbers from 5 to 1 below the name of each tests according to the following definitions)

5 I feel I have done extremely well on this test.
4 I feel I have done quite well on this test.
3 I feel I have done moderately well on this test.
2 I feel I have not done well on this test.
1 I feel I have done poorly on this test.

General Information	Figural Reasoning	Mathematical Reasoning	Analytical Thinking	English	The Entire Psychometric Examination
☐	☐	☐	☐	☐	☐

10. How did you react emotionally to the tests?
(Write numbers from 5 to 1 according to the following definitions)

5 During the test I felt very relaxed.
4 During the test I felt relaxed.
3 I had neither positive nor negative reactions toward the test.
2 I felt uncomfortable and tense throughout the test.
1 During the test I felt frustrated, anxious and very tense.

The Entire
Psychometric
Examination

☐

11. In your opinion, was there any evidence of prejudice or bias against any particular group of examinees?
(Write numbers from 5 to 1 according to the following definitions)

5 The test was very fair and I was not aware of any bias.
4 The test was fair.
3 There was no apparent bias in the test.
2 There were a few biased items in the test.
1 There was a definite bias in the test against certain groups of examinees.

General Information	Figural Reasoning	Mathematical Reasoning	Analytical Thinking	English	The Entire Psychometric Examination
☐	☐	☐	☐	☐	☐

12. How would you evaluate the behaviour of the test proctors, administrators and supervisors, especially with regard to explaining test directions and setting a pleasant and relaxed atmosphere?
(Circle the number of the answer of your choice)

5 The behaviour of the test administrators and proctors was excellent.
4 The behaviour of the test administrators and proctors was satisfactory.
3 The behaviour of the test administrators and proctors was moderately satisfactory.
2 The behaviour of the test administrators and proctors was unsatisfactory.
1 The behaviour of the test administrators and proctors was completely unsatisfactory and may even have caused confusion.

13. How would you evaluate the physical conditions of the examination: room temperature, lighting, silence, air conditioning, sitting and writing arrangements etc.
(Circle the number of your choice)

5 The physical conditions were excellent.
4 The physical conditions were satisfactory.
3 The physical conditions were adequate.
2 The physical conditions were unsatisfactory.
1 The physical conditions were inferior and completely unsatisfactory.

14. The psychometric examination is only one of the available selection tools. There are many others for student selection.
(Please list from 5 to 1 according to the following definitions)

5 I think this method is very suitable for student selection.
4 I think this method is suitable for student selection.
3 I think this method is moderately suitable for student selection.
2 I think this method is quite unsuitable for student selection.
1 I think this method is completely unsuitable for student selection.

Psychometric Examination	
Personal Interview	
Matriculation Grades	
Specific tests for each major area of study	
Letters of recommendation	
Personality tests	
Averages of grades in last year of high school	

Other Method . . . .

CHAPTER 5

Defining the Task of Assessment: Implications for Teaching

INTRODUCTION

The scene for this and the chapters which follow has been set in Chapter 1. The models of the assessment-curriculum process defined a new role for the teacher in higher education as a manager of learning. Every teacher in higher education is responsible for curriculum design and evaluation, and assessment is an integral part of that process which is about student learning. Ralph Tyler summarized these basic tasks of the educator as long ago as 1949 thus:

(1) To determine the objectives which the course should seek to attain;
(2) To select the learning experiences which will help bring about the attainment of these objectives;
(3) The organization of those learning experiences so as to provide continuity and sequence for the student and to help the student integrate what would otherwise appear as isolated experiences;
(4) The determination of the extent to which the objectives are being attained.

It is evident that these tasks can only be fulfilled if a systems approach is adopted in which the focus is student learning. A student has to learn the objectives of the programme and, as we saw in earlier chapters, these relate, on the one hand, to the more general aims which society has for education, both latent and manifest, and, on the other, to those factors of temperament and interest which influence the path of student achievement.

Necessarily the teacher (curriculum designer) has to define the significant aims and objectives on which his or her programme is to concentrate. Much of this chapter is concerned with arguments for and against the so-called objectives approach. The first part considers the emotional commitments which teachers have to the aims of their subjects as well as higher education. The internalization of new commitments to assessment and course design requires considerable time for assimilation. Fortunately, there are many pathways to this end.

Nevertheless, many teachers have been influenced by *The Taxonomy of Educational Objectives* (Bloom *et al.*, 1956) (see below), and the categories of the cognitive domain have had a profound influence on educational thinking in the Western World. The principal categories of the cognitive, affective and psychomotor domains are tabulated, as is a taxonomy of experiential learning. The relevance of these taxonomies to assessment and the design of instruction is demonstrated.

Important criticisms of the *Taxonomy* have been made. The categories of the cognitive domain are not all-embracing and it seems to introduce an unreal divorce between the cognitive and affective domains. Syllabuses which embrace the two are likely to be less precise but more in keeping with the emotional commitments of the teacher (for example, history). It also pays little or no attention to the role of values in human behaviour.

Eisner (1979) argues that we do not always preformulate goals. We undertake activities in anticipation that something will happen. In all human endeavour there are unintended as well as intended outcomes. In contrast, it is argued that the establishment of strategies, as, for example, in projects, is to preformulate objectives, even if they are broadly defined. These 'focusing' objectives are sufficient criteria and the teacher can and should evaluate what happens when they are evaluated. This does not mean precise and continuing measurement, but that the teacher in higher education should develop skills in what Eisner calls educational criticism and connoisseurship, or what others have called self-assessment through reflective thinking.

Many approaches are to be found to the specification of tasks. The 'objectives approach' discussed in this and Chapter 6 provides one valuable resource. It reminds us that education is as much about the development of learning skills as about the recall of knowledge. The art of learning necessarily contains its own objectives. It is also a reminder that education is as much about values as about knowledge and skills. Goals are inherent in the value positions we adopt. If student powers of critical thought are to be developed attention has to be given to all three dimensions.

THE IMPORTANCE OF AIMS

The institutions and teachers of higher education owe their existence to the social belief that education is of benefit to the community. Exactly how it benefits the community is a matter of debate. At least six perspectives on educational excellence have been identified by the American writers Morgan and Mitchell (1985), all of which hold that an important aim of higher education is the development of a highly trained workforce.

Aims of this kind create tension in institutions between academics, more especially between those in the humanities and the technologies, since public resources are likely to be given to the technologists in the belief that there is a direct relation between certain activities undertaken in the university and economic performance. If these activities are not perceived to be the ones required then the academics in those disciplines will have to adapt if they are to receive resources. This has been seen to be the case in both Britain and the

United States, where research has been directed away from the pure to the applied as well as to greater association with industry.

Many academics would argue that higher education is not primarily for the creation of a workforce, and in this they are supported by the definition of excellence given in the report of the National Commission on Excellence in Education (NCE, 1983):

> We define excellence to mean several related things. At the level of the individual learner, it means performing on the boundary of individual ability in ways that test and push back personal limits, in school and work place. Excellence characterizes a school or college that sets high expectations and goals for all learners, then tries in every way possible to reach them. Excellence characterizes a society that has adopted these policies, for it will then be prepared through the education and skills of its people to respond to the changes of a rapidly changing world.

These assertions can be increasingly refined until they are open to measurement, and the pressure, at least in the United States, is for this to happen so that the concept of multiple-strategy assessment in the Governors' report relates to the many measures which would have to be made to determine excellence as defined. Such goals are directed at the level of the institution as well as that of the teacher. They will either conflict with or enhance those aims of education held by the teacher. Even though they may not be thought through, they nevertheless form a key emotional attachment which is interrelated to the teacher's views of the nature of student learning. Dressel (1980) reminds us that college professors do not all subscribe to the same conception of higher education. Some believe that its purpose is to convey the knowledge and truths established by the great minds of the past; others that it is to help students to learn how to learn; some hold that it is the aesthetic experience of education which matters, and others may hope that the experience of college will develop the person who will radically change the community.

I emphasize these points because it seems that those who have been concerned with the development of systems approaches to assessment and curriculum have paid too little attention to the goals (aims) to which teachers in higher education are attached. Moreover, it is for this reason that the objectives movement did not take off in higher education. That is why the model in Figure 3 (Chapter 1) incorporates aims as well as objectives.

However, this omission is easily understood, since those who first developed the objectives approach began with a dissatisfaction with terms like 'critical thinking', which were so broad as not to be useful in planning a teaching programme. What has to be found is something which is apparently more measurable to which a teacher's emotional attachment can be transferred and this process will take a long time (Dressel, 1976; Fitzgibbon and Heywood, 1986; Murphy, 1976). There is no doubt that some instructors in higher education have found this attachment in *The Taxonomy of Educational Objectives* with which the objectives movement is associated. Equally, for many others it is anathema. Fortunately, there are other pathways to this end. So why objectives, and why is critical thinking not enough?

A PROBLEM OF TERMINOLOGY: MEANINGS OF THE TERM 'OBJECTIVE'.

Just as 'aims' and 'goals' are used interchangeably so too is the term 'objective'. There is no way round this difficulty because they are deeply embedded in our thought. For those of us who work in the education field 'objective' usually means something more focused and precise than an aim or a goal. When the term 'behavioural' is attached (i.e. a 'behavioural objective') it means something which can be measured. Sometimes 'educational objective' is used in the same sense as 'behavioural objective'. At other times it is used to signify non-behavioural objective. More recently, public examination boards in England have begun to distinguish between objectives which define the aims of a course and assessment objectives which will be tested in examinations and coursework. Multiple-strategy assessment as defined by the US Governors embraces both. Dressel (1976) writes of instructional goals which seem to have the same purpose as educational objectives. That is, they are both related to the curriculum activity. All describe preformulated goals which have to be obtained by the learner. In this sense Eisner's term 'outcome' is perhaps the best, since the outcome is not always specified.

Eisner (1979) has argued that in the United States the shift in terminology (educational to instructional to behavioural to performance) is not accidental. He argues that 'it reflects an increased emphasis on the manifest behaviour of the student and on discrete forms of student activity'. It is a move away from the general to the specific and a prohibition on expressive outcomes.

Notwithstanding his view, I believe that, whichever terminology we take, we can see that the goals of higher education are set at too broad a level for them to dictate the curriculum process. More precise statements of purpose have to be drawn from them to form the operational goals of a department or the courses which it runs. At a third and very concrete level are the objectives for specific units of instruction (for example, lectures, practicals, seminars).

In the section which follows the concern is primarily with objectives at the level of the course.

THE TAXONOMY OF EDUCATIONAL OBJECTIVES

One approach to the specification of objectives which has had an all-pervasive influence on educational thought is the so-called *Taxonomy of Education Objectives* (Bloom *et al.*, 1956). The authors of the *Taxonomy* attempted to describe the abilities involved in cognitive information processing and at the same time to illustrate how they could be tested (see Tables 11 and 12). They maintained that these abilities were hierarchically ordered and that they were not learned automatically. Therefore careful instruction had to be given if these abilities (skills) were to be learnt. They also produced a handbook for the affective domain, which has not inspired much interest. Other authors have produced taxonomies for the psychomotor domain and experiential learning.

Table 11. *The Taxonomy of Educational Objectives.* An outline of the major categories in the cognitive domain

---

1. *Knowledge*
1.10   Knowledge of specifics
1.11   Knowledge of terminology
1.12   Knowledge of specific facts
1.20   Knowledge of ways and means of dealing with specifics
1.21   Knowledge of conventions
1.22   Knowledge of trends and sequences
1.23   Knowledge of classifications and categories
1.24   Knowledge of criteria
1.25   Knowledge of methodology
1.30   Knowledge of universals and abstractions in a field
1.31   Knowledge of principles and generalization
1.32   Knowledge of theories and structures

2. *Comprehension*
2.10   Translation
2.20   Interpretation
2.30   Extrapolation

3. *Application*

4. *Analysis*
4.10   Analysis of elements
4.22   Analysis of relationships
4.33   Analysis of organizational principles

5. *Synthesis*
5.10   Production of unique communication
5.20   Production of a plan, or proposed set of operations
5.30   Derivation of a set of abstract relations

6. *Evaluation*
6.10   Judgements in terms of internal evidence
6.20   Judgements in terms of external criteria

The principal categories of these taxonomies are shown in Tables 11 and 13–16.
   The categories in the cognitive domain are given detailed descriptions. For example, the category Comprehension contains three subcategories:

   Translation
   Interpretation
   Extrapolation

Each of these is then analysed in more detail. The subsection on translation reads:

   Comprehension is evidenced by the care and accuracy with which the communication is paraphrased or rendered from one language or form of communication to another. Translation is judged on the basis of faithfulness and accuracy, that is, on the extent to which the material in the original communication is preserved, although the form of the communication has been altered.

The ability to understand non-literal statements (metaphor, symbolism, irony, exaggeration).

Skill in translating mathematical verbal material into symbolic statements and vice-versa.

Table 12. Examples of medical faculty questions according to the six levels of Bloom's taxonomy (from Foster, 1983)

Knowledge
What was the heart rate?
Where is the primary lesion?

Comprehension
When would you use that type of hernia repair?
Why is the fracture in the same place it was before?

Application
You are watching the patient and she falls. What would you do?
Here is a lady with no vibratory sensation. What problem does this pose?

Analysis
What are the most significant aspects of this patient's story?
That is a curious bit of information. How do you explain it?
How would you divide that information into ways of looking at it?

Synthesis
How would you summarize this?
What are your conclusions?

Evaluation
Why is that information pertinent?
How valid is this patient's story?

Table 13. The Taxonomy of Educational Objectives; affective domain

---

Outline of the major categories in the affective domain (Krathwohl et al., 1964)

1.0 Receiving (attending)
    1.1 Awareness
    1.2 Willingness to receive
    1.3 Controlled or selected attention
2.0 Responding
    2.1 Acquiescence in responding
    2.2 Willingness to respond
    2.3 Satisfaction in response
3.0 Valuing
    3.1 Acceptance of a value
    3.2 Preference for a value
    3.3 Commitment (conviction)
4.0 Organization
    4.1 Conceptualization of a value
    4.2 Organization of a value system
5.0 Characterization by a value or value complex
    5.1 Generalized set
    5.2 Characterization

Table 14. Example of the Development of a Category

5.1 Generalized Set

Readiness to revise judgements and to change behaviour in the light of evidence.

Changes his mind when new facts or insights demonstrate the need for revisions of opinions formerly held.

Willingness to face facts and conclusions that can be logically drawn from them.

Views problems in objective, realistic and tolerant terms.

The habit of approaching problems objectively.

Acceptance of objectivity and systematic planning as basic methods in arriving at satisfying choices.

Relies increasingly upon the method of science in finding answers to questions about the physical world and about society.

Changes his opinion on controversial issues when an examination of the evidence and the arguments calls for revision of opinions previously held.

Confidence in his ability to succeed.

Judges problems in terms of situations, issues, purposes and consequences involved rather than in terms of fixed, dogmatic precepts or emotionally wishful thinking.

It is fairly easy to see how these abilities can be tested (see, for example, Table 12, which relates to medical education). Testers argue that questions will be more valid if they are designed to obtain a particular ability. *The Taxonomy's* most significant contribution may well be the debate which it caused about the value of declaring objectives. This debate continues.

TO DECLARE OR NOT TO DECLARE OBJECTIVES

It is now customary for the examining boards in England to require detailed statements of aims and objectives. Validating authorities like BTEC and CNAA require general statements. The examining boards became interested in the *Taxonomy* very early on, when R. A. C. Oliver influenced the JMB to develop a GCE A level in General Studies which would test the categories of the *Taxonomy* but for which *no* syllabus would be required. Its nearest equivalent would be the GRE in the United States. The success of General Studies undoubtedly influenced other committees in the JMB which were concerned with the development of new or the redesign of subjects in the curriculum.

Some of these subject committees used the categories of the *Taxonomy* as they stood. Others found it necessay to modify them to better express what it was they wanted to achieve. Nevertheless the influence of the *Taxonomy* is clear, as the example in Table 17 shows.

The first problem was that the titles of the main categories were the choice of the authors and summarized what they thought the abilities involved in a particular ability were. These titles did not necessarily represent the abilities necessary for performance in a subject as perceived by the subject specialist.

Table 15. A taxonomy of the psychomotor domain: principal categories (Harrow, 1972)

1.00 Reflex movements
  1.10 Segmental reflexes
    1.11 Flexion reflex
    1.12 Myotatic reflex
    1.13 Extensor reflex
    1.14 Crossed extension
        reactions
  1.20 Intersegmental reflexes
    1.21 Co-operative reflex
    1.22 Competitive reflex
    1.23 Successive induction
    1.24 Reflex figure
  1.30 Suprasegmental reflexes
    1.31 Extensor rigidity
    1.32 Plasticity reactions
  1.33 Postural reflexes
    1.331 Supporting reactions
    1.332 Shifting reactions
    1.333 Tonic-attitudinal reflexes
    1.334 Righting reactions
    1.335 Grasp reflex
    1.336 Placing and hopping
         reactions

2.00 Basic fundamental movements
  2.10 Locomotor movements
  2.20 Non-locomotor movements
  2.30 Manipulative movements
    2.31 Prehension
    2.32 Dexterity

3.00 Perceptual abilities
  3.10 Kinesthetic discrimination
    3.11 Body awareness
      3.111 Bilaterality
      3.112 Laterality
      3.113 Sidedness
      3.114 Balance
    3.12 Body image
    3.13 Body relationship to
        surrounding objects
        in space
  3.20 Visual discrimination
    3.21 Visual acuity
    3.22 Visual tracking
    3.23 Visual memory
    3.24 Figure-ground
        differentiation

3.25 Perceptual consistency
3.30 Auditory discrimination
  3.31 Auditory acuity
  3.32 Auditory tracking
  3.33 Auditory memory
3.40 Tactile discrimination
3.50 Co-ordinated abilities
  3.51 Eye–hand co-ordination
  3.52 Eye–foot co-ordination

4.00 Physical abilities
  4.10 Endurance
    4.11 Muscular endurance
    4.12 Cardiovascular endurance
  4.20 Strength
  4.30 Flexibility
  4.40 Agility
    4.41 Change direction
    4.42 Stops and starts
  4.43 Reaction–response time
  4.44 Dexterity

5.00 Skilled movements
  5.10 Simple adaptive skill
    5.11 Beginner
    5.12 Intermediate
    5.13 Advanced
    5.14 Highly skilled
  5.20 Compound adaptive skill
    5.21 Beginner
    5.22 Intermediate
    5.23 Advanced
    5.24 Highly skilled
  5.30 Complex adaptive skill
    5.31 Beginner
    5.32 Intermediate
    5.33 Advanced
    5.34 Highly skilled

6.00 Non-discursive communication
  6.10 Expressive movement
    6.11 Posture and carriage
    6.12 Gestures
    6.13 Facial expression
  6.20 Interpretive movement
    6.21 Aesthetic movement
    6.22 Creative movement

Table 16. A taxonomy of experiential learning: principal categories (from Steinaker and Bell, 1969)

Exposure
Seeing, hearing, reacting and recognizing

Participation
Observing, discussing, listening and ordering

Identification
Classifying, explaining, experimenting, writing and drawing

Internalization
Generalizing, comparing, contrasting and transferring

Dissemination
Communicating, debating, presenting, motivating and influencing

---

Table 17. Aims of practical work in GCE Engineering Science at A Level (Carter *et al.*, 1986)

Evidence should be produced of the student's appreciation of aims in the following areas:

(i) Technique
(a)   The development of the facility for making accurate observations and the ability to make reasonable estimates of the errors incurred in making such observations.
(b)   Familiarization with the facility in the use of scientific apparatus and equipment.

(ii) Originality
The development of the ability to:
(c)   Formulate hypotheses from given sets of observations;
(d)   Formulate experiments to test hypotheses;
(e)   Devise and improve upon experimental procedures;
(f)   Appreciate the relative importance of errors in differing situations.

(iii) Analysis
The development of the ability to:
(g)   Discriminate between possible alternatives;
(h)   Formulate problems in a form appropriate for investigation;
(i)   Recognize assumptions made and assess their importance;
(j)   Extrapolate.

(iv) Synthesis
The development of the ability to:
(k)   Produce a unique communication;
(l)   Produce a plan or proposed set of operations;
(m)   Derive a set of abstract relations;
(n)   Design and evaluate.

Teachers in the subject committees were asked to change the terms to which they were emotionally attached, but it was more than this, for the *Taxonomy* did not always possess the particular abilities required for performance in the subject or which the subject had to offer in the general development of individuals. This is particularly well illustrated in a similar statement for geometrical and engineering drawing from the same board, which includes categories for Visualization and Interpretation. These convey an emotional expression of what has to be done, whereas comprehension does not. The power of visualization is lost. Technique is a practical category which could also have been included in the category application.

Similarly, the syllabus designers of engineering science also used *technique* but added *originality* to their objectives for practical work (Carter *et al.*, 1986). In the general introduction to the subject it was stated that: 'A course in Engineering Science should be concerned with physical skills: the co-ordination of hand–eye'. The skills contributing to this are specified as making observations, estimating errors, handling equipment, maintaining concise and accurate records and sketching quickly and meaningfully. That the *Taxonomy* has no category for originality (creativity) is a serious impediment to its use by teachers in subjects like Art, where such qualities are valued.

If the subcategories in the objectives for laboratory work are compared with those in the *Taxonomy* it will be found that they do not all correspond with the major categories. For example, extrapolate (which is listed under Analysis) is in the comprehension category in the *Taxonomy*. It is for this, among other reasons, that the *Taxonomy* has been criticized, for in a real taxonomical classification the categories should be mutually exclusive. This is clearly not the case with the *Taxonomy*, and it raises the question as to whether it is hierarchically ordered. One study has suggested that it is sequentially ordered as far as 'analysis'. My own findings are ambiguous. On the one hand, task analyses suggest that it is not sequentially ordered, whereas on the other, the assessment of projects suggests that students find the skills of evaluation and self-assessment the most difficult to acquire. It is possible from mine and the work of others to state categorically that specific instruction is generally required in these areas.

In this respect much work has been done in the United States to relate domain, level of learning and instructional method to objectives, as Weston and Cranton (1986) in a substantive review have shown (Table 18).

A third criticism of the *Taxonomy* (and this follows from the above) is that it is not all-embracing. It does not cover every eventuality, but I doubt whether that matters. What matters is that the curriculum designer should focus on a few significant categories and allow (possibly predict) that there will be other important learning outcomes. Objectives should provide a focus for assessment design, which is why I have called the objectives of the subtests for the engineering science examination 'focusing objectives'.

Table 18. Matching objective domain and level of learning to appropriate methods of instruction (from Weston and Cranton, 1986). (Reproduced by kind permission of the Editor of the *Journal of Higher Education*. © 1986 by the Ohio State University Press. All rights reserved)

Domain and level	Method
Cognitive domain	
Knowledge	Lecture, programmed instruction, drill and practice
Comprehension	Lecture, modularized instruction, programmed instruction
Application	Discussion, simulations and games, CAI, modularized instruction, field experience, laboratory
Analysis	Discussion, independent/group projects, simulations, field experience, role-playing, laboratory
Synthesis	Independent/group projects, field experience, role-playing, laboratory
Evaluation	Independent/group projects, field experience, laboratory
Affective domain	
Receiving	Lecture, discussion, modularized instruction, field experience
Responding	Discussion, simulations, modularized instruction, role-playing, field experience
Value	Discussion, independent/group projects, simulations, role-playing, field experience
Organization	Discussion, independent/group projects, field experience
Characterization by a Value	Independent projects, field experience
Psychomotor domain	
Perception	Demonstration (lecture), drill and practice
Set	Demonstration (lecture), drill and practice
Guided response	Peer teaching, games, role-playing, field experience, drill and practice
Mechanism	Games, role-playing, field experience, drill and practice
Complex overt response	Games, field experience
Adaptation	Independent projects, games, field experience
Origination	Independent projects, games, field experience

A more important criticism of the original *Taxonomy* is that, by separating the two domains, the authors have made a separation between the affective and the cognitive, which does not happen in reality. It is easy to demonstrate that the cognitive involves the affective. Consider, for example, the statement of aims and objectives for the syllabus in history in Table 19. Although it is not expressed in the form of the *Taxonomy* it is nevertheless a statement of behaviours which can be realized. At the same time, these behaviours cut across the affective domain and are intimately related to it thus:

To be objective in interpreting historical material	The ability to examine critically
To respect the right of others to be different and to hold different points of view	The ability to evaluate the relative merits of different interpretations of historical phenomena
	or
	The ability to evaluate different historical points of view

Critical thinking, be it in engineering, history or medicine, necessarily involves value judgements, and it is an important task of the tutor to make sure that the students understand that this is so. That not all medical students are likely to have suitable skills for dealing with patients has been demonstrated on several occasions (Strassman *et al.*, 1967; Walton, 1967).

Table 19. Aims and objectives of a syllabus in history[a]

Knowledge and comprehension
Students should be able to recall, recognize and understand the principal events, trends and issues of the periods of history set out in the syllabus. They should have some understanding of the recent evolution of the world in which they live.

Skills
Students should be able to practise, at a level suitable to their stage of development, the skills used in history; more particularly:
  (i) The ability to locate, understand and record historical information;
 (ii) The ability to examine critically and discuss statements on historical matters encountered in their textbooks and in everyday life.

Attitudes
Students should feel a responsibility:
  (i) To be objective in interpreting historical material;
 (ii) To find rational explanations for historical events and developments;
(iii) To respect the right of others to be different and to hold different points of view.

---

[a] Originally written for the school syllabus in History by the Department of Education in Ireland. I have substituted 'student' for 'pupil' in each case.

Just how important this is may be judged from Thompson's (1969) comments on partiality and prejudice in history:

> Sometimes major historical events breed their own forms of prejudice and bias. French historians of all political hues would agree that 'contemporary history' dates from 1789 and that the upheavals of the French Revolution are an immensely significant landmark in the history of modern Europe. They tend even to share a propensity (which it took an Italian historian of the Revolution, Geatano Salvemini, to point out) to personify the Revolution and to accredit 'it' with having proclaimed the Rights of Man or dethroned Louis XVI. Thomas Carlyle, Jules Michelet and Jean Jaures could write of the Revolution as if 'it' were an independent agent, instead of a historian's shorthand term for a vast sequence of events; even as if it were a thing of flesh and blood. On the basis of this double referral the hypothesis would have to be rejected.

There is an obligation on us to be clear about the value systems which we hold and the assumptions we make. There is an equal obligation to make these clear to our students and to recognize the prejudices deriving from our own professional studies and contacts. This we did, for example, in a programme of industrial studies at the University of Liverpool (Carpenter and Heywood, 1973; Heywood, 1974a).

Table 20.

(a) *Extract from a statement of aims and objectives of a course in industrial studies for students of engineering science*

Basic areas in which knowledge is to be acquired	Understanding and skills to be developed	Attitudes which it is desirable the student should develop
Factors contributing to the social and economic behaviour of individuals or organizations. Attitudes to economic growth and technological and social change. Problems of innovation and achievement and the motivation of individuals and groups. Applications to current problems such as advanced and underdeveloped countries, pollution, population growth resource and conservation	Ability to relate individual and corporate acts to their global consequences. Understanding of real facts in situations which are currently highly charged with emotion	Appreciation of the value and limitations of historical studies in explaining current situations. Appreciation of the interactive nature of our economic and social situations and problems: of the need for analysis and synthesis in situations where controlled experiments are impracticable: recognition that real gains are seldom won without corresponding concession and of the frequent need for compromise

(b) *Examples of examination questions set in this area of the curriculum*

'In the eighteenth and early nineteenth centuries science did not initiate industrial trends.'
'The inventions of the early stages of the industrial revolution were effects not causes.'
'What evidence is there to support these statements? How true do you think these statements are of science progress in the twentieth century?'

'The enemy is not change itself but the fact that the direction of change has become rigidified. And science is our great ally, if by science we mean the whole field of empirically verifiable knowledge and not merely the older more mechanistic technologies.'
'What does Maurice Temple Smith mean by the direction of change and how does he envisage that science can help alter the direction of change? Advance your reasons for agreement or disagreement with the thesis.'

I have no doubt that the value system, general approach and selection and interpretation of material by economic historians is different to that which we used, nor that, while we had an obligation to be aware of these differences we also had a duty to pursue our goals which were not only concerned with inventions and innovation but with their prosecution through entrepreneurship in industry. It is also significant that in another part of the programme we considered the problem of prejudice. The statement of objectives (Table 20) shows our position just as it shows the relationship between knowledge, skills and values. In a strict behavioural approach we would not have used the terms 'understanding' and 'appreciation'. The examples in the lower half of the table show how an individual's or a teacher's dispositions are intrinsic to the response to questions set to meet these objectives.

Many of us would probably think that the more important 'affective issues' relate to our dealings with people, especially those concerning the medical profession. These range from empathy to decisions about transplants and genetic engineering. We would expect a taxonomy of medical education to embrace such matters and for practitioners to be assessed in these personal and ethical domains.

Dressel (1971, 1976), who was vociferous in his criticism of the *Taxonomy*, felt that it completely underestimated the role of values in human behaviour. An education which ignores this dimension at the expense of the cognitive fails:

> The values themselves, no matter how well stated, do not resolve these conflicts which will yield, if at all, only through intellectual efforts directed by value concerns and conducted in full awareness of the fact that value-free intellectual exchange is an ideal unachievable by man and probably undesirable in any case.

However, these are not reasons for not stating objectives if by this we mean a full awareness of our own position and the goals we hope to achieve. When subject specialists seek to clarify their own position and methods they necessarily make statements from which definitions of the skills required for the pursuit of understanding in their particular subject can be derived. The trouble is that we have assumed that we and our students know where we are going. We have also assumed that students acquire the range of skills inherent in such statements of aims of higher education as those in the American reports on excellence in higher education or in *The Idea of a University* (Newman, 1854; 1947). Unfortunately, there is plenty of evidence to suggest that we do not achieve these cherished ideals. If nothing else happened, the publication of the *Taxonomy* created a climate in which many teachers were forced to think about what it was they were trying to do, and some found great stimulation from trying to achieve their aims through its application to their courses. It is clear that while it is an important source of objectives, it is not the only one. Eisner (1979), who was one of its critics, also gave us a concept of the teacher as evaluator which brings Tyler's requirement for objectives into perspective. It is with some of Eisner's views that this chapter concludes.

INTENDED VERSUS UNINTENDED OUTCOMES

Eisner (1979) distinguished between three kinds of objectives—behavioural, problem-solving and expressive. He attached the terms 'objectives' to the first two and 'outcomes' to the third. This was because the term 'objective' implied a preformulated goal, whereas 'outcome' suggested the result of what happened. He argued that while there was a case for preformulated goals there were many activities for which we did not formulate specific goals. We undertook them in the anticipation that something would happen, even though we could not specify what. For example, we do not think much beyond the data, even though we could predict from the ample criteria at our disposal. What we do is to evaluate retrospectively what happened against these criteria. From this he deduces that teachers should be able to plan activities which do not have any specific objectives.

This leads him to express the view of many educationalists who would say with him that

> Expressive activities precede rather than follow expressive outcomes. The tack to be taken with respect to the generation of expressive outcomes is to create activities which are seminal; what one is seeking is to have students engage in activities that are sufficiently rich to allow for a wide, productive range of valuable outcomes. If behavioural objectives and activities constitute the algorithms of curriculum, expressive activities and outcomes constitute their heuristics.

Such a statement would surely be met with approval by teachers in the arts. My difficulty is that even to establish a strategy which will allow things to emerge is to formulate a goal in the expressive domain in which the cognitive and the affective are especially merged. I would argue that this is the purpose of 'focusing' objectives, and call on the methods of project assessment described in Chapter 11 for history and engineering as examples to demonstrate this point. Given criteria, I can evaluate what happens, and I should. There can be no rigid distinction between criteria and objectives.

CRITIC AND CONNOISSEUR:
THE ART OF SELF-ASSESSMENT IN TEACHING

Eisner, who accepts that behavioural and problem-solving objectives have a role to play in curriculum and instruction, removes the ruthlessness of the systems model which so many teachers seem to perceive. In his model of evaluation the teacher is a critic and connoisseur who undertakes a task which is essentially qualitative in nature. The model he takes is that of the art critic and connoisseur.

By 'criticism' he means the 'illumination of something's qualities so that an appraisal of its value can be made'. The activity of criticism depends on the critic's powers of perception, and therefore on skills of looking, seeing and appreciating. Connoisseurship is the art of appreciation. I take the view from Eisner's perspective that, while teachers in higher education should be willing to open themselves to critical evaluation, ultimately the teacher has to become his or her own critic. Through experience they will have to develop skills in reflective thinking. Thus Eisner argues;

> Prior to actual teaching: planning at home, reflecting on what has occurred during a particular class session, and discussing in groups ways to organize a programme. Theory here sophisticates personal reflection and group deliberation. In so far as a theory suggests consequences flowing from particular circumstances, it enables those who understand the theory to take those circumstances into account when planning.
>
> In all of this, theory is not to be regarded as prescriptive but as suggestive. It is a framework, a tool, a means through which the world can be construed. Any theory is but a part of the total picture. . . In one sense all teachers operate with theory, if we take theory to mean a general set of ideas through which we make sense of the world. All teachers, whether they are aware of it or not, use theories in their work. Tacit beliefs about the nature of human intelligence, about the factors that motivate children, and about the conditions that foster learning influence the teachers' actions in the classroom. These ideas not only influence their actions, they also influence what they attend to in the classroom: that is, the concepts that are salient in theories concerning pedagogical matters also tend to guide perception. Thus, theory inevitably operates in the conduct of teaching as it does in other aspects of educational deliberation. The major need is to be able to view situations from the varied perspectives that different theories provide and thus to be in a position to avoid the limited vision of a single view.

The development of the art of educational criticism requires a continuing and reflective exchange between theory and practice. Self-evaluation by the teacher may be thought of as painting a picture of his or her students. It can only be an impression. Our goal is their learning, and we like to bring certain experiences to this activity. The greater the variety, the more detailed the impression and the better the understanding. Just as the painter experiments with colour so too can we experiment with learning. To use Eisner's distinction, our experiments will be directed as much at expressive outcomes as they will at behavioural and problem-solving ones.

A compromise position has been suggested by Anderson (1975) and a number of colleagues, which Miller (1979) suggests will probably be acceptable to both advocates and opponents of the behavioural objectives approach. It reads:

> (1) Objectives expressed in measurable, behavioural terms are appropriate for basic skills and for other areas where there is agreement about the components of an instructional program. (2) For most purposes, behavioural objectives need not be reduced to trivial detail. The degree of specificity may vary and should relate to the purpose of instruction and the understanding of students and instructors. (3) The use of behaviourally stated objectives should be contained in an instructional model which recognizes and provides for individual differences. (4) Complex and long-range objectives should be included in a set of objectives, even though they cannot be described in precise terms or measured with a high degree of accuracy. (5) Educatonal objectives must be appropriate to the social milieu at a given time, and students should participate with their instructors in finding objectives that make sense to them. (6) In times like the present, when technological and social

changes are rapid and the future is uncertain, the desired behaviours should be adaptable to situations other than the existing one. The ultimate usefulness of behavioural objectives will depend upon how effectively they may be adapted to quite different learning needs and situations.

However, let the case for defining the task adequately rest with the university student who wrote:

> Looking back on my university career I see it as having a series of important landmarks.
>
> The first was the writing and marking of my first essay. I felt that, this being university, something more must be required than seemed to have been acceptable at school. The essay was to be 'about' a famous book of a foreign literature, and I thought to use for it two famous and important contemporary essays, quoting from them in the original. To my great disappointment and bewilderment I only got a 2/2 result.
>
> The second occurred during the revision period for first-year exams; it simply dawned on me that what was wanted was not a piece of writing 'about' something but an argument about same; that exam questions were intended to prompt an argument in response. Second-year essays were developed as arguments relating to the questions, but I could only ever get the same sort of high 2/1 mark.
>
> The third step was made during the second-year revision period. The concentrated effort of reading through many notes about numerous propositions, and of thinking about potential exam arguments about them, led of itself to the asking of questions about the material and to the discovery of potential new approaches or ideas.
>
> The final year was spent on developing this realization. I found it much easier to develop ideas and questions for some topics than for others; at the same time, although I had become interested primarily in the history and politics of one of the countries (which unfortunately was not part of my language and literature course) I found it virtually impossible to develop ideas and questions about interesting items in these spheres. I could not thereby establish, for example, meaningful patterns to relate and interpret, to put a pattern on, apparently current events and developments.
>
> In wanting to do a further degree which concentrated on these interests I saw the main initial goal to be to learn how to do exactly that: to interpret phenomena through the development of questions and ideas. I feel that the fourth important point was to have come to see a degree course simply as a process of learning *to ask*, rather than to answer questions and to acquire as knowledge the resultant interpretations. The task of submitting a dissertation was at times a frightening exercise in this learning process: learning by the experience of unsuitable ideas for a topic how to ask research questions; learning how to handle data and reorient the dissertation on the basis of modified and new questions.
>
> My dissertation concerned in part the relationship between politicians and managers, and objectives set by the former for the latter. This raised for me the importance of a general need which is present in many situations: the need for clearly defined and stated tasks, and clearly defined criteria for evaluating their achievement.
>
> This can and should apply to a university course. At the beginning there should be discussion of
>
> 1. the purpose of a university education;
> 2. the purpose of exercises such as essay writing and exam answer writing.

It is evident that many approaches are to be found to the specification of tasks. 'Objective' approaches provide one valuable resource. It reminds us that education is as much about the development of learning skills as it is about the recall of knowledge. It follows that objectives will be decided by the position we adopt in regard to learning, for the art of learning necessarily contains its own objectives. The debate about the *Taxonomy* is also an important reminder that education is as much about values as it is about knowledge and skills. Goals are inherent in the value positions we adopt. If student powers of critical thought are to be developed, attention has to be given to all three dimensions.

Chapter 6 continues this exploration of aims and objectives in higher education.

Finding Objectives for Learning and Competency

INTRODUCTION

There are many sources of objectives. In this chapter the concern is with the generation of educational objectives similar to those in *The Taxonomy of Educational Objectives* (see Chapter 5). Its critics have produced a variety of similar lists and categories. Examples are given of lists emanating from the domains of philosophy and psychology that analyse the concept of critical thinking which is so often used to describe one of the major goals of higher education. Taxonomies (lists) of critical thinking skills have been developed and courses specially designed to teach critical thinking in both schools and colleges. Programmes in philosophy have been developed for schools.

Research studies can be used to derive and modify objectives. The *Taxonomy* (or modifications of it) have been used in evaluation and classroom research. Examples of its use in the evaluation of 'discussion' in higher education classrooms are given, and these show how the *Taxonomy* can influence training techniques.

Teachers have to derive their own objectives if they are to internalize them, for which reason some techniques for deriving objectives among groups of teachers and of teachers and students working in disciplines and otherwise are considered.

In professional studies the *Taxonomy* can be applied to analyse the work done by persons in their field (for example, engineering and management). However, such models are closed: an open-system approach is to be preferred in which live analyses of the work done by individuals are used to derive training objectives. A technique for such studies is described. However, it suffers from the weakness that, while it demonstrates skill requirements, it does not show how the principles learnt in an educational programme are applied in practice or, for that matter, what principles are essential to such practice. A possible solution to this problem is the critical incident technique, which is used to study work proficiency. In certain fields like dentistry and medicine it is essential that the practitioners have mastery in the tasks they have to do. For this, both domain and specific behavioural objectives have to be defined.

In subjects like medicine, dentistry, engineering and teaching there is considerable interest in competency-based learning. Tasks have to be mastered before the student can proceed to the next section of the course. Assessment of such courses is aimed to produce high grades and fails, not a normal distribution. The advent of the microcomputer is likely to increase interest in mastery learning and individualized instruction.

Because the objectives of instruction are relatively precise there has been some interest in providing profiles of student performance as distinct from grades. The generation of profiles is itself a mechanism for developing and sorting objectives. It is concluded that the 'objective movement's' great advantage has been that it has forced teachers in higher education to define what they mean when they speak of concepts as 'problem-solving', 'creativity', and 'critical thinking'.

Nevertheless, hundreds of objectives can be found. It is for the teacher to develop those domain objectives with which he or she has affinity, since without it the commitment to the new methods of teaching and learning made necessary by a systems approach is unlikely to be found.

CRITICAL THINKING:
A PHILOSOPHICAL PERSPECTIVE

Perhaps one of the most striking developments in American schooling in the last decade has been the introduction of philosophy into schools. One of those who has developed courses in philosophy for children is Matthew Lipman, whose aim was to improve children's reasoning abilities by having them think about thinking as they discussed concepts of importance to them.

The basic assumptions of such a course rest on the argument that children are, by nature, interested in philosophical issues such as truth, fairness and personal identity, and therefore, that they should learn to think for themselves, to explore alternatives to their own points of view, to consider evidence, to make careful distinctions, and to become aware of the objectives of the educational process.

The challenge of this work to teachers in higher education is immense, for it is saying that a child does think about fundamental problems appropriate to its age and experience. An excellent demonstration of this point is to be found in a book by a philosopher (Matthews, 1980), who recounts conversations with his young son in order to illustrate this argument. Such approaches to the curriculum also challenge the views of Piaget. Needless to say, they are not without their critics.

Lipman, Jacobs and Coleman, working with the New Jersey Board of Higher Education, developed a Taxonomy of Thinking Skills, because the Board felt that the guidelines of the College Board on critical thinking did not wholly describe the characteristics of thinking/reasoning. When it was completed it was decided that both lists were necessary because of the need to examine both the broad and the specific nature of the skills involved. Neither list (taxonomy) was exhaustive, there was no hierarchical order, and they were not mutually exclusive (Lipman, 1984; Morante and Ulesky, 1984).

Table 21. The New Jersey Task Force taxonomy of thinking skills. Compiled by Matthew Lipman, Paul Jacobs and Jerry Coleman, listed by Morante and Ulesky (1984). (Reproduced by kind permission of the Editors of *Educational Leadership*, the journal of the Association for Supervision and Curriculum Development)

Mental acts	*Reasoning skills*	*Inquiry skills*
associating	concept formation	observing
assuming	sorting	narrating
pretending	grouping	describing
supposing	classifying	explaining
guessing	defining	estimating
speculating	grading	formulating problems
wishing	seriation	forming hypotheses
surmising	using criteria	measuring
conceding	exemplifying	predicting
remembering	generalizing	designing experiments
choosing		verifying
judging	recognizing relationships	inductive reasoning
deciding	distinguishing dissimilarities	methodical doubting
comparing	logical	reciprocally adjusting
contrasting	existential	means and ends
and so on	discovering similarities	seeking comprehensiveness
	resemblance of terms	distinguishing among
	identity of terms	casual, contingent and
Cognitive states	resemblance of	correlated relationships
knowing that one knows	relationships	formulating conclusions
knowing that one doesn't	understanding systems	looking for relevant
know		evidence
comparing, wishing and	applying criteria to reasoning	and so on
hoping	consistency	
realizing one understands	validity	
and so on	completeness	
	truth (definitional)	
Combinations of	inferring	
mental acts and	formal	
cognitive states	immediate	
doubting	ordinal (relational)	
knowing	categorical syllogistic	
wondering	conditional	
understanding	informal	
and so on		
	generating logical alternatives	
	utilizing matrices	
	utilizing contradictories	
	understanding perspectives	
	and frames of reference	
	constructing arguments	
	formulating questions	
	providing reasons	
	assumption-finding	
	relating premises to	
	conclusions	
	standardizing sentences	

With this taxonomy (Table 21) as a framework, the New Jersey Task Force set out to examine the validity and reliability of three tests of critical thinking among a sample of 2200 freshmen in eight colleges. The results indicated that there were items in each test which were not very productive, that many of the students were functioning below the level of formal reasoning assessed by the tests, and that there were strong positive correlations between each thinking test and the three sections of the basic skills test (Reading Comprehension, sentence sense, computation, elementary algebra and essay).

One of the tests used was the Cornell Critical Thinking Test, which was designed by Ennis and Millman (1971, 1986). Ennis (1962), who is a philosopher, has had his work much discussed in recent years. He believes that critical thinking is the result of interactions between our willingness (interest) to think critically and the critical thinking abilities which we have. It is in a sense psychological, since the disposition to think critically to which he attaches importance clearly embraces what many teachers call motivation. A person with a disposition to critical thought will, according to Ennis,

(1) Want a clear statement of the problem;
(2) Want to seek reasons;
(3) Try to be well informed;
(4) Try to remain with and pursue the main point of the argument.

The cognitive and the affective cannot be differentiated in such dispositions.

Ennis suggests that the abilities of critical thinking can be grouped into five main categories, which he calls:

(1) Elementary clarification;
(2) Basic support (evaluation of the credibility of sources);
(3) Inferencing (evaluation of own deductions and deductions);
(4) Advanced clarification;
(5) Strategy and tactics.

Some of the tests commonly used to test critical thinking in the United States are listed in Table 22.

CRITICAL THINKING:
A PSYCHOLOGICAL PERSPECTIVE

Sternberg (1984) has published a taxonomy based on the psychological skills involved in critical thinking. His approach is to look at the underlying processes which contribute to intelligence, of which three are identified. He calls them components:

(1) Meta-components;
(2) Performance components;
(3) Knowledge-acquisition components.

Table 22. Tests of critical thinking commonly in use in the United States, listed by Morante and Ulesky (1984). (Reproduced by permission of the Editors of *Educational Leadership*)

New Jersey Test of Reasoning Skills   50 items, untimed

Virginia Shipman

    IAPC—Test Division   Conversion
    Montclair State College   Standardization
    Upper Montclair, NJ 07043   General reasoning
                         Assuming
                         Induction
                         Good reasons
                         Syllogism
                         Contradiction
                         Hypothetical reasoning
                         Casual relationships
                         etc.

Whimbey Analytical Skills Inventory   38 items, untimed

Arthur Whimbey

    Franklin Institute Press   Differences and similarities
    Box 2266   Following directions
    Philadelphia, PA 19103   Solving problems
                         Analogical reasoning
                         Mathematical analogies
                         Trends/patterns
                         Sorting
                         etc.

Cornell Critical Thinking Test, Level X   76 items (5 sample), timed or untimed

Robert Ennis and Jason Millman   Hypotheses
                         Deduction
    University of Illinois Press, 1982   Reliability of authorities
    Box 5081, Station A   Assumptions
    Champaign, IL 61820   Relevance

Cognitive Abilities Test, Form 3   25 items per section, timed
(Level H)

Robert Thorndike, Elizabeth   VERBAL
   Hagen and Irving Lorge   Similarities
                          Sentence sense
    Riverside Publishing Co.   Classification
    8420 Bryn Mawr Ave.   Analogies
    Chicago, IL 60631   QUANTITATIVE
                          Relating
                         Seriation
                    NON-VERBAL
                         Classification
                         Synthesis
                         Analogies

Table 22 (*cont.*)

Watson–Glaser, Forms A and B	80 items, timed or untimed
Goodwin Watson and Edward M. Glaser	Inference
	Assumptions
Psychological Corporation	Deduction
757 Third Ave.	Interpretation
New York, NY 10017	Evaluation of arguments

Ross Test of Higher Cognitive Processes	105 items, timed
John D. Ross and Catherine M. Ross	Analogies
	Deduction
Academic Therapy Publications, 1976	Missing premises
20 Commercial Blvd.	Abstract relations
Novato, CA 94947	Sequential synthesis
	Questioning
	Relevance
	Analysis of attributes

The meta-components are higher-order executive skills which we use to plan, implement and evaluate tasks. Organizing our work at the beginning of an examination is an example of this process. At the other end of the operational time-scale would be strategic planning by the senior administration of a higher-education institution. Performance components help us to carry out the job which we have decided to do. For example, they control the steps taken in writing an examination answer. At the lowest level of his taxonomy are the processes which we use to learn new things.

Sternberg claims that these processes of intelligence can be trained and commends (but only after careful choice in respect of the population on which they are to be used) the instrumental enrichment technique philosophy for children and Chicago Mastery Learning Programmes. The principal skills which underline intelligence listed by him in *Educational Leadership* are the ability to:

(1) Recognize and define the nature of a problem;
(2) Decide upon the processes needed to solve the problem;
(3) Sequence the processes into an optimal strategy;
(4) Decide upon how to represent problem information;
(5) Allocate mental and physical resources to the problem;
(6) Monitor and evaluate one's solution processing;
(7) Respond adequately to external feedback;
(8) Encode stimulus elements effectively;
(9) Infer relations between stimulus elements;
(10) Map relations between relations;
(11) Apply old relations to new situations;

(12) Compare stimulus elements;
(13) Respond effectively to novel kinds of tasks and situations;
(14) Effectively automatize information processing;
(15) Adapt effectively to the environment in which one resides;
(16) Select environments as required to achieve a better fit of one's abilities and interests to the environment;
(17) Shape environments so as to increase the effective utilization of one's abilities and interests.

So the list of skills ('taxonomies', as some people call them) increases, yet, as Sternberg has recognized, they all include operations from each other's lists. This suggests that there is probably a core of thinking skills. My own studies would support this view, for in my classes I have given to my students, each year, a sheet of paper on which four empty squares are printed, spaced one from another. I have then asked the students to make up a model of their decision-making process. Almost all of them, independently of the subject they study, produce a model of decision-making which is similar (for example, hypothesis-forming, selecting alternatives, etc.), although the terms they use to describe them differ widely and are, to some extent, a function of the way the question is put. Almost all of them omit feedback.

More recently, Joan Gubbins, of the Connecticut State Department of Education, has compiled a list which is intended to reflect the skills which have been published by numerous theorists who have made suggestions in this area (Table 23). This point was made long ago by Saupe (1961), who, while not restricting himself to this model, suggested that critical thinking required the ability to:

(1) Recognize the existence of a problem;
(2) Define the problem;
(3) Select information pertinent to the problem;
(4) Recognize assumptions bearing on the problem;
(5) Make relevant hypotheses;
(6) Draw conclusions validly from assumptions, hypotheses and pertinent information;
(7) Judge the validity of the processes leading to a conclusion;
(8) Evaluate a conclusion in terms of its assessment.

Many would find those lists which have their origin in the philosophical domain preferable to the *Taxonomy* and possibly to Sternberg's. This is certainly true of the students I mentioned above. Even so, the authors of the *Taxonomy* could argue that everything in that list is contained within their two volumes. These lists focus on the same kinds of skills but categorize them in a different way. Thus their terminology has different effects on our emotions as they, in turn, are influenced by our particular language usage. The category titles in the taxonomies which derive from the philosophical domain approxi-

130

Table 23. Joan Gubbins' matrix of critical thinking skills cited by Sternberg (1985)

I. Problem solving

  A. Identifying general problem
  B. Clarifying problem
  C. Formulating hypothesis
  D. Formulating appropriate questions
  E. Generating related ideas
  F. Formulating alternative solutions
  G. Choosing best solution
  H. Applying the solution
  I. Monitoring acceptance of the solution
  J. Drawing conclusions

II. Decision making

  A. Stating desired goal/condition
  B. Stating obstacles to goal/condition
  C. Identifying alternatives
  D. Examining alternatives
  E. Ranking alternatives
  F. Choosing best alternative
  G. Evaluating actions

III. Inferences

  A. Inductive thinking skills
    1. Determining cause and effect
    2. Analyzing open-ended problems
    3. Reasoning by analogy
    4. Making inferences
    5. Determining relevant information
    6. Recognizing relationships
    7. Solving insight problems

  B. Deductive thinking skills
    1. Using logic
    2. Spotting contradictory statements
    3. Analyzing syllogisms
    4. Solving spatial problems

IV. Divergent thinking skills

  A. Listing attributes of objects/ situation
  B. Generating multiple ideas (fluency)
  C. Generating different ideas (flexibility)
  D. Generating unique ideas (originality)
  E. Generating detailed ideas (elaboration)
  F. Synthesizing information

V. Evaluative thinking skills

  A. Distinguishing between facts and opinions
  B. Judging credibility of a source
  C. Observing and judging observation reports
  D. Identifying central issues and problems
  E. Recognizing underlying assumptions
  F. Detecting bias, stereotypes, cliches
  G. Recognizing loaded language
  H. Evaluating hypotheses
  I. Classifying data
  J. Predicting consequences
  K. Demonstrating sequential synthesis of information
  L. Planning alternative strategies
  M. Recognizing inconsistencies in information
  N. Identifying stated and unstated reasons
  O. Comparing similarities and differences
  P. Evaluating arguments

VI. Philosophy and reasoning

  A. Using dialogical[a]/dialectical approaches

Gubbins, E. J. "Matrix of Thinking Skills." Reprinted in Sternberg, R. Critical thinking: its nature, measurement and improvement published in *Essays on the Intellect* (Link, Frances R., ed.), pp. 45–65, by ASCD 1985. Reprinted by permission of the Association for Supervision and Curriculum Development.

[a] Dialogical: a term due to Paul (1986), which means the ability to see things from another's point of view.

mate much more to the way we perceive people to behave than those of the *Taxonomy*. Taxonomies are very much the product of the personal disposition (cognitive and temperament) of their authors. What would seem to matter for effective learning is that the learners are of (or can be persuaded into) a similar disposition. In this respect the terminology (language) used is very important.

To be fair, testing and experience suggests that students are 'light' on critical thinking skills when they enter higher education. King (1986) has suggested that this is because the liberal arts are undervalued because many teachers do not understand what thinking entails. He believed that there has been too much emphasis on empirical reasoning at the expense of interpretation and evaluation, and that training in these skills may help students with their studies. The evidence for this will be considered in Chapter 9. Others have suggested that, in the event, teachers are not yet ready to develop skills in critical thinking (Schenkat and Tyser, 1986). As far as higher education is concerned, all the evidence is that teachers in higher education need to be clear about their goals.

Saupe's list above has the great merit of simplicity. There is a danger that lists generate more goals than either the teacher or the students can handle (see Chapter 7). As will be seen in Chapters 10 and 11, Saupe's list has informed much of the work that I have done on the assessment of essays and projects. Nevertheless, students need to be shown not only how to assemble arguments but how to assess them as well.

The critical thinking project in higher education described in a later section in this chapter has this twofold approach as its aim. If questions are set to elicit these skills and learning experiences devised to assist their development then improvements may occur in the reliability of marking and the validity of essays. Chapter 10, on the marking of written assignments, is therefore in part a paraphrase of these sections on critical thinking.

As an instrument for research the *Taxonomy*, directly or in modification, can be used to analyse the teaching–learning situation in a variety of ways, as the examples which follow show.

USING THE *TAXONOMY* IN EVALUATION AND ASSESSMENT RESEARCH

Three examples of the use of the *Taxonomy* in the lecture/classroom situation in higher education follow. The first relates to an investigation in engineering which set out to compare the relationship between lecture and self-study programmes, especially in relation to class size. It was found that self-study methods aided the development of knowledge, the skills of comprehension and application while the classroom offered more potential for the development of the higher-level skills, although this advantage disappeared as class size increased. This resulted in the introduction of a hybrid system of teaching which employed a range of instructional strategies. The associated study aids were not valued by the students (Lindenlaub and Nunke, 1981).

In another study of classroom discussion in medical classes Foster (1981, 1983) showed that the level of discussion as indicated by the *Taxonomy* was a function of the level at which the instructor led the discussion. A low level produced low-level verbal interaction, and a high level of instructor input produced a high level of discussion. Foster found that student response level was related to the level at which the questions are put. If the level is changed to analytical discussion students will make a conscious effort to respond. It was also found that those who participated at higher levels of cognitive activity in discussions were also those who scored higher in the entry tests. Student-entry characteristics contributed very significantly to performance, whereas participation in discussion contributed very little variance to the outcome measures.

Very similar findings were made by Fischer and Grant (1983) in a study of the classroom behaviour of professors and teachers in education. For this they used two instruments, one of which, *The Florida Taxonomy of Behaviour*, was developed from *The Taxonomy of Educational Objectives*. This is a series of categorical statements. The person being observed reads . . . cites a rule . . . gives reasons, and it is thus a checklist of behaviour, with 55 items. The category of interpretation includes the following:

(1) Gives reason (tells why);
(2) Shows similarities, differences;
(3) Summarizes or concludes from observation of evidence;
(4) Gives analogy, simile, metaphor;
(5) Performs a directed task or process.

It is based on the assumption that the role of the teacher is to guide students in the acquisition of knowledge and towards the development of abilities defined by the categories of the *Taxonomy*. The major result of the study was to suggest that students received very little practice in applying higher-order thinking processes to the issues under instruction.

Examples of this kind show the value of the *Taxonomy* or its modification in the assessment and evaluation of what is going on in the classroom, not that the results will always be clear (Barker and Hapkiewicz, 1979; Lindenlaub, *et al.*, 1981). In these studies and those of D. G. Smith reported in the same volume (*Instruction and Outcomes in An Undergraduate Setting*, pp. 83–116) it seemed clear that cognitive development could be fostered by high-level intellectual interchange in the classroom in which the students are actively involved. Such investigations can throw light on the competencies required for effective teaching.

Just as objectives for the education and training of teachers can be derived from studies of teachers at work, so too can such studies be undertaken with professionals in any field. In the sections which follow some other techniques which have been used to derive aims and objectives are described.

GOAL CLARIFICATION USING THE DELPHI TECHNIQUE AND OTHER METHODS OF GROUP PROBLEM-SOLVING

Group techniques can be used by teachers and students in any field of academic endeavour to derive objectives. For example, in one enquiry a group of instructors and students joined together for the purpose of evaluating their courses in the second year of the life of a new university in England. They began by writing down what they would like the examination system to assess. When consensus was reached the following areas of assessment emerged:

(1) Creativity: absorption, assimilation, synthesis, application;
(2) Objectivity: transferability of values and methods;
(3) Perception: analysis, speed, depth;
(4) Knowledge: of facts or of sources, memory, understanding;
(5) Coherence: communication, both written and spoken.

These seemed to be generally accepted as a breakdown of the quality which was unanimously agreed should be assessed, namely 'academic ability'.

The students then designed a questionnaire which was distributed to all the students in the university. This took into account some of the underlying concerns of the students and, in particular, the three-subject first-year curriculum, which they believed was causing unnecessary stress (Dew-Hughes et al., 1966).

Dressel (1980) has pointed out that there are continuing tensions between faculty and students about the level of learning required. In respect of technical programmes he drew attention to the distinction between rote knowledge of a technique and its use, knowlege of the technique's rationale, the ability to demonstrate its validity, and depth knowledge, which will enable the student to handle it in unfamiliar situations. Students are often not clear what is expected of them and often staff expect what is not necessary. We found that subject teachers in programmes which required two or more subjects to be studied expected the same workload and depth from students as if they were studying a single subject, which is the usual approach to undergraduate study in Britain. Levine and Wright (1987) have demonstrated how the Delphi approach can be used to reconcile the views of students and their teachers, in order to develop a measure of teaching effectiveness in a specific subject area.

The Delphi technique is a particular one for obtaining an agreed view from a number of people, and it has been tried in higher education on several occasions (Balaram and Venkatakrishan, 1980; Pradeep and Rubenstein, 1973; Winstead and Hobson, 1971). The participants do not necessarily have to come together for the purpose.

Each participant anonymously rates items on a questionnaire. In this case the items would be about goals. The participants are then given detailed information about how the others responded to the items. They are then asked to respond to the same items but with this new information in front of them. The purpose of this iteration is to find out the level of commitment to the items. The process is repeated on several more occasions until a consensus is reached. A series of workshops may then be used to work out the details of a particular curriculum or, for that matter, objectives for use in a management-by-objectives approach for institutions in higher education.

A modification of this method was used to derive an engineering curriculum by a group of engineers and teachers of engineering. The participants met first as a group to produce an outline course. Each of them was then interviewed by the co-ordinator who, on completion of the interviews, circulated a draft text. This was followed by further meetings with the participants and subsequent redrafting until a consensus was reached. Several persons not involved in the group were consulted as the activity continued. A complete curriculum was drawn up in this way (Heywood et al., 1966).

In ophthalmology a list of behavioural goals was obtained from teachers in the University of Iowa Hospitals, but they were not specialists in the field. Spivey (1971), the investigator, argued that his technique has greater validity than the usual one when a specialist department sets and evaluates its own objectives internally.

Another technique used to evaluate short in-company management training courses was to bring a group of teachers together for a week in a university context to try to get them to relate the experience of their training to the objectives for courses to be run in the future. From the belief that their own jobs and experiences were unique, by the end of the week they had come to the position where they were prepared to provide a list of six broad behavioural categories that were common to them all, and which would meet their needs (Heywood, 1973; Heywood and Fitzgibbon, 1987).

The fact that they took five days to come from very different positions to agree a limited number of objectives shows how difficult the understanding and internalization of educational aims and objectives is. It is not therefore surprising to learn that de Winter Hebron (1979) did not obtain agreement among 81 staff from 12 educational institutions about 46 carefully chosen objectives which, he thought, spanned the disciplines.

A CRITICAL THINKING PROJECT

This particular project, which was designed by Alverno College to study how critical thinking ability is defined, taught and assessed within particular academic disciplines, is an example of group work in which 36 faculties from many institutions meet in four groups over three years to try to answer the issues raised by the study.

During the period of the project these teachers experimented with instructional strategies, teaching styles and methods of teaching. The impact of their experience has been recorded in reports from the three groups (Cromwell, 1986;

Halonen, 1986). In their groupwork the members discussed various aspects of critical thinking within their subjects.

A major assumption that they made was that critical thinking was a complex activity that must be learned through a specific discipline which will be defined differently by each discipline. They found support for this assumption in the work of McPeck (1981). It is a view which is increasingly supported by research, and is futher substantiated by the fact that the approaches in the two published reports on psychology and the humanities use substantially different terminologies.

Table 24. Profile of the critical thinker in the arts and humanities. (Reproduced by kind permission of Cromwell (1986))

Foundational knowledge, abilities and attitudes
The critical thinker:

1. Asks significant and pertinent questions and states problems with specificity. Arrives at solutions through hypothesis, inquiry, analysis, and interpretation.

2. Assesses statements, insights, and arguments according to the knowledge and skills provided by formal and informal logic and by the principles of aesthetic judgement.

3. Derives meaning through an educated perception, whether propositional, systematic, or intuitive.

4. Formulates propositions or judgements in terms of clearly defined sets of criteria.

5. Strives to acquire knowledge of the various disciplines, knowing that such knowledge is a necessary, though not sufficient, condition for critical thinking.

6. Understands the different modes of thought appropriate to the various disciplines. Can apply these modes of thought to other disciplines and to life.

7. Is aware of the context or setting in which judgements are made, and of the practical consequences and values involved.

8. Thinks about the world through theories, assessing these theories and their contexts to determine the validity of their claims to knowledge of reality.

9. Seeks and expects to find different meanings simultaneously present in a work or event. Is intrigued and curious about phenomena others might avoid, disavow, or ignore.

10. Recognizes and accepts contradiction and ambiguity, understanding that they are an integral part of thought and creativity.

11. Constructs and interprets reality with a holistic and dialectical perspective. Sees the interconnectedness within a system and between systems.

12. Is aware of the problematical and ambiguous character of reality. Understands that language and knowledge are already interpretations of phenomena.

13. Tolerates ambiguity, yet can assume a committed position.

14. Is aware of the limitations of knowledge and exhibits epistemological humility.

Knowledge, abilities, and attitudes related to self-awareness
The critical thinker:

1. Demonstrates capacity for continuing intellectual developmental and lifelong learning. Sees the development of critical thinking as an aim and as a process of self-assessment and correction.

136

Table 24. (*cont.*)

2. Recognizes own intellectual potential and limitations in dealing with different tasks. Constantly evaluates the limitations and strives to develop the potential.

3. Extends the range of experience by educating the self in a variety of realms of meaning.

4. Recognizes the style of one's own thought in its creative potential as well as its boundaries. Is willing to explore the style of others to augment one's own perceptions.

5. Treats one's own thinking with dignity.

6. Can apply insights from cultures other than one's own.

7. Is self-directed, with the courage to criticize both society and self.

8. Assumes responsibility for thought and action by being able and willing to explain their meaning and consequences.

9. Demonstrates commitment to a specific world view, while having the capacity to understand and accept others. Is open to the interchange of ideas and to the possibility of changing one's own views.

10. Finds joy in the activity of thinking critically.

Knowledge, abilities, and attitudes related to the social dimension to the critical thinking
The critical thinker:
1. Is aware of the development and production of knowledge and critical thinking as a historical and social process of co-operation among human beings. Knows that thought and knowledge have relevance and meaning only in a social context.

2. Is aware that critical thinking is a social process, and so actively seeks critique from others to increase both self-awareness and understanding of society.

3. Enters willingly into the give and take of critical discussion. Is ready to be called upon to justify and defend thoughts and actions, and is willing to call upon others to do the same.

4. Is sensitive to audience, taking seriously the task of communicating with others. Listens carefully and is able to express thoughts clearly, to argue cogently and appropriately, and to edit sensibly.

5. Examines the assumptions and validity of every communication. Is committed to reflection about the assumptions that guide our construction and interpretation of reality.

6. Goes beyond own interests or the interests of own particular culture to understand other interests and points of view and to foster, when appropriate, synthesized or ecumenical views.

7. Uses knowledge and skills to intervene and support critical and intelligent positions on controversial issues facing the community. Is specifically committed to defend and promote those individual and social relations that will guarantee the possibility of the continuous development of critical thinking in any human being.

At the graduate level Powers and Enright (1987) have shown that faculty have different perceptions of the reasoning skills required for graduate study as a function of discipline. What is important in one subject is not in another. For example, 'breaking down complex problems into simpler ones' was perceived as extremely important in computer science and engineering but not at all in English. Examples like these show why it is necessary to develop critical thinking skills within the context of specific subjects.

The focus of the Alverno study was on the student and, in consequence, the teaching and assessment of critical thinking rather than its definition. Nevertheless, the arts and humanities group began their work with the profile of the critical thinker (reproduced in Table 24). It will be noticed that this profile is of student abilities. In a second part of their general statement the group identified and discussed the pedagogical principles of teaching critical thinking, and these are listed in Table 25. It is instructive to compare this list with Saupe's, for together they show a remarkable consistency over the years about what constitutes critical thinking. Items 12 and 13 suggest, as does all the evidence, that little notice has been taken of these axioms. The system of higher education continues to rely largely on the lecture technique. If it does not then, in Britain at least—where a very able population studies higher education—it must explain why half the output are given degrees which rate their skills of critical thinking as poor, for that is the meaning of a poor second or pass degree. The balance of argument must favour the view that more effective teaching and curriculum design could improve performance considerably. Once again, the value of determining objectives and its implications for instruction are demonstrated. Nevertheless, these were based on the views of teachers in the arts and humanites. In the professional sphere analyses of the jobs done by professionals at work can contribute to programme objectives, as the examples in the next section demonstrate.

Table 25. Pedagogical principles in teaching critical thinking in the arts and humanities discussed by the Alverno Study Group. (From Cromwell (ed), 1986). (Reproduced by kind permission)

1. Be sensitive to individual students.
2. Be an example of a critical thinker.
3. Provide criteria to specify the conduct involved in demonstrating critical thinking abilities.
4. Develop and use as large a range of activities in the class as possible.
5. Open the class to student participation.
6. Provide guidelines for the activities you wish to encourage.
7. Use small groups.
8. Involve every aspect of the student.
9. Use your discipline in teaching critical thinking.
10. Encourage transference.
11. Stress the open-ended quality of critical thinking.
12. Be modest.
13. Be courageous.

Table 26. Example from a role analysis of a unit manager in a steelworks using the taxonomy of educational objectives. (Due to W. Humble, simplified; in the original version, affective behaviours were classified but not described—Heywood (1970))

Objective: To plan and maintain work schedules to secure the required production of goods and services.[a]

	Knowledge	Application				
		Comprehension	Application	Analysis	Synthesis	Evaluation
1. Planning for and causing the required quantity and output to be maintained	Targets tolerances, customer preferences etc.			Ability to recognize when plan is not being met. Skill in causes of disruption		
2. Assigning employee to meet work schedules.	Schedules, policies, methods, limits of authority	Skill in interpreting and translating policies and predicting outcomes	Skill in predicting probable effects of changes			
3. Obtaining and/or checking the availability of the necessary materials, tools, machines and services in accordance with policies and procedures.	Procedures, sources, policies					
4. The proper care and use of materials, tools, machines and equipment within his unit	Familiarity with equipment			Ability to instruct in proper use and maintenance of equipment		

5. Recommending and controlling overtime	Criteria agreements, limits of authority	Skill in interpreting and translating agreements and predicting outcomes		
6. Providing adequate materials and tools to meet the work programme of the following shift	Work programme. Sources of tools and materials. Methods			
7. Recording status of work and general conditions at the end of each shift.	Criteria	Skill in communicating		
8. Checking performance against standards and taking corrective action	Criteria, standards, schedules	Skill in interpreting standards	Identifying causes of non-achievement	Ability to take corrective action

[a] There are eight similar schedules for each of the roles of the model manager.

Table 27. Partial derivation of a taxonomy of industrial objectives derived from a typical works situation in which managers and workmen were in confrontation to some degree

---

The ability to adapt involves:

The ability to perceive
  (i) That organizational structure and formal/informal relationships, value systems and languages and therefore its needs, knowledge of the technical, human and financial aspects of the system or situation;
 (ii) The different thought processes involved in the solution of human or technological problems;
(iii) Our own (self) attitudes and needs.

The ability to control involves:

1. Knowledge of
     (i) How the skills of those who have to be controlled should be used;
    (ii) His or her requirements in relation to needs for communication, competence and excellence;
   (iii) What people ought to be doing;
    (iv) Whether or not they are doing it effectively;
     (v) How to create a climate in which jobs will be done effectively.
2. The ability to make things happen.
3. The ability to discriminate between relevant and irrelevant information, etc.

Ability to relate with people involves:

1. Knowledge of rights, responsibilities and obligations;
2. Knowledge of ways of thinking (determinants of attitudes and values) of people in all parts of the organization;
3. Ability to understand when action in the key environment is right and acceptable in those circumstances (i.e. to understand the effect of his or her behaviour on a situation);
4. Ability to be able to predict the effects of his or her behaviour and that of others on a situation;
5. Ability to create the feeling that the job is important, etc.

USING THE *TAXONOMY* IN JOB ANALYSIS

The *Taxonomy* has been directly applied to the analysis of jobs for the purpose of designing training schemes by W. Humble of the British Steel Corporation (Heywood, 1970). The striking features of this model are the relatively 'passive' expression of the operations and the complexity of the total study (Table 26). It is an example of what Morasky (1973) called a closed system in that the objectives were designed by the trainers to meet a model of what it was believed happened in these particular jobs. An open-systems approach derives its objectives from the nature of the work actually done. The taxonomy shown in

Table 27 was derived from live evaluations of behaviours in some typical work situations in which managers and workmen were in some form of confrontation. In my view it is more dynamic: at the same time it highlights skill areas for training. Notice how each category is a mix of cognitive, affective and value dimensions grouped so as to describe a dominant need (Adapt, Control, Relate). Like the *Taxonomy*, they overlap and some are broader than others. Unlike the *Taxonomy*, they cut across the affective domain which might in the area of management be called the domain of action.

A similar contrast may be seen between two much more sophisticated studies. Meuwese (1968) of Eindhoven University used the categories of the *Taxonomy* to derive 300 behavioural statements from his colleagues in the Department of Industrial Engineering. The same teachers then rated and classified them after which they were factor- and cluster-analysed. The factorial analysis yielded six main factors: these were objectives related to:

Factor 1: The social system components of industrial engineering;
Factor 2: Machine shop technology;
Factor 3: Systems analysis;
Factor 4: Critical analysis and synthesis in industrial situations;
Factor 5: Organization and planning;
Factor 6: The management of mechanical systems.

At the same time the ratings were subjected to a hierarchical cluster analysis. Some of those in what might be described as the area of communication are shown in Figure 16.

This methodology was used to design a first year course in mechanical engineering in the Keller style (Meuwese, 1971). Each of the course units contained the stated objectives, a list of references to specific pages in books which could be used, supplementary texts, a series of study questions, answers to these questions, and six diagnostic multiple-choice tests of approximately twelve items each:

> After an introduction to inform the students about the system and to ask their cooperation in evaluation procedures, all students were given their first unit. This test was randomly chosen for each student from the six tests for that unit. If the score was below the norm, advice was given about material to be studied again. This advice was strictly on the basis of item responses, and was given by a graduate assistant who selected adequate advisory statements from a list of possible statements, following a specific description. After a period of study the student could do a second test and the procedure was repeated. If the results at the third try were still below the norm, then the student was tutored by the professor. Two afternoons a week were available for testing. For each group of 15 students an assistant was available, who scored tests, monitored the advice procedure and distributed materials (Meuwese, 1971).

This design is an example of mastery learning.

142

Short description of item

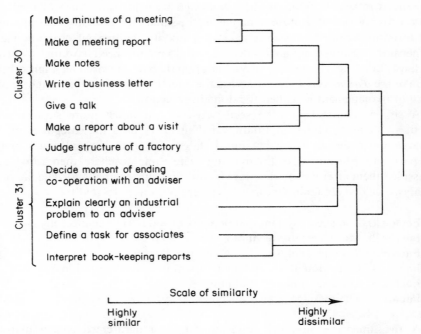

Figure 16. Part of the hierarchical analysis derived by W. Meuwese from teacher ratings of behavioural objectives for industrial engineering. (Reproduced by kind permission of W. Meuwese)

DERIVING EDUCATION AND TRAINING PROGRAMMES FROM JOB ANALYSES

The objection to Meuwese's technique for deriving a curriculum is that it is not based on the jobs which people actually do at work. One study which attempted to do this took into account the fact that job performance, independently of the effectiveness with which it was done, would be influenced by both organizational structure and attitudes (Youngman *et al.*, 1977). A detailed study of two firms in America by Barnes (1960) supported this view.

The investigators argued that the operations derived by Meuwese (and a similar set derived by E. Matchet, unpublished) were too broad. It was necessary to be even more precise. To obtain this degree of precision they interviewed a sample of persons in engineering functions in the firm in which the study was completed to obtain their views about the jobs which they did. Apart from the fact that the interviews were long (and recorded), the novel feature of the interview technique was its modification of the repertory grid technique developed by G. A. Kelly for his theory of personal constructs (Bannister and Mair, 1968).

Kelly was not concerned primarily with any ideal way of anticipating events but with the ways in which individual men choose and anticipate the events of which they are aware: 'Different people may anticipate different events and formulate different modes for anticipating similar events.' For this reason, we thought it essential to obtain information about attitudes to job and self as well as data about the structure of the organization, for the resulting behaviour of an individual is a result of the interaction between the individual and the organization. Kelly described his model of man thus:

> Man is a form of perpetual motion with the direction of the motion controlled by the ways in which events are anticipated. The ways in which a person anticipates events are defined by his personal constructs. A construct is a way in which some things are interpreted as being alike and at the same time different from other things. The substance that a person construes is itself a process. It presents itself from the beginning as an unending and undifferentiated process. Only when man attunes his ear to recurrent themes in the monotonous flow does his universe begin to make sense to him. Like a musician, he must phrase his experience in order to make sense out of it. The phrases are distinguishing events. The separation of events is what man produces for himself when he decides to chop up time into manageable lengths. Within these limited segments, which are based on recurrent themes, man begins to discover the bases for likenesses and differences.

The investigators sought to find out how the engineers interviewed anticipated their work by asking them to indicate the differences and similarities in their jobs over time and with the people with whom they were associated both horizontally and vertically in the organizational structure.

Analysis of the interviews yielded 434 operations, which were then clustered into 14 segments. These were called engineering activities (Figure 17). The operations within one of the clusters are shown in Table 28.

Table 28. Details on one of the clusters of engineering activities. Activity 10: facilitate manufacturing (14 operations)

Operations

Examine design schemes for manufacturing problems.
Identify possible production difficulties.
Examine designs for possible assembly difficulties.
Examine manufacturing implications of new techniques.
Anticipate possible side effects of machining processes.
Consult design engineer regarding alterations for manufacture.

Recommend design alternatives.
Examine manufacturing implications to assist manufacture.
Obtain co-operation from engineer regarding design change.
Consult with engineer regarding adjusted tolerances.
Obtain information regarding machines/tools available.

Issue notes on problem solutions to others.
Use own experience of production methods.

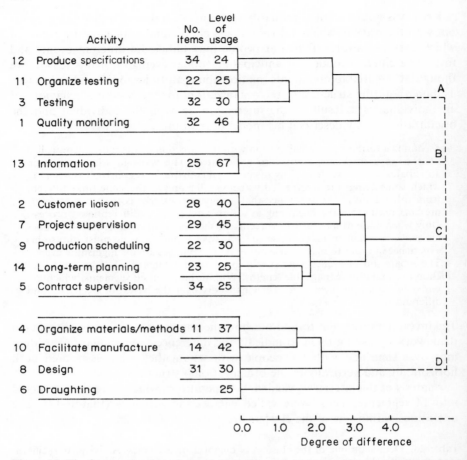

Figure 17. The fourteen engineering activities. The activities are ordered so that adjacent activities are relatively similar, whereas a large separation is indicative of dissimilarity. The list shows the four subsets

After the respondents had completed the checklist they were interviewed. During the interview they were asked to comment on the first results and to complete instruments using the semantic differential technique which sought to explore their attitudes to their jobs and themselves. These were subsequently factor analysed along with data concerning their opinions on industrial training also obtained during this interview. A section of one of the semantic differentials is shown in Table 29. Fifty-two bi-solar scales were included in the two instruments.

Seven factors were identified in relation to job perceptions and these differentiate among engineers doing different types of work. The titles given to the factors were: subjective job evaluation, variety, satisfaction, objective job evaluation, responsibility and authority, stress, job involvement and complexity.

Table 29. Examples of items from the semantic differential used to rate engineers' attitudes to 'themselves' and to their 'jobs'

			My job					
Involves working as a member of a team	1	2	3	4	5	6	7	Does not involve working as a member of a team
Frustrating	1	2	3	4	5	6	7	Satisfying
Inventive	1	2	3	4	5	6	7	Uninventive
Requires experience	1	2	3	4	5	6	7	Does not require experience
Unpleasant	1	2	3	4	5	6	7	Pleasant
Precise	1	2	3	4	5	6	7	Vague
Exciting	1	2	3	4	5	6	7	Disappointing
Well defined	1	2	3	4	5	6	7	Ill defined
Relaxed	1	2	3	4	5	6	7	Tense
Involves diagnosing trouble	1	2	3	4	5	6	7	Does not involve diagnosing trouble

Two examples from the factorial analysis of the semantic differential and training attitude inventory showed its power in relation to the derivation of staff-development programmes. First, the analysis indicated differences between the perceptions of the technicians in the sample and those in the remainder of the sample. The technicians did not think much of their jobs, for they consistently gave high ratings to individual semantic items such as 'tedious', 'involves little responsibility', 'requires little intelligence'. These responses underlined the debate about status in the professional institutions which was going on at the time. They felt that their opportunities for promotion were limited. The second and perhaps more important point was that in respect of attitudes to job, age and job level were more significant variables than educational qualifications.

Other analyses were undertaken in respect of the tasks undertaken by particular groups of engineers (tasks and job level). It was also demonstrated that studies of this kind can show up inconsistencies in organizational structure. (Similar kinds of study have been made of dental technicians (Butler, 1978).)

However, the question to be put in this context is whether it is worthwhile turning these operations into a behavioural taxonomy. If there is an advantage it would seem to lie in the perception it gives of skill categories, even though the titles are arbitrarily chosen.

One of the engineering activities shown in Figure 17 is reclassified in Table 30. While it shows some relation to the *Taxonomy* the categories are not the same. It is not (nor can it be) hierarchically ordered. It also shows the possibility of other important categories in a taxonomy. For example, diagnosis is an important skill in other professions such as medicine. It should be noticed that, like the Florida Taxonomy, each of the operations begins with an action/ initiation term (for example, use, assess, discuss). It is these action words which

Table 30. A subjective analysis of engineering Activity 1 (see Figure 17) in terms of operations contributing to skills of application, communication, diagnosis, evaluation and management (direction and control)[a]

Application
Use test reports from other firms.
Use test reports on earlier components.
Use Pert chart.
Prepare rig for testing.[b]
Simulate normal working conditions for component.

Communication
Discuss testing requirements with technician.
Consult regarding cause of service fault.
Pass report to another engineer.
Notify designer regarding existence of fault.
Advise production department concerning faults.

Diagnosis
Identify deviations from specifications.
Interpret performance graphs.[c]
Interpret test reports supplied by technicians.[c]
Confirm existence of fault by appropriate checks.
Monitor investigations into fault diagnosis.

Evaluation
Assess whether existing component meets customer specifications.
Assess success of fault removal attempt.
Examine test reports supplied.
Assess validity of continuous budgets.[b]
Assess customers' real timing requirements.[b]

Management (direction and control)
Initiate diagnosis of fault.[c]
Suggest modifications to testing specifications.
Give advice to technicians on test results.
Observe dismantling of part failing in service.
Decide measures required to eliminate faults.

---

[a] In activity 1 there are 32 operations in all. These are assigned as follows: Application—2; Communication—5; Diagnosis—11; Evaluation—3; Management (direction and control)—8.
[b] Operations taken from other derived activities to make up groups of five operations.
[c] Illustrations of overlap between the behavioural groups in the table arising from the subjective nature of the method of assignment.

make the operations classifiable. There are those who would object to *Management* as a category, for it is more often than not associated with age and function rather than with behavioural activity. If we ask ourselves the question 'what is management?', we find that the *Shorter Oxford English Dictionary* defines a manager as 'one who has direction and control'. Thus those operations which indicated direction and control were placed in the management category. Those statements generally began with such terms as Initiate, Suggest, Observe, Advise, Request, Decide, etc. In my submission the development of the behavioural classification from the ability groups illuminates the education and training needs in that particular enterprise. It also throws some light on more general needs, for we all accept or acquire tasks which we have to decide how to do, to implement and to evaluate, i.e. we all direct and control. Learning, like management, is an activity which requires direction and control, but it is also an activity which requires motivation. Satisfaction in learning (not necessarily success) is a measure of the extent to which individual needs for direction and control are satisfied.

THE VALUE-ADDED DIMENSION OF ASSESSMENT

The investigations by Meuwese and Youngman et al. described above did not complete the system. In the Dutch study the objectives were generated by the staff in the absence of any study of what actually happens in industry, whereas that of engineers in the aerospace industry described a set of abilities which could be used by trainees to design training schemes. In neither case was a relationship between principles and practice established.

Since 1976 the American Assembly of Collegiate Schools of Business has been concerned with the development of outcome measures which would show how much value was added to a student's performance as a result of their stay in college. What is the effect of college on students' achievement and their ability to function effectively in society? Can measures be designed to show increases in competence which are a result of college training? Alternatively, as the jargon now goes, what value is added to the students' knowledge?

The American Assembly of Collegiate Schools of Business, which is an accrediting body for some 800 institutions, conducted a three-phase project that identified and classified the knowlege, skills, abilities, aptitudes, personal characteristics and values which every business school graduate should possess independently of area of concentration. In the first phase which was conducted both in academia and business, cognitive areas (for example, accountancy, economics) deemed important were identifed. In addition 90 skills and personal charateristics were found which were grouped into six clusters. These were administrative, organization and planning, interpersonal skills (ranging from leadership to oral communication), intellectual stance (range of interests, general intelligence), stability of performance (for example, resistance to stress), work motivation, and values of business (AACSB, 1980).

The second phase focused on the development of alternative strategies for the assessment of skills and personality characteristics. It used assessment centre techniques which use simulations to elicit and measure behaviour. In business the assessment is done by observers who are senior managers, but in this study videotaping was used in order to keep down the costs. In this respect it is very similar to microteaching. The report suggests that these techniques can be transferred to the academic situation.

During this phase attempts were also made to develop pencil and paper tests for this purpose. While it is argued that these measures can be used in academic settings the respondents felt that the tests did not have face validity (AACSB, 1984).

During the third phase knowledge tests for the cognitive areas were developed by ACT and non-subject tests were designed by Development Dimensions International. These included the Edwards Preference Scale (AACSB, 1987).

The cognitive tests were administered to 100 entering and 100 graduating students in each of 14 schools. Comparability between the two groups was investigated by the Student Opinion Survey, which assesses the backgrounds of the students. Chi-squared tests assessed the similarities. From the scores obtained it was found that schools with lower entering scores obtained substantially higher gains (as measured by the difference in means between the entering and graduating scores) than did those with higher ones. This phenomenon is one which the researchers intend to investigate further. Fifty-nine percent of the undergraduates and 45% of the graduates believed that the test content covered a broader area than their course. The percentages who thought their courses were broader than the test were 15% and 27%, respectively. There was a high degree of dissatisfaction with the use of this test for assessment, although the investigators suggest that this is not surprising, since each student saw only one-seventh of the items. In contrast, the students found the exercises used to assess non-subject matter characteristics very valuable. Reliabilities for these measures ranged from 0.77 to 1.0, which is very high for this kind of assessment (i.e. perfect agreement between raters). Graduate students scored significantly better than entering students in decision making, information gathering/problem analysis, written communication and analysis, and from these results it is argued that the instruments to discriminate. The intangible which is always present in such studies is the influence of maturation on performance.

WORK AND PROFICIENCY:
THE CRITICAL INCIDENT TECHNIQUE AS A
MEANS OF DERIVING OBJECTIVES

Another technique which was designed primarily to measure job proficiency has also been used to derive assessment objectives in medicine and education (Flanagan, 1949; Blum and Fitzpatrick, 1965). Called the Critical Incident Technique, it sets out to determine what are the critical factors in a particular task (for example, the principal of a school) (Diggins, 1979). Such studies avoid routine activities and concentrate on what is essential in a task. Data are obtained from stories and anecdotes about how individuals handle certain situations.

A school manager would be asked to think back over a period of six months and focus his or her attention on any one thing that the principal has done which made one think of him or her as an outstandingly good or very effective principal. One should consider a critical incident which has added considerably to the success of the school, and describe the circumstances which led up to the incident, what the principal did at the time, and how this contributed to the success of the school. In the research mode the names of persons are not usually known. Teachers could, for example, be asked to describe critical incidents which they had observed when they had served under other principals. From such pictures it is possible to derive essential functions and behaviours which can be used to compile behaviour rating sheets, assessment schedules, and education or training strategies.

Subsequent to the development of the Critical Incident Technique, D. C. McClelland developed the Behavioural Event Interview (Boyatzis, 1982). This asks the interviewee to describe past job situations in which he or she felt effective or ineffective and then describe those situations in detail. It will be seen that the interview's aims are very similar to those employed by us in our study of engineers. McClelland argues that the qualities (abilities) demonstrated in these situations are the competencies required for the job. This technique has been used to study the role of the operations manager in a high-technology company and personnel in a branch of the US Foreign Service.

It was found that Foreign Service Office examinations did not test for the attributes which the behavioural analysis demonstrated were required. Objective tests designed to meet the derived competencies (in the areas of non-verbal sensitivity, speed in learning political networks and positive expectations of people) predicted outstanding performance (McClelland and Dailey, 1973).

COMPETENCY-BASED ASSESSMENT AND LEARNING

In professional jobs like those of medicine and dentistry there is considerable interest in task analyses as a means of deriving curriculum objectives for areas in which the professional person should be competent. The question of grading does not enter into the issue if a person must be able to do a task if it is essential to the job. It is for this reason that there has been much interest in competency-based learning in medicine in training institutions throughout the world. It is also the reason for the development of competency based education in teacher education in the United States (Houston 1980). There is now substantial interest in competency-based education in the liberal arts and, as we have seen critical thinking is regarded as an important competency in this area of study (Cromwell, 1986). The phrase 'minimum competency' has been used to describe the minimum requirements for a task. At the second level some authorities have suggested that all students should attain a minimum competence before they leave school. The problem is to define what that minimum competence should be.

Competency-based education begins with a description of the broad-based competencies which describe how a competent educator or professional person would perform. It attempts an answer to the questions, what is a competent doctor or what is a competent teacher? Or, as we have seen, what is a critical thinker? A curriculum designed to develop competencies assumes that they can be described and that the competencies which are chosen are the focal points for future learning. In respect of medical education, McGaghie *et al.* (1978) have written:

> The competencies are many and multifaceted. They may also be ambiguous and tied to local custom and constraints of time, finance and human resources. Nevertheless, a competency-based curriculum in any setting assumes that the many roles and functions involved in the doctor's work can be defined and clearly expressed. It does not imply that the things defined are the only elements of competence, but rather that those which can be defined represent the critical point of departure in curriculum development. Careful delineation of these components of medical practice is the first and most critical step in designing a competency based curriculum.

The view taken by those authors is that this necessarily leads to mastery learning. I would contend that, as far as engineering is concerned, this need not be the case and would support it by the case study described in Chapter 13. The weakness of the studies by Meuwese and by myself and colleagues was that while the former concentrated on the knowledge and skills required for the college course on the basis of college data, the latter looked at the tasks done—how the college learning influenced the tasks undertaken was not examined. That is, we still need to know how a person actually applies in practice the principles learnt in college. The attainment of objectives and their assessment depend on the selection of instructional strategies to obtain those objectives. Those who practise mastery learning would argue that it necessarily resolves this problem.

Among the approaches used for competency-based education in the United States in particular are the Keller (1968) plan of personalized instruction (PSI), which has its origins in the pupil–teacher system operated in Britain in the nineteenth century. Bloom's method of mastery learning is a similar system (Bloom, 1976). The learning principles which underly both approaches are:

(1) Given that aptitude is normally distributed, then variations in the amount and quality of instruction can bring every student to the same level in a particular subject.

(2) Anyone learns best when they know what is to be expected of them.

(3) Anyone learns best when they have learnt the procedures which have to be followed in learning new material. For this reason, it is important to relate the new learning to what the student already knows.

(4) Programmes should be designed to respond to the learning strategies which the students bring to the problem. Students learn in a variety of ways, therefore a variety of ways of learning should be provided.

(5) Learning is most proficient when it is undertaken in relatively small units which are undertaken regularly and for which feedback is given at the time. Regular assessment of small bodies of knowledge is therefore a prerequisite of efficient learning.

(6) Because learning proceeds in a sequence of logical steps the units should be designed to move from the simple to the complex. The learner should complete each step before moving to the next. Therefore feedback should be provided at each step. Tutoring should be provided to help students over difficult hurdles.

Both systems are criterion-referenced. That is, the grading is against mastery of the criterion (objectives) and it is not related to the performance of other students. A typical self-paced system is shown in Figure 18.

F. S. Keller's scheme embraces the following features:

(1) The student proceeds at his or her own pace.
(2) Complete mastery must be obtained.
(3) Lectures are used as a means of motivation. (Students qualify for lectures which are used as a reward: the material in the lectures is not examined.)
(4) Proctors are more senior students to whom the students bring their work.

A course is divided into units and each unit takes about one week. On completion the student is given a 'readiness' test for the next unit by the proctor. If students fail they repeat the unit and take another test (not the original). This process is repeated until they pass the unit. The proctor provides tutoring, as did monitors in the British system of school education in the nineteenth-century.

Many teachers in engineering have modified the 100% criterion to 90% or even 80% because a student could show that he or she knows how to solve the problem yet make a mistake in the arithmetic and get a wrong answer which would normally lead to a repeat of the unit. Bloom's mastery learning uses an 80–90% criterion.

Keller's method originally relied on printed materials, but it is now widely held that any type of material can be used. Related audiovisual materials have been used with success (Pearson and Carswell, 1979). It is particularly appropriate for computer-assisted instruction.

In contrast to Bloom's mastery learning, which is undertaken in groups, lectures, and group discussion supported by reading assignments, Keller's scheme is for individual study by the student (hence the term 'individualized learning'). The mastery-learning programmes are teacher-paced whereas the Keller units are self-paced, which is made possible by the use of proctors. In mastery learning the tests are taken at the same time. Students score their own tests, copies of which can be returned to the tutor. The tests are given in class and usually of the objective type (Blair, 1977; Stice, 1979b).

Related to the concept of 'immediate assessment and evaluation", Belbin and Belbin (1972) described a self-evaluation system used by the Centre Universitaire de Co-operation Economique et Sociale at Nancy in France for training adult men and women in mathematics and science, developed by Bertrand Schwartz in 1964. This comprises evaluation sessions in the evenings of the

152

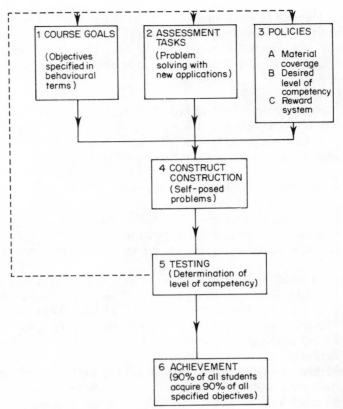

Formal requirements

Each student may work along at his own pace. On Friday of each week those students who feel they are ready to be tested on the chapter they studied may elect to take a test. Each test will consist, in general, of one problem and will be taken on a closed-book, closed-note basis (open appendices). A common test question will be written for each chapter, and students who take a test are obliged on their honour not to divulge its concepts.

The tests will be graded and returned on the following Monday. If a student receives a grade of 75% or higher, he may continue on to the material in the next chapter. If he receives a grade of less than 75% he must review the material on which he was tested and prepare himself for a re-examination on Friday (or on the following Friday if he feels that he needs more time for preparation).

As a minimum requirement each student must complete the first eight chapters by the end of the quarter. The final grade-point average will be computed by adding the scores of all tests and dividing the sum by the number of tests taken. A final grade-point average between 75 and 87 will earn a B grade for the course; an average between 88 and 100 will earn an A grade. No final examination will be given.

Figure 18. An approach to self-paced learning described by Gessner, F. B., *Engineering Education*, **64**, (4), 368. (Reproduced by kind permission of the Editors of *Engineering Education*)

course at the end of each term and at the end of the year. In the evening session a discourse is given for about 40 minutes: group work organized by an assistant involving discussion of the lecture or exercises in application to their daily work takes place for 40 minutes at the end of the session. In between these two periods 20 minutes are devoted to self-evaluation, after which questions are set. The answers are given when the test is completed. The students have to mark their own answers and record one of:

(1) Failed to understand the text of the question;
(2) Made an error in the calculation;
(3) Misused or used a wrong formula;
(4) Forgot something;
(5) Made an error of reasoning;
(6) Failed in some other way.

The assistant analyses the papers (which are unnamed) and also makes comments if necessary. The teacher is given an analysis so that he or she can judge the effectiveness of this teaching and decide whether to repeat parts of the course.

It is the self-assessment within the scheme that sets it apart from mastery and individualized instruction programmes described above. It is not criterion-referenced. (See also Chapter 11 for a further discussion of self-assessment.)

In the Keller scheme any test form may be used, including oral questions and essays. One research project has reported that they are usually 30 minutes or so longer than the equivalent mastery-learning units. The students took twice the number of tests in the Keller programme as were taken in the mastery programme. The same research reported that while the intention of the Keller approach is to test all objectives the time required to solve difficult problems meant that the tests had to sample knowledge.

The Keller scheme usually requires that students re-study the same material, which is a characteristic of most teaching and learning. In mastery learning alternative materials are provided on the assumption that repeating the same instructional approach is not likely to be effective.

It is expected that students who have followed the Keller scheme will perform either well (A and B) or fail (F). Few Cs or Ds are expected, although the number of fails is likely to be significant. The grade is determined by the number of units taken (75%) and a comprehensive final examination (25%), which is not repeatable.

In contrast, the grade obtained from a mastery-learning programme depends on the score obtained in a summative examination at the end of the course. The grading is determined by the mastery criterion set at the beginning of it. If it is 85% then all students with 85% and over get A. It is intended in the ideal situation that no-one should fail and most should get A.

Both Keller and mastery courses require a substantial development effort on the part of any teacher who wishes to implement such schemes. Some idea of their value is therefore important.

The first point to make is that mastery learning has its exponents throughout the world and in a variety of subjects. In England a basic mastery course in physical geography contributes 15% to the final examination mark. Another advanced module which contributes 20% of the final examination mark is entered via a 2000-word essay. Innovative ability is tested by an investigative design project of 200 words (Clark and Gregory, 1982). All this is to be compared with a single examination at the end of the year. It is not surprising that students should find such courses hard work, as is reported in another study in geography from Australia (Cho, 1980).

It is a fact of life in higher education (worldwide) that teachers are always critical of any new developments while enthusiasts always find an excuse to modify the original idea. One investigation reports that all student suggestions were against the principles of PSI even though the drop-outs from the PSI course were fewer. The author concluded that if it can be introduced into the normal academic environment it will be done well. It seems from a metastudy by Hereford (1979) that the type of pacing can influence the drop-out rate as well as lead to procrastination. One might start with small innovations. For example, in an accounting course detailed study guides with statements of behavioural objectives were used with a small-group discussion and multiple-choice tests. Although there was not much individualized learning the students felt that there was some improvement in their learning and development (Stewart, 1980).

Students have to be persuaded, for usually, when offered choice of a new technique of instruction or assessment, they tend to prefer the traditional (i.e. the approach to which they are used) (Cameron and Heywood, 1985; Kaplan, 1978). Nevertheless, several reports say that students do better in their final performances however these are accounted when they have experienced mastery (Clark et al., 1983) or Keller-type programmes (Guthrie et al., 1985), although in Canada the suggestion has emerged that the PSI may only be suitable for certain kinds of chemistry courses (Vaughan, 1982). Various papers have reported the value of self-paced instruction in diagnosis and remedial work. It has also been reported that the spread of examination marks has been reduced (Dorey and Wilkins, 1977).

A review of work in mathematics in Australia and New Zealand suggests that mastery learning has limitations in university courses in the context of 'problem-solving'. Imrie et al. (1980) argue therefore that the assessment should be two-tiered to incorporate mastery and problem-solving levels (see also Brook and Thomson, 1982).

Early experiments in science and technology with computer-assisted instruction suggest that quite sophisticated problem-solving strategies can be accommodated in mastery and individualized learning packages. As with non-computerized approaches, it has been found useful in remedial instruction

(Shale and Cowper, 1982; Mihkelson, 1985) to improve performance (Pazder-nik and Walaszek, 1983), and one interesting study in chemistry showed that while there was a positive change in attitudes toward computers among women students there was not corresponding change in attitudes toward chemistry (Cavin *et al.*, 1981).

At the level of the institution, computer-based instruction has, it would seem, not been very effective (McCord, 1985), while at the level of the subject the majority of the studies show that student achievement is better in examinations than with that in conventional classes. Its effect on the relationship between aptitude and college achievement has been small. It has not had much effect on drop-out rates but it saves around 50 minutes of instructional time for a conventional 3 hours. Nevertheless, the meta-analyses by Kulik and colleagues (1980) of some 180 reports were, in most cases, of work with mainframe computers. The microcomputer may make a difference in the future (Nadler and Seirig, 1982; *Engineering Education*, February 1986).

It seems from another meta-analysis by Kulik and colleagues (1979) (61 studies) that in PSI the improvement in student performance is the same for low-aptitude students as it is for high-aptitude ones. In this respect the Keller approach seems to be much superior to CBI as things stand. Moreover, there is some (but not very reliable) information to the effect that essay performance is improved with PSI. Drop-out rates appear to be higher from Keller-type courses.

I offer these examples instead of a more detailed summary of the meta-analyses because they show that there is a continuing flow of small-scale innovations which are recording successes. It seems from analyses of all the data that when a teacher is involved in innovation, to quote McCord (1985), the quality of his or her teaching is improved and that, moreover, there may be a Hawthorne effect on some of the students. Students value those teachers who are committed and such commitment is essential if individualized instruction in any of its forms is to be effective (Pearson, 1983). However simple the innovation (as, for example, in the development of audio-tutorial methods), more work will be required of the teacher. However, as Lower (1981) shows, the reward can be increased by personal contact with the students. These and other examples also show that students do not necessarily respond to the same learning treatments in the same way. Some may respond better to the tightly controlled Keller type of individualized study whereas others might respond to truly independent study (Melton, 1981). These differences extend to instructional aids and methods of presentation, for several studies have shown that different methods of presenting programmed instruction vary in their effect on student attainment of objectives. For example, with visual material the more simple it is, the fewer the differences between high, low and medium reading comprehension groups. The more realistic, the greater the improvement among the 'high' group (Dwyer and Parkhurst, 1982). Similarly, in the evaluation of a mastery-learning package in microbiology in which the students were distinguished by their performance on a test designed to meet the six levels of the

Taxonomy of Educational Objectives, Whiting (1982) found that the attitudes of the high-level students became more favourable toward the package, whereas those of the low-level subjects became less so between the pre- and post-test questionnaire. Neither group was favourable toward the assessment test.

We do not have a general theory of instruction. This is because student response to instruction and student ways of learning are complex. No acceptable matrix has yet been proposed which enables a foolproof prediction of what will happen in a specified set of circumstances. There is little doubt that in many cases mastery learning, personalized instruction and computer-based learning cause students to perform well and often better than in conventional courses and exams.

The fact that they are competency-(criterion)-based has led some authorities to suggest that the results from criterion-referenced measures could be used as profile in place of grades. The activity of generating profiles for assessment one way to approach the derivation of projects. Profiling is discussed in more detail in Chapter 11.

CONCLUSIONS

A variety of objectives have been described which can be used to design norm competency- and criterion-referenced measures. However, there is not much research on the validity and reliability of criterion measures (Berk, 1980; Harris *et al.*, 1974). In the United States, researchers have not been able to equate them with the measures which they customarily use to assess general learning abilities. Their great advantage has been that they have forced teachers higher education to think what they mean when they use terms like 'problem solving', 'creativity', and 'critical thinking'.

Any brainstorming activity will produce hundreds of skills dependent on the perception that individuals have of the things they do well in critical thinking and or problem-solving. The difficulties begin with the fact that teachers of the humanities do not understand problem-solving while those of the sciences not understand critical thinking to be the same mental dimension which functions in the subject context in which they work. This is not to suggest return to a set of undefined aims but that teachers isolate the domain objectives which are essential to them if they are to become committed to new approaches to teaching which derive from the need to define objectives. They will still have to make these decisions within a framework which is dictated (or derived, dictated is too strong a word) from their beliefs about the overall purposes learning on the one hand, and the conceptual structure of the subject to taught, on the other. It is these aspects which are considered next.

CHAPTER 7

Concept Learning and Curriculum Objectives

INTRODUCTION: TOWARDS THE CLARIFICATION AND ASSEMBLY OF GOALS

In Chapters 5 and 6 the development of what might be called the 'objective' movement was traced. This was a response to much loose thinking about the goals of higher education, which assumed that such concepts as preparation for life, the development of critical thinking, and problem-solving skills in their higher orders were achieved when it was patent that they were not. Although it has been greatly criticized, the publication of *The Taxonomy of Educational Objectives* was an important landmark in thinking about assessment. Since then, as we have seen, philosophers and psychologists have contributed their own lists of thinking skills. The response to these developments has been divided. It seems that scientists and technologists find them more useful than teachers working in the humanities, and this is apparently due to the emotional commitments which teachers have to the language and purposes of their subjects. These commitments prevent the insight necessary for them if they are to attempt to develop their instruction along these lines. However, this is no excuse for them to hang their goals on loosely ordered terms like critical thinking, for research using these taxonomies in a variety of contexts suggests that in many subjects high-level skills (abilities) are not tapped. The Alverno studies (to which reference was made in Chapter 6) illustrate the potential of this approach in the humanities (see Chapter 13).

Many other investigations suggest that the assessment procedures which we use are equally limited. For this reason, there is an obligation on every teacher in higher education to design teaching and assessment strategies which will bring about the learning necessary for the attainment of course objectives. However they are derived and from whatever philosophical position, there has to be goal clarity. As we saw in Chapters 5 and 6, there has also to be goal simplicity. The aim has to be to produce a relatively small number of significant 'focusing' or 'domain' objectives.

Dressel (1971) has drawn attention to the fact that groups of teachers often formulate more goals than student teachers during their training when they plan their lessons. He urged that a single well-defined objective may ensure that the other aims essential to a course of study are achieved: for example, 'the ability to appreciate the thought structures (modes of thinking) in an unrelated subject to those studied' (Heywood and Montagu-Pollock, 1976). Tests should be designed to ensure that this is the case.

We can arrive at these objectives by what Furst (1958), one of the authors of *The Taxonomy of Educational Objectives* called 'screening', which is a process of sifting objectives for their significance, and also to avoid contradictions between them. This is accomplished by rating (evaluating) them against the philosophical (values), social (as derived from sociological), and psychological (learning) aims of education (Cromwell, 1986; Heywood, 1966, 1976, 1981; Fordyce, 1986; Halonen, 1986).

Many contradictions can be found in the first three chapters in the comments on educational policy. The activity of screening is to select a non-contradictory list of essential aims. For example, a major question at present concerns the relationship between what is learnt in higher education and what is required in industry. Should there be a close relationship between education and industry? If there is, how should the curriculum and learning strategies be designed to meet the goals specified by such a relationship? Aspects of this particular issue will be considered in one of the illustrations in Chapter 13.

From discussion at this level should come a statement which can be reformulated into operational goals, as can be the case with Newman's statement on the education of a gentleman in *The Idea of a University*.

As we have seen, it is a major problem for institutions and departments to reconcile the beliefs which teachers have about the role of the curriculum in higher education. Compromises have to be reached in all subject areas. For example, in the humanities, teachers who value the subject for its own sake are likely to have very different views from those who see their subjects as having real-use value in respect of contemporary social issues, or who are even more radical and want to use them as a force for social change (Duguid, 1984).

The views that teachers have of the functions of instruction have epistemological foundations, which have a profound bearing on their approach to student learning (Shulman, 1970; McMahon, 1988). For the moment, it suffices to say that the psychology of learning and human development has a major role to play in the screening of educational objectives, since it indicates factors likely to impede or enhance learning. For this reason, Furst (1958) argued that:

> Every instructor and every school [college] should also formulate and use a defensible theory of learning. The theory should consider the conditions under which learning best takes place, the role of student interests, some conception of the instructor's functions and so on.

The particular theory held will necessarily influence the choice of objectives.

The exercise of screening may also result in entirely different ways of stating goals for part or even the whole of the curriculum. It is the primary purpose of Chapters 7–9 to consider the implications of recent research in learning theory for the derivation of assessment and curriculum objectives.

LEARNING THEORIES

Unfortunately, there is a gulf between psychologists who work in the field of learning as described by such authorities as Hilgard and Bower (1981) and those who study learning in higher education. The former are not primarily concerned with linking theory to instruction whereas the latter are.

Learning is that process by which experience develops new and reorganizes old concepts. It is something we do, whether we like it or not. It is an exchange with experience past and present in order to understand and control the future. Learning is goal-directed behaviour. Some of it may be involuntary, but it is never informal. The particular asset that higher education institutions should bring to learning is the organization of experience, so that the skills of learning can be better organized to sample the knowledge thought to be appropriate. In this respect, to quote Fincher (1985), learning in higher education is 'a process of acquiring and integrating through a systemized process of instruction or organized experience, varying forms of knowledge, skill, and understanding that the learner may use or apply in later situations and under conditions different from those of instruction'.

From these definitions I understand the aims and objectives which my model of the curriculum requires to embrace knowledge, skills and values. It equates with Fincher's, since it involves a person in knowing, doing and feeling.

Unfortunately, there is no grand theory of learning which embraces all these facets. It is for this reason that Furst can only say that teachers should adopt 'a defensible theory of learning', and this, it seems, is what happens. Teachers become interested in and adopt a particular model. Thus in Britain many teachers have experimented with the Anglo-Scandinavian model of learning styles (Chapter 8). In the United States there has been interest in the Perry model of development (Chapter 9). Still others have become hooked on the behavioural approach. Each of these represents a particular domain of learning theory, and these domains relate to an amalgam of behaviourists, gestaltists and associationists who have sought general principles from empirical studies, cognitive psychologists whose concern has been to describe the processes of decision-making and problem solving who gave a particular meaning to the phrase 'cognitive style', and developmental psychologists whose concern has been with the person and (in higher education) the student.[1]

In the 1950s the following principles, quoted by Saupe (1961), were widely held to be the rule:

(1) Without appropriate readiness a learning experience will be inefficient. Learning will not occur (entering characteristics).
(2) Learning will be more effective when the motivation is intrinsic (as opposed to extrinsic).
(3) Learning proceeds much more rapidly and is retained much longer when that which has to be learned possesses meaning, organization and structure.

(4) The learner learns only what he himself does.

(5) Only those responses which are learned are confirmed.

(6) Transfer can only occur when there is a recognized similarity between the learning and the transfer situations.

(7) Transfer will occur to the extent that students expect it to.

(8) Knowledge of a model(s) of problem finding and solving or aspects of critical thinking can contribute to its improvement.

McKeachie (1974), whose speciality has been learning in higher education, now argues that there are only two principles which hold consistently. These are that involvement in learning is better than passive reception, which covers axioms (2) and (4) above, and that meaningful learning is still more effective than rote memory (axioms (3) and (8)). He would not disagree that the entering characteristics of students are important (related to (1) above) but he would argue that other principles do not hold, because learning is an interaction between a variety of complex variables.

INTRODUCING CHAPTERS 7–9

In this and the two chapters which follow it is suggested that these rules continue to have meaning. At the same time, it is clear that the factors which influence learning are complex, and that at present there is no general theory which describes this complexity. These chapters therefore look at the problem from several perspectives but not in historical sequence.

Suffice it to say as an introduction that, traditionally, teachers in higher education have held that it is what the individual does for himself or herself that matters. Students were thought to be well motivated or not. This student studies hard, that one does not, and so on. Now we understand better the nature of extrinsic and intrinsic motivation (Entwistle, 1981). As far as research in the United States was concerned, by 1946 (Robinson, 1946) attention had been drawn to the fact that individuals demonstrated characteristic study behaviours, so that by 1966 Brown and Holtzman had introduced an inventory of study skills. There continued to be interest in what Sherman (1985) has called stable variables. These are aspects like intelligence, achievement, personality which belong to the individual and factors that are controllable like teaching methods (characteristics at entry, class size, etc.). Much of this book so far has been concerned with these variables and the potential for their control. In the United States there has been considerable interest in these aspects of learning during the last ten years and several of the studies in this book are of this kind. This chapter is especially concerned with what the instructor can do to help concept learning.

In school education much attention has been paid to Piaget's work. Teachers find his stage-development theory in which children move from pre-operational, concrete operation and formal operation (abstract reasoning) helpful in designing instruction for young children. Many of them also adopt Bruner's strategies, which suggests that the relevance of the psychology of learning for them is an amalgam of these theories. Piagetian tests have been given in higher education, with the surprising result that some students are found to be at the level of concrete operations in some subjects of the curriculum (Chapter 9). A theory of development in higher education which has provoked much interest is due to Perry (1970), who believed that students evolved through nine stages. His study was based on students at Harvard and Ratcliffe in the United States. In Australia Biggs (1979) developed a taxonomy which identified five levels of intellectual development. There are other theories which are developmental. In particular, Lonergan (1954) has described a theory of development which he has related to particular subjects of the curriculum (for example, history, philosophy or theology). Perry's and Lonergan's theories are discussed in Chapter 9 because of their implications for the design of curriculum and instruction.

Table 31. Academic learning skills listed by Sherman (1985). (Reproduced by kind permission of the Editors of the *Journal of Higher Education*. © 1985 by the Ohio State University Press. All rights reserved)

Preparation skills	*Memory skills*
Survey skills	Organizing skills
—read topic markers	chunking
—read topic sentences	discovering organization
introductory, and summary	
paragraphs	Meaning skills
—read large sections of materials	Imaging
Study goals	Analogies
	Restating
Learning information skills	Story schemes
Attending skills	Memory tricks
Study questions	Acronyms
Active reading	Loci
Relating to current knowledge	Rhymes
Organizing skills	Practice skills
Outlining	Overlearning
Network representation	Rehearsal/recitation
Notes	Reconstruction
Reviewing skills	
Restating	*Follow-up skills*
Summarizing	Summarizing skills
Answering questions	Study summaries
Rereading	Test-like situation
	Reviewing skills
	Cramming
	Periodic review

Interest among some of those concerned with learning skill development has shifted from stable and institutionally controlled variables to what Sherman (1985) calls 'learner-controlled' variables. Learning is understood for what it is,

162

an activity undertaken by the learner with skills owned and managed by him or her. Clearly, the stable variables such as intelligence and personality will influence performance with these skills. The difference between institutional and learner-controlled efforts to improve learning are shown in Figures 19(a) and (b). Sherman has produced a list of learning skills which are reproduced in Table 31.

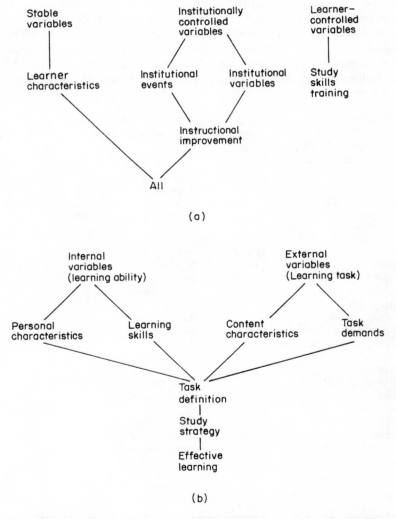

Figure 19. (a) Institutionally and (b) learner-controlled variables. (From Sherman, T. M. (1985). Learning improvement programs: a review of controllable influences. *Journal of Higher Education,* **56**, (1), 85–100. Reproduced by kind permission of the Editors of the *Journal of Higher Education.* © 1985 by the Ohio State University Press. All rights reserved)

In Chapter 8 I try to move into this area by linking what is variously called 'cognitive' or 'learning' style to concept learning (the subject of this chapter) via a discussion of the factors which influence our perception and thus our understanding of our environment.

Early in the 1950s Witkin (1976) proposed that cognitive style was important, and introduced the concepts of field-dependence and field-independence. Subsequently, there was considerable interest in creative thinking, as represented by divergence on a continuum of divergence–convergence. Most recently, attention has focused on surface versus depth processing, and it is this Anglo-Scandinavian work (Marton *et al.*, 1981) coupled with that by Sherman and others in the United States which has given the impetus to the learner-controlled perspective.

The review articles by Fincher and Sherman are in great contrast to each other, and both merit attention. The learner-controlled perspective has developed at a time when in Australia and Britain, many academic staff are beginning to take an interest in learning, and for this reason it has received much attention.

The purpose of Chapters 7–9 is not to present an all-embracing critical review of these theories: faults can be found with each of them. It is to show by illustration first, the complexity of learning and its implications for assessment and second, that these theories are objectives, as it were, in their own right. For example, the adoption of Perry's model will lead to a particular curriculum structure and teaching methodology, or an awareness of Piaget's ideas may cause the teacher to use a particular instructional strategy (Chapter 9). Commitment to the perceptual learning point of view may lead to important changes in instruction at the beginning of a course (Chapter 8). Focus on concepts may lead to a concept network (map) approach to curriculum structure (this chapter).

Taken together, theories of learning do have implications for the teacher, and these are considered at the end of Chapter 9.

THE IMPORTANCE OF CONCEPTS AND PRINCIPLES: INSTRUCTION AND THE CURRICULUM

Understanding depends not on the acquisition of facts but through the continuing organization and reorganization of concepts and principles into new frames of reference:

Knowledge of things is not produced in us through knowledge of signs, but through knowledge of things more certain, namely principles ... For knowledge of principles produces in us knowledge of conclusions; knowledge of signs does not (Thomas Aquinas).

Unfortunately, not everyone uses these terms in the same way. This arises from the fact that some concepts are very large in every sense of the word (for example, democracy or learning how to learn), and are therefore open to interpretation.

Gagne (1976) distinguishes between concepts and principles. He gives the example 'Birds fly'. The concepts are birds and fly. Linked together, they form a principle. With principles we can solve problems, which is the highest form of learning.

The difficulty with Gagne's theory is that it is in the language of science and not the humanities. Teachers in the humanities are more likely to use terms like 'understanding', 'concepts', and 'critical thinking'. A concept like democracy is built up from a number of principles. The important point is that teachers in the humanities should be able to explain the process at work in their scholarship (learning) so that it is readily perceived by their students.

I use 'concepts' and 'principles' interchangeably: whenever we look at an issue without some basic category which identifies common characteristics we have no means of linking what would otherwise be discrete items or events. Their understanding is the key to learning. Concepts create the structure of content (knowledge): without content there can be no learning.

The Characteristics of Concepts

The functions of concepts are therefore to help us to reduce the complexity of the environment through the identification of the objects in the world around us, and with these to build up networks (maps, trees) of concepts with which to examine the world in which we live and appraise the new knowledge which 'comes' at us daily.

A concept is a class of stimuli which have common characteristics. Concepts are identified by their attributes (colour, form, size) and each of these attributes can vary. The colour of an object is usually inadequately described by the primary one—red can vary from scarlet to crimson. These variations describe the value of the attribute, and some attributes are more dominant than others. When the attributes and values are added together a conjunctive concept is produced (for example, car as compared with motorcycle or bicycle). Disjunctive concepts are produced when attributes and values are substituted one for another. Many concepts (for example, distance, time) are equally difficult to comprehend (De Cecco and Crawford, 1974; Howard, 1987).

Conjunctive concepts are the most used. It is in higher education where disjunctive and relational concepts are likely to be in common use. We can get some idea of the problem from Ericksen (1984), who records how in *Zen and the Art of Motor Cycle Maintenance: an inquiry into values* the author, Persig (1974), 'steadily evolved the concept of quality from a set of attributes of a satisfactory term paper—such as unity, vividness, authority, economy, sensitivity, clarity, emphasis, suspense, brilliance, precision, proportion, depth and so on . . . to the point where quality ended up as a philosophy of life'. At this stage a high level of abstraction is reached, and this is the essential problem in higher education; the higher the level of abstraction, the more difficult it is to define its boundaries.

Gilbert and colleagues (1982) have suggested that one of five things happen to learners when they are learning concepts:

(1) The learners' concepts remain unchanged although a technical language is adopted.
(2) The learners' concepts remain unchanged but the concepts and propositions taught are retained for examination purposes.
(3) The learners are confused such that presented concepts and propositions reinforce incorrect or naive interpretive frameworks.
(4) The concepts and propositions taught are assimilated into appropriate interpretive frameworks but not transferred to others.
(5) The concepts and propositions taught are correctly understood and so modify all interpretive frameworks.

There is a continuing flow of evidence to confirm that students have difficulty in learning concepts in higher education.

Examples of Difficulties in the Classroom

In the final assessment of a course in evolutionary theory and the philosophy of biology of 23 third-year Australian undergraduates 16 were failed by all three authors of the questions, a zoologist, an educator and a philosopher. Brown and Caton (1983) could not find evidence of a critical understanding of the concept of natural selection. The students regarded it as a dogma. They also had difficulty in understanding the significance of refutable propositions in science. In an earlier study in England (Brumby, 1979) only 18% of first-year undergraduates were able to apply this concept to common environmental problems, in spite of the fact that they had GCE A level Biology. The authors of the former study concluded that the students' problems were due to a specialization in biology which lacked theoretical underpinning, while the latter suggested that discussion of the wider issues of the evolution debate increased the problems students had in understanding the fundamental concept of natural selection. In another study by Prosser (1979), of Griffith University, an attempt was made to isolate the major instructional and prerequisite concepts of part of a short physics course taught to first-year biology students for the purpose of determining the intellectual level at which these concepts were defined. A Gagne-style task analysis was performed on a set of instructional objectives, which showed that the concepts were too abstract for many students. Prosser suggested that such courses should be arranged so that less formal reasoning would be required, or that the central focus of science courses should be intellectual development. A similar study among freshman chemistry students in three institutions in Australia and the United States concluded that students may not only need to learn concepts but the language of chemistry (Hill et al., 1980).

It seems from other studies that some of the difficulties which students have with concept learning could have been removed in school education.

THE ENTERING CHARACTERISTICS OF STUDENTS

If students have misunderstood concepts and principles in the school courses on which subsequent college programmes depend it stands to reason that they will be in difficulty. This is particularly important in subjects like maths and science in England, which depend on what is learnt in school.

One or two studies have suggested that, in England, mathematical learning in undergraduate studies is impeded by a lack of understanding of concepts in school education which could be helped by teaching students how to learn more, especially through discovery learning (Walkden and Scott, 1980). In the learning of integration it has been found that the concept of integration as the limit of a sum is extremely difficult to comprehend (Orton, 1983).

At GCE A level Price (Heywood, 1976) described what happened when a student in engineering science was asked to design an experiment to verify a hypothesis, which he was to formulate, regarding water discharge through an orifice in terms of pressure difference or total pressure. The student had not met this topic before. What happened, for the scientific reader, was that the student suggested that the velocity of discharge would increase more rapidly than the potential difference. When asked why by the teacher, the student answered, "because it seems reasonable". When asked what form of increase, the reply given was 'that the velocity of transference from one pressure to another lower pressure is proportional to the square of the pressure difference', and again it was put forward as 'reasonable'.

The non-scientist will appreciate the teachers' dilemma, because the mathematical formulation was wrong in terms of the physics. The graph (Figure 20) agrees with the mathematics and not with the physics, and includes both positive and negative values of flow.

Figure 20. Problems in the transfer of learning between mathematical technique and physical explanation

Evidently, the transfer of learning between mathematical techniques and physical understanding is not accomplished with ease. The technique, it seems, 'swamps' the understanding of the physics. This implies that in written examinations care should be taken to devise questions which ensure the assessment of understanding, even at the expense of mathematical techniques, otherwise the mathematical technique may swamp the need to understand. Such findings have equally profound implications for teaching method.

That such misunderstanding may be widespread is illustrated by Cowan (1983), who asked students to write *protocols*. These are records of thinking set down by students shortly after they have concluded a problem-solving event (Table 32). He found that undergraduates, faced with sketches which, for example, illustrated problems relating to the loading of beams that are not attached to given values and dimensions, rely on the quantitative methods taught in class to solve the problems. This they do by attaching numbers or symbols to the diagrams. Few develop qualitative strategies based on past experience. Even practising engineers tend to favour one overworked qualitative strategy. All this is in keeping with the finding of Luchins (1942) that, once students are taught a problem-solving strategy, they keep to that strategy to solve all problems.

Table 32. John Cowan's technique for deriving protocols of student thinking processes (*Engineering Education* January, 1983). (Reproduced by kind permission of Professor John Cowan)

1. The 'subject' is encouraged to talk out and record on an audiotape his problem-solving thoughts, listen to these recordings, and reflect (in private) on their accuracy and completeness. He then discusses the experience informally with other subjects of roughly the same age and status. When satisified that he is producing a reasonably accurate spoken record of his problem-solving, we proceed to the next stage.
2. Subjects are then invited to record protocols for new problems, play back the recordings immediately, in private, and supplement the record of the protocol with written notes. They often add missing information or explain something that is badly conveyed on the tape. Immediate replay is essential, so that the additional information can still be recalled.
3. The subjects go on to discuss and clarify their self-analyses with a fellow subject. They may discover they share common difficulties or have used a tactic of interest to the other.
4. Finally, the subjects discuss their findings with a researcher. That analysis is also tabulated, so that the protocols can be replayed later and checked against all parts of the record.

In much more recent research, Thoms and Bain (1982) reported that among student teachers there was considerable consistency in the strategies used in various learning contexts. They did not vary their strategies to meet the requirements of particular situations. Cowan (1983) developed self-study packages to overcome this problem with his engineering students and claims a very significant increase in post-test scores.

Other studies in statistics and maths have tried to find out how undergraduates solve problems using think-aloud techniques, which allow the observer to analyse their strategies in terms of the errors made (Allwood and Montgomery, 1979). An American study in the area of mechanics found that the novice tended to solve the problems by assembling individual equations, while the expert solved them using a process of successive refinements (Larkin and Reif, 1979).

Champagne *et al.* (1983) have suggested that, for a few students at least, misunderstandings begin in childhood. Naive concepts of such ideas as 'force' and 'energy' accompany the pupils' understanding throughout their school career, but they never fully grasp these.

In these circumstances it is not surprising to find that there has been interest in the use of pre-knowledge tests although, if the pattern of deficiencies shown by the tests remains the same over the years (as Sutton (1977) reports for a physics test), it is difficult to see the point in their retention. It is perhaps surprising that, generally, teachers in higher education do not seem to pay sufficient attention to the entering characteristics of students. It is perhaps all too easy to blame schools for such deficiencies.

Apart from these remedies, there are several studies which suggest that alternative strategies of teaching and curriculum design may help the learning of concepts.

ALTERNATIVE INSTRUCTIONAL STRATEGIES

That some teaching strategies may be more suitable than others for learning concepts is illustrated by two experiments. In the first, Thune and Ericksen (1960) described the teaching of calculators by rote and abstract (conceptual) methods. The rote learners practised the operations on a particular desk calculator, the concept learners were limited to the use of a schematic diagram of the operations of calculators in general. The first test of learning with the calculator used by the rote group showed them to have the advantage. However, another test at a later date revealed that they had lost their advantage and the concept learners showed a 50% transfer advantage in the new situation. The ability to abstract (conceptualize) enables us to look beyond the immediacy of the environment. Thus when students complain that courses are not immediately relevant (as they often do) we need to have examples before us which will help to demonstrate the case that concepts and principles are best learnt at a distance from a particular situation which might cloud what is to be learnt.

Relevance may not only be a function of the perceptions which students have of the subject but of the way a course is taught. For example, in a first-year undergraduate course at the University of New South Wales first-year biology students completed one-third of their practical work at home. One reason for this was to allow them to work at their own pace and pursue their own interests (Adamson *et al.*, 1979). In another investigation McConnell (1983) invited students to complete the different components of a course in human biology. Two components accounted for 68% of the total variation. Anatomy and physiology were construed as relevant and related to the core of the course, whereas genetics and biochemistry were found to be irrelevant, boring and unenjoyable. In contrast, physiology lay in a different direction, where the students' constructs related to a variety of teaching methods that allowed for a diversity of opinion.

One of the earliest experiments to show that alternative instructional strategies might improve learning was described by Abercrombie (1960) in *The Anatomy of Judgement*, demonstrating the value of discussion groups. Her concern was with the factors which influence the making of judgements, and particularly judgements in science. She hypothesized that we may learn to make better judgements if we can become aware of some of the factors which influence their formation. To test this hypothesis, she designed a course of eight sessions of $1\frac{1}{2}$ hours each for 12 students in which the emphasis was on observing and thinking as opposed to results. She wrote:

> In traditional teaching the student makes an observation and finds it to be correct or incorrect by comparison with the teacher's (or the currently accepted) version. He learns by discovering disparities between his result and that obtained by more experienced and skilful persons. In the discussion technique of teaching the student learns by comparing his observation with those of ten or so of his peers. He compares not only the results, but how the results were arrived at and in doing this the range of factors taken into consideration is much wider than is usual in didactic teaching. What the student learns, it is hoped, is not only how to make a more correct response when he is confronted with a similar problem, but more generally to gain firmer control of his behaviour by understanding better his own ways of working.

The kind of hypothesis tested by Abercrombie on medical students was whether they could be made aware of the assumptions and preconceptions which influence the receipt of information, visually or otherwise, and so improve the skill of observation.

Two groups, an experimental and a control, were instructed on the thorax and the arm. The control group dissected these, whereas the experimental subjects were given exercises in interpretation and discussion. Tests of observation of X-rays showed the experimental group to have superior knowledge (James *et al.*, 1956).

Abercrombie's study created considerable interest in discussion group techniques in Britain. Clement (1971), for example, has suggested that student-led discussion may only be advantageous for complex learning involving organization and manipulation of concepts, which is to suggest that care needs to be taken with its use. A study by Dreyfus and Lieberman (1981), at the Hebrew University of Jerusalem, suggested that for discussions to be successful there has to be an issue at stake, so that there can be an expression of opinion which is backed by relevant data, otherwise the opinion will be prejudice. There has to be an exchange of opinions through the clarification of questions, and finally the outcome has to be identifiable and be seen to be the outcome of the discussion.

Much work has been done with syndicates which are structured modifications of the open-discussion method. Collier (1969, 1983) wrote that:

> Although syndicate methods are not a panacea, no other method generates and combines the independence, motivation and involvement of student groups in systematic academic study. Furthermore, by requiring students to make reports

with cross-references and cross-comparisons of readings from very contrasted sources, interdisciplinary integration may take place within their own minds.

Collier has not changed his mind over the intervening years.

Role playing, especially in the affective domain of the medical and behavioural sciences, has been found to be very effective, but, as several authors have pointed out, this has to be planned and introduced with great care, especially that which is concerned with values as opposed to calculations (Lee, 1982). Attitudes have certainly been changed in management role-playing exercises, although there is not much information about their spillover into the actual work situation (Lake, 1983). Some teachers assess role plays, others do not. Chapters 8 and 9 consider the possibilities further in relation to a variety of instructional techniques.

Concept learning may be reinforced by curriculum arrangements which help students to understand the totality of their subjects in terms of key concepts.

CURRICULUM STRUCTURES FOR CONCEPT LEARNING

Taba (1964), who introduced the phrase 'key concepts', defined them as procedural devices to help teachers in the selection and organization of content. They are, therefore, 'objectives', and as such have important implications for the teacher because they create the learning strategy requirement and thus the time requirement and therefore the syllabus. They may also be regarded as themes which pervade the whole curriculum, as the examples in Table 33 from an occupational therapy curriculum show.

Table 33. Key concepts in a course for occupational therapy

Perception:	The individual's assimilation and modification of data presented by the environment through the senses.
Learning:	The process by which experience develops new and reorganizes previous concepts and patterns of behaviour.
Activity:	Any process through which an individual engages in living.
Communication:	The effective transmission and reception of relevant information.
Design:	A process in which problems are formulated, analysed, solutions planned, treated, tested and the outcomes evaluated.
Management:	Direction and control over self and/or others.
The individual:	A human being with unique needs and potential for adaptation and control of self and environment.

The way the key concepts of a subject link together is likely to differ between the subjects of the curriculum. This point is illustrated by Donald's (1982) work in the United States. She investigated 16 college courses, 11 of which used concepts in a linear hierarchy. The most important concept was the most inclusive one. In all but one of the courses the key concept had the pre-ordinate

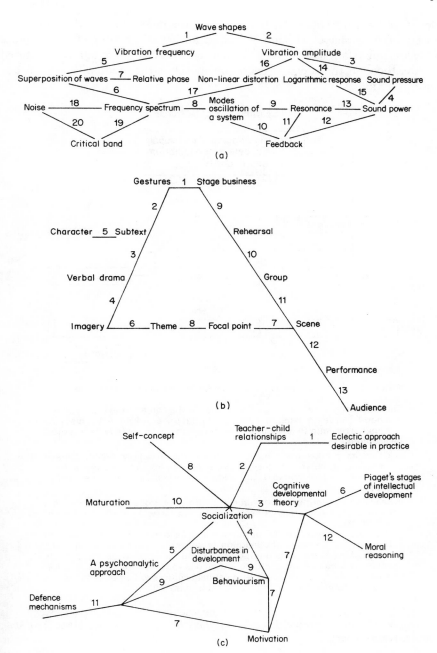

Figure 21. Key concept structures in (a) physics, (b) English and (c) developmental psychology. (From Donald, J. G. (1982). Knowledge structures: methods for exploring course content. *Journal of Higher Education*, **54**, (1), 31–41. Reproduced by kind permission of J. G. Donald and the Editors of the *Journal of Higher Education*)

role. In physics, for example, the whole of the course was built around the concept of 'wave shapes' (Figure 21). The branches of the tree go from the more to the less important aspects. The key concepts in science are tightly structured whereas those in the social sciences are loosely structured, with certain key concepts acting as pivots or organizers.

TERMINAL BEHAVIOUR

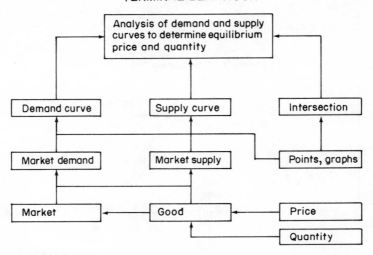

A student respondent used this approach in the teaching of economics:

The students are required to be able to analyse the demand and supply curves of a good in order to determine the equilibrium price and quantity. This is the terminal behaviour. Before this can be done certain concepts and skills must be acquired.

> *Concepts:* market, good, market demand, market supply, graph, demand curve, supply curve, intersection. (*Note*: the equilibrium price and quantity are found where demand and supply intersect, i.e. where demand = supply.)

In teaching this terminal behaviour to a fifth-year group one assumes that some subsets have already been acquired, e.g. drawing a line, the idea of 'equal to', etc.

> Thus the behaviour to be acquired must be preceded by a number of subsets, which comprise the learning of concepts, e.g. 'demand', and the learning of skills, e.g. graphing points. During the process certain of these concepts will be defined and their definitions may be forgotten, e.g. price, quantity, market, but since the terminal behaviour is to find the equilibrium price and quantity, the students may be able to do this.

Figure 22. A student-teacher's concept tree for teaching fifth-year economics, with his explanation. (From Heywood, J. (1982). *Pitfalls and Planning in Student Teaching*, London: Kogan Page)

The argument from 'grammar' hypothesized above suggests that students will better understand concepts if they understand their grammatical as well as perceptual roles. Most student teachers have so internalized them in their previous learning that they fail to see the need for explanation. It is therefore a salutary exercise for them to work out the key concepts in their subjects (Figure 22). Suggestions as to how this might be done have been made by Sutton (1980) and Posner (1977). The latter includes concept mapping in addition to clinical interviews, word-association, generation of propositions and problem solving tasks.

Moreira (1985) has given examples for physics and English, and another which asks 'What kind of a liar are you?' (Figure 23). However, he also gives examples of student-generated concept trees which can be used to study their misconceptions and meaningful learning. They can be particularly helpful in establishing prior knowledge and, as we have seen, this is of considerable importance (see also Novak and Gowin, 1984).

The design of interdisciplinary and integrated programmes is greatly facilitated by the use of key concepts. Seven used to integrate a programme in geography, history and social studies are shown in Table 34. These provide an integrating theme, even though the subjects retain the distinctive nature of their disciplines. While they are at a high level of abstraction and overarch the disciplines, they do not possess a special epistemological status, and if they were to do so they could impose on the students an idiosyncratic structuring of ideas which is not merited.

Table 34. Key concepts for an integrated programme in history, geography and the social sciences. Although relevant at any level of interpretation these particular concepts were applied to the development of a programme for 8–13-year-olds. (Reproduced by kind permission of Blyth, 1973, and his colleagues at the University of Liverpool)

1. Communication:	The significant movement of individuals, groups or resources or the significant transmission of information.
2. Power:	The purposive exercise of power over individuals and society's resources.
3. Values and beliefs:	The conscious or unconscious systems by which individuals and societies organize their response to natural social and supernatural disorders.
4. Conflict/consensus:	The ways in which individuals and groups adjust their behaviour to natural and social circumstances.
5. Similarity/difference:	Classification of phenomena according to relevant criteria.
6. Continuity/change:	Distinction of phenomena along this essentially historical dimension.
7. Causality:	The notion that change in a state of affairs can be attributed to the phenomena preceding.

174

What kind of a liar are you?
People lie because they don't remember
  clear what they saw.
People lie because they can't help making a story
  better than it was the way it happened.
People tell 'white lies' so as to be decent
  to others.
People lie in a pinch, hating to do it, but
  lying on because it might be worse
And people lie just to be liars for a
  crooked personal gain.
What sort of a liar are you?
Which of these liars are you?

(Carl Sandburg)

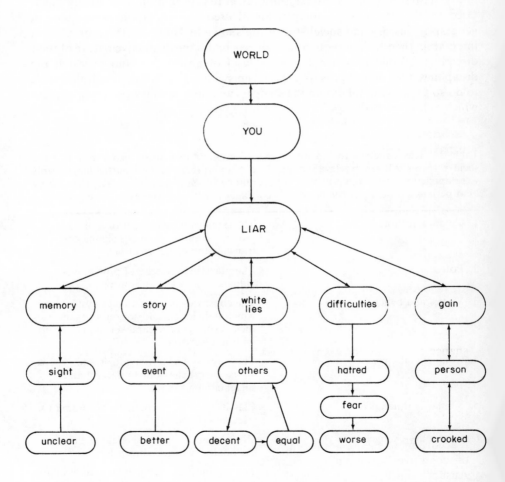

Figure 23. A concept map for 'What kind of a liar are you?' (Reproduced by kind permission of M. Moreira)

Concepts like cause, chance, and uncertainty have different meanings in their usage in geography, history and social studies which need to retain their integrity in an integrated programme. The effect of integrated programmes should be to broaden the boundaries of perception which the student brings to the understanding of new issues and problems.

Of the general principles which learning theorists attempted to describe in the past, the above sections of this book illustrate the importance of understanding entering characteristics and the factors which contribute to readiness (i.e. without appropriate readiness a learning experience will be inefficient and to the extent that learning will not occur). They also point to the need for intrinsic as opposed to extrinsic motivation, as is evident from the success of group discussion and role-play. Finally, they suggest the importance of meaning, organization and structure to learning.

Changes of this kind will make considerable demands on the teacher, but involvement at this level is likely to be its own stimulus. It is by no means the only way of looking at the problem.

Note

1. *Associationism*: the view that concepts are connected through the action of association by contiguity in experience. Associationism is closely related to behaviourism.

   Behaviourism: All behaviourist theories of learning are associationistic. Perhaps the best-known behaviourists are Pavlov and Skinner, the latter whose work provided the basis for programmed instruction. Behaviourists hold that almost everything that a child does has to be learned, and that learning is achieved by conditional responses. An adult behaves through a system of response habits which are reinforced by continuous repetition. These habits are capable of modification by new conditioning. Behaviourists derive their conclusions only from observations of overt human behaviour, and the key to behaviour control is reinforcement. In Skinner's theory the tendency to repeat certain acts and therefore to learn is a function of the degree to which an act is rewarded. This is called 'operant conditioning', because the learner operates on the environment. Voluntary actions are shaped by the environment. Behaviourism is criticized because it oversimplifies human development.

   Cognitive psychology: arose in response to the criticism that learning theorists of the behavioural school paid insufficient attention to the cognitive determinants of human development. In the Piagetian view of cognitive development children (individuals) explore the environment and respond to it according to their comprehension of its essential characteristics. The level of cognitive development determines the complexity of understanding. Ausubel and Bruner are examples of cognitive psychologists.

   Gestalt: A German word translated as form, pattern, configuration or structure. *Gestalt* psychologists hold that we do not just add together impressions but grasp how they are related. There is a tendency to view things as more simple, regular and complete than they are, and, as such, they may or may not be an advantage. Teaching becomes the assistance given to helping students to grasp relationships. Bruner, a cognitive psychologist, argues that students should be helped to grasp the structure of a field of study, and in this way they will be able to apply the principles and consequences learnt in a variety of situations.

Bruner advocates a planned discovery approach to learning, and in this way the concepts and principles grasped will be more meaningful. Step-by-step study following expository teaching limits children's thinking and may lead them to believe that learning is undertaken simply to obtain a reward. (For a recent work which includes assessment of these different approaches to human development as well as studies of information-processing theory, the Soviet tradition, and humanistic approaches see Murray Thomas, 1985.)

CHAPTER 8

Perception, Learning and Studying

INTRODUCTION

This chapter continues with the theme that, because learning is a complex activity, no one perspective (theory) suffices for its understanding. Experience is a powerful influence on learning, and may enhance or impede it. The fact that it can impede learning is seldom discussed. The idea of experiential learning can all too easily lead to the view that all that matters is experience, even though that idea is far removed from the intentions of the theorists. This chapter begins with a commentary on the role of experience in perceptual learning. It takes into account the acquisition of data, sampling and personal value systems. How these become problematic in the teaching learning situation is discussed and particular reference is made to the problem of cognitive dissonance.

It seems that we have preferred ways of organizing what we see, remember and think about (Messick, 1976) or different styles of conceptualization and patterning of activities which may be the most important characteristics of an individual (Tyler, 1978). These cognitive or learning styles (as some authors prefer to call them) have been thought to play an important part in learning and studying.

Four styles are discussed in this chapter (i.e. field-dependent–independent, convergent–divergent, Kolb's experiential learning, and depth–surface). However, because spatial ability is an influence on perception, and because there is some indication that it may be related to field-dependence–independence, the discussion of style is preceded by a brief description of recent thinking about spatial skill.

Because cognitive styles may be related to study habits this chapter includes a brief discussion of recent work in the area of learning how to learn.

The investigations reported in this chapter have considerable implications for teachers in higher education. Learning may be influened by them in a number of ways, and there is a great need for them to understand how they can enhance rather than impede learning. All the investigations reported confirm the view that there should be variety in assessment, instruction and learning.

The clarification of objectives that such an approach demands may be helped by the use of an inventory which investigates learning styles and is correlated with the assessment procedures in use. Reflection on the results may help the teacher better to understand the impact of the curriculum on students through his or her teaching. The teacher who is seen to be committed to the instructional enterprise is likely to be valued by students.

LEARNING AND EXPERIENCE

All learning is a result of an interaction between the self and the environment. 'What' students bring from their education in school can influence their subsequent learning. Experience is a powerful ally of perception and misperception, for all learning is rooted in experience and is substantially influenced by our perception.

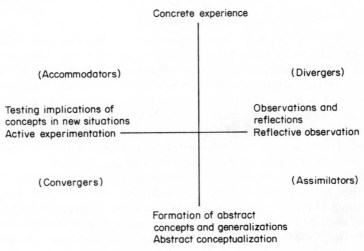

Figure 24. An adaptation of Kolb's experiential learning model. (From Fitzgibbon, A. (1987). Kolb's experiential model as a model for the supervision of classroom teaching for student teachers. *European Journal of Teacher Education*, **10**, (2), 163–78. Reproduced by kind permission of A. Fitzgibbon)

Kolb's model of experiential learning illustrates the function of experience. An adaptation of this model to the supervison of trainee teachers (discussed in detail later) is shown in Figure 24. It will be seen that this model of learning follows a four-stage cycle. It begins with our concrete experience which is the basis for observation and reflection. These data are assimilated into hypotheses about future action, and it is this which helps the learner to create new experiences. The cycle is very similar to the model of decision-making shown in Figure 25. Kolb (1984) suggests that learners need four kinds of abilities, which he calls *concrete experience, reflective observation, abstract conceptualization, and active experimentation* (Kolb *et al.*, 1984).

The first sections of this chapter are primarily concerned with what the learner brings to the environment, particularly in respect of observation and reflection, and more especially in terms of experience, which is a collective of past and present responding to the demands of the learner on the one hand, and the environment on the other.

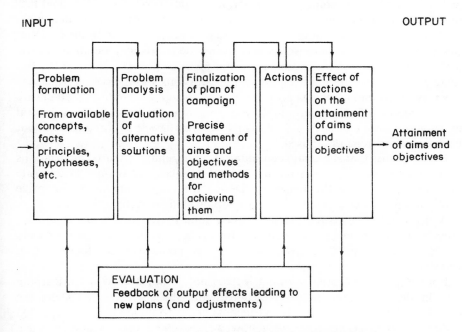

Figure 25. A model of decision making (problem solving)

INTERPRETING THE OUTER WORLD

In order to interpret the outer world and more especially the questions in tests we have to have some internal frames of reference so as to relate new to old information. These frames of reference (or schema, as they have been called) may be regarded as tools which help us to see, evaluate and respond. Allport described such categories as accessible clusters of associated ideas in the mind which serve as a frame of reference for fresh perceptual samples of immediate modes of behaviour.

Champagne (1983) distinguishes between micro- and macroschema. The former is a mental structure that guides the analysis and interpretation of an identifiable class of phenomena. A microschema generally incorporates concepts, propositions, and more or less integrated networks of these two elements. The latter is a mental structure which encompasses several microschema.

Hirsch (1987), in his best-selling book *Cultural Literacy*, employs the term 'schema' but the items which he uses to describe schema are concepts, and he builds up concept trees and principles to show their importance in understanding language. Moreover, he attaches the same functions to schema that others have given to concepts, i.e. that they aid us to store knowledge in a retrievable form so that it can be applied rapidly and efficiently. His views relate to Saupe's principles for both meaning and transfer, for he points out the self-evident fact that, without appropriate background knowledge, people cannot adequately understand written or spoken language. Hirsch draws attention to the fact that we cannot model how we use schema in any detached way but that we use different types of schema. Some are static pictures (for example, birds), but there are also procedural schema related to occasions about birds on which the memory draws. Some schema are directly available to the mind while others are in the recesses of the mind and take a long time to retrieve. Thus general information about birds is at a deeper level than specific information about birds, which is most often used.

Hirsch argues that successful communication depends on shared associations which necessitates an extensive knowlege of specifics and is thus an opposite view to educators in the Rousseau–Dewey tradition, who favour intensive study in a few cases as the basis of developing skills in critical thought.

Apart from the linkage made between concept learning and perception, Hirsch's views present a clear problem for curriculum designers and certainly challenge the notion that specialist knowledge necessarily develops skills of transfer.

For my part, perceptual learning focuses not so much on concept learning but on the interaction between ourselves and the environment. There are techniques of instruction which will help us better to understand concepts. At the same time, we need to know how we are influenced by and, in turn, influence the environment. It is for this reason that I prefer the phrase 'frames of reference': this focuses on the relationship between ourselves and the environment, which, in the first instance of observation, is holistic. Moreover, 'frames of reference' embraces the emotional commitment involved in the extraction and internalization of data from the environment.

If learning is that process by which experience develops new and reorganizes old concepts it follows that this is more difficult in situations where the learner's frames of reference are limited.

Therefore a general education should provide for the acquisition of the widest possible frames of reference, which is an axiom that supports the view that in higher education the curriculum should be broad.

MEANINGFUL LEARNING AND THE ACQUISITION OF CONCEPTS

Meaningful learning depends on our ability to sort things out from the mass of data which presents itself to us in life and in the formalized learning situations provided by an educational system. It is the fact that these data have to be sampled, which is the source of many learning problems. In order to understand those data we *impose* meaning on the objects of knowledge, and that meaning is determined in no small measure by our previous experience.

Because of our particular dispositions there is no guarantee that we will each see the same attributes in a concept (object), and it is by no means a matter of autistic thinking. It is important to recognize that we are all too easily deceived by what we see, as studies of the techniques of a television production show (Baggaley *et al.*, 1980), and it applies as much to our perception of people as it does to objects. For example:

> A student had to make a work sampling study of chargehands in a fairly confined factory, without complete introduction. He started on a Monday morning. A new product was assembled and production was under time stress. Because he often spoke to the chargehands and was continually making notes he appeared to most of the young assembly workers as a controller of their bosses. His appearance near their assembly lines was welcomed with some satisfaction: they became bolder towards the chargehands: made jokes and nudged each other when he was approaching. To the chargehands he became a menace; they became uncertain and nervous and they concerned themselves more with the production process itself than with their group of workers. To the departmental manager he became a scapegoat: he blamed several production faults on this work sampling study and he walked about the factory more than usual (Hesseling, 1966).

This kind of event happens between teachers and their students in college classrooms with varying levels of response. For example, at one American college a course evaluation showed that while female instructors were given higher formal ratings than men they were also required to offer greater interpersonal support because they were perceived as warmer and more potent individuals. This finding was considered by Bennett (1982) to arise from culturally conditioned gender stereotypes and is an excellent example of the prior conditioning of experience.

It seems that under certain conditions conflicts between the values of the teacher and those held by the student can impede learning. When this occurs it is called 'congitive dissonance'.

VALUE DISPOSITIONS AND COGNITIVE DISSONANCE

Value dispositions begin to be formed when children are young. One study which illustrates this point reported of students at Bath University that social science students were anti-industry when compared with those of economics, engineering and management. Consistent with these values, they also wanted non-industrial jobs. From the data, Duff and Cotgrove (1982) concluded that their choice and career was a function of their experience in early adolescence.

In both Australia and the United States differences in the attitudes of students to academic subjects have also been found. At the University of New England Watkins (1982) obtained evidence which suggested that the different academic environments in the various faculties may attract and satisfy students of different personality types. Another US study by Long (1976) found that conservative and liberal students viewed academic subjects differently and did not use the same dimensions when describing academic subjects. The costs of a 'poor' choice could be great if the values which a student brings to the class are in conflict with those of the teachers and such cognitive dissonance can be an impediment to learning. It is a problem which has worried teachers in the humanities because they believe that such conflicts might lead students to evaluate their courses poorly.

If, for example, a first-year student is introduced to cognitively complex material about a value system which is foreign to him or her, as might occur in political science, learning may be impeded or resisted. A student's consistent like or dislike for an instructor occurs when:

(1) The student likes the instructor, and agrees cognitively and affectively with the message given by him or her which is understood;
(2) The student dislikes the instructor and disagrees affectively with the message from him or her which is understood.

Learning takes place in either case, and, as Marshall (1980) has pointed out, this consistency is sometimes maintained because the student imposes his or her own understanding on the message so as to comport with the feelings he or she has about the instructor.

The more difficult the problem, the more likely is inconsistency or cognitive dissonance (Canter and Meisels, 1971; Marshall, 1980). In this case, while the student may like the teacher in the beginning, untenable views on the teacher's part may cause him or her to change the understanding of the instructor's message and perhaps to dislike the instructor. Cognitive dissonance is particularly acute when the level of cognition required is difficult and the conclusions run counter to the student's disposition.

Hesseling (1966) called this mode of thinking, in which 'truth' is confused with desire or in which there is a fusion of subjective and objective, 'autism'. Such autism, he maintained, always interferes with logical thinking. Moreover, there is no clear borderline between autistic and ordinary thinking. In this sense, our experience is prejudiced, and we are not free and unbiased to engage in 'open' interplay with our experience.

One of the skills which contributes to Kolb's concrete experience abilities is the ability to free ourselves from prejudice. We have to learn that there are likely to be discrepancies between our perception and the actuality of the incoming data. Of more importance is the fact that our previous experience contributes to these discrepancies.

It is in this sense that an individual's specialization may impede learning. Hesseling gives the example of how different functionaries look at the problems of an industrial organization:

A production manager may categorize information in terms of technical process and work performance. When a sociologist, for example, points out to him interpersonal rivalries in his department, it can be a surprise for him. This interpersonal relations concept did not yet fit into his system of categories and had mainly been seen as differences in performance.

In any situation a specialist has to be open-minded. Thus the production manager in the example would require a *choc des opinions*. It is for this reason that some curriculum designers have established learning strategies and curricula to meet the goals of perceptual learning.

MEETING THE GOALS OF PERCEPTUAL LEARNING IN THE CURRICULUM

Carpenter and I at Liverpool University believed that the engineering students coming to us with the habits and skills developed during several years of scientific study would not only lack the alternative skills needed for the study of less numerate subjects but would be intellectually and emotionally unable to accept that their learning skills could be incomplete. We believed it to be essential to remove this mental 'roadblock' and arranged our first few meetings almost as 'shock tactics'. The students were exposed in the early practical sessions to behavioural exercises in which they effectively experimented on each other (Carpenter and Heywood, 1973). These began with exercises in perception and insight derived from ideas put forward by Dinkelspeil (1971), who had organized a similar course for business students in the United States. In his course students demonstrated to themselves that their perceptions of a given situation differed substantially from one student to another, that the differences were, to a fair degree, predictable according to their experience, age, sex and cultural background, that insight into a problem or situation was coloured by their perceptions and other factors, and that any question or statement is almost inescapably structured so that it predetermines the attitudes and frame of reference of the responder. These tactics—somewhat differently applied in our course—had a considerable effect on most of the students. Initially, they exhibited a marked degree of confusion, but this quickly settled down into a growing confidence in the open-minded study of themselves and of their environment, in which there was a pleasing absence of undue scientific rigidity. These free-thinking techniques were extended and reinforced by exercises in brainstorming, which led to the value analysis of both products and systems, role-playing (which culminated in the playing of company roles in a competitive business game), and in the making of short closed-circuit television recordings on a chosen aspect of the study programme. The latter was a modification of the syndicate technique. The formal outcome of student-organized work was the planning and making of the closed-circuit television recording. The lecture programme which accompanied this course was designed to highlight impediments in perceptual learning, particularly as they influence behaviour in industry. (A more sophisticated approach to language learning using this method has been described by Knudson (1969). An experimental course was run on these lines but the students were rotated betweeen the roles. They did not write the scripts.)

The authors of the Images course at Little College believed, like us, that the capacities of freshmen were unused and that the freshman curriculum had a stifling effect (Roller *et al.*, 1972). After seminars with the students they decided to initiate a course on 'the processes by which man conceptualized his universe and in turn both shapes his experiences and is himself shaped by his images or concepts'. We decided to call the course 'The Making and Manipulation of Images', a title inspired in part by one of Kenneth Boulding's books on our list of core readings. Rather than organize our course around a topical division of materials or disciplines, we developed a generic model of the image-building process and adopted that as a broad outline for the course. In essence, the model and outline were a simplified version of the 'scientific method' intentionally stated in terms so general as to be almost universally applicable:

(1) *Encounter*: meeting with new and unexplained phenomena;
(2) *Articulation*: the formulation of an explanation tentatively held until tested;
(3) *Conflict*: discovering the inadequacy of the image to explain the phenomena and/or discovering in the implications of newly validated image a conflict with a previously held image;
(4) *Internalization*: acceptance (whether by an individual or a society) of the new image, a conflict with previously held and validated images;
(5) *Rule and Reign of Images*: guiding thought and conflict to establish and elaborate image systems, sometimes even when some portion of that image system is in conflict with or fails to explain newly encountered phenomena.

> We expected freshmen, at least out of boredom or anxiety, to eventually insist on ordering phenomena in some fashion or other. We expected a crisis to develop which would then lead them to formulate some kind of testable explanation of their experiences with the readings, the discussions, or other classes. That we could explain as *articulation* and we would then be on our way into an examination of the systems of knowledge known as 'disciplines'. After almost three weeks, the looked-for crisis arose; not among the students, but among the four instructors who could no longer endure in so meaningless and unstructured universe . . . if our error as undergraduates had been to hold rigidly to certain verities, theirs was to reject the desirability and utility of creating knowledge. As knowledge is somehow relative, they reasoned, we therefore live in a world of uncertain opinion. They understood that ideas could be analysed and the facts could be tested and then synthesized. But, when you have done all that, they argued, you reach a tentative statement subject to repudiation by some additional factor, some new experience. Like younger brothers and sisters of Sisyphus, who had watched their older brother futilely press his question up the slope of knowledge, they decided to leave their own questions untouched in the sure valley of unverified opinion.

I found this to be true of science and engineering graduates who were asked to discuss the conclusions of a book describing a substantial strike. They were not prepared to be objective.

Students cannot, it seems, be left on their own to develop stuctures unless they are clear that this is what they are expected to do. It is unfortunate that 'satisfaction with courses' may be related to the perception of structure (Kozma, 1982), but this is what we have to expect from perceptual learning theory. They have to be trained to cope with unstructured situations. So in a second course Roller and his colleagues introduced a project:

> The second course had the aim of focusing on what each student was now thinking, and on what they had learned in the last twenty-odd years about his own perceiving, thinking and communication processes. This was achieved first by exposing the students to a range of experiences, and then analysing their processes of thinking about these experiences in relation to such questions as 'Can different or personal ways of perception be communicated? How do different cultural backgrounds and different group situations affect people's perceptions? To what extent does the English language restrict our abilities to think of, or even imagine, other ways of seeing the world?' The students were then asked to devise exercises. Anything was allowed so long as it involved creative effort. Many students found the initiative and responsibility with which they had to cope more than they could handle. The project also broke up the group experience but nevertheless it seemed to be a powerful educational experience which, while not a panacea, is consonant with the broadest aims of liberal education in that it enables the student to gain comprehension and control over his present capabilities and some perspective on this present value.

There is a great deal of misperception in learning and it contributes to misunderstandings which can make good grades difficult to get. Neither do such misunderstandings necessarily relate to the intelligence of the perceiver. We can see from the example that what is perceived depends not only on what is to be perceived but on the state of the perceiver, i.e. the internal organization of perception. How often does the internal state of an examinee lead to a misinterpretation of an examination question?

Fortunately, one study among a large group of students concluded that cognitive dissonance is a weak framework for understanding course evalutions. What mattered more than the recruitment of interested teachers was the building and reinforcement of reputations for teaching interested classes (Granzin and Painter, 1976). Marshall (1980), in his investigation mentioned above, found among a group of students taking politics some who changed position away from those of the instructor and yet learnt. At the same time, their post-course ratings of the instructor went down. He put this down to good instruction.

Nevertheless, as Marshall indicates, such good instructors might have to put up with lower performance ratings. What matters in all evaluation is that the objectives are perceived by both teacher and student to have been achieved. Thus teachers should seek to secure the co-operation and understanding of the students (Cross, 1976). Many teachers are finding that if they have some understanding of how students learn their performance is helped. Students bring other things as well as experience to their perception, and not least among these are intelligence and learning styles, which are the topic of the next section.

SPATIAL ABILITY

Apart from the influence of the environment on the mental mechanism of sampling, it is evident that intelligence plays an important role, however it is defined. In the traditional British view of intelligence it was supposed that there was a general factor which underpinned two major groups of factors, one of which was responsible for verbal and numerical abilities and the other for spatial and mechanical ones. In 1964 Macfarlane Smith published an important and controversial thesis, which argued that the shortage of qualified engineers and scientists in Britain was due to the fact that the grammar schools of the time emphasized teaching in subjects which help to develop verbal and numerical abilities at the expense of those which could develop the spatial and mechanical abilities essential for performance in technology. Incidentally, mathematical ability was held to be different from numerical ability and to depend on spatial ability. A variety of test data was adduced to support this thesis. The biographical data of such persons as Einstein was also used to defend the argument.

It had already been suggested by Zangwill (1961) that the left and right hemisphere dominances of the brain were related to the 'symbolic' and the 'visuo-spatial', respectively. By 1967 it seemed to be understood that the right hemisphere is largely concerned with integrating data from our senses not only to orient us in space but also to enable us to integrate our external perceptions (Warrington et al., 1966).

In 1969 a striking demonstration of the different functions of the two hemispheres of the brain came from Bogen (1969). He had surgically divided the organ which connected the two spheres as a treatment for intractable epilepsy and found among eight patients that their right hands were able to write normally but were not able to copy a geometrical figure, whereas the opposite happened to the left hand. From this he argued that the two sides of the brain performed different functions.

Bogen was led to believe that the individual with two intact minds had the capacity for two distinct modes of thought. Propositional thought was lateralized in one hemisphere and appositional thought was the specialization of the other. MacFarlane Smith (1969) assumed that the verbal/numerical abilities (which were associated with analogical reasoning) depended on the left hemisphere, and that the capacity for relational thinking depended on the right.

Most recently, Gardner (1983) has argued that spatial intelligence is one of a number of fundamental competencies which are relatively autonomous but fundamental to our thinking. He calls them *frames of mind*. These ideas have been taken up in school education, especially in the United States, where there is developing interest in the use of imagery skills (Galyean, 1983).

FIELD-DEPENDENCE AND FIELD-INDEPENDENCE

Many factors come together to influence our perception. Cognitive or learning style is the particular mode of perception which an individual brings to the understanding of his or her world. In the United States in the 1950s Witkin (1976; Witkin and Goodenough, 1981) suggested that individual dispositions toward their perception of their environment lie on a continuum, the polar ends of which he called field-dependent and field-independent. Those who are field-dependent look at the world in a global way, while those wo are field-independent would see it analytically. The reactions of the field-dependent to people, places and events are undifferentiated and complex. In contrast, the events (objects) in the environment are not associated with the background of that environment by the person who is field-independent.

Using the embedded figures test (Witkin *et al.*, 1971), which was developed to test for field-dependence and independence as well as other tests, Zocolliti and Oltman (1976) described an investigation which set out to examine the relationships between these two dimensions and the right and left brains. They were not able to confirm that the two dimensions were related to one side of the brain in particular but they concluded that the field-independence–dependence dimension was probably related to the degree of segregation of functioning between the two hemispheres. In another study Sigman and Oltman (1976) came to the conclusion that the two dimensions were characteristic perceptual strategies, each of which could be adaptive in certain conditions.

Some studies of the response of students to visual material might have been illuminated had they taken a test for field dependence–independence. For example, in one study visual aids with different amounts of realistic detail were compared (Dwyer and Parkhurst, 1982). It was found that different methods of programmed instruction were not equally effective in obtaining different types of educational objective and, similarly, that different types of visual representation are not equally effective. The achievement of a high-level reading comprehension group of students improved as the degree of realism in the visuals increased, whereas the opposite was found to be true of the low-reading comprehension group. In another study two groups were presented with the same graphical information. They were then given a task, the complexity of which differed between the two groups. The results of a post-test relating to these graphical data suggested that the type of cue (task) influences learning in various ways. For example, some cues may cause cognitive overload (Kirk and Eggen, 1978). Even if a relationship with field-independence–dependence is not immediately apparent, the significance of perception is. It also brings home the point that the instructional apparatus (in this case, visuals) requires careful design (Garrick, 1978).

Directly related to the educational context is the fact that several investigators, including Witkin (1976), have claimed that an individual's location on the continuum between the two poles contributes to academic choice, success and vocational preference. Field-dependent persons require their learning to have more structure, direction and feedback than field-independent ones, who tend to dislike collaborative learning. This would explain the everyday experience of teachers who find that some students who do not like group work are nevertheless good at academically analytical work. Tyler (1978) has pointed out that the same may apply to teachers in higher education, and this woul account for the liking that some teachers have for lectures and others for grou discussion.

For a detailed study of this approach to cognitive styles the reader is referre to the GRE study by Witkin and others (1977). This contains a substantia bibliography as well as the results of a major study. The field-dependence independence dimension is shown to be slightly related to verbal skills an unrelated to overall academic achievement. Choice of academic study doe however, appear to be related to cognitive style, especially in mathematics an the sciences. One study has gone so far as to suggest that the Embedded Figure Test measures cognitive ability rather than cognitive style (Highhouse an Doverspike, 1987).

CONVERGENT AND DIVERGENT THINKING STYLES

Probably the best-known cognitive styles are those described on the continuu of convergent–divergent thinking. Divergent thinkers are commonly describe as creative. These descriptions originate with Guilford's (1954) study of th intellect, but were given prominence in Britain by Hudson's (1966) report of th test results of students in sixth forms in British schools. He found that thos who were studying arts (the humanities) subjects were much more creative tha those who studied science. This led to a furore at the 'political' level, becaus lack of divergence among scientists might have been a contributory factor t Britain's poor industrial performance (Gregory, 1972).

The Guilford model assumes that creativity and intelligence are differe things and that creativity is as important as intelligence. Convergent thinke tend to concentrate on test questions which require a single answer, wherea divergent ones do not like the confines of conventional tests: they are more home in generating many solutions. It is said that they perform well in activiti like brainstorming.

One of the problems with the tests used by Hudson was that they were of t pencil and paper variety. Scientific creativity is difficult to measure with suc tests. Guilford considered that effective thinking resulted from the sequenti use of convergent and divergent processes. In Britain Whitfield (1975) show models of the engineering process which illustrated this point. In general, it held that there has to be a balance between convergent and divergent thinkin If the student leans too much toward convergent thinking he or she is likely experience difficulties with problem-solving.

Freeman (1968), who has been associated with creativity studies amor undergraduates in architecture, economics, and medicine, used a 'hypothese test of divergent thinking and several others (including a test of skills ar attitudes) with electrical engineering students, and found that balance betwe convergence and divergence was an important predictor of post-test perfor ance.

Torrance (1962) holds the view that above a threshold level of IQ 120 t correlation between convergence and divergence falls away, and performance may be as much due to divergence as to convergence. Freeman's studies support this hypothesis.

Creativity studies seem to have gone out of fashion. However, in recent work I have found that student teachers, when asked to implement activities in the classroom which would develop creativity, found that the strategies which they developed gave them insight into their pupils learning and also helped them to develop other teaching styles.

One investigator who has used Hudson's ideas in the development of a learning styles inventory is David Kolb. It is to the learning styles related to his experiential model of learning that we now turn.

KOLB'S LEARNING STYLES

Attention was drawn to Kolb's (1984) model of experiential learning in an earlier section of this chapter. This derives from his particular view of learning as a 'process whereby knowledge is created through the transformation of experience'. While it seems to comprehend the same dimensions as the definitions of learning given by Fincher and myself, it is important to repeat it here, since, as stated, it leads Kolb to adopt a particular terminology. 'Prehension' is the grasping of knowledge which is 'transformed' (transformation) when grasped. The way individuals grasp and transform their knowledge is their learning style. The model may now be described in two dimensions. The X axis is a continuum between abstract and concrete and the Y axis one between active and reflective. For effective learning the learner has to use all the four skills necessary for the completion of the cycle. Kolb believes that each learner has a preferred style related to one of these experiential learning skills. This is in keeping with everyday observation. It is not surprising to think that learning style and personality disposition are related or that while there may be one dominant style all the others have to be used in learning. As the situations change, so the learners have to choose which set of abilities they will use in the specific circumstances they face.

The four styles are:

(1) *Convergers*: Their dominant learning styles are abstract conceptualization and active experimentation. It is the mode of learning which has often been associated with the classroom and caused by traditional assessment. People with this style do best in tests where the problems require single solutions. Not very emotional, they tend to prefer things to people. Convergence relates to that part of problem-solving which is related to the selection of a solution and the evaluation of the consequences of the solution.

(2) *Divergers*: These are the opposite of convergers. Both terms come from the early research in creativity, and Kolb cites Hudson's study in particular. Divergers are best in the situation of concrete experience and reflective observation. They like to 'imagine' and generate ideas. They are emotional

and relate well to people, and do not perform as well in tests which demand single solutions. Divergence relates to that part of the problem-solving process which identifies differences (problems) and compares goals with reality.

(3) *Assimilators*: Their dominant learning skills are abstract conceptualizations and reflective observation. They are not so much concerned with people as with abstract concepts. They are interested in the precise and logical development of theory rather than with its application. Kolb describes them as pure rather than applied scientists. Assimilation relates to the solution of problems and the considerations of alternative solutions in the problem-solving process.

(4) *Accommodators*: These are the opposite of the assimilators. Their dominant learning strengths are concrete experience and active experimentation. They like doing things and want to devise and implement experiments. Such individuals take more risks than those with the other learning styles. Kolb says 'we have labelled this style "accommodator" because he tends to excel in those situations where he must adapt himself to specific immediate circumstances'. Such individuals are at ease with people, although they are relatively impatient. Accommodation relates to the choice of goal(s) and the execution of solutions in problem-solving.

Kolb and his colleagues devised a self-assessment inventory to measure the learning styles of individuals (The Learning Styles Inventory), which has been substantially revised. Using the original version with 800 managers for whom they had undergraduate data only, they found that those who had studied business were accommodators. Nursing and engineering undergraduates were convergers, history, political science, English and psychology students were divergers, and economics, and those studying mathematics, sociology, chemistry and physics were assimilators. Kolb argued that undergraduate education was a major factor influencing style while at the same time recognizing that his results might be due to the selection process. Our interest here is that divergers and accommodators could be disadvantaged by some techniques of assessment.

Kolb related his learning styles to problem-solving. His model shows quite clearly that all four skills are required in the solution of problems. In this respect it is consistent with Whitfield's (1975) finding on creativity in industry. Industrial problems require both convergent and divergent thinking styles at different stages of the process. The same argument derives from our study of engineers at work (Youngman *et al.*, 1977). Kolb cites two American studies in support of his thesis.

There is a difficulty with this thesis, for if a person selects a field which is consistent with their learning style they may try to mould their subsequent work to fit that style rather than allow the job to force the individual to learn other styles. For example, Plovnick (1971) found that the major style in physics education was convergent. Ten years later, studies at Rutgers University by

Enyeart *et al.* (1980) found that deductive logical ability contributed more to achievement in an introductory college physics course than inductive logical ability.

Plovnick predicted that those undergraduates who were divergers would be uncertain of physics with a career, and this was found to be true. The assumption here is that physicists entering careers in physics will find that jobs in physics require convergence. However, if Whitfield is correct they will have to function at some time or another in all four modes.

Kolb's model provides additional insight into Hesseling's theory of autism and our views of the effects of experience in industrial situations in that it suggests that it (autism) is due to the overuse of one dominant style. A *choc des opinions* might have been given to the production engineer and sociologist in Hesseling's example had they been given the Learning Style Inventory and asked to discuss the results together.

As we have seen, an interesting feature of research in problem-solving is the fact reported by several authorities that, once taught a problem, students use the same technique to solve all others. This 'problem set', as Luchins (1942) calls it, is extremely limiting and can prevent effective transfer. The same seems to be true of learning styles (Thomas and Bain, 1982).

Grasha (1984) argues that the assumption that an individual's learning style should be matched to particular instructional strategies is without foundation. If individuals are always in the same environment they will soon become bored. Moreover, such an environment will limit their skills of adaptability: 'In building an environment compatible with a preferred learning style, one may miss the opportunity for significant learning.'

In regard to assessment in higher education, given that a person should enter into all the modes of learning even though some tension might be created, it follows that students should be exposed to a variety of assessment and instructional techniques (Cross, 1976) designed to meet the learning objectives inherent in the model.

The Learning Skills Inventory has been used in higher education as part of a self-assessment process designed to help students learn how to learn. Loacker and her colleagues (1984) report on the Alverno experience with Kolb's LSI thus:

> The identification of experiential validation of knowledge and theory as a significant cause of learning relates to the student's awareness of learning as a process of experiencing, reflecting, forming new concepts, and testing one's judgements and abilities in action...At entrance students showed a marked preference for 'concrete experience' over 'abstract conceptualization' and for 'reflective observation' over 'active experimentation'. Eventually students showed that they had come to rely equally on concrete and abstract models and to use a similar flexibility in choosing either reflective or active approaches.

Fitzgibbon (1987), from studies with graduate trainee teachers for secondary schools, has shown how Kolb's model can be applied to the supervision of classroom practice. In her teaching students are seen on five occasions during the training period. Each of these is assessed: one at least will be by another supervisor. After the lesson there is a conference between the supervisor and the student. A written evaluation is submitted one week after the conference. She suggested that the application of Kolb's model to the supervision of teaching practice would have considerable advantages to both the teacher and student. The model as adapted by Fitzgibbon for this purpose is shown in Figure 26 and its relationship to learning type is given in Table 35. Fitzgibbon does not comment on the problem of assessment. It might be assumed from this model that there would be personal growth, in which case the five assessments could not be given equal weight. Competency rather than graded assessment would seem to be more appropriate.

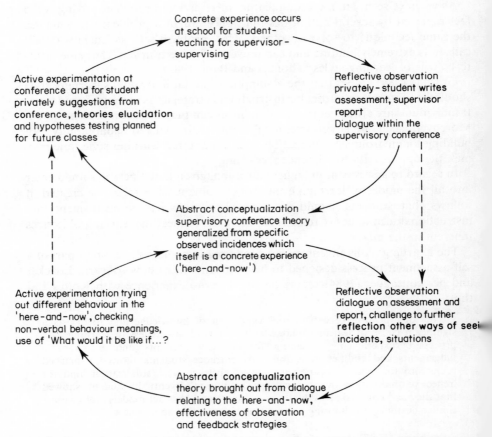

Figure 26. Kolb's experiential model of learning applied to the classroom supervisor of trainee teachers. (Reproduced by kind permission of A. Fitzgibbon and the Editor of the *European Journal of Teacher Education* (see Figure 24))

Table 35. Kolb's model of experiential learning applied to student teaching showing the strengths and weaknesses of each learning type within its quadrant for (A) the student and (B) the supervisor. S—strength; E—excess; D—deficiency. (Reproduced by kind permission of A. Fitzgibbon and the Editor of the *European Journal of Teacher Education*)

(A) Concrete experience is the supervised class

Accommodation

S: Writes lesson plans incorporating desired skills and class needs, teaches lessons adapting plan as required, takes appropriate risks.

E: Overplans, fits class or content to suit skills.

D: Cannot use points elucidated in supervisory conference in plans, cannot adapt plan to suit class.

Convergence

S: Able to select skill needing improvement, able to test hypotheses priorities.

E: Premature closure, excessive focusing on small area.

D: Unable to select priority areas unable to focus attention.

Divergence

S: Generates data from observations and subsequent reflection, analyses causes of actions and incidents.

E: Produces too much data to manage, creation of sense of hopelessness.

D: Inability to recognize problems/opportunities, rationalization of difficulties.

Assimilation

S: Identifies theory underlying actions, defines problems, suggests conceptual basis.

E: Sees theories everywhere, attempts total integration of difficulties.

D: Not able to identify theoretical basis of actions, unable to learn from successes or mistakes.

(B) Concrete experience is the supervisory conference

Accommodation

S: Invites student to set own goals for teaching and development; challenges student to take risks; affirms student in own decisions.

E: Be totally directive.

D: Be totally non-directive.

Convergence

S: Stimulates student to think through implications of theory in relation to practice; helps student to prioritize.

E: Forces premature closure; avoids interpersonal issues.

D: Allows student to float in an undifferentiated mass of theories; fails to focus student.

Divergence

S: Identifies and exposes the 'here-and-now' situations; allows ambiguity and variety in interpretation; invites different perspectives on data.

E: Invades privacy of student; dominates; too many points made.

D: Ignores opportunities of 'here-and-now' situations; alternatives not suggested nor allowed.

Assimilation

S: Helps in the relating of data observed to current theories; creates models; integrates points.

E: Suggests too many theories; ignores practicalities in evaluating ideas.

D: Allows student's statements to stand outside of theoretical body of knowledge.

Kolb modified the first edition of his inventory because of evaluation research which proved to be non-supportive. The second instrument has also been criticized for lack of reliability and stability (Sims *et al.*, 1986). Highhouse and Doverspike (1987) have tested its construct validity by correlating it with field-independence–field-dependence and the Vocational Preference Inventory (Holland, 1978). They concluded that it measured preferences rather more than cognitive style.

Nevertheless, as the studies by Loacker and Fitzgibbon show, independently of what it actually measures this inventory can be used by teachers to better understand their students and to design their courses. This latter point is particularly well illustrated by Svinicki and Dixon (1987), who relate the many different types of instructional activity to the components of the cycle most likely to support that method (for example, concrete experience—fieldwork; reflective observation—discussion; abstract conceptualization—papers; active experimentation—homework). They agree with Kolb that there are fundamental differences in the nature of the disciplines, and because of these differences the discipline itself can circumscribe an instructor's choice of learning activities. They demonstrate how the application of the model might work in pharmacy, history, public policy, architecture, engineering and psychology.

High psychometric reliability and validity are not necessarily required to illuminate the problems which the teacher has in the classroom. In recent years many psychologists interested in learning in the classroom have followed Parlett and Hamilton (1972) into more rigorous methods of illuminative evaluation, especially in the area of learning styles.

STUDY SKILLS: LEARNING HOW TO LEARN

Related to cognitive/learning style are the study skills which students bring to their learning. In 1966 Brown and Holtzmann described a study habit inventory in the United States and reported a correlation of 0.4 between study habits and Grade-Point-Average. Lower correlations using the same inventory were reported in England by Cowell and Entwistle (1971). In general, it seemed that the more organized a student's study work habits, the more likely they were to get good grades. This in turn led to the view that students could be helped to learn how to learn. Specialist courses were developed for this purpose and counsellors with a knowledge of learning skills were introduced into institutions of higher education (Nelson-Jones and Toner, 1977, 1979). In the United States *College Survival* has produced a programmed text to help students to investigate themselves and develop learning skills (Ellis, 1985). In Britain the view was widely held that schools could do more to develop study skills, and within-subject guides were produced. In the vocational sector special attention was given to learning how to learn, since learning disabilities were thought to be a major factor impeding success at this level (FEU, 1981). Advisory notes were produced for college lecturers and students in higher education (Main, 1980). Interest in improving study skills continued (Hartley, 1986).

One aspect of study which received particular attention was note-taking in lectures. In one study the notes taken in first-year technology lectures were photocopied and analysed. A questionnaire was given to the students after three weeks to see what use had been made of the notes. This was followed by a test of factual recall. Every set of notes contained 40% of the information necessary for the test. Quantity and long-term recall seem to have been related. The amount of use made of the notes also correlated highly with test scores. However, the author concluded that the majority of students made little use of their notes. Intention and action were quite different things (Norton, 1981).

In veterinary studies it was found that the proportion of important points omitted from the notes was as high as one-quarter. Handouts did not improve note-taking, although students provided with diagrams labelled them more than those who had to draw their own, and those who did not draw diagrams did not use them to help them to answer examination questions (McDonald and Taylor, 1980). Could this be due to limited spatial ability?

Another study in New Zealand by Collingwood and Hughes (1978) showed that, from pre- and post-course questionnaires, students with no experience of partial handouts move from a position of not perceiving them to be valuable to a preference for full handouts. Also in New Zealand at another university Nye (1978) found that women took more notes than men, although there were no significant differences in their examination results. However, those who took rough notes scored 5.4% lower than those who took full ones, which says a great deal about the method of lecturing and examining.

Locke (1977) obtained data from 161 students in twelve different courses. He found that virtually all the errors in the notes were errors of omission, and, as might be expected, that 'completeness' dropped steadily as the lecture progressed. Completeness was also related to the characteristics of the data presented. Again, it might be expected that new information would cause more complete notes. A significant positive relation was found between completeness and course grades. Other studies suggest that lecture presentation (for example, pauses, pacing) are likely to influence note-taking and memory (Morgan and Puglisi, 1982).

The movement to generalize study skills so that mechanical techniques of studying could be taught was challenged by Gibbs (1979, 1981), then at the Open University. He argued that the theories of learning which teachers use to train students in study methods may be far removed from what they do when they learn. For this reason, they may not be willing or able to take up what is suggested. He argued that directive advice and training could interfere with a student's natural ability to learn. Therefore any approach to learning should begin with where the student is and show him or her what the purposes of the study (goals) are. It should not concentrate on the mechanics of study. This requires that teachers should be clear about their aims and objectives.

Similarly, in relation to formal attempts to improve study patterns Rees and Reid (1977) concluded, from studies of over 400 students at a polytechnic and university in England, that formalized courses are not likely to be as successful as those tehniques which build on the skills students possess and at the same time help students to acquire self-confidence.

As was noted in Chapter 7, the general move in research has been away from institutionally controlled to learner-controlled research, much of which has been due to Entwistle and Marton (Marton *et al.*, 1980) in Britain and Sweden and Sherman (1980) in the United States.

Analysing research from both sides of the Atlantic, Sherman concludes that if students are to manage their own learning they have to recognize their potential for learning, obtain or have a sufficient skills repertoire to handle the learning, possess the skill of judgement with which to evaluate the learning task, match their skills to the tasks, and monitor what they do. All of which is yet another way of describing the cybernetic model of decision-making or the skill morphologies of people at work. Nevertheless, it gives different insights into the issues.

It would seem to support Saupe's view that academic learning skills appear to be most successfully acquired when they are presented in explicit models (Dansegrau, 1979; Day, 1980; Sherman, 1984). As we have seen, there are many such models, among the best known of which is Polya's heuristic for mathematical thinking. Unfortunately it is extremely difficult to get student teachers to explicate these skills when asked so to do. Told to help students acquire problem-solving skills, I have found that the majority of student teachers feel it sufficient to set a problem! Research in the United States and Britain supports the view that if there are to be changes in ways of thinking which are embedded they will only occur if students are exposed to them frequently over a long period of time (Ford, 1980). One-week courses at the beginning of a college career will not suffice. While this supports the views of those who say that it should begin in school, it does not excuse teachers in higher education from designing learning strategies which continue this process of learning skill development.

Learning skill development may be facilitated by the assessment procedures. It is clear from my work that one reason for the response which I had to the demand to develop problem-solving skills could well have been the way in which the question was set. Marton and Säljö (1976) make it clear that students' perceptions of requirements influence the quality of response, and Elton and Laurillard (1979) suggest that the quickest way to change learning behaviour is to change the external environment. These findings give independent support to the view expressed in the first edition of this book in 1977, that the most powerful way of influencing teaching and learning is through the structure of the examination.

The recent work increases our understanding of Saupe's generalization concerning extrinsic and intrinsic motivation, for not only does it help the teacher to understand the factors which contribute to positive motivation but it also reminds them of the elements which demotivate task failure (Kozeki, 1984). It is not merely a question of success breeding success but of enabling success to happen through formative rather than summative assessment.

Entwistle and Wilson (1977) found three groups of students who achieved above average and another which did very badly. They were described as 'fear of failure', 'self-confident and hope for success', 'radical and extroverted', and 'idle and unmotivated'.

Entwistle (1981) defines competence motivation as a positive orientation towards learning created by the repeated experience of successful learning activities. He concludes within his definition of intrinsic motivation McClelland's (1953) concept of achievement motivation as well as perceived interest and relevance. Fransonn (1977) believes that intrinsic motivation is something that the learner finds. Thus intrinsic motivation will occur when the task is related to interest, and this applies to any method of teaching (Hodgson, 1984; Gibbs et al., 1984).

Implicit in the studies of learning style and explicit in the Anglo-Scandinavian work as well as that of Pask (1977) is the fact that students differ in their perceptions of what learning is (see below). It follows from this that they use different strategies. Although it is not clear if these strategies are inherent dispositions, it does seem that there is a range of strategies available, and that those who have high levels of achievement are able to consciously select the skills most appropriate for the attainment of specific objectives. If a person does not have control skills of this kind he or she is likely to perform badly in academic tasks (De Charms, 1968; Lefcourt, 1976). Learners need to be made more versatile. Thus the training programme devised by Kolb for his experiential learning model requires the learner to develop four domain skills. At the same time, it has to be remembered that learners are very idiosyncratic, and Gibbs' view that learners should be helped to understand their own strategies cannot be overlooked lightly.

All of this places an important onus on the teacher who sets the task, and in particular, when this task is for assessment, to ensure that it is well defined in learning-skill terms. It is confirmation of Saupe's dictum that learning occurs best when it is given organization, structure and meaning. To this we now add—in such a way that task and learning skills are matched (Brown, 1978).

From these investigations insight is also obtained into Saupe's axiom concerning reinforcement, for it is found that if students are to learn effectively they must not only reinforce the knowledge content through evaluation but must monitor and evaluate their skills in learning. In this respect the current work on self-assessment (see Chapter 11) is of importance.

This work throws light on the use of the various taxonomies described in Chapters 5 and 6, for they clearly relate to the list of learning skills described by Sherman. Just as students are idiosyncratic, so are teachers. There is a great danger that this is forgotten. Teachers acquire a language of learning with which they become familiar early on: it is soon embedded. They will inevitably select those ideas which they perceive to be of interest and relevant to them. In these circumstances their obligation is to ensure that they understand precisely what their tasks involve and be prepared to explain and elicit strategies from the students which will help the task to be met. A beginning is to remember that many teachers and students perceive the task in terms other than problem-solving, and they are unlikely to get involved in something which is headed 'problem-solving'. The same is true of the phrase 'critical thinking'.

DEPTH AND SURFACE APPROACHES TO LEARNING

Entwistle, who was among the first in Britian to use the Brown–Holtzman study-habits inventory, came to criticize this approach because it led to a tendency to explain performance from the perspective of the lecturer. Thus a poor student is one who is not interested. The approach does not focus on the responsibilities of the institution and its teachers for what is learnt. Therefore he and his colleagues set out to investigate other approaches to learning and became associated with the work of Marton (1976) in Sweden. Together they have had a profound effect on research in higher education in Australia and Britain with their approach to learning styles (Ford, 1981).

In order to discover how students learnt, Marton and Säljö gave them an article to read on which they would be questioned about its content and how they tackled the task. The influence of this approach on Cowan's protocols (Table 32) will be clear.

Several methods were used: in one a text was given to students to read and then they were asked to recount it, answer questions on the content, describing how they had read it and went about remembering its content. On the second occasion they were asked to recall as much as they could of the text. A second revised and enlarged text was given and the procedure repeated. In another investigation a split-group technique was used with independent halves. On the first occasion one half was given questions on particular points in the text, the other half received no guidance. For the second occasion half the group were given instruction as to how they should read while the others were given no instructions. A free recall was requested, and questions were asked about the text immediately after reading and after 65 and 85 days. Students were also interviewed in similar studies who were not in the experiment. An examination was also set. Further variations in technique were used and questionnaires and interviews administered. The samples were 30 first-year students in education and 29 in political science and economics. Marton and Säljö concluded that

> the students who did not get 'the point' failed to do so simply because they were not looking for it. The main difference which was found was whether the students focused on the text in itself or on what the text was about; the author's intention, the main point, the conclusion to be drawn.

They were led to distinguish between two different approaches to understanding which they called deep-surface (related to the students search for meaning) and holistic/atomistic (related to the way the students organized the information in the article for reading).

Marton suggests that, apart from anything else, these are indicative of different perceptions of what is wanted in learning in higher education. For some, 'learning is through the discourse and for others learning is learning the discourse'. Those who adopt the former strategy get involved in the activity while those who take the latter view allow learning to 'happen' to them. It is this group who are surface learners who pay but superficial attention to the text, who are passive, who do not reflect and who do not appreciate that understanding involves effort (to paraphrase Marton).

What we would appear to see is the traditional distinction between active and passive learning which is intrinsically understood by academics even if not explained when they talk about study in depth. Learning through discourse is exactly how Newman (1947 edition) described the effects of university education in *The Idea of a University*.

The technique is open to criticism, for the phenomenology on which it is based is a form of empiricism. By itself it cannot say if and when the levels of consciousness are raised by the 'surface group' (see Chapter 9 on Lonergan). Or does it imply that they are never raised by persons in this group? It might also be objected that the technique depends on reading and therefore neglects reflective thought. Nevertheless, it has shown the care, for example, with which examination questions should be designed and it has also produced other research which supports the general thesis. For example, in Australia studies among senior-year students have suggested that deep-level students were more likely to perceive their courses as encouraging independence in both attitudes and approach to learning and as not being overburdening (Watkins, 1981).

An important issue is whether students can use both depth and surface approaches. One of the early investigations suggested that all students could surface but only some could depth-process (Fransonn, 1977). Later investigations by Ramsden (1979) have suggested that students can do both.

Given the view that learning is the process by which experience develops new and reorganizes old concepts, it would mean that 'surfacing' (if we may call it that) would be an essential strategy in perceptual sampling. The key issue is what triggers the commitment to a particular aspect of the perceptual sample.Within the formal learning context the approach used is likely to depend on their perception of the demands of the context of learning (Laurillard, 1979), and this is a point which is taken up by Wilson (1981).

Entwistle believes that the way instructions are interpreted is an important factor in determining the approach adopted. They create an *intention* to learn in a certain way which determines the level of processing. Wilson (1981) queries this emphasis on intention, and argues that it is the conception of what learning involves which is one of the most important factors affecting the approach the student adopts:

The approach they actually do adopt will depend upon several factors:

First is likely to be the difficulty of the subject matter: some texts can be skimmed over while others can only be understood by systematically setting out the arguments, evidence and conclusions. Second is the interest and importance of the text: a 'set' book will receive a closer look than supplementary reading, but especially if its subject matter appeals to the student. Third may be the student's natural preference of reading in a particular way: the studies so far reported have not really clarified whether there are in fact basic differences in approach or whether the approaches actually used reflect the fourth factor, viz. the student's conception of what it takes to learn complex subject matter.

My own work with examination questions which attempts to relate theory to what was done in practice depended in no small way on student understanding of instructions given during the course (Heywood, 1982, 1984). While it caused certain things to be done by the students, the significant factor in relating theory to practice was that they could stand back from their own opinion in the written papers. The key factor seems to be interpretation, and some students do not respond to combinations of written or spoken instructions in the way anticipated.

Ramsden and Entwistle (1984) developed the Lancaster Approaches to Studying and Course Perceptions Questionnaire to further these investigations. The headings shown in Table 36 indicate that this embraces other theoretical positions. For example, they found that several of the items compared with those in Bigg's Structure of Learning Outcome Inventory (SOLO), and included these in the final version. It derives from an attempt to describe the development of the child in terms of how questions are answered. These levels are:

(1) *Pre-structural*: in relationship to the prerequisites given in the question, the answers are denying, tautological and transductive. Bound to specifics.
(2) *Uni-structural*: the answers contain 'generalizations' only in terms of one aspect.
(3) *Multi-structural*: the answers reveal generalizations only in terms of a few limited and independent aspects.
(4) *Relational*: characterized by induction, and generalizations within a given or experienced context using related aspects.
(5) *Extended abstract*: deduction and induction. Generalizations to situations not experienced or given in the prerequisites to a question.

They also used Hudson's (1970) concept of the syllabus-bound (Sylbs) who work within the confines and structure of the academic framework, while Sylfs are syllabus-free and treat the academic frameworks either as a point of departure or as a curb to their wider academic interest. There are questions as to whether these concepts describe a short-term disparity in styles of adaptation or more deep-seated differences in the case of personality. Wilson argues that Sylbs and Sylfs are likely to have characteristic approaches to study corresponding to their pathologies, although this theory has as yet to be confirmed.

The serialist and holist concepts derive from the work of Gordon Pask. Serialist learners approach a learning task on a step-by-step basis. Holists attempt to seek globally. These strategies reflect broader 'operational' and 'comprehension' learning styles. The former is that aspect of learning concerned with the mastery of procedural details. Operational learners, while picking up rules, methods and details, may not see the subject as a whole. Comprehension learners are concerned to see the topic as a whole, and can describe the internal relationships between various aspects of the topic.

Table 36. Summary of the areas evaluated in the Lancaster Approaches to Studying and Course Perceptions Questionnaire

Approaches to studying
1. Deep approach
2. Use of evidence
3. Relating ideas
4. Intrinsic motivation

A. 5. Meaning orientation
composite of 1, 2, 3, and 4
(Deep approach to studying)

6. Surface approach

7. Syllabus boundness
8. Fear of failure

9. Improvidence
B. 10. Reproducing orientations
composite of 6, 7, 8 and 9

11. Extrinsic motivation
12. Strategic approach
13. Achievement motivation
C. 14. Strategic orientation
composite of 11, 12, 1

15. Comprehensive learning

16. Operation learning

17. Disorganized study
methods
18. Negative attitudes
19. Globetrotting

D. 20. Non-academic orientation
composite of 17, 18 and 19

Course perceptions
21. Good teaching
22. Freedom in learning
23. Workload
24. Openness to students
25. Social climate
26. Formal teaching methods
27. Clear goals and standards
28. Vocational relevance

E. 29. Student-centredness
composite of 21 and 22

F. 30. Control-centredness
composite of 23 − 22

The summary and numbers are mine and not the authors. High scores on A indicate that students understand what they are studying. In contrast, high scores on B mean that students intend only to 'reproduce' what they are going to study. High scores on C represent the grade-getters in other studies. They are obtaining qualifications for employment. Almost the opposite is true of D, where high scores indicate little regard for academic requirements and who have study difficulty related to poor academic performance. E indicates whether students feel that the courses and teaching are presented in an effective way, and D contrasts restricted choice and heavy demands with perceived choice and reasonable pressure.

The fact that it appears to be so all-embracing makes it very appealing to teachers. Haigh (1986) has described how he used it to define the aims of a general systems approach to physical geography and then to evaluate whether they had been achieved. His aims were:

(a) to increase the *meaning orientation* scale. By the end of the course the students should have broken away from compartmentalized thinking and should be more inclined to *relate ideas* from different parts of this course and from other courses. They should be better at assembling and *using evidence* to support their conclusions. They should be more inclined to a deep approach to study.

(b) to reduce reliance on superficial memorization. There should be a reduction in all of the sub-scales of the *reproducing orientation* scale. The scores for the sub-scales: *surface approach, syllabus-boundness* and *improvidence* should be reduced.

(c) to decrease sub-scales such as *fear of failure* and *negative attitudes* and to increase sub-scales such as *good teaching, good social climate,* and *openness to students.*

While the results in terms of the achievement of goals could be said to be disappointing in the sense that many students did not achieve the intellectual leap to general systems theory, the analyses did reveal a number of important findings which would merit further study in conventional courses. In relation to assessment, the initial results suggested that the course had not caused students to adopt a more meaningful approach to study, and that those with a non-academic orientation and disorganized study habits performed significantly poorly on the course. This might be predictable for a conventional course but not necessarily for a novel one. What appeared to have happened is that the stress created by the novel teaching strategy caused the better students to change in a positive direction. It did not benefit the poorer students and may even have confused some. The best indicators of performance were the ability to use evidence to generate conclusions and a strong commitment, and the will to understand and succeed.

Taken together, the investigations reported in this chapter have considerable implications for teachers in higher education. At the very least, there is a great need for them to understand the factors which influence learning. All the investigations reported lead inevitably to the conclusion that there should be variety in assessment, instruction and learning.

The clarification of objectives which such an approach demands may be helped by the use of an inventory which investigates learning styles and is correlated with the assessment procedures in use. Reflection on the results may help the teacher better to understand the impact of the curriculum on students through his or her teaching. The teacher who is seen to be committed to the instructional enterprise is likely to be valued by students.

CHAPTER 9

Learning and the Role of the Teacher

INTRODUCTION

This chapter brings to an end the trilogy of chapters on aspects of assessment related to learning. If learning is to be improved, teachers in higher education will have to participate in the process of learning far more than they have before. This will involve them in fundamental changes in their approach to assessment, curriculum, and instructional design. Each teacher will require a defensible theory of learning, and the starting point for such a theory is examined in the final section of this chapter.

We begin with brief descriptions of some developmental approaches to student learning, including those of Piaget, Perry and Lonergan. Their implications for curriculum and instructional design are considered. Since development and personality are intimately connected, some aspects of personality as it relates to the teaching and learning environment are also studied. An example of the insight which personality indicators can provide instructors about their classes is given. The implications of recent work on learning for the role of the teacher in higher education are considered and complete the chapter.

PERSONAL AND INTELLECTUAL DEVELOPMENT

Most teachers in higher education subscribe to the view that one of its functions is to aid the personal development of the student. However, in reality the subject which they have to take dominates learning, and even in the domain of intellectual development the student is often left to find his own way through the maze. The development which takes place could simply be the outcome of physical and mental maturation independently of teaching, and it is a matter of observation that such maturation differs between individuals. Ultimately, students will, if asked, be able to summarize what happened to them in college.

In Chapter 6 the views of a student about his experience of college were described. Clearly, his development was aided by the circumstances in which he found himself. Without having to do the tasks which were set there would have been no development in understanding of what was sought by those responsible for his education. The question at issue is whether teachers can do anything to assist intellectual development, more especially through the design of assessment. The evidence, some of which is in the preceding chapters, crude though it may be, suggests that they can, but that it demands a knowledge of the theories of learning and development if judgements are to be made about the state of development of a particular student.

There is a variety of developmental theories. Like the lists of objectives, they have both psychological (Bruner, Piaget) and philosophical (Lonergan, White-head) origins. Some are concerned with the student's cognitive ability to handle abstractions (Perry, Piaget), while others relate to the developmental heuristic within subjects and problem-solving (Lonergan, Polya). Whitehead (1932) is generally concerned with the rhythm of learning. The student moves from a stage of romance and curiosity in the world to the study of the grammar of the subject, to emerge into new romances in which the interaction with the grammar brings about a new synthesis. His stages are shown in Table 37.

Table 37. Whitehead's (1932) stages of rhythm in education

(a) *The stage of romance* is the stage of first apprehension. The subject-matter has the vividness of novelty; it holds within itself unexplored connections with possibilities half-disclosed by glimpses and half-concealed by a wealth of material. In this stage knowledge is not dominated by systematic procedure. Such a system as there is must be created piecemeal, *ad hoc....*
(b) *The stage of precision* also represents an addition to knowledge. In this stage, width of relationship is subordinated to exactness of formulation. It is the stage of grammar, the grammar of language, and the grammar of science. It proceeds by forcing on the student's acceptance a given way of analysing the facts, bit by bit. New facts are added, but they are the facts which fit into the analysis....
(c) The final *stage of generalization* is Hegel's synthesis. It is a return to romanticism with added adventure of classified ideas and relevant technique...

Following in the footsteps of Piaget, Lawrence Kohlberg has described a stage theory of moral development. The outlines of some of these different approaches to development are shown in Table 38.

PIAGET'S THEORY OF COGNITIVE DEVELOPMENT

The essence of psychological (cognitive) theories of development is that children have to go through well-defined stages of mental growth before they are able to reason in the abstract. Piaget distinguished three stages of development. These were sensory motor, concrete operations, and formal operations. He also believed that the second stage was divided in two. Up to about the age of seven in the pre-operational stage 'the thought processes that result are "concrete" in the sense that they deal only with objects which can be handled or imagined in concrete form, and not with more abstract materials such as hypotheses or purely verbal propositions', to quote from Wallace's review of concept development in children. After this there is a substage of attainment in which the child begins to develop elementary logical thought structures. In the final stage of formal operations, which begins around the age of 12, the adolescent develops the powers of abstract reasoning.

An important feature of Piaget's theory is the mechanism for change between one stage and the next. Throughout life people *adapt* and *organize*. These operations are promoted by *assimilation, accommodation* and *equilibrium*. The state of equilibrium is a temporary one which constitutes a new point of departure. This would imply that the need to adapt promotes a disequilibrium which becomes an equilibrium when the adaptation has been made. So the same process is undergone in moment-to-moment encounters as well as in the transfer from one stage to another of any development. In this dimension, Hesseling's 'choc des opinions' would seem to be a mechanism which deliberately engenders disequilibrium (see Murray Thomas, 1985, for a discussion of Piaget's uses of the term 'equilibrium').

Like any other theory of development, there are difficulties with Piaget's model. Nevertheless, it is found to be helpful to student-teachers who find that it makes them aware of the entering characteristics which students have. Often they try to teach at a level of abstraction above that of which the students are capable.

Those investigations which have attempted to analyse the level of Piagetian operation among students in higher education have found that many students are not at the level of formal operations when they come to freshman classes. Renner has suggested that as many as 50% of students are at the concrete level, and that this might account for the many drop-outs from higher education in the United States. Of 4500 undergraduate liberal arts students attending an introductory course in astronomy focused on the stage of formal operations, only 21% were thought to be capable of such thinking. (In line with the arguments on spatial ability it was found, as might be expected, that skill in spatial-visualization greatly helped performance (Renner, 1964; Renner and Lawson, 1973).) A study of 800 male and female first-year students in Italy came to similar conclusions (Cinquepalmi, Fogli-Muciaccia and Picciarelli, 1983).

Blanc (1982) has reported that there is a first-year drop-out of 40% from 11 000 students at one American university. It is highest during the first six weeks. A supplemental study programme in reasoning, reading and study skills is provided. Experience shows that there are profound differences between students operating at the concrete and formal stages of the Piagetian model: 50% are at the concrete level on entry.

These and other studies not only indicate the importance of entering characteristics but the fact that even in the constraints of higher education teachers have to cope with what in school education is called 'mixed ability' instruction. This arises in part from the expectations of teachers who are training students to be like themselves.

Phillips (1982), faced with the difficulty that 'if students are not ready they cannot be taught, and if they are ready, they don't need to be taught, proposed that teachers should concentrate on 'consolidation' of the structures which result from an equilibration when that equilibration involves only routine accommodation. That is, if students are to be changed they have to be prepared for change and be challenged to do it.

Table 38. Outline of the stage structures of some theories of development as they relate to learning and instruction

PIAGET (Kohlberg)	WHITEHEAD Stages of Mental Growth	LONERGAN Experiencing and Knowing	LONERGAN Understanding and Knowing	BRUNER Representations (modes) for coping with the environment
Pre-formal operations	ROMANCE	AUTOBIOGRAPHY	PRE-CRITICAL HISTORY Artistic Ethical Explanatory Apologetic Prophetic	ENACTIVE (learning through action)
Concrete operations	PRECISION	BIOGRAPHY	CRITICAL HISTORY Heuristic Ecstatic Selective Critical Constructive	ICONIC (learning through perceptual maps which follow a route from where we are to where we want to be)
Formal operations (handling abstract concepts)	GENERALIZATION	HISTORIOGRAPHY	SECOND LEVEL CRITICAL HISTORY (Professional)	SYMBOLIC (to aid the translation of experience into the word)

PERRY (development in higher education)	SHERMAN (excellence in teaching)	BRUNER — Theory of instruction (method)	
DUALISM	(1) Learning is right or wrong; (2) Concern is with right answer rather than method for obtaining answer.	(1) Telling (little influence on student learning).	Specify experience which most effectively implants in an individual a predisposition to learning.
MULTIPLICITY	(3) Main concern is with methods of learning. Answers perceived as right, wrong, not yet known. (4) Begin to see difference between an opinion and a supported opinion.	(2) Hoping students will learn (directs students to proper materials and information).	Specify ways in which the body of knowledge should be structured so that it can be readily grasped by the learner.
RELATIVISM	(5) Endorse variety. Acquire new capacities for detachment and self-processing. (6) Begin to see the necessity for commitment. Fear being narrow if they make a choice. (7) Make an initial commitment. (8) Experience the implications of commitment.	(3) Transmitting knowledge (learning is influenced if student characteristics are present). (4) Complex interaction which is unique and dynamic (learning influenced by interactions between student, teacher and content).	Specify the most effective sequences in which to present the material to be learned. Specify the nature and pacing of rewards and punishments in the learning and teaching (i.e. evaluation).

There is confusion in the stage theories over the time-scale of operation. The student-teachers who find that their children are not at the stage of formal operations are describing a situation that is subject-language specific. Generally, in regard to life a child may be quite capable of philosophic reasoning, but in their own terms, as Matthews (1980) and others have shown (Chapter 6). Depending on the problem to be solved and the issue to be faced, we bring a set of skills to its solution. There is no reason not to suppose that we do not begin with the concrete before moving to the abstract in very short as well as very long cycles, or that we do not require romance before we can get excited about the grammar. Emphasis on the longer cycles of growth may detract from the arrangements made for teaching and learning in the short run of a classroom period.

If, according to the theory a teacher has chosen, students are found to be at a lower stage of reasoning than the teacher selected for his or her exposition, then in terms of assessment and performance that teacher has a problem.

Two theories which have attracted much attention are those due to Kohlberg and Perry.

KOHLBERG'S THEORY OF MORAL DEVELOPMENT

Kohlberg's scheme is shown in Table 39 (Kohlberg and Turiel, 1971). It has been challenged by other studies, more especially Lyon's (1983), who argues that, in contrast to man's notion of morality as 'having a reason', the woman's sense of morality is a type of 'consciousness', which produces a sensitivity toward others. Caring predominates. These distinctive ways of making moral choices lie on a continuum and are not dichotomous. Moran (1984) has contributed a substantial critique of the theories of Piaget and Kohlberg from the perspective of religious development. Moral development does not just end in stage. It must continue throughout life, otherwise atrophy will occur. The educational journey does not end until death.

PERRY'S THEORY OF DEVELOPMENT IN HIGHER EDUCATION

Perry's (1970) studies of students at Harvard and Ratcliff in the United States led him to propose a nine-stage model of intellectual and ethical development which has proved attractive to many teachers. In this theory a student progresses from a simple dualistic view of life and knowledge, in which absolute answers exist for everything, to relativism, in which knowledge and value judgements are seen as relativistic (position five). Following this, an adjustment is made to the relativistic world, and in the last three stages the student begins to experience commitment, and at first make an initial commitment in an area such as career selection, values and regligious belief. In the ninth position commitment becomes 'an ongoing unfolding activity through which the student's life style is expressed'.

Table 39. Kohlberg's stages of moral development simplified. (Reproduced by kind permission of the author)

---

1. *Stage 0. Premoral stage*

2. *Pre-conventional level*
   Stage 1. The punishment and obedience orientation.
   Stage 2. The instrumental relativist orientation. (Right action consists of that which instrumentally satisfies one's own needs and occasionally the needs of others.)

3. *Conventional level*
   Stage 3. Interpersonal concordance . . . good behaviour is that which pleases or helps others and is approved by them . . .
   Stage 4. Law and order orientation . . . right behaviour consists of doing one's duty, showing respect for authority and maintaining the given social order for its own sake.

4. *Post-conventional, autonomous, or principled level*
   Stage 5. Social contract legalistic orientation . . . right action tends to be defined in terms of general individual rights and in terms of standards which have been critically examined and agreed upon by the whole society . . .
   Stage 6. The universal ethical principal orientation. Right is defined by the decision of conscience in accord with self-chosen ethical principles appealing to logical comprehensiveness, universality and consistency.[a]

---

[a] At this level there is a clear effort to define moral values and principles which have validity and application apart from the authority of the groups or persons holding these principles and from the individuals' own identification with these groups.

It is argued that by the end of their experience of higher education many students do not develop as far as stage four. Higher education impedes student development by the methods of assessment and instruction which it uses. The lecture method reinforces the dualism (right–wrong) of the first two stages. The professor is the authority, the bible, the textbook. The curriculum is received and is reinforced both by the structure of the timetable and the organization of knowledge within the traditional disciplines. In engineering, for example, this leads students away from an understanding of what real-life problems are, i.e. a 'smorgasborg of several subjects' to quote Culver and Hackos (1982). Students, they say, do not learn how to define problems or work through to an open-ended solution. Even at positions three and four of the model they have only a limited ability to evaluate evidence. The solution of real-life problems requires students to operate at higher-order positions.

The implications for instructional and curriculum design are considerable, and there have been several attempts to validate curriculum strategies designed to meet the specifications of the Perry model. The instructional procedures used assume that, for development to take place, dissonance or conflict has to occur if individuals are to alter their perspectives (Widick *et al.*, 1975). For example, in one freshman social science course the instruction emphasized challenges to the students' values and cognitive constructs but within a supportive instructional framework. In the same study a parallel group of students in a humanities and an English course considered the same content but without the cognitive-developmental treatment. Even though the groups of students selected themselves into the different courses, the differences in outcomes were so large as to suggest that the experimental course was having the desired effect (Stephenson and Hunt, 1977).

Another study which provided an instructional procedure appropriate to the dualistic mode of thinking for freshmen together with another strategy appropriate to the relativistic mode of sophomores showed considerable gains from input to output among both groups on an instrument designed to assess development on the Perry scale. The problem is that these changes could have been due to maturation (Miller and Prince, 1978). Lonergan's theory is in contrast, and is considered next.

LONERGAN'S THEORY OF HUMAN KNOWING

Lonergan (1954) believed that human knowing is not a single act but the totality of a number of acts, which include seeing, hearing, smelling, touching, tasting, inquiring, imagining, understanding, conceiving, weighing the evidence and judging. In each cognitional activity there is a basic pattern of operations which belongs to one of four levels of consciousness, and these are summarized in Table 40.

Table 40. Summary of Lonergan's cognitional structure

Levels of consciousness	Principal operations	Operations
1. Empirical	Experiencing	Seeing, hearing, touching, smelling, remembering, imagining
2. Intellectual	Understanding	Inquiring, insight, understanding, formulating, conceiving
3. Rational	Judging	Judging, checking, weighing the evidence, marshalling the evidence (reflective insight)
4. Responsible	Deciding	Evaluating, deliberating, deciding, doing (the good)

Inherent in Lonergan's scheme is the development of a value position. The empirical level operates on the data presented to the senses. All the levels require the person to be attentive, thus the presentation of data requires attention if the level of consciousness is to be raised. Once the data are available, an inquiry is undertaken in order to transform the unknown into the known. This product is called an 'insight'. Understanding involves experience and inquiry in which the data are rearranged as a result of the questions asked and answered about them. This conforms with the definiton of learning given previously. What is being experienced is one's intelligence. To have an insight demands that a person is learning.

Judgements at the rational level should not be made in the absence of experiencing and understanding, for that is to set aside fact. Unfortunately, it is a matter of everyday observation that people make judgements without reflection. The value dimension enters forcefully at this level of consciousness, for operating on the rational is to engage in the philosophic pursuit of truth. It is a level for reflection. At the final level, having reflected on the data, responsibility is experienced through deliberation, evaluation, decision and experience. Lonergan's scheme does not embrace a relativistic approach in the sense emphasized by Perry. His model has been used to devise both lessons and curriculum in religious education (Topley, 1982).

A GENERAL CRITICISM OF THEORIES OF DEVELOPMENT

A general criticism of theories of cognitive development has been made by Bunzl (1978), who has pointed out that there are two possible explanations for someone not thinking like ourselves. Either the person tested agrees with and understands the terms used or the respondent understands the terms differently. If a person does not understand then no measurement is possible. Kohlberg's scheme (see above) may be considered to be a series of shifts in content from psychology to law to morality, and may not therefore represent a set of transformations within the domain of moral thinking. The changes which occur may simply be of subject matter. For a change in stage to be transformational the previous stage has to be dissolved. What is more likely in complex behaviour is that some transformations take place alongside some shifts in subject matter.

It will now be understood that each model of development is a particular perspective on what happens to students within the context of their higher education. Piaget's theory relates in particular to the problem of concept learning, but the other theories mentioned in the previous chapters are equally relevant perspectives. Wilson (1981) has attempted to integrate them into one model, which is shown in Figure 27. In Witkin's terminology complete development is implied by a move from field-dependence to field-independence. The other components of the model which relate to the ideas discussed in Chapter 8 are self-explanatory.

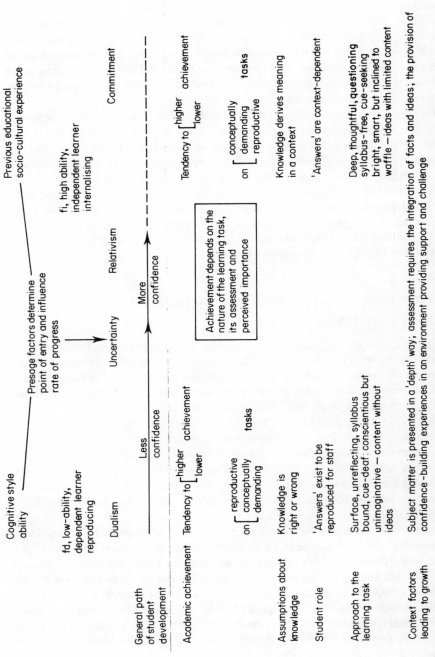

Figure 27. John D. Wilson's developmental model of student learning. (Reproduced from Wilson, J. D. (1981). *Student Learning in ...*

THE LANGUAGE OF SUBJECTS:
THE IMPLICATION OF DEVELOPMENT THEORY
FOR THE CURRICULUM

The language which teachers use is very much bound up with the psychology of development. Oakeshott (1962) wrote that a 'university education is unlike either a school or a "vocational" education, because it is an education in "languages" rather than "literatures" and because it is concerned with the use and management of explanatory languages (or modes of thought) and not prescriptive languages'. By language, Oakeshott meant manner of thinking. It is the distinction between manner of thinking in a subject (for example, poetic imagination) and a poem or a textbook. My purpose in this section is to argue that acceptance of this view is also an acceptance, in part, of a psychology of development, and that there is no real difference between the language of subjects and the demands of cognitive development.

Lonergan (1971) quite specifically applies his theory to the methodology of learning subjects, more especially history, philosophy and theology. His stages for understanding history are called pre-critical, critical and second-level critical (professional) history. The alignment between Whitehead's romance, grammar and generalization is evident, but it is also obvious from what Lonergan has to say about them that they are also movements from the concrete to the abstract.

On pre-critical history Lonergan writes:

> Its vehicle is narrative, an ordered recital of events. It recounts who did what, when, where, under what circumstances, from what motives, with what results. Its function is practical ... it is never just a narrative of bald facts. It is *artistic*, it selects, orders, describes ... it is *ethical*, it not only narrates, but also apportions praise and blame. It is *explanatory*, it accounts for existing institutions by telling of their origins and development and by contrasting them with alternative institutions found in other lands. It is *apologetic*, correcting false or tendentious accounts of the people's past, and refuting the calumnies of neighbouring peoples... It is *prophetic*, to hindsight about the past there is joined foresight in the future and there are added the recommendations of a man of wide reading and modest wisdom.

A little later in the same essay he described the process of critical history thus:

(1) *Heuristic*: The bringing to light of relevant data.
(2) *Ecstatic (imaginative)*: The leading of the inquirer out of his original perspectives and into perspectives proper to his object.
3) *Selective*: Selects from the totality of data those relevant to the understanding achieved.
4) *Critical*: Remove from one use or context to another the data that might otherwise be thought relevant to present tasks.
5) *Constructive (synthesis)*: Data are selected and knotted together by the vast and intricate web of interconnecting links that cumulatively come to light as understanding progresses.

Within each stage there is a process of development just as there is development between the two stages. Of greater significance is the idea that the methods of two stages are different. Pre-critical history is dependent on the narrative method. It is a stage of romance, and therefore one of motivation.

To grasp the role of history in understanding the social and cultural process one may possibly begin with existential history, i.e. with one's self, a view which is underlined by the French historian, Bloch (1954) who wrote:

> For here, in the present, is immediately perceptible that vibrance of human life which only a great effort of the imagination can restore to the old texts. I have many times read, and I have often narrated, accounts of wars and battles. Did I truly know, in the full sense of that word, did I know from within, before I myself had suffered the terrible sickening reality, what it meant for an army to be encircled, what it meant for a people to meet defeat? Before I myself had breathed the joy of victory in the summer and autumn of 1918 ... did I truly know what was inherent in that beautiful word?

Through autobiography and biography a student can be shown the problems of self-evaluation, of the third person and personal beliefs, of fragmentary data and of uncertainty.

The biographical method overlaps with critical history, for it is applied to the community. It is a process which 'proceeds from the data made available by research, through imaginative reconstruction and cumulative questioning and answering towards related sets of concepts so that there is seen a developing and/or deteriorating unity constituted by co-operation, by institutions, by personal relations, by functioning and/or malfunctioning good or order, by a communal realization of originating and terminal values and disvalues'.

The psychology of development highlights the importance of method in both the development of skills in a subject as well as the limitations of those particular skills at the particular stage of development which a student has reached. It demands a theory of instruction to match its theory of learning. Thus the teacher is required to begin by specifying the experiences which will effectively implant in an individual a predisposition toward learning and to design assessment procedures which will evaluate what was learnt.

An Application of the Perry Model to the Curriculum

Mention has already been made of adaptations which have been made of particular curricula to fit them to Perry's model. The implications of Kneffel-kamp's adaptation for English are shown in Figure 28.

Culver and Hackos (1982) were very critical of engineering curricula because, as we saw above, they did not encourage open-ended problem-solving similar to that which engineers would have to face in their careers. However, they appreciated that the introduction of open-ended problem-solving could make the students unsure of themselves because of the loss of structure. Therefore they proposed that the traditional subjects should be the tools for problem-solving while the 'trunk' of the course should be the problem-solving activities designed to bring students along the stages of Perry's model (Figure 29). In this way content and process become linked. A similar approach, but from different premises, has been proposed earlier by a group of British engineers, who suggested that engineering synthesis and analysis could be taught by means of the project method. An example of their approach is shown in Figure 30 (Heywood *et al.*, 1966). The organization is quite different to a traditional course. An important problem for the teachers would be to ensure that the key concepts/principles in the matrix are understood in such a way that they will be applied to radically different problems. Culver and Hackos felt that some of the problems arising from the dissonance that such courses create can be overcome if behavioural objectives are specified so as to show that the complexity lies in the subject matter rather than the organization of the course.

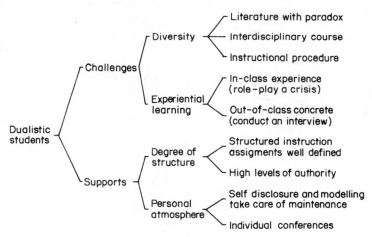

Figure 28. A representation of Knefflekamp's (1974) model of course design as described by R. S. Culver and J. T. Hackos. (Reproduced by kind permission of the authors and the Editors of *Engineering Education*)

One response in the United States to the theory of development has been demands from students akin to those of Fawthrop (Chapter 1) for courses and laboratories on such topics as human potential, group processes, communication skills, non-verbal communication, etc. However, Fincher (1985) argues that quasi-curriculum solutions in critical thinking, personal adjustment and speed reading did not find adjustment and speed reading did not find 'a suitable place in the curriculum *per se*, and each has been subject to cycles of erosion and rediscovery'. As we saw in Chapter 6, critical thinking skills have to be developed within subjects. Transfer of learning is not easy to achieve.

Moreover, like learning skills, it is unlikely that development can be speeded up, as attendance at such courses seems to imply. It requires a sustained attack. Wilson's model suggests that if learning skills are acquired over a long period of time, aided by assessment and learning carefully designed to meet specific objectives, then development will take place and the goals of instruction for development achieved.

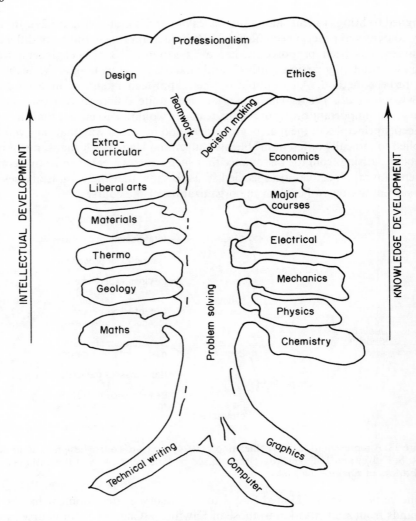

Figure 29. An alternative model of technical education which takes into account theories of intellectual development described by R. S. Culver and J. T. Hackos. (Reproduced by kind permission of the authors and the Editors of *Engineering Education*)

LEARNING, PERSONALITY AND THE TEACHER

It is clear that many factors contribute to learning and development, and not least among them is personality. In Chapter 4, Furneaux's (1962) pioneering study in this field was described. It seemed that introverts would tend to do better in examinations than extroverts, given existing strategies. Similar tests led to Wankowski's (1973) model of student motivation and to the conclusion that the 'problem of student wastage is largely the problem of teaching'. In the United States the idea that students who persist in engineering might have different personality characteristics to those that do not was put by Elton and Rose (1974) as well as by Wankowski. That examination success is not simply a matter of introversion was demonstrated by Entwistle and his colleagues by the fact that a group of students whom they described as 'radical and extroverted' achieved above-average degree results (Cowell and Entwistle, 1971). Once again the principle seems to be that 'in certain circumstances some students will . . .'

Resources / Operations	Energy (a)	Space (b)	Force (c)	Materials (d)	Men (e)
(1) Forms and properties	Heat: CO2: effective temperature				
(2) Location and acquisition	In wings – off main power units				
(3) Measurement			Compressor characteristic pressure/flow/temp.		
(4) Control		Navigators, pilots passenger, steward, compartments			
(5) Transformation and conversion	Cooling: heat removal from fluid			Filters in order to remove dust, etc.	Number of passengers and crew
(6) Transmission		Recirculated air for heat balance	Method of recirculation	What has to be recirculated? What has to be lost ?	

(a)

	Energy (a)	Space (b)	Force (c)	Materials (d)	Men (e)
(2) Location and acquisition	☐	Wings	Torque shaft	Normal steels except for blading	Design organization of sub-contract
(3) Measurement	Kerosene fuel and ram air	Determined by available space left in wing and flow and pressure of ram air	☐		

(b)

Figure 30. An example of the application of a matrix approach to curriculum design in engineering based on the problem of ventilating an aircraft. (Adapted from Turner, B. T. (1958). High altitude passenger flying with special reference to air treatment. *J. J. Inst. E.*, **68**, 219; in Heywood *et al.* (1966)). (b) is an example of the expansion of items (2) and (3) in (a)

One interesting study of students in the United States, where there is interest in the effects of the university environment on student performance, investigated the personality characteristics of students in halls of residence (Miller and

Prince, 1978). The Omnibus Personality Inventory, which was also used by Elton and Rose, was employed in an investigation which examined the interpersonal effects of one student on another in shared rooms. The sample was structured for similar cumulative achievement and ability patterns. It was found that personality difference or similarity could influence cumulative achievement among students of different ability levels. A low-ability student with a personality profile similar to that of a high-ability one in the same room may benefit through such grouping in terms of achievement. At the same time, the highly able student may be adversely affected if he or she has to room with a low-ability one with a dissimilar personality profile (Ainsworth and Maynard, 1975). Several American studies support the view that a peer context (in residence) of high achievement has a unique, positive influence on individual achievement (Pascarella and Terenzini, 1982), and there has been one study which suggests that residential units designed to foster study can be more beneficial than ordinary residence units (Blimling and Hample, 1979) (see also Pascarella, 1985).

In the context of this general study of assessment and given the difficulties which there have been with personality tests together with the sometimes low correlations obtained, the teacher might question the validity of their use.

Several inventories have received a lot of attention. One of these is the Myers–Briggs indicator (Briggs and Myers, 1976; Thompson and Borello, 1986). Its potential as an aid to instructional and assessment design is demonstrated by a practising teacher, Philip Rutsohn, who examined in a business education seminar programme the idea that personality plays an important part in the determination of a student's responsiveness to a particular learning technique. Admittedly, the sample was very small, but the ability of the instrument together with other assessments to provide profiles is evidently powerful.

In this class (for which there was no textbook) the majority of the learning resulted from group interaction. The students were not told that they were the subject of research, which was conducted around the following design:

(1) Students took the Myers–Briggs Indicator;
(2) At the end of each class they recorded their beliefs about their learning for that particular class;
(3) The instructor recorded behavioural patterns of each student during the classroom period.

During the course four different instructional strategies were used. These were an unstructured seminar, an assigned structure, an assigned structure with assigned group leaders, and the instructor as group leader. In an assigned structure the group was provided with rules of order. They were assigned to a particular group, and the leaders emerged informally. Each group was given the opportunity to present and defend their findings in front of the whole class. The instructor actively participated by asking questions after the group had presented their positions, summarized the class consensus, and commented on the problems. When the instructor acted as group leader the class formed one large group and the instructor was very directive.

Rutsohn drew up profiles of personality versus student preference for class type and observed behaviour. For example, a student labelled by the Myers–Briggs indicator as introverted, intuitive, feeling and perceptive was profiled for Assigned Group with Emerging Leadership as follows:

> Did not feel that this technique was satisfactory. His major criticism was the lack of monitoring and guidance in the specific areas for discussion. An inordinate amount of time was spent on irrelevant ideas. This severely limited the time to concentrate on solving the problem.

Contrast this with another student profiled for Assigned Group with Emerging Leadership who was classified as extraverted, sensing, thinking and judging. This student found the learning experience:

> Quite rewarding. The involvement factor was quite high and the group interaction most rewarding. This individual preferred a structure which was informal and lacking an assigned leader.

The four profiles described by Rutsohn are summarized in Table 41. Even within a very small sample it shows that there is no one instructional technique preferred by a particular personality type. Rutsohn suggests that in selecting a learning technique the instructor could benefit from a profile of the class personality. Perhaps it would be necessary to try several techniques during the course in order to reach all the personalities in the class. Student-teachers in my studies found that techniques designed to encourage divergent thinking release much new information about the pupils in their classes.

One of the most interesting studies in recent years was by Freeman and colleagues (1982), who related the personality characteristics of teachers to those of their students. In this case the respondents were postgraduate medical students preparing for general practice and the teachers their instructors. The test used was the Eysenck Personality Inventory, and 76 trainees and 76 teachers participated. Among the measures with which the Inventory was compared were a Multiple-choice Questionnaire and a Modified Essay Question test (see Chapter 13). It was found that between pre- and post-course tests there was a significant correlation with personality variables of their teachers and the 25 students who showed the most change in MCQ scores. However, no such relationship was observed with 25 students who recorded the least change in MCQ and MEQ scores. This study supported other enquiries which showed a consonance of personality variables between teachers and trainees, and suggests that in this kind of teaching situation it might be possible to match instructors and students.

Freeman's study relates to the concept of the person/environment fit. That is, academic success may depend on the degree of fit which the student experiences with the environment. The studies by Tinto and others on wastage (see Chapter 2) are also based on this concept, which has its origins in the theories of Lewin

Table 41. Relationships between personality type, instructional strategy and leadership role in a business studies class. (Adapted from Rutsohn (1978))

Personality type	Unstructured learning experience	Assigned group Emerging leadership	Assigned group Assigned leader	Instructor as group leader
Extraverted, sensing thinking, judging	Excellent learning experience	Quite rewarding	Good learning experience. Restrictive structure	Perceived as valid learning experience
Introverted, sensing thinking, perceptive	Perceived as fruitful	Responded positively	Learning experience minimal	Best technique
Extraverted, intuitive feeling, perceptive	Viewed quite favourably	Did not like structure as a learning technique	Satisfactory[a] learning but believed group too small	Best of all structures
Introverted, intuitive feeling, perceptive	Completely unsatisfactory	Not satisfactory	Excellent learning experience	Excellent learning experience

[a] This person was elected group leader.

(1936). Studies in the 1960s led to the view that the relationship is rather complex. Using a variety of measures, Pace and Baird (1966) derived scales to measure the Intellectual/Humanistic/Aesthetic press (IHA), and from these they concluded that the strength of the association between needs–press congruence was moderated by personality requirements.

The reality of most teaching situations is such as to prevent the one-to-one luxury. However, taken together, the work on learning indicates the need for calculated variety in assessment and instructional techniques in courses. It also suggests that such calculations will depend on a much greater understanding of pedagogy than in the past.

ASSESSMENT, INSTRUCTION AND THE ROLE OF THE TEACHER IN HIGHER EDUCATION

There is evidence of much experimentation by teachers with techniques and theories. Rutsohn's work is a case in point. Nevertheless, it is small compared with the magnitude of the criticisms which research in teaching and learning in higher education implicitly level against the system.

In a situation where no formal training is required and where there are beliefs about the 'rightness' of what is done a start can only be made if teachers evaluate the position that they are at in terms of research that is available. It is an exercise in epistemology, for, as Shulman (1970) says about the debate over the merits of discovery and expository teaching, 'it is much more than a mere disagreement concerning pedagogical policy'. It can, he says,

> best be understood in terms of certain basic controversies relating to the manner in which *anything* becomes known. These issues of the nature of knowledge and the knowing process are the domain of epistemology.

For example, MacMahon (1988) has evaluated recent development in learning in the light of underlying theories of knowledge. He argues that the new approaches depend on an 'active' as opposed to a 'passive' view of learning. Passive learning, a term which he derives from Holloway (1987), is based on a static conception of knowledge of reality which has to be commuted in its present form to the learner. In the extreme, it can be learned passively by rote, association and conditioning. MacMahon writes:

> Underlying these theories of knowledge are two distinct philosophies of man. A theory of knowledge which views facts as objective reality is related to a static concept of the universe and a consequent concept of man as reactive, formed and shaped by the world around him. Alternatively a theory of knowledge which proposes that facts are contextually dependent is related to a dynamic concept of the universe in which changes occur depending on one's perspective. Consequently man is seen as creative, acting upon, interpreting and bestowing meaning on perceived reality. In the first of these approaches learning is concerned with the acquisition, retention and recall of factual information, the meticulous analysis of such data for logical consistency, and the drawing of logical implications and

conclusion. In the alternative approach learning is concerned not merely with facts and their logic, but also with understanding these facts, ascribing meanings and interpreting them in the light of one's own experience, with the result that, on occasions, one comes to a totally new understanding of oneself or one's world.

If there is difference between the two, then it lies in the phrases in italics. I suspect that many in the 'static' category would claim to achieve what is in the dynamic one. Nevertheless, the two categories are apparent in the different approaches to the curriculum and instruction observed in institutions of higher education.

MacMahon argues that, in the dualist concept of knowledge, surface processing, serialist and operation approaches are predominantly related to a theory of knowledge which sees factual knowledge as absolute and unchanging. On the other hand, a relativistic concept of knowledge, depth-processing, holist and comprehension approaches relate to a theory of knowledge which stresses the understanding and meaning achieved by the individual. He goes on to argue that both trends are evident in learners, although some may tend toward a more relativistic concept than others. It is these, he suggests, who will be more capable of dealing with uncertainty.

One of the strange features of research in this tradition is that no-one suggests that students should, as a necessary part of general education, be faced with the problem of knowledge. It is assumed that by the time they reach university they will understand what knowledge is. My experience is that student-teachers in their junior freshman year simply cannot grasp that there is such a problem. If they could, would they take a different approach to learning? I take it that they would, although their disposition to learning might not change, because the way in which they arrive at the ownership of knowledge is something that is only partly related to learning style.

If it is important that students should come to a view of the nature of knowledge it is equally so that teachers should be aware of the implications of their own positions. It is difficult to see how change can be evaluated and implemented except from an instructor's present standpoint. Moreover, it is equally important for institutions to appreciate that they create the press in which change takes place. Some institutions and departments may make it impossible for anything other than a teacher-directed model of lecture presentation to take place. MacMahon argues that institutions which are mechanistically organized and relatively 'closed' as systems are less likely to be open to change than those which are more 'open' and organically structured for vertical and lateral responsibility.

Unfortunately, as Kloss (1987) has pointed out, many instructors are entangled in metaphors about higher education which influence their perceptions of how students learn and thus their methods of teaching. Bruner (1986) believes that these metaphors are influenced by a cultural tendency which views knowledge as intact and complete and which has to be transmitted by those who know to the ignorant. The consequences of this view are (1) that learners are regarded as beings who have to be changed, and (2) that institutions as well as the individuals in them acquire their own metaphors which reinforce each other's views about how they should be organized as well as how the task of education should be accomplished. If students are drilled and continually tested the task of helping them to become autonomous learners is made all the more difficult (Abercrombie, 1980).

For individuals to change their metaphorical systems new metaphorical concepts have to be introduced (Lakoff and Johnson, 1980). Thus instructors will only change their metaphors if they can be persuaded that other positions are possible. One possible starting point is with the four instructional models which Tracy and Schuttenberg (1986) derived from a study of literature on adult learning. They lie on a continuum, the ends of which clearly relate to the two philosophical dispositions described by MacMahon. The four models are:

(1) Instructor-direction of both the *what* and *how* of instruction;
(2) Instructor-direction of the *what*: collaboration on the *how*;
(3) Instructor/learner collaboration on the *what*; instructor-direction on the *how*;
(4) Instructor/learner direction collaboration on both the *what* and the *how*.

The investigation and those of others suggest that adults are likely to choose the first model, because that is the model with which they are familiar. It is Bruner's metaphor, described above. Adults may come to feel that classes directed by the instructor represent the expected roles of both the instructor and the learner. Certainly, young undergraduates would seem to have this set.

It may provide an optimal learning environment for students with low levels of conceptualization. This is what I have found student-teachers come to believe about low-ability pupils in schools when they compare their performance in expository and guided conditions, in spite of evidence to the contrary. The point has been made that persons who require a well-structured environment may become rigid in a system with too many options. Such persons may not be helped, for example, if there are too many questions on an examination paper.

The fact that pupils in school are thought to have these characteristics suggests that some students in higher education will require their courses to be highly structured, since they bring that metaphor with them to higher education (Gruber, 1973; Kloss, 1987). The second model requires an agreement with the students about the method of teaching. It assumes that learners are capable of understanding their own learning styles.

Tracy and Schuttenberg suggest that the methods with which this model is associated are very suitable for teaching specific skills (for example in 'interviewing' in management courses). Some students may learn best 'by observing others carry out the process, others by seeing themselves on videotape practising the skills, and others by gathering samples of good interview questions'.

The collaborative-instructor directed model is also used with skill-learning. It is particularly relevant to adult learning, where a student enrols on a course to achieve a specific goal. The instructor has to incorporate the student's needs into the course objectives and content. Some authorities argue that this is the most appropriate approach for the in-service education of teachers. Neither this nor the *what* and *how* collaborative model remove the ultimate responsibility for course-effectiveness from the instructor. It does require that, at some early stage, students are helped to understand their own learning styles.

Tracy and Schuttenberg's model was based on studies of adult learners. It will be seen that it applies equally to any cognitive developmental model of learning. To achieve the changes which the Perry model requires of undergraduates during their university career would require that many teachers make substantial changes in their modes of instruction and thus in their metaphors.

Sherman and his colleagues (1987) have argued that teachers who focus on teaching their discipline as well as its content may develop through stages that reflect increasing awareness of action strategies which will allow them to accommodate an increasingly complex view of themselves as decision-makers *vis-à-vis* their instructional mission. Excellence, they argue, is a concept which is developmental. They suggest four stages in the development of excellence in teaching:

(1) Teaching is telling;
(2) Teaching is hoping students will learn;
(3) Teaching is transmitting knowledge;
(4) Teaching is a complex interaction which is unique and dynamic (see Table 38).

The similarity between this model and that of Tracy and Schuttenberg is evident. Just as Tracy and Schuttenberg argue that the advantages of their models are that they recognize the formal role which instructors have to play in the institution but, at the same time, they allow adult learners to be involved more or less directly in the decisions regarding the instructional process, so Sherman and his colleagues would say the same of college teachers and their students.

Given that many undergraduates are able to pursue dissertations and projects of their own choosing, and that in some instances they are able to assess themselves, there are clearly moves in college education toward this end. Assessment and instructional techniques may be regarded as resources which will help the instructor to evaluate, and, if necessary, to change his or her approaches to teaching and learning. Chapters 10–12 examine the assessment techniques available and their potential for obtained prescribed objectives of learning.

CHAPTER 10

Written Examinations and Assignments (Content, Structure and Marking)

INTRODUCTION

This and Chapters 11 and 12 are primarily concerned with techniques of assessment. For convenience, the term 'practical' is taken to embrace aurals, orals, seminars, role-playing, etc., in addition to laboratory practicals, field-work and projects. A section on profiling follows the discussion of projects and a complete chapter is devoted to objective testing.

In this chapter the concern is with written answers and open-book and prior-notice methods of assessing such answers. These answers may be long (essay) or short. Particular attention is paid to the short-answer technique called the Modified Essay Question (MEQ), commonly used in medicine.

The issue of essay marking and its reliability is considered from two perspectives, those of the marker on the one hand, and the perception of students, on the other. The need for careful design of questions is reinforced by the fact that students will tend to do what they perceive a question will tell them to do.

Marking schemes should reflect the objectives sought and will vary as the purposes differ (for example, narrative, role-playing, creative thinking, critical thought). The schemes discussed here relate in particular to creative thought, and, as such, the discussion here is an extension of those sections on critical thinking in Chapter 6. Differences between problem-solving and the application of critical thought to problem-solving will be seen in the discussion on the modified essay question.

LITERACY AND NUMERACY

The levels of literacy and numeracy of entrants to universities and colleges in the United States are of particular concern (Call, 1982; Miller, 1985; White, 1985). Even Ivy League institutions find it necessary to run remedial courses (Callas, 1985) and the literature abounds with the descriptions of these. Iyasere (1984) has called for minimum requirements to be defined, and expresses these in a statement of common goals for courses in composition which might be similar to those in Table 42.

Table 42. Suggestions for common goals in language usage in higher education. (From Iyasere, (1984). *Improving College and University Teaching*, **32**, (4), 173–9.) Reprinted with permission of the Helen Dwight Reid Educational Foundation. Published by Heldref Publications, 4000 Albemarle St., N.W., Washington, D.C. 20016. Copyright © 1984.

By the end of a term of instruction in basic composition the student should be able to:

1. Control English grammar, usage, and syntax.
2. Spell English words and use them appropriately.
3. Punctuate according to accepted conventions.
4. Employ concrete illustrations (avoid abstraction).
5. Use a topic sentence as the basis for a coherent paragraph.
6. Create a minimum of one paragraph showing competence in all of the above areas.
7. State the thesis of an essay and develop that thesis appropriately
8. Demonstrate the ability to use various modes of paragraph development.
9. Organize at least five coherent paragraphs into a coherent essay on a single subject.
10. Use transitions appropriately and effectively.
11. Demonstrate ability to work with all rhetorical modes (definition, example, process, etc.).

By the end of the second term of instruction in basic composition, the student should be able to:

1. Use a variety of sentence structures.
2. Use exact and concise words and phrases.
3. Use logical development throughout an expository paper.
4. Use logical development throughout a persuasive paper.
5. Present appropriate details, examples, definitions.
6. Analyse the nature of a potential audience and use a style that will appeal to that audience.
7. Use basic library research topics.
8. Abstract important information from sources and take useful notes.
9. Outline, draft, write and edit a persuasive college-level term paper.
10. Document a research paper using a recognized form of documentation.
11. Identify and avoid plagiarism.

In Britain there was equal concern about the teaching of English, and a committee was set up in 1987 to look at the school curriculum. It has always been assumed that students going to university would have the minimum competencies described in Iyasere's list, although an enquiry by Hewitt (1967) suggested that many students in the science area would fail school English if they had had to take the O level examination. As far as Iyasere's second term is concerned, there is little doubt that some students in England and Ireland experience study difficulties in these areas, as the research reports referred to in Chapter 9 indicate.

The College Entrance Examination Board has drawn attention to the poor reliability and validity of tests and suggested how better tests might be devised (Breland, 1983). The Educational Testing Service has also been active and has produced a set of guidelines in this area. It is interesting to note that they advocate as many as three scorers for their programmes. Multiple-judgements, they believe, are better than one, and, like objective tests, they believe that pre-testing is important, for it enables the weaknesses in a topic to be spotted. A highly selective essay test might find 20 minutes for its writing sufficient. There is a need to put standards on paper (ETS).

Another experiment was conducted among a small group of freshman students who had been enrolled on computer-assisted language courses. The program presented information, responded to answers and evaluated student input with a programmed response. Pre- and post-tests were given of sentence structure, error analysis and sentence types used in written compositions. Although there were few significant differences between the experimental and control group, those that there were favoured the experimental one (Evans, *et al.*, 1966).

These requirements for language capability should not be confused with Hirsch's (1987) demand for cultural literacy. His book is far more concerned with general education and the knowledge that is important in general education. It has many similarities with a study by Richmond in 1963 in Britain, which tested such knowledge.

Some interest has been stirred by American and then British studies of the influence of Latin in learning English. There is the suggestion that when less-able students learn Latin they increase their lexical bar, which in turn may lead to greater fluency in English (Corson, 1982; Masciantonio, 1977).

In higher education in Britain the essay is a standard form of examining. Nevertheless it is widely used in the United States, and whereas in Britain it was the major vehicle in written examinations it is now increasingly used for assignments which range from one or two to 30 pages (variously called projects, dissertations, minor theses, etc.). The reasons for these changes have been documented in Chapter 4.

We saw in Chapter 3 that essay examinations tended to be unreliable, and the evidence for this continues to abound (Byrne, 1979; Edwards, 1979; Ford, 1977). An interesting variation of the standard type of reliability study was reported from the University of Keele, which attempted to relate examiner-personality to marking. The particular inventory used was the Eysenck Personality Questionnaire, which gives scores for Extroversion and Neuroticism and is accompanied by a lie score (Branthwaithe *et al.*, 1981). The investigators found that the marks on the essay were unrelated to any of the personality correlates but were positively related to the lie scale. This raises concern about the nature of staff–student interactions as they are exposed in marking, especially when the candidates are known to the assessor.

One act of despair reported by Bell (1980) arose from a survey of 388 social science students, who wrote an essay on one of ten topics. They were marked by 13 assessors, who each scored two or three topics. Taking all the limitations into account, the investigator concluded that the differences between them were such that the only action which could be taken would be to reduce the weighting of the award for essays. Undoubtedly, the perceptions which staff have of the purposes of study in their subjects are likely to influence their perceptions of what marks should be given. There have been occasional newspaper articles in Britain which have reported that those who return scripts with a certain ideological bias in the literary and social subjects do better than those who do not.

Hake and Andrich (1975) make an important contribution to the debate about teacher-marking, for they argue that *the grader is creating the essay in much same way as its writer*. Their thesis about marking is based on this assumption as well as the view that the abstract generalization of the whole (in this case, the essay) generates its own parts:

> We assume that teachers or graders have a conceptualization of the essay as a whole; therefore, they, when reading an essay, expect an integrated whole with meaningful and logical connections in the writing, paragraphs, sentences, syntactical, and phonological structures. If the concept of the essay as a finished product suggests that the essay is made up of integrated parts, then the whole essay should have harmony among its parts. Because breaks in harmony stand out, flaws should be the conspicuous feature for the reader.

They argue that graders notice blocks or flaws in the communication from the student and correct them by fitting it to their concepts of the correct:

> We must be aware that there are many ways to correct a flaw in language. The way the grader decides to correct the flaw will affect the way he classifies the flaw and even if or when he will perceive another flaw.

They suggest an observation scheme for graders which has four hierarchically ranked dimensions:

(1) Essay continuity and organization, relationships independent of symbol. For example:
  (a) 'The statement has a meaningless or ambiguous relationship among its components because (i) an incorrect or inconsistent definition is included, (ii) a term for which no definition has been offered or implied is included ... etc.'
  (b) 'An objective usage flaw because of (i) an incorrect comparative or superlative, (ii) no comparative or superlative ... etc.'
  (c) 'A semi-colon (i) used incorrectly, (ii) omitted ... etc.';

(2) Statement of paragraph continuity; transformation to symbol;
(3) Mechanics and usage transformation among symbols;
(4) Punctuation inflectional or referential; signals among symbols.

The resultant scheme is very elaborate, but its advantage is that it should help students to construct better essays. The scheme is designed to, first, assist the marker to recognize the components of the essay, their relationships and functions in respect of each other, and second, to assist the marker in the grading of flaws within those specific dimensions. According to their theory, the more flaws there are in dimension (1), the more there will be in the other three dimensions.

Hake and Andrich claim only to have scratched the surface of the problem and have therefore undertaken other investigations. Nevertheless, they say that if:

> ... teaching composition is to be considered a professional activity, it must move closer to the concerns of rhetoric and language and away from excessive attention to correctness. We claim that if these concerns are taught, correctness will be a result and what is important is the sequence of invention, arrangement, organization and style.

Their views serve once again to emphasize the need for a correspondence between course and assessment objectives.

Notwithstanding the mass of candidates in the middle of the ability range, the problem remains. Whatever they do, it seems to be extremely difficult to differentiate one from another. There is no doubt that many students of all levels of ability experience difficulty in writing essays, and it is with this aspect as a function of marking that the second part of this discussion is concerned.

THE MARKING OF ESSAYS AND PROBLEM-SOLVING EXAMINATIONS

There is no reason to suppose that because essays are marked during a course the assessment is any more reliable than it would be in a terminal examination using the same question. At the same time, criticisms of essay examinations should not overshadow the positive role that these have in the testing of important skills (for example, the ability to write narrative history, to synthesize historical material or to write creatively). How, then, can their marking be improved?

First, examiners must have in mind the difficulties inherent in the marking of essay examinations. Second, great care should be taken in question design. Third, it follows from the study mentioned above as well as those of Geisinger (1980) that the assessors should be aware of their own prejudices, and that these may not only relate to content but to grammatical presentation. Some examiners bother about spelling and grammar, others do not (Marshall and Powers, 1969; Chase, 1979). Some are happy if the meaning is clear and justify their approach on the grounds that one cannot expect students under stress to perform perfectly. There is no doubt that scripts sometimes show evidence of stress. It may also be that the length of a script influences assessment (Hall and Daglish, 1982). My own experience is that an overlong script poses problems when one is tired and/or when it is difficult to read.

For all these reasons, it is suggested that markers should prepare detailed marking schemes which detail the content and skills to be assessed and indicate the balance between the two. There is a danger of 'drift' in the marking, and such a dictate reminds the examiner from time to time that this can happen.

Formal schemes also take into account the 'fudge' factor in written examinations, which is the equivalent of 'guessing' in objective tests. It may be due to verbosity, poor writing or a combination of both. Little is known about assessor-reliability as a function of tiredness when marking large numbers of scripts.

Some kind of structured marking scheme would therefore seem to be necessary. The success of such schemes is likely to depend on the clarity of objectives and the extent to which the questions are specifically designed to meet these. In this way a high degree of similarity may be obtained between answers either in respect of style, or content or both.

Table 43. Iliffe's guide for the marking of essays (Iliffe and Heywood (eds), 1966)

80	Outstanding answer: shows independent reading and thinking.
70	Best possible organization of all expected material.
60	Well organized use of most major points.
50	Sensible use of some major points.
45	Clear signs of understanding, but material thin.

(pass)
40	Some relevant material but incomplete grasp.
30	Not an answer to the question set, but shows some understanding of the general field.
20	Very muddled, but shows some understanding of the general field.
10	Poorly organized and almost completely lacking in relevance.

Various schemes have been suggested which might improve marking. I have used one suggested by Iliffe (1966) to try to improve the number of first-class marks awarded (Table 43). While I have found it a valuable aid in marking university examinations, I still discovered that I tended to mark towards the centre of the scale. It seems as though there is always that essay which I saw last year (or the year before that) which was just that little bit better than those in the present pile. Bias of this kind may play a large part in the reluctance of examiners in the humanities to produce a wider dispersion (i.e. one which approximates to the normal curve). One thing is clear; the good scripts usually stand out from the rest, as do the poor (Hall and Daglish, 1982).

Another difficulty with this scheme is that it does not take into account every eventuality. One procedure which I have used is to select, say, ten scripts from the bundle of 140 or so, mark them and add notes to the scheme and then mark the main bundle and revise the ten. Recent studies in the United States also suggest that the ten scripts should be re-assigned to the batch and re-marked. This would mean that no marks should be put on the script in the first round (Mitchell and Anderson, 1986).

I have also used content lists alongside the Iliffe scheme. There is not time to use them in detail with every essay, but if they are regularly consulted they seem to provide both a check and a balance. I have also employed a shorthand version of the project-marking scheme for history for long essays (see Chapter 11). The scheme was divided into two. Part I gave up to 15 marks for organization of material, up to ten marks for content: Part 2 gave up to 15 marks for analysis. This proved difficult to use under examination marking conditions.

It is probable that we are also influenced in marking by the script which came before, and I would hypothesize that many difficulties occur in the mid-range. It is also possible that we might be influenced by the first answers in a script when marking the second in the same script (Hales and Tokar, 1975).

Ultimately, marking will have to be holistic because of the large number of scripts involved. The development of the marking schemes should be regarded as part of self-training for the task and self-checking during it.

One or two multiple-marking exercises have been undertaken which lend some support to these inferences but which are of interest in their own right. Two are described in the section which follows.

AN APPROACH TO THE MARKING OF LARGE NUMBERS OF SCRIPTS

Some colleges and universities have very large numbers of students taking tests, and the examination administration comes to resemble that of a schools examination board in England. In the early 1970s one method developed by the University of Georgia to assess the essay-writing competence of students wishing to enter university brings the assessors together to 'mark' under the same conditions. Thompson and Rentz (1973) described the scheme which coped with 4500 scripts, and used model answers designed to illustrate expected performance at three points on a four-point scale. The model answers are written to obtain behavioural specifications which describe performance at these three levels:

> The '4' [level] theme clearly and effectively states a thesis that relates directly to the assigned topic. The theme concentrates on this central idea and has a clear overall organization plan. The major points in the theme are developed logically and are supported with concrete specific evidence or detail that will arouse the reader's interst. The theme should reveal the writer's ability to select effective, appropriate words and phrases, to construct and organize sentences and paragraphs, to make careful use of effective transitional devices, and to maintain a consistent appropriate tone. The theme should also be free from mechanical errors.

The model answers were developed against this set of pre-specified character-istics of quality writing. The organizational structure of this system is of special interest, more especially because Thompson and Rentz claim that a high degree of reliability was achieved.

Seventy-five raters are located in seven centres, and mark 3000 essays per day. This means that if 10% of all scripts were reviewed in a national system of moderation with 40 000 candidates the raters would not be involved in more than two days' work in a particular subject. Working in groups the raters are:

> ... instructed to read each essay quickly to gain an overall impression of its quality in relation to the three model essays and to assign a rating based on that comparison. Three raters judge each essay independently to ensure reliable results. This approach to scoring does not require a rater to thoroughly evaluate a paper analytically but merely to compare the paper with pre-selected models.

In respect of reliability the investigators report that: 'for 91% of the essays graded at least 2 out of the 3 raters agreed exactly on the score that the essay ought to have'. The authors do not tell us whether the markers knew the previous rating. As we have seen, McVey (1975) suggests that where this is known the reliability of the second marker is influenced by this knowlege in such a way that he or she will tend to agree with the first score.

The scale is also crude, but this would tend to increase reliability, since the area of potential agreement is widened with this general approach to marking (Cronbach and Gleser, 1965). Research by the ETS on multiple-assessor rating is, however, far from sanguine. Even with their methods of calibration they did not think that reliability could be much improved because of the unpredictable habits of examiners (Braun, 1986).

History teachers working with our project found it difficult to write model answers to meet the content requirements of history at the four threshholds. Instead they wrote model answers for the pass/fail and the good/excellent regions. They provided example marks and comments to assist the school-based assessors, and in the following year they reverted to a structured scheme and did not give advice or comment. These outcomes should not, however, be regarded as a repudiation of the Thompson–Rentz approach in which every teacher marks, for we did not give the moderators the opportunity to mark scripts under the conditions operated by Thompson and Rentz. 'Reliable' gradings of essays by comparison have been found to be reliable for classroom work in Canada (Nyberg and Nyberg, 1978).

More recently (1986) the Association of American Medical Colleges has evaluated the reliability of holistic scoring on the Medical College Admission Test (MCAT) (Mitchell and Anderson, 1986). This test was introduced in 1985 to provide examinees with an opportunity to demonstrate skill in (1) devel-oping a central idea, (2) synthesizing concepts and ideas, (3) separating relevant from irrevelant information, (4) developing alternative hypotheses, (5) present-ing ideas cohesively and logically, and (6) writing clearly.

Twenty scorers, who were trained by a method suggested by White (1985), participated in scoring sessions which marked a sample of 3117 papers. Each essay in a batch was rated on a six-point holistic scale by two readers. Papers which were more than one score point apart were read by a third. Such was the comparability that third readings were required on only 5.3% of all the papers. The mean score of all the ratings was 3.4 and the standard deviation 0.94. The analyses showed that 66% of the variation in scores was due to the table at which the readers were sat, the reader, the batch and other unexamined factors.

The rating took place over three days. The means for day 2 were lower than those of days 1 and 3. The means for days 1 and 3 were also closer to the theoretical mean for a six-point holistic scale. During the scoring there were calibration exercises. However, these were more frequent on day 1 than on days 2 and 3. The authors suggest that calibrations should be frequent and that other activities should be introduced to reduce the effects of boredom and fatigue.

QUESTION DESIGN AND THE DESIGN OF ESSAY EXAMINATIONS

Question design is of considerable consequence. Apart from the fact that questions can be ambiguous they can also be so vague as not to be understood. Edwards (1984) gave examples of questions he would not want to set in systems analysis:

1. Discuss the importance of the evaluation phase in systems design. Describe a system which you have assessed and discuss your conclusions.
2. Describe briefly the term systems design. Give a brief description of five different techniques which you feel are important in systems design, stating when they can be used to advantage.

He objected to these questions on the grounds that he would find them difficult to answer himself. He wanted to test the students' ability to do rather than describe. His first point underlines the need to draft model answers or at least outlines at the time of drafting the questions. The second point focuses on the value of coursework procedures. Sometimes, however, the goal is good but the institutional means for attaining the goal difficult. For example, I wanted to get students to apply the theories of the psychology of instruction in their course in the classroom. At the same time I could not visit 140 students on at least four occasions to check that, in addition to their normal lessons, they tested out these theories. Therefore they were informed that the examination would test their knowledge of the theories and of recent research on them. However, it would be expected that they would give an illustration of how they had applied them in the classroom, together with an evaluation of what happened and what influence the theory was likely to have in the future. The results showed that real experiments were undertaken. Over a three-year period enough examples were obtained to publish two books in which the examples provided the advanced organizers for each chapter (Heywood, 1982, 1984). As institutional arrangements have changed, so we have been able to implement formal procedures in the classroom for coursework assessment. The length of the formal examination has been reduced but this, in its turn, has created problems in question design.

I do not share Edwards' view that the writing of an essay is an unnatural act of communication. It is a view which seems to stem from the idea that tests are unnatural. Such reductionism seems to me to be implausible.

Some investigators, even when they find that objective tests produce better predictions from among a battery of tests, believe it necessary to retain the essay (Johnson, 1985). However, if they are to be used, questions should be avoided which test low-level skills and, like many others, Collier (1986) shows questions in electrical engineering which, at the low level of cognitive skill, could be tested in other ways.

Questions in the sciences are normally intended to be problem-solving, but, as Laurillard (1984) showed, many of the tasks faced by students in engineering and science did not call for much more than comprehension. Moreover, this influenced the style of learning which they adopted. For many tasks they adopted a standard procedure and did not engage in thinking at a deeper level. Laurillard found that many questions did not demand hypothesis-testing or explanations of theory. It was precisely this assumption, that the examinations evaluated by Furneaux in his 1962 study of engineers were all testing the same 'thing', which led the designers of engineering science at A level to try to formulate questions which would test at the higher level of cognitive skill (see Chapter 13).

Marton and Säljö (1984), working with students in the social sciences, also found that the type of question influenced the learning strategy. They used questions which, on the one hand, required a precise recollection of what was said and, on the other, were devoted to major lines of reasoning. The participants had to give evidence that they understood how the conclusions developed from the argument and provide judgements as to whether the reasoning was correct and consistent.

As Gibbs and his colleagues (1986) point out, not all essays are of this kind. For example, a design essay may benefit a person with a different orientation. This does not nullify the conclusion which says students adapt their learning to suit the task. However, not all those responding to a question set to produce a deep approach did so. Those who did not interpret the demands as intended focused on the conspicuous tasks which they would *have to do* after reading the material on which the question was set. This led them to summarize rather than understand. Thus to obtain the understanding required it would seem necessary to ensure that the students know how the marks will be allocated.

We may expect to learn better how to write essay questions if we understand what students expect an essay to be within the context of our subject.

In addition to designing questions which have the same facility (difficulty), examiners need to have information about the popularity or unpopularity of questions. When a question is particularly unpopular, choice is to restricted.

Morrison (1974) has developed both choice and facility indices for essay examinations which take into account the ability of the candidates answering particular questions (given in the Glossary). These indices, together with a discrimination index, can provide useful feedback to examiners when relatively large numbers of students are involved. With small numbers the assumptions on which they are based are a useful reminder to examiners of what they should seek to obtain when designing questions.

QUESTION SPOTTING: PERCEPTIONS OF ASSESSMENT AND PERFORMANCE

Nowhere is the influence of assessment on learning more apparent than in the weeks immediately before an examination, when students attempt to spot the questions likely to come up in the examinations, and they do this by looking at previous examination papers. It was this understanding of the role of examinations which led me to experiment with questions which would cause the students to respond in different ways and so demonstrate how they could obtain different objectives in Engineering Science at A level in 1969. The fact that we could not obtain all the objectives we wanted without a project led to the inclusion of practical work which included one. This marked a major change in GCE A level examining (Heywood and Kelly, 1973). By 1973 we had learnt that we had overloaded the students considerably, and so a substantial reduction in syllabus and assessment requirements was made. Thus the systems model of the assessment–curriculum process was born (Heywood, 1984).

What we did not know was how the overloading affected student performance. Light on what might have been happening has now been thrown on this problem by Ramsden and Entwistle (1981), Gibbs (1981) and Hounsell (1984). From their studies of 57 students in six university departments Ramsden and Entwistle confirm that perceived assessment requirements are major influences on the approach to learning which a student adopts. Moreover, if students believe that they are threatened by the assessment situation they are more likely to adopt a rote-learning approach to tasks. The issue at hand, to which reference has already been made, is that the mere substitution of one technique of assessment for another (as from, say, a written examination to continuous assessment) is no guarantee that the objectives of learning will be obtained unless attention is paid to the interacting components of the system. Ramsden (1984) and others in the Anglo-Scandinavian school found that overloaded syllabuses and inappropriate assessment techniques simply caused students to adopt a memory (reproductive) approach to learning. Continuous assessment can be as pernicious as an examination, and needs to be carefully designed, particularly so if it is to get the best from high-achieving students (chapter 4).

Haigh's (1986) investigations supported these points. At Oxford Polytechnic he and Gibbs discovered an adverse relationship between contact hours and approach to study. Although students may not perceive that they are overloaded, they may in fact show stress associated with information overload. He wrote of his own course that it had a much larger contact pattern than the human geography course which preceded it, and so it might have encouraged unwanted superficial learning styles at the expense of more contemplative study habits. Students also (and this is consistently true of my courses) find new approaches to learning difficult and some experience a decline in performance.

STUDENT PERCEPTIONS OF ESSAY WRITING

Using an interview approach, Hounsell (1984) investigated the perceptions which students have of essays. Some idea of the significance of essay writing in the British context may be had from the fact that some history students may have had to write 18–20 essays over a year as a whole. In the module which Hounsell investigated, three 2000–2500-word essays were handed in during the first two terms with an extended essay of 3000–3500 words in the final one. The students spent between 13 and 15 hours on the essays. One student quoted by Hounsell said 'Basically I am a full-time essay writer'.

Among the students he found three perceptions of the purposes of the essay. These were the essay as argument, as viewpoint and as arrangement, i.e.:

(1) An ordered presentation of an argument well supported by evidence;
(2) An ordered presentation of a distinctive viewpoint on a problem or issue;
(3) An ordered presentation embracing facts and ideas.

It is interesting to evaluate Iliffe's scheme of assessment from these different perspectives. Does it cover all three perceptions or does it cover one at the expense of another?

Hounsell found among these first-year students that when their coursework marks were combined only two got more than 65%, and these were from among five who were classified as 'argument'. All those classified as 'viewpoint' obtained between 60% and 64%, and four out of five classified as 'arrangement' obtained marks of less than 60%. These results were not related to final-degree results, since the module contributed only part of a score which was heavily weighted by the results of an examination.

Hounsell suggests that those who perceive the essay to be an 'argument' are able to articulate and discuss the activity as they see it, and because it involves 'argument' they see themselves as 'makers of meaning'. There is, he says, in this as in the deep approach 'a concern to abstract and construct meaning through an active engagement with subject-matter'. This is in contrast with the perception of the essay as 'arrangement', where regurgitation is the order of the day. It parallels the surface approach described by Säljö (1979) and is essentially reproductive in character. Those who have a 'viewpoint' see 'essay writing as a medium for self-expression'. These three dispositions can be seen quite clearly in student-teacher responses to questions about the relationships between theory and their actual practice in the classroom.

Given that first-year students were told that 'writing an essay is an exercise in handling historical evidence and building it into a convincing argument' the existence of two groups who do not see it in this way creates a problem for the tutors. If students do not share the same premises as the teachers then they may fail to understand what the teacher wants them to understand. How then, does one get student-teachers to comprehend this fact of learning, particularly if the orientations to learning of the kind described in Chapter 9 are embedded? Clearly, some kind of specific training is necessary, and this is consistent with the view of cognitive learning as a process of development.

FEEDBACK

There is much evidence that short initial training courses at the beginning of higher education do not work. A sustained effort is required, and this is consistent with the idea of continuous assessment as a means of feedback and development. Yet, as Hounsell reports in another article, such studies as have been done on individual guidance suggest that teacher-comments on essays can be very cursory. He says that the remarks on essays which he has seen amount to summary judgements rather than specific diagnosis, and this was my experience in the counselling role. It was also my experience when programmes were organized to discuss learning how to learn that it was the better students who attended. Like Hounsell, I believe that the essential ground for diagnosis lies between the subject-tutor and the student. Lecturers have to learn to guide students towards the goal through the remarks they make in lectures, the personal advice they give, and the lectures/seminars they present.

Often both lecturers and students find it difficult to articulate their views. One possible way forward is to be found in the work of Gibbs, who has used the following technique in workshops. Students are given two contrasting essays about the same topic. One is intended to require a deep approach and the other a surface one. Each student assesses the answer and judges which is best. Then, in pairs and then in fours, the students compare their views and consider the intentions which underlie the two essays. In this way the students learn skills of exploration and analysis and obtain a wider perception of the issues involved. Lecturers should adopt this or a similar technique within their own subjects.

Hounsell (1984), in another report on how students plan their essays, found that five different strategies were used, including a 'no plan'. These he related to the conceptions that students had of essay writing. The basic, extended or evolving plan plus the argument conception type produced the highest number of students with upper second-class degrees. He suggests that advice on planning lectures will not be very helpful if students do not know what an essay means.

If Gibbs' method is translated to the subject seminar by the subject specialists such explorations would be done within the framework of the subject and teachers could, in summaries, explain their expectations. A one-off approach is unlikely to suffice.

An interesting development in this respect is the publication by the GCE Examination Boards of A level questions together with candidate responses and examiner comments in both the humanities and the sciences. They provide an invaluable resource (Bryant, 1983; Ridd, 1983).

For the student who is working alone or for the lecturer who only sees a large lecture group, the scheme of assessment might also be given, together with some explanation (Campbell *et al.*, 1982; Clanchy and Ballard, 1983). Alternatively, students might be given a checklist of the kind produced by Fitzgibbons (1981), shown in Table 44.

The connection between the approaches to critical thinking in Chapter 6 and this procedure for assessing arguments should be clear. My own view is that the lists may be helpful in the design of questions, whereas Fitzgibbon's procedure is likely to be of greater use to students who wish to develop skill in critical thought.

At Murdoch University lists of criteria called 'assignment attachments' were made available to students before assignments as well as being distributed afterwards. Most of the students liked this method. They felt that it helped them to understand the grades and also their strengths and weaknesses (McDonald and Sansom, 1979). Several writers have drawn attention to the value of the essay in continuous assessment as a means of diagnosis. For this to be successful, Henderson (1980) believes that care needs to be taken in the design of questions which should help students to cultivate a learning style.

SHORT-ANSWER QUESTIONS

The phrase 'short answer' has many meanings. Generally, it describes a question for which the answer is no more than two or three lines. Sometimes the total problem is set in such a way that a series of short answers are generated. This technique is commonly employed in comprehension exercises, where the candidates have to read an article during the examination and answer specific questions relating to their understanding of it. In England 'short answer' is sometimes related to problem-solving exercises which are intended to be completed in 10–15 minutes. The 'short answer' in this case arises from the comparison which is made with the more traditional 30–40-minute question. Short answer questions should have greater reliability than essays, although this may not be true if a very simple grading system is used (for example, A, B, and C). One investigation by Mowbray and Davies (1967) suggests that the greater reliability in marking short-note answers is at the expense of examiners' time, which, they suggest, demands more concentration. This is certainly the writer's experience in marking comprehension tests of the kind set in Engineering Science at A level.

Very often, short answers are used when the question at issue could be put in the objective form. This is particularly true of test questions in second-level education (Heywood *et al.*, 1980).

Table 44. Evaluating Arguments in Essays (adapted from R. E. Fitzgibbons, (1981))

In your work	In someone else's work (*especially when acting as an assessor or in a debate*)
1. Outlining the argument	
List the premises (hypotheses/propositions which you wish to demonstrate or prove). State the conclusion(s). List the reasons for the conclusions.	Identify the premises (hypotheses) and conclusion(s). Establish which sentences do not add to the argument. List the reasons given for the conclusion.
2. Examining the argument for clarity	
Check that the key terms (concepts, principles) are stated clearly. Do not attempt to fudge the issue.	When any terms and phrases are unclear ask for clarification in a live argument. In an examination write a note at the side of the script to check that you have not misperceived what is being said. Look out for fudging.

NB An argument whose key concepts and principles are not clear, or which contains ambiguities is not a good argument. A good argument should be brief and to the point.

3. Asserting and checking the truth of premises	
You must be able to stand over each premise you use and, where necessary, cite supporting evidence and its course. Don't throw false premises into an argument, because they are easily spotted.	Any questionable premises must be defended by another argument. In an examination answer look for false premises as a foundation for your own assessment. List the reasons which make you think that the proposition is false (see 5 below).
4. Ensuring that the premises are necessary and relevant to the argument	
Check that each premise is both necessary and relevant to the argument. Eliminate premises which are not.	In debate the person offering the argument must be able to show the necessity and relevance of each answer. In scripts look out for circular argument and tautologies.

Any person involved in a disputation must have sure grounds for the claims which are made.

5. Testing the strength of an argument	
Predict the counter argument and test your conclusion for validity against the alternative. If the alternative view has strong merits then your conclusion may be wrong.	In debate and examination scripts look for weaknesses in the logic of the argument, and the data used to support the conclusion

Short-answer examinations are held by many teachers to be reliable. However, in medicine it has been found by Wakeford and Roberts (1984) that while markers can agree about the rank-order of candidates, consistent idiosyncratic behaviour leads to odd pass/fail and pass/distinction decisions in such tests.

Short-answer questions are used to test clinical problem-solving in the *Modified Essay Question* (MEQ). MEQs derive from the work of McGuire (1971) in the United States. Knox (1975), who has prepared an excellent pamphlet on the design of these questions, wrote:

> In the developing situation of a given case, questions can be devised to explore, among other things, perceptions of salient factors influencing decision-making and attitudes thereby demonstrating the candidates' stated behaviour in relation to his daily professional work. It is thus possible for a candidate to indicate not only the *outcome* in terms of his stated actions that he might take, but also some of the thought *processes* leading to these actions.

Freeman and Byrne (1976) show part of one of their questions to illustrate the technique. It begins:

> In 1957 Mrs A, a slightly built woman aged 32 with two girls (aged three and six), moved into your area and registered with your practice. She told you that as a child she had (a) rheumatism, (b) valvular disease of the heart (no adequate records are available).
> 1. What further four questions would you have to put to the patient to elaborate these two facts?
> 2. You learn that the valvular disease may have occurred at five years old and that she had raised blood pressure with both her pregnancies. She has reported because she is about to have a dental anaesthetic for the removal of 10 teeth and is afraid she might still have raised blood pressure.
> On examination you find pulse regular at 90, BP 150/90, a slight displacement of the apex beat to the left. One feature of ausculation of the heart suggested she may have mitral stenosis. List three sounds you might have heard that would suggest this diagnosis.
> . . . .etc.

Subsequent items go on to evaluate other aspects of skill in patient management such as aftercare, occupational advice, etc.

Knox suggests that the best approach to the design of a Modified Essay Question is for a doctor to draw up an example which tests both content and skills. A matrix aid may prove useful (Table 45(a)).

The MEQ designer puts the subquestion numbers appropriate to the abilities in the box. (Inspection of many of the books on objective testing shows this approach as a means of selecting the items to be included in the test is often used.)

Knox (1976) suggests that the draft question be circulated among a group of experienced doctors. *They are asked to answer the questions.* In this way a bank of responses is built up. When this is done the group should meet to determine acceptable and unacceptable responses. Marks may then be allocated (see Table 45(b)). There is no need for each subquestion to carry the same number of marks. Nowadays it is common practice to show the total number of possible marks on the printed paper, even though students may be misled by this procedure.

Table 45.

(a) *Matrix scheme for the design of modified essay questions (simplified from Knox, 1975)*

Subject Area	ABILITIES EXERCISED				
	Recall	Formulation of hypothesis	Plan formation	Synthesis	Totals
1					
2					
3					
4					
Totals					

(b) *Example of mark scheme for a subquestion of an MEQ (from Knox, 1975)*

5. Patient management requires:
    Exploration of her reasons   2 marks
    Possible counselling   1 mark
    Suggest discussion with her husband   1 mark

   No marks for:
    'Explanation'
    Telling her she must go to hospital
    Refusing to confine
    Removing her from list of patients
    or other responses

   Total possible: 4 marks

The advantages claimed for MEQs are that they avoid the cueing inherent in multiple-choice questions which are used widely in medicine, they can provide an element of reality, and the scores can be weighted if answer Z is dependent on the previous answer Y.

Unfortunately, little is known about what they test, although they would seem to have considerable face validity. Reasonable reliability has been reported by Feletti (1980). It has also been found by Fabb and Marshall (1983) that experienced doctors do better than trainees when answering MEQs and that sometimes one question is a better predictor of final performance than others. At Belfast, where the latter was found, it was also discovered that women did better than men in the MEQ but that it had a poor correlation with other parts of the final examinations. One evaluation of the MEQ by Weinman (1984) suggested that changes in cognitive behaviour in quite specific clinical teaching were associated with the teaching.

Freeman (1982), who gave pre- and post-test MCQs (multiple-choice questions) and MEQs to trainee practitioners, found an increase in both, but the greater increase was with the MEQ. He also showed among practitioners that experience of the MEQ was likely to influence performance positively. He expressed concern that, in spite of revision of the questions, the examinees obtained an undue percentage of marks in terms of their attitudes toward patient management rather than their fundamental problem-solving skills. If such skills are related to certain attitudes and qualities of mind then the problem is acute.

He reports that, whereas the marks tend to be rather high on the pre-entry test, there is a fairly good overall scatter of scores. To offset the tendency to high marks he suggested that a greater degree of weighting was necessary at the lower end of the marking scale. In spite of these difficulties, the MEQ seemed to be an effective measure of the change in trainee performance during the course. Freeman and his colleagues argue from their data that a number of MEQ questions are essential if the technique is to be valid (see Chapter 13).

One of the criticisms levelled against this technique is that no chance is given to candidates to demonstrate individual approaches to hypothesis formation because the scheme is based on a consensus of panel members. Nevertheless, the same critics claim that the MEQ can be used as an aid to learning and as a self-audit service arising from the study of the documentation of the cases. They have been used as aids to group discussion, to illustrate topics prior to a lecture and effectively in diagnosing student weaknesses (Feletti, 1980). It has the advantage that it can be designed to give immediate feedback. Multiple-choice questions may be used instead of short answers.

Clearly, the technique could be used in other scientific subjects which require problem-solving. Freeman suggests that it is better used where there is a possibility of several *sensible* and *considered* alternatives. The scoring would depend on how far the examiner decided that the examinee met these criteria, even though this presents scoring problems. Freeman has attempted to redesign a teacher-comprehension test in history to illustrate the potential of the technique at school level (Heywood, 1977). It would seem that, if problem-solving skills are to be tested in this way, the examinee has to be prepared to go beyond the information given.

OPEN-BOOK EXAMINATIONS

Another approach to reducing stress which also has the objective of reducing the amount of recall of factual data is to allow candidates to bring books into the examination. The objectives of open-book examinations will differ between subjects. One American evaluation of the literature on open-book examinations concluded:

(1) No change, or slight increase in achievement resulted when open-book examinations were administrated.
(2) Students liked open-book examinations better. The possible reason is that they were less anxious.
(3) Better study preparation resulted when open-book examinations were used.
(4) Different abilities were tested in the open-book examination. Students were not tested on memory only but also on reasoning.
(5) Slight increase in validity, variance, and reliability values were found in open-book set examinations over closed-book set ones (Feldhusen, 1961; Kalish, 1958; Michaels and Kieran, 1973; Tussing, 1951).

Among those studies were papers which suggested that students were less prone to cheating in open-book examinations. Michaels and Kieran (1968), who conducted this review, also made a study among 600 mathematics students, but these were in high school. They obtained open- and closed-book examinations scores, anxiety scores for open- and closed-book examinations, as well as attitudes (during a neutral period) to the different types of test and to mathematics. The open-book setting used by them was conservative in that it was a multiple-choice test designed for a closed-book situation. Their results seemed to indicate that the open-book setting may increase achievement as measured by the test score in areas such as knowledge and comprehension. The closed-book test resulted in the highest level of anxiety. Nevertheless, they concluded that there was some evidence that open-book settings could create an environment in which there was an optimal level of stress.

Some science and mathematics examinations include tables and formulae and so avoid recall which, if it is at fault, causes an unnecessarily wrong answer. At the National Technical High School in Bergen, Norway, the engineering students have access to terminals linked to the mainframe computer during their one-day final examinations. They can access any computer program they like, and it is argued that this enables them to solve complex engineering problems. As Gibbs and his colleagues (1986), who reported this work, suggest there is much more scope for this type of examination than might have been thought possible in the sciences. This view is also held by Brewer and Tomlinson (1981), who describe how they used an open-book examination in anatomy at the University of Sydney. Questions for this examination were unseen and no previous papers were published. They ascertained from other investigations of their course that memory of recall was poor. Moreover, it was not found to be an important indicator of student learning. Therefore they argued that books should be allowed. Many distinguished scientists, they say, have poor recall.

Open-book examinations in English Literature at GCE A level in England were held in 1971 and 1972 by the JMB. Results indicated that the effectiveness with which candidates used this facility was related to their ability. The most able improved their performance, while some of the least able used the texts very little or wasted time paging ineffectively through them. The teachers involved generally considered that the prospect of open-book examinations would improve the quality of work throughout the course.

The main cognitive benefit to be expected from open-book exams would seem to be the raising of the level of skills tested. By eliminating many knowledge items from the material to be examined more time is left for more testing items. It must also influence teaching and learning, since texts would be studied and examination questions set in ways appropriate to this kind of testing. It would seem, from both English and American experience, that the use of open-book examinations helps the strong student more than a weak one. There is some evidence that too much information may confuse the candidates. It is essential, therefore, to be clear about the precise objectives which this additional information is to achieve. If open-book examinations were to be introduced the preparation for them would have to start at the beginning of the course, and teachers would need briefing and perhaps training if they are to take advantage of them to the full.

THE TIMING OF EXAMINATIONS: PRIOR-NOTICE (SEEN) QUESTIONS

One of the objections to the traditional examination is that it is a single measure of the student's performance. Thus, in addition to the unreliability of scoring, a student may produce a poor performance within the tight constraints of time imposed by the traditional 2- or 3-hour paper. To overcome this objection at university level some teachers have introduced prior-notice questions.

Such questions have been used in both the training of teachers and undergraduates. In the former experiment (Flood Page, 1967) the questions were given out one week in advance. This procedure reduced anxiety among the students, although they thought that the examination tended to be too much a test of memory. In the latter experiment the intention was to get science students on a humanities course to read. Eighteen questions were related to the understanding of required reading and issued at the beginning of the academic year. Candidates were told that the questions in the final examination would be taken from that test. Motivation was enhanced and reading was undertaken (Heywood, 1974). This technique may be helpful in the development of learning skills with under-achievers.

In a recent experiment on two occasions graduates in a teacher-training course were allowed to opt either for a prior-notice or for a traditional 3-hour examination (Cameron and Heywood, 1985). On the second occasion a list of six questions would be given to those students who chose the prior-notice condition. They would be given two to do in the examination, and there would be no choice. After the first test the 'rumour' got around that taking a prior-notice examination was more difficult and it caused a much smaller group to volunteer for the second. As far as was possible, the unseen and seen questions were designed to test the same content and skills. There was no statistically significant difference between the results of the two groups. It might be objected that the groups were self-selecting. However, if the aim is to reduce anxiety among those students who perceive themselves to be anxious then self-selection would be the better approach. The major objections are that the 'unseen' group could decode the examination and that the papers may not have been totally equivalent. They were difficult to design.

In a later experiment in the same university department undergraduates from three associated colleges who took a common course within the department were given a prior-notice examination. It was found that groups of students in each of the colleges collected together to produce model answers, and the examination became a memory exercise. It was also found that the preparation for the paper took place the week before the examination. In such circumstances it is difficult to see what value the open-book examination had.

Several other teachers have reported variations in the technique. Chansarkar (1985) has described an experiment with business studies students in which part of the answer was seen, but he did not outline the technicalities of administration. All examinations taken included a seen component in years 1 and 2 except one. Of the 100 students who responded to a questionnaire, 50 thought that knowing the topic helped preparation, which could be done under relaxed conditions. At the same time, most students felt that, like our students, it caused too much time to be spent in preparation. They wanted the system changed. Seventy per cent preferred a combination of continuous assessment and unseen examinations in most subjects.

Unlike our study, statistically significant differences in marks were obtained, the better marks being for the 'seen' question, and this was particularly true of the weaker students. There is also an improvement in the 'seen' marks between years 1 and 2, and this might be assumed to be due to the self-training element.

The teaching staff who designed the questions to test the ability of students to gather, assimilate and write about a subject area which they could not do with unseen questions preferred this scheme, as it removed some of the causes of dissatisfaction associated with continuous assessment. Presumably, they did not mind students working in groups. It was also administratively convenient.

Another approach, reported by Edwards (1984) and used in examinations in systems analysis at both undergraduate and graduate levels, included a question on a case study which was distributed before the examination. It contained the solution and the question was set to obtain criticisms of the solution and suggestions for improvement.

A modification of this technique in English Literature at the University of York allowed students 14 days in which to prepare the answers to a question. Students could talk to each other but not to staff, and they could use any material at their disposal (Brockbank, 1968). Although no evaluation is available this technique might encourage creative writing or skill in the reviewing of books (critical précis) under time pressure.

Gibbs and his colleagues call this the '168-hour exam', because the students have one week to submit their answers (Gibbs, 1986). The advantages claimed for this examination in addition to the elimination of memorization and question-spotting are reduction on anxiety, higher-quality answers and the testing of something more worthwhile. It is quite likely that some students would be very anxious during the week period of the examination. Gibbs notes (and this would be a universal concern among educators) that it could be open to plagiarism, and students could obtain substantial help. Like so many test forms which might motivate students, there is a price to pay. The question is always whether in a particular learning environment it is worth doing.

CHAPTER 11

Practicals, Projects, Profiles and Self-assessment

INTRODUCTION

This chapter continues the discussion of techniques commonly in use. Aurals and orals are discussed with particular reference to assessment in modern languages and medicine. Role-playing and simulations are playing an increasingly important part in assessments, and evaluations suggest that there is a need to train the assessors and, if possible, those involved in the simulations. Equally, students are likely to benefit from role-playing in situations which they themselves have designed.

Although there has been relatively little work done on assessment in laboratory and on projects, many ideas have been implemented and much time has been spent on working out objectives. The problem is not so much finding objectives but determining which ones to use. A case study of the assessment of both laboratory and project work is included in this chapter. Most of the assessment schedules are semi-criterion referenced, and they are shown to have reasonable reliability and validity. They are essentially profiles. The chapter ends with a brief discussion of the potential for and purposes of self-assessment in higher education.

Viva-voce (or oral) examinations are commonly used by external examiners in the British system of examining. At the doctorate level the candidate's thesis is explored with the candidate. This may be an act of 'confirmation' on the part of the examiner, or to see if things were done which should have been done but are not reported, or it may be to 'take issue' with the candidate. It is not meant to be a defence by the candidate of his or her thesis, as it was in the Middle Ages and still is in the Church today. There are no universally agreed guidelines for this procedure except for the fact that an internal examiner who may have been the candidate's supervisor often participates in the *viva*.

Fong (1987) has drawn attention to some work by Granville Johnson who devised a rating scale for masters' orals which has not, unfortunately, been published. He believes that it might be a useful basis for the development of scales at the undergraduate level. In Britain at the undergraduate level, students, particularly those who are considered to be in danger of failing, may be interviewed by an external examiner to see if they can do themselves justice.

Sometimes candidates are interviewed at the borderlines of grades. In these circumstances, external examiners often find themselves troubleshooting and, in consequence, helping departments with particular problems, but this happens independently of the interview. Again, there are no universally agreed guidelines. The examiners do not think of these interviews as oral examinations.

In the United States oral examinations may be a feature of comprehensive examinations. This chapter begins with a discussion of aural and oral examinations.

AURALS AND ORALS IN FOREIGN-LANGUAGE TEACHING

Aural and oral examinations are of importance in foreign-language teaching at all levels of education, more especially as substantial attention is now paid to the language aspect. In Britain and Ireland the polytechnical institutions have moved away from courses with a heavy orientation towards literature to studies that have commercial relevance (White, 1980).

In the United States the National Association for Self-Instructional Language Programs has designed an individualized course in foreign languages not regularly offered in the institutional curriculum whose aim is oral proficiency. It provides resources such as written and taped materials and arranges for native speakers who live in the vicinity of the students to act as tutors (Fong, 1987). Outside examiners not only examine each student's work at the end of each term (Coffin, 1975) but also play a key role in troubleshooting and help to diagnose problems with individuals and their tutors (Morehouse and Boyd-Bowman, 1973).

Field tests with the US State Department's Foreign Service Institute's criterion-referenced tests which evaluate the language competencies of college students suggest that they have reliability for this population (Frith, 1979).

In Britain the Secondary School Examinations Boards have completed several studies of the assessment of orals and aurals and precise regulations for the conduct of such assessments have been worked out (for example, AEB, 1982, 1985).

The traditional aural test was a dictation administered in the examination room. Now it is very often a radio broadcast transmitted in the language laboratory. In such an aural the students can play the tape backwards and forwards as many times as they like in a specified period of time (for example, 40 minutes). White (1980) reports that students make as many as four times the errors they would make in a traditional test in this kind of comprehension test. It discriminates sharply between good and weak students.

In some higher education examinations the student listens to a text intended for speaking, after which he or she answers questions on, or makes a summary of, the text. Such tests are scored by an error count. Some institutions complicate matters (as some do with objective tests) by weighting the errors.

Oral examinations are used in foreign-language teaching, medicine and dentistry. In some foreign-language examinations in higher education the oral may act as a hurdle, or count for as much as 30% of the score (Chaplen, 1970).

Oral tests in languages are of several kinds. For example, the 15-minute conversation is normal, but there may be translation-at-sight tests (in either direction), tests of speed of transfer, simulated role-playing tests, and telephone tests. As with the aural, the trend is towards the real situation.

White (1980) reports that there were so many problems about oral examining that in the early 1980s some teachers felt that they should be abandoned. However, the poor oral performance of candidates in Britain and Ireland means that the oral examination is likely to remain. In both countries the examining boards in both the second- and third-level sectors have taken a lead in this respect (BTEC, 1980).

The Royal Society of Arts (RSA) Diploma for Bilingual Secretaries described by White puts them through a role-playing situation in which, for example, a visitor to a firm requires help from a secretary-linguist. A mark scheme is provided and a technique of standardization similar to that used by the Institute of Linguists is employed (Table 46). This consists of a sample taped oral examination with a commentary on the performance of both the candidate and the examiner. The marking scheme is biased against the candidate who does badly and includes a scale for language-quality adjustment.

White (1980) reports that there is a conflict about whom should examine. Some say that it should be the student's teacher, but the RSA reports that when the teachers did assess, the pass rate became too high. One approach which has been suggested in the area of business education is to integrate written, oral and aural tests within a single task-oriented examination.

ORAL EXAMINATIONS IN DENTISTRY AND MEDICINE

As in modern language examining, oral examinations play and have played an important part in the assessment of medical students. The medical profession has used orals with and without patient involvement (clinicals). Many studies have shown these examinations to be very unreliable, and several have also shown that the same topics could be tested by other methods, and much more cheaply (Kelly et al., 1971). Studies in dentistry and medicine have also shown that the student's personality as perceived by the examiner (Wigton, 1980) as well as anxiety can influence performance in the viva-voce situation (Holloway et al., 1967). Other investigations suggest that the marks given changed during the day: for example, they improved as the day went on (Green et al., 1967). One investigation, while not finding a personality correlate, showed that the grade awarded was closely related to the number of words spoken in the examination (Colton and Peterson, 1967). Seventy-six per cent of the questions were of the recall type.

In the traditional oral the candidate was sent off to examine the patient and report back. Surprisingly, the examiner did not witness the examination of the

Table 46. An extract from an oral examination for bilingual secretaries (Diploma of the Royal Society of Arts) (See White, 1980, for a discussion)

Diploma 4. Task: To deal with a foreign visitor and general conversation

$\frac{1}{2}$	
1	
$1\frac{1}{2}$	
2	Very poor.
$2\frac{1}{2}$	
3	Poor—misunderstands much of what is said—response incomprehensible to native speaker.
$3\frac{1}{2}$	
4	
$4\frac{1}{2}$	
5	Not adequate—misunderstands a significant proportion of what is said, or is unable to respond sensibly or comprehensively to native speaker.
$5\frac{1}{2}$	
6	
$6\frac{1}{2}$	Not quite adequate performance—less than 80% understood, or too much hesitation or answers only just comprehensible.
7	
$7\frac{1}{2}$	Adequate performance: Understands at least 80%, sensible answers without too much hesitation; no difficulty in understanding candidate.
8	Quite good performance: Understands completely, does not lose thread of conversation. Responds clearly and sensibly.
$8\frac{1}{2}$	Good performance: Has no difficulty in conversing, does more than just respond to questions.
9	Excellent performance: Converses with ease; keeps conversation going. Shows mature level of ideas.
$9\frac{1}{2}$	Performs as well as one would expect of an educated native speaker. Takes initiative in conversation, not thrown by interruptions; mature level of ideas.
10	

Diploma 4 and 5   Language quality adjustment marks

Balance of factors: fluency; accuracy/range of structures; accent/intonation   Language quality adjustment

	+5	Exceptional. Educated Native Speaker quality. Would get a high 1st on oral perfomance.
	+4	Excellent. Near native performance. Would get a 1st on oral performance.
	+3	Very good. At least 2 of the 3 factors well above average. Would get a high 2(i) on oral performance.
	+2	Good. At least 1 of the 3 factors well above average. Would get a low 2(i) on oral performance. Combined Mark
Half marks	+1	Above average. Would get a high 2(ii) on oral performance.
may be	0	Average for this level. Adequate in all 3 factors. Would get a 2(ii) on oral performance.
used	−1	Below average. 1 factor may be weak but would get a 3 on oral performance.
	−2	Weak in 1 or 2 of the 3 factors but would gain a marginal pass at degree level.
	−3	Poor. Probably weak in all 3 factors. Fail at degree level. Grade D at A level oral.
	−4	Very poor. Very weak in all 3 factors. Bare pass at A level oral.
	−5	Abysmal. Would fail at A level oral.

patient. In view of these difficulties, several approaches were taken to improving the examining. One of the earliest attempts at this was the development of the diagnostic interview at the University of Illinois. In this interview one examiner role-plays a patient while another observes. It was found to be important to match the sex of the examiner with that of the patient. In a short interview (15 minutes) the candidate is expected to get to the heart of the problem quickly: 30-minute interviews provide for a more complex situation. The candidate is expected to explain to the patient his assessment of the patient's problems. A quite detailed procedure is followed. Ratings of the relationship which the candidate has with the patient are made by the role-playing examiner whereas those relating to data collection and diagnosis are performed by the observing one.

In order to improve reliability a rating scale with 15 or so behavioural items is used. Each one is marked out of ten so they are not strictly criterion-referenced (Evans et al., 1966). Developments in oral examining also show how the 'objectives' movement has pervaded medical education worldwide.

Another type of oral examination which has been developed in medicine by the College of Family Physicians of Canada and described in full by Fabb and Marshall is *The Formal Oral Examination*. It lasts for 25 minutes and constitutes 20% of the total examination marks. A case is selected which represents a common condition in family practice: its solution is intended to require a stepwise approach to the evaluation of the problem and is made complex by the inclusion of interfamily relationships. The solution will involve a consultant physician and workers in the paramedical profession. A major goal of the technique is to cause the candidate to create options, which is in contrast to the situation in most written examinations, where the options are presented so as to cause a particular choice. Creative problem-solving in this context is achieved by getting the candidates to ask for the data so that their problem-solving abilities are observed. It also allows the examiner to stimulate the candidates' thinking.

Once again, a comprehensive rating schedule is provided. Fabb and Marshall claim that, because of content validity, the method of scoring, and the training of examiners, it allows for accurate assessment of the candidate. As part of examiner training videotapes to demonstrate good and poor techniques have been prepared.

The idea of training examiners in medicine seems to be increasingly acceptable. Newble says that the unreliability of clinical tests is due in part to the complexity of skills being assessed, the mix of the patients being tested, and the variance of the examiners. The last of these is the most intractable. Thus the problem is to select examiners who are inherently consistent and to provide them with an objective rating form (Newble et al., 1980). To this end, he and his colleagues developed a training scheme in which the examiners examined simulated patients.

An interesting aspect of the use of videotape in preparing for clinical studies arises from a course taught in small groups by films to show the complexity of human relationships (doctor–patient interviews). Evaluation showed that the films used for teaching were not suitable for testing. While ambiguity was required for teaching it was not helpful in the testing of students at this phase of their education (Pearson *et al.*, 1977). The examiners also required some training.

SIMULATIONS

According to Corley (1983a), 'role playing is the most versatile of all simulation formats, equally adaptable for teaching and for evaluation'. That may be so in medicine, but there are role-playing activities (for example, in the management of people) where assessment might be difficult, especially when self-evaluation is the purpose.

In the medical situation the role-plays are well defined, the candidates' expectations clear and the marking schedules precise. Those shown in Fabb and Marshall's book are not criterion-referenced but confined-domain dominant. Examiners may comment and somethimes they have to give a mark. As soon as that happens there is room for error. For example, what variations in answer produces differences in an allowable score of 5 when an examiner is asked 'does he take a proper history?' It is, as the project case study in engineering science at the end of this chapter demonstrates, extremely difficult to design a criterion-referenced system at this level. The designers of the project assessments in engineering science and history described at the end of this chapter began with 'yes' or 'no' dichotomous schedules and ended with multiple-choice systems.

Many teachers prefer to use a scale from 'very good' to 'unacceptable', or a differential such as 'thorough' to 'incomplete'. The trouble with such scales is that unless things are demonstrably good or bad there is a tendency for the assessor to score around the mean. This may not matter in the assessment of clinical practice but it does in a system where course marks contribute a reasonable percentage in a distributed mark (honours) system. For these reasons, the multiple-choice format was eventually chosen for the coursework in engineering science and history.

One of the most interesting developments has been the in-training test for psychomotor skills in South Carolina, United States. This oral is now conducted on real patients and lasts for one hour (5 minutes to meet the patient; 20 to conduct the physical examination; 5 for the examiner to score; 15 for feedback; 10 for the examinee and the two examiners to discuss the complexities of an adequate routine physical examination, leaving 5 minutes for preparation for the next oral (Corley, 1983b). The activity embraces evaluation, provision of immediate feedback and teaching. They were fortunate enough to have real patients. They had previously tried to train simulators but the range of physical abnormalities which could be simulated successfully for a judgement of psychomotor performance was found to be limited. Others have found that simulated patients can be trained with self-instructional materials (Meier *et al.*, 1982).

Role-playing and simulations are now quite common in many subjects. They are at the heart of the Assessment Center technique, which is widely used in business in the United States. The Assessment Center (in Britain the term implies a centre where children and adolescents go for psychological assessment) technique is a method used in business to assess management performance. It utilizes simulations which are designed to elicit important behaviours from the participants. Senior managers observe the performance and rate against a criterion-referenced scale for which high reliabilities have been claimed (Thornton and Byham, 1983).

It is not surprising that this idea should be adopted by business schools (AACSB, 1987), teacher-education departments and medical schools (Weiner, 1987). Teacher-training institutions are familiar with microteaching, where the trainee teaches a small class of pupils and is videotaped during the performance. Systems of microteaching take the trainees through a variety of skills (Brown, 1975) (for example, questioning). An assessment centre introduces criterion-referenced observer assessment into the technique. In medicine a self-assessment centre has been developed at the University of New Mexico (Obenshain and Rezler, 1987). The assessment centre concept developed independently by the college played a key role in the developments at Alverno College described in Chapter 13.

The in-basket test is among the best known of the simulations used. This is open to assessment, and recent work has led to a simplified method of scoring which may make it available for wider application. Hakstian (1986) and his colleagues, who did this work, believe that as a test it has a significant contribution to make when it is used in a multiple-strategy situation (for example, interview data, previous work performance information). In some populations such as the hourly workers they tested it may have 'morale-boosting face validity' and 'improved predictive validity'.

In the Outcome Measurement Project of the American Assembly of Collegiate Schools of Business (AACSB, 1987) the measures used to assess non-subject matter characteristics included the in-basket exercise in a role-playing situation, unit start-up exercises (the participant plays the role of a manager charged with establishing a word-processing unit), and a group discussion exercise in which funds have to be allocated in a swift, orderly way. Reliabilities of between 0.77 and 1.00 were obtained between raters. Case studies are often used.

Beveridge and Matthews (1986) have reported that they have found it difficult to assess case studies in engineering because it is not easy to obtain evidence of effective participation in the learning experience, which is the aim of the case study. In one programme in a master's degree in education the students, who are experienced teachers, contract to write a role-play. It is intended that this should be from their own experience but suitably changed to avoid knowledge of who the real-life persons are. Each member of the course is given a role to play but the case study writer and the tutor act as observers. The debriefing follows this pattern:

(1) The case study writer:
    (a) Gives his or her impressions of the role-play;
    (b) States what actually happened in the situation on which the case was built.
(2) Each contributor gives his or her views of the case.
(3) Each contributor states the most significant thing learnt from the case study.
(4) The tutor reviews the case and then draws attention to appropriate management practices and theory.

One of the objectives of the programme is to develop a high level of skill in self-assessment. It is thought that such programmes cannot (nor should not) be assessed. To achieve a credit on this course the whole exercise must be completed together with a 3-hour written examination based on set-reading and prior-notice questions (Fitzgibbon and Heywood, 1986).

Students are afraid of this course, which ensures that there are never more than the maximum allowable number of nine. It is the only course in a heavy programme of study which is experiential, and very few of those who take the programme go away dissatisfied. It is highly praised and the course seems to be taken for its own sake, for few register for the examination.

Such role-playing might be of use in the undergraduate curriculum in a situation like that described by Bishop (1981), who reported that there was a change in student behaviour across three clinical undergraduate years when interviewing simulated patients. The junior students displayed more personal concern for the patients, whereas the seniors conducted a more controlled and structured interview.

Lee (1982) has described role-plays which accounted for 20% of the course mark. The grade depended on the factual content of the statements and presentation, and he found that more time was needed for debate and role-playing.

The interview is also widely used in education, and, in particular, in *viva-voce* examinations with postgraduates. The same problems in orals and observations are likely to arise when students are placed in an interview situation. Various studies have shown that shy students as well as those who are highly voluble can be disadvantaged. It has been observed that in such situations the highly anxious report a greater incidence of task-irrelevant thoughts than less anxious persons (Holloway et al., 1967; Ganzer, 1968). Their preoccupation with the task may be accompanied by irrelevant comments which are of a self deprecatory kind (Sarason and Stoops, 1978).

Much has been written about interviewing in management. This shows the need for clarity of goals. Interviewing can be very unreliable: for example, interviewers obtaining the same information are likely to interpret it differently.

In the exam situation it seems that interviewers tend to be influenced more by unfavourable than by favourable information. It is also important to consider if the information could be obtained in a different way. If large numbers of students are to be interviewed it is important to maintain the same structure both cognitively and affectively in each interview. Although reliability can be high, validity may be low. There is also a danger that if the interview is unstructured the examiner will talk more than the candidate. Structuring interviews has been shown to increase inter-rater reliability. In any case, an interview should be supported by other performance data (Holdsworth, 1981; Mayfield, 1964). It is possible that candidates may feel that two examiners are preferable to one, and as there is evidence to show that interviewers need training, so is there need to train interviewees.

The rise in interest in continuous assessment in Britain brought with it the idea that 'everything should be assessed... tutorials... seminars... discussion...' Again, the same first rule applies and that is to state the purpose of the assessment and to consider if it can be achieved in any other way. Very similar problems to those discussed here apply to orals, observations and interviews in the laboratory and project situations.

LABORATORY PRACTICALS

Once again, it seems that there has been relatively little research on the assessment of laboratory practicals. It has been well reviewed by Boud (1986) Kempa (1986) and others. Nevertheless, there has been much discussion and criticism of laboratory assessment procedures which has given rise to considerable interest in the objectives of laboratory work.

At GCE A level laboratory practicals required the student to conduct the practical and submit a report to external assessors for subsequent marking. In these circumstances the assessor marked the report rather than the practical. Thus the ability to do a practical (as opposed to the ability to report one) was not assessed.

It was for this reason (among others) that in Engineering Science at A level the JMB examiners moved to a system of coursework assessment in 1968. They defined three kinds of practical and stated the objectives which they were expected to obtain (Carter et al., 1986). These definitions are shown in Table 47. This threefold classification has been adopted by various authorities in higher education with the occasional refinement. Lee (1970), who seems to have made the first effort to determine the objectives for practicals in engineering by obtaining the views of practising chartered mechanical engineers, also related what he had found to the JMB classification. Since then there have been many statements of objectives, and Carter and Jordan have summarized them in the list shown in Table 48 (Carter et al., 1980).

One aspect of Lee's work which is seldom discussed is the finding (contrary to both our opinions) that engineers liked traditional laboratory work. It seems that they did not criticize it because they believed that it was the one part of their course where they felt they were experiencing real engineering. It enabled them to identify with what they believed engineering to be. This is a point which should not be forgotten in discussion of the value of laboratory and project work in subjects which are perceived to be practical but are nevertheless highly academic.

Table 47. Definitions of controlled assignments, experimental investigations and projects for engineering science at GCE A level. (Extracts reproduced by kind permission of the Joint Matriculation Board, Manchester, *Notes for the Guidance of Schools on Engineering Science* (A level))

(i) *Controlled assignments*
Controlled assignments are of short duration and normally accomplished within a two hour period; they are intimately connected with the subject matter. Pupils may work singly or in groups. Such assignments will:

(a) Reinforce and illuminate lesson material;
(b) Familiarize students with the use of scientific equipment;
(c) Develop a reliable habit of faithful observation, confirmation, and immediate record in a journal style;
(d) Introduce the techniques of critical review, analysis, deduction and evaluation;
(e) Promote good style amd presentation in the formal technical report.

(ii) *Experimental investigations*
An experimental investigation poses an engineering or scientific problem and involves the student in an analysis of the situation and an appropriate selection of procedures and techniques for solution. The end point of the particular investigation may or may not be known but the means for its achievement are comparatively discretionary.

The time needed for an investigation of this type should normally lie in the range 6 to 12 hours.

A record of an investigation should include:

(a) A clear account of the analysis of the problem;
(b) Brief report and comments on the work as the experiment proceeded;
(c) Comment upon the results;
(d) An appraisal of what has been achieved.

Projects
The project is a major undertaking for which it is suggested that 50 hours of laboratory time would be suitable. The pupil will be required to design a device or design and conduct an investigation to fulfil a specification and to evaluate the degree of fulfilment achieved.

Projects call for mental connective abilities rather than for craft skills and the time spent on construction or practical investigation should be kept at a minimum, the emphasis being on design and the formulation of problems, literature search in its widest sense and evaluation.

Table 48. The aims of laboratory work and some behavioural objectives. (Reproduced by kind permission of Jordan and Carter, 1986)

Aim	Behavioural objective capable of being tested and of being observed
1. To stimulate and maintain the student's interest in engineering.	Student likes working in the laboratory, is often to be seen there, arrives early, leaves late.
2. To illustrate, supplement and emphasize material taught in lectures.	Student uses lecture material, in laboratory problems and vice versa, has knowledge of methods learned.
3. To train the student to keep a continuous record of laboratory work.	Student keeps well-laid out notebook for this purpose rather than loose sheets of paper.
4. To train the student in formal writing of the experimental procedures adopted in laboratory practicals, and the writing of technical reports.	Student hands in well-written reports on time, discusses them with tutors and attempts to improve them.
5. To teach the student how to plan an experiment so that he derives useful, meaningful data.	Student comes to laboratory having read necessary references and with prepared plan of operation.
6. To give the student training in the processing and interpretation of experimental data.	Student uses graphs and tables intelligently, draws fair conclusions from them and deals sensibly with errors.
7. To train the student to use particular apparatus, test procedures or standard techniques.	Student shows competence in handling common laboratory equipment and learns how to use new equipment quickly.
8. To improve the learning/teaching process by improving the communication and rapport between staff and students.	Student talks with the staff, initiating discussion on the experiment and other matters.
9. To strengthen the student's understanding of engineering design, by showing him that practical work and design work must be integrated to achieve viable solutions to design problems.	
10. To develop the student's skill in problem-solving in both single and multi-solution situations.	Student progresses from 'dashing off in all directions' methods to planned attacks on problems.
11. To provide each student with an opportunity to practise the role of a professional engineer so that he can learn to perform that role.	Student exhibits responsible, truthful and reliable attitude towards data, use of time, care of equipment, etc.
12. To provide the student with a valuable stimulant to independent thinking.	Student creates his own solution to problems, does not wait to be told what to do. In discussion student puts his own points clearly.

13. To show the use of practical work as a process of discovery.

14. To demonstrate use of experimental work as an alternative to analytical methods of solving engineering problems.

15. To help students understand that small models of plant or processes can aid greatly in the understanding and improvement of such plant and processes.

16. To familiarize the student with the need to communicate technical concepts and situations—to inform and persuade management to certain courses of action—to disseminate technical knowledge and expertise for the benefit of all.

   Student can explain clearly what he has done and why using proper technical concepts, using graphs, tables, sketches, etc. as seems most useful.

17. To help student bridge the gap between the unreality of the academic situation and the industrial scene, with its associated social, economic and other restraints which engineers encounter.

18. To teach the student how accurate measurements made with laboratory equipment can be; to teach him how to devise methods that are precise when precision is required.

   Student can determine and report errors correctly, can devise more accurate methods of measurement and demonstrate them. Student also guesses correctly and knows when to ignore errors and when to 'round-off' numbers.

19. To teach the student what 'Scientific Method' is and how it is applied in an Engineering laboratory.

20. To give the student confidence in his ability to imagine a concept or hypothesis, to plan an experiment, to test it, to carry out that experiment and report its results to others.

   Student acts confidently yet sensibly and safely in the laboratory.

Lee's enquiry was part of a team exercise in which an attempt was made to derive objectives for the curriculum in engineering in education. Criticisms of these projects and the JMB project led to attempts to derive objectives from the task analyses of the work done by engineers in industry which were described in Chapter 6 (Lee, 1969; Monk, 1972; Moon, 1968).

The importance of this general movement to derive objectives was that aims came to be stated in behavioural terms against which it was possible to devise criterion and semi-criterion referenced measures. Numerous grade schedules have been developed and, like the essay schedules described in Chapter 10, they can be used during a course to provide students with feedback about their performance.

Boud (1986) has pointed out that, when the aim of assessment is feedback, students themselves can provide each other with useful feedback and reinforcement. While this often happens in the laboratory it does not do so universally, so he argues that peer-assessment should be formalized in the laboratory. In this way, students begin to take responsibility for their own learning and gain insight into their own performance through having to judge the work of others. They are therefore a useful adjunct to assessment by staff.

The choice of objectives from among so many is always a matter of compromise, and this should be determined by the major aims which the course designers have in mind. Contrast the list in Table 47 with assessment criteria for the experimental investigations in JMB Engineering Science at A level (Table 49). The focus of the latter is very sharp. Note that one of the items required self-assessment.

Table 49. An assessment procedure for experimental investigations used for Engineering Science (JMB) A level GCE

QUESTIONS ON THE EXPERIMENTAL INVESTIGATIONS
1. Has the candidate made safe use of the apparatus involved?
2. Has the candidate succeeded in making accurate observations within the limits of the apparatus used?
3. Has the candidate presented the observations in a clear and workmanlike manner?
4. Are the findings of the investigation consistent with the observations made?
5. Does the final report contain an account of the essential features of the work?

Form B1

CRITERIA WITH RESPECT TO THE TWO EXPERIMENTAL INVESTIGATIONS

1. **Theoretical understanding**   Grade
   In relation to his depth of understanding of the theoretical aspects of
   the problem the candidate has shown sufficient understanding of the
   problem to enable him/her to plan the approach competently   3
   sufficient understanding of the problem to be seldom in need of help 2
   limited understanding of the problem   1
   little or no understanding of the problem   0

2. **Planning the investigation**
   In determining the activities to be undertaken the candidate considered a range of appropriate possibilities with respect to the type
   and scope of measurements to be made and came to a reasoned
   conclusion   3
   considered a range of possibilities and came to a less well-reasoned
   conclusion   2
   considered an inadequate range of possibilities   1
   exercised little judgement   0

3. **Procedures and equipment**
   In selecting the experimental procedures and equipment to be used
   the candidate made a reasoned assessment of the alternatives available and came to a well-argued conclusion   3
   lacked depth in determining the final choice   2
   made some attempt to consider alternative approaches   1
   unthinkingly adopted standard procedures or relied entirely on the
   teacher's advice   0

4. **Errors**
   The report includes a statement of errors together with estimates of
   magnitudes and a discussion of their relative significance   3
   a statement of errors and estimates of the magnitude of each error   2
   a statement of errors (including the most important errors)   1
   no explicit statement of errors   0

5. **Critical review**
   In considering the investigation in terms of the results obtained and
   the conclusions reached the candidate made a thorough appraisal
   including a thorough estimate of the effects of the assumptions made
   and including suggestions for improving the approach and/or taking
   the work further   3
   as above but with one of the features missing   2
   made a significant appraisal of the work done   1
   made no significant appraisal of the work done   0

6. **Personal contribution**
   In planning and executing the investigation the candidate exercised
   initiative and judgement throughout   3
   lacked initiative and judgement at times   2
   made little personal contribution   1
   relied entirely on external help   0

The engineering science scales are not the only possible dimensions for measurement. A more popular approach is to grade a statement against a scale as, for example, good, satisfactory, barely adequate, not suitable for this work. (This scale is taken from part of the classification used to assess the work of examiners by the JMB.) Reliability diminishes with increasing scale points, and there is also a tendency to regress to the mean. The principles relating to such scales are the same as those for grading set out in Chapter 3 and the Glossary.

In certain areas of practical work it is desirable to ensure mastery. In engineering science candidates must pass a hurdle (scheme A on the forms, Tables 49 and 50) but this is not an assessment of true mastery because not all of them have to be given 'yes' to pass the hurdle. However, if required, quite precise criteria may be established to check that a student possesses basic laboratory skills. Keller-type schemes provide for those who fail to repeat.

Table 50. An assessment procedure for projects used for Engineering Science (JMB) A level GCE

QUESTIONS ON THE PROJECTS
6. Did the candidate produce a work plan (Project Outline)?
7. Has the candidate used the work plan with intelligence?
8. Has the candidate worked consistently for appreciable periods during the conduct of the project?
9. Has the candidate made use of relevant and independent sources of information available to him, e.g. has he consulted books to which he was not directed and mentioned them in his report?
10. Does the final report contain an account of the essential features of the work?

Form B2

CRITERIA WITH RESPECT TO THE PROJECT

	Grade
7. **Planning**	
In planning the project the candidate recognized relevant factors, discussed their importance sensibly, drew up a detailed specification in practical terms and mapped out a reasoned plan of campaign	3
as above but lacked one significant feature	2
made some attempt to analyse the problem in practical terms	1
made little attempt to analyse the problem	0

8. **Execution**
In executing the plan the candidate gave thorough consideration to realistic alternatives at every stage, and made a reasoned selection of the optimum solution in each case — 3
gave consideration to realistic alternative solutions with inadequate reasons for selection — 2
gave some attention to the consideration of alternative solutions — 1
paid little attention to this aspect of the work — 0

9. **Design activity**
In relation to the design for all or part of the project with respect to procedure or artefact the candidate produced a markedly significant and original contribution — 3
an original contribution — 2
a new device by applying a standard design technique — 1
little or no design activity during his work on the project — 0

10. **Use of resources**
In relation to the resources and time available the candidate used them well throughout the project — 3
used them reasonably well for much of the project — 2
failed to make reasonable use of them over significant periods of the project — 1
made little use of them throughout the project — 0

11. **Critical view**
In comparing the final product or outcome with the original specifications the candidate has produced a thorough and objective discussion in which consideration has been given to all major aspects of the

work including suggestions for further development and a critical appraisal of the conduct of the project with a clear indication of the lessons learnt 3

a reasonable depth of discussion which, however, lacks either objectivity or coverage 2

some significant comparison 1

a discussion of little significance 0

12. **Personal contribution**

In planning, executing and appraising the project the candidate exercised initiative and judgement throughout 3

lacked initiative and judgement at times 2

made little personal contribution 1

relied entirely on external help 0

An area of controversy is created by answers to the question, how much practical? This can only be decided when the purposes for which it is desired are clear. Answers to this question may lead to the view, as they did in engineering science, that only certain activities should be assessed. However, the student was required to keep a journal in order to demonstrate that he or she had completed experimental work in other content and skill areas of the course.

A variety of techniques are used to assess practicals. For example, the engineering science assessment requires a written report with teacher comments on the assessment schedule. Pencil and paper tests using multiple-choice questions have also been used, as have interviews and straightforward observation. The type of test used will depend on the outcome required. Thus manual skills will require a practical test, interpreting data will need some kind of written report, and so on. As in medicine, the candidate may be interviewed. The same general principles outlined elsewhere apply to tests of whatever kind in the laboratory situation.

Criterion-referenced tests which seek mastery do not pose a problem for scoring. However, as soon as grades are required to discriminate between students, problems arise. Boud has pointed out that if objectives are carefully written then the same index of discrimination which is used for the analysis of multiple-choice tests in the classroom is applicable. This assumes that only a limited number of objectives are deployed and that the extent to which they are achieved can be assessed.

As in the humanities, the marks given in coursework in science tend to be high when compared with other forms of assessment. One of the major developments in the last 30 years has been the inclusion of project activities at all levels in higher education and in a variety of subjects.

PROJECTS AND PROJECT WORK

Like continuous assessment, the meaning and requirements for projects between departments varies, even with the same university (Harris and Smith,

1982; Samuelowicz, 1983). Projects are a feature of education in engineering and science. The large and compulsory project in diploma in technology courses in the late 1950s gave a great impetus to this kind of activity (Heywood, 1969, 1971b). The dissertation in the humanities is the equivalent of the project in science.

Projects are advocated for interdisciplinary studies because real-life situations require a variety of knowledge and resources for their solution and also because people have had to work in teams. Thus at Aachen Technische Hochschulen in West Germany teams of students had as their objective the making of video recordings which seemed to enhance their sense of independence and responsibility (Brandt, 1976).

It is also argued that the unseen examination in sociology as a technique for assessing research methods is unsuitable because it constrains teaching and assesses the ability to talk about rather than do research (Marsh, 1981).

Projects have been used in mathematics to open up real situations for investigation (Hall, 1982) and have also been employed in the first year to encourage students to read literature. For example, at Napier College, Edinburgh, a librarian and a biologist have collaborated to help students to prepare three projects of increasing complexity involving detailed literature searches. They claim that the technique increased the student's ability and willingness to read scientific literature, and that these attitudes persisted throughout the course (McElroy and McNaughton, 1979).

It seems that electrical engineers in Britain believe that there are three groups of students in any first-year cohort. They are those who will do well as practical engineers whatever the teaching method used; those who cannot do project work; and a large group whose performance may be improved by carefully designed strategic and experimental studies (Carter and Lee, 1981).

Project work has not been confined to full-time study. It has been used by the Open University in distance learning and seems to have found favour among staff and students (Bynner and Henry, 1984; Henry, 1977). Some of the problems found seem to be general, and these relate to the amount of time required by tutor and student for guidance and work. The role of the supervisor at both graduate and undergraduate level has been identified as an issue (Moses, 1985). Open University students also needed guidance in choosing a viable topic and in identifying, locating, and collecting information. This is also true of students in undergraduate and school courses. The Open University finds, as do many others, that the amount and organization of individual support is problematic (Cook, 1980; Silk and Bowlby, 1981). For some departments it could be too costly (Harris and Bullock, 1981). There is no doubt that some project work can be expensive.

The general impression of project work is that it is favoured by many students. Most of them are motivated and many feel that the independent involvement in their own learning is of value (Armstrong and Shanker, 1981). However, a paper by Gabb (1981) suggests that it is not all plain sailing. He evaluated the work of 28 students at a British university and found that a profound hidden curriculum was at play. The students reported that their efforts were directed to getting a good mark rather than in using the project as a learning experience. From his study he drew up a set of rules for the project game. For example:

> 1.1 *Supervisor*—a topic must be chosen on the basis of who is supervising it rather than for any intrinsic interest. Important criteria for choosing a supervisor are helpfulness, approachability and friendliness.
> 2.1 *Assessment Procedure*—discover as much information as possible on the assessment procedure. It is supposed to be secret but friendly staff members will reveal it if encouraged.
> 2.4 *Results*—most assessors are more interested in results than any other aspect of the project—results make projects easy to mark. Advise your supervisor of any results obtained. If no results are forthcoming, don't tell your supervisor until it is absolutely necessary.
> 3.2 *Length*—the report should be approximately 30 pages in length. Padding may be necessary to obtain sufficient words but do not exceed the 30 page limit as you will be marked down for 'waffle'.
> 3.3 *References*—a long list of references. These can be obtained from abstracting journals, which provide enough information for a decision to be made (Gabb, 1981).

Gabb said that these students took a strongly instrumental view towards their project. In the circumstances in which the projects seem to have been administered they had a right to be cynical. Once again, the power of beliefs about assessment is all too clear.

Problems in assessment have been discussed in various reports, and Boud and his colleagues (1986) conclude that the reason why project work so often contributes little to the overall grading is because the reliability of assessment can be very low. He accounts for this in two ways: first, the projects can vary in difficulty, and second, because a supervisor may use different criteria to other supervisors when assessing projects of the same group of students. To overcome this difficulty some universities have developed fairly precise statements of what is required to obtain a grade (Black, 1975; Prosser and Oliver, 1983). Boud, who has examined two of them, suggested that they do not take content into account. An alternative view is that content matters only in so far as the content used is correct for the problem to be solved and that is necessarily inherent in the scheme. Unfortunately apart from Engineering Science at A level, which has been the subject of a 17-year evaluation (Carter *et al.*, 1986), there are few evaluative studies of project work.

Coursework in Engineering Science at A level began in 1967 for first examination in 1969. At that time it included four experimental investigations and one 50-hour (laboratory) project. In order to try to obtain reliability and validity a scheme of assessment was designed to meet the stated behavioural objectives of the course. In its original format a series of criterion-referenced questions were put to the teachers to which they had to respond 'yes' or 'no'. The assessments were undertaken by the teachers and until 1986 the project reports were independently examined by moderators appointed by the JMB:

the moderators also made periodic visits to the schools. In the early years all projects were seen by the moderators because the number of students involved was small. Two moderators remained with examination throughout the period 1967–86.

It should be noted that each student was expected to have a copy of, or access to, *Notes for Guidance on Engineering Science*, published by the Board. It was also expected that they would fully understand the criteria for assessment. There is not much evidence that the *Notes for Guidance* were read: there was plenty to show that the criteria in the assessment schedules (Tables 49 and 50) influenced performance.

During the first year the moderators were able to ask the students to volunteer to do an experiment in their presence and that of the teacher. They were assessed by the published scheme and it was found that four items gave rise to considerable difficulty. While it was clear that some change would be necessary, it was considered that an indication of student perceptions of the criteria would be useful before making any revision. Thus in 1970 candidates were asked to give an example, from their own experience, of the type of response they thought was required to gain an affirmative answer to the particular assessment question. The teacher was asked to indicate agreement or disagreement with the candidates' examples, as was one of the moderators. A similar exercise was conducted in 1971, and by 1974 the strict criterion-reference questions had given way to scaled multiple-choice questions, and the format of the scheme became that shown in Tables 49 and 50. With one or two minor modifications it remained in that form until 1986.

The schedule is based on a model of what it was thought that engineers did in industry (Figure 31). It is a compromise, and highlights some features at the expense of others, for engineers do more than the scheme reflects. It was felt that the skills of planning implementation and self-assessment (critical review) were the qualities on which to focus. Content was assessed in relation to the understanding of the problem set. The examiners did not believe that they could judge the aesthetic merits of a design, or that they should be a primary function of the activity.

The selection of these objectives illustrates several points which were made previously, especially with reference to lists of critical thinking and the relationship between aims and objectives. First, the quantity of assessments which can be made are severely limited by instructional time and teacher workload. Any criterion-referenced list has to have the merit of simplicity and focus on key domains. Second, one well-chosen aim (in this case, the simulation of an engineer at work) will lead necessarily to the key behaviours which should be drawn into focus.

Perhaps the most important and persistent problem of this project work has been its overall contribution to the total course mark. In the first year 12.5% of the total mark come from coursework, but it was evident that it was worth much more. Thus in 1970 it was raised to 20% and remained at that figure. It is interesting to note that in some GCE examinations quite high percentages are now allowed for coursework, in spite of problems with its reliability.

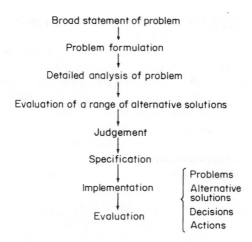

Figure 31. The cycle of the engineering design activity

It was also found that the amount of coursework required for submission was excessive. Accordingly, the requirement for four experimental investigations was reduced to two. The problem of 'how much' was a continuing question for evaluation throughout the period. It was a problem which also applied to the syllabus, and a significant reduction in its content was made without damaging the course, so its authors believed. Given the findings of Ramsden and Entwistle and Gibbs and Haigh reported in Chapter 10, it shows that significant reductions in content can be achieved without detriment to the syllabus.

In the first year it was found that some students had great difficulty in formulating a suitable topic for the project, and this was always found to be the case. Those who could not formulate a proposal in terms that were sufficiently precise and practical tended also to be those in difficulty in the written examination. Finally, it was clear that many of the students were intrinsically motivated. Many hours were spent in producing projects and some vied with postgraduate work for quality.

The moderators felt it necessary to try to help students plan projects better and at the same time try to control the amount of time spent on this work. To this end, they produced a form called the 'Project Outline', which had to be completed by each student before commencement of the project. The teacher was required to confirm that the project was feasible and the moderator to judge the appropriateness of the project for submission. The scheme is shown in Table 51. It was open to the moderator to reject the submission and to offer advice on alternatives and the 'Project Outline' was resubmitted with the project report. These outlines are normally completed in the preceding summer of the two-year course.

So, how well did the system work? The first change from a dichotomous scheme of marking to a scaled response caused the distribution at the lower end of the mark scale to be raised. This meant that some competence on the part of the weaker candidates was recognized.

In general, over 17 years the results of the moderation have been shown to be reasonably consistent from year to year. It has been found to discriminate well between the candidates. Some fail to pass the hurdle each year but the numbers in this group are very small.

Table 51. Extract from the Engineering Science Project Outline. (Reproduced by permission of the Joint Matriculation Board, Manchester)

THE CONTENTS OF THE OUTLINE

Title
This should be a clear statement of the problem to be tackled. While the title should be brief, it must not be vague or so general that it does not convey the essence of the project.

Analysis of the problem
The problem to be dealt with in the project should be analysed as fully as possible. A general statement of the problem should be given, and where possible, quantities laid down together with the limitations under which you will be working, such as restraints of size, cost, use and availability of workshop facilities and assistance. For example, if an engine test bed is to be constructed, the size and nature of the engine test bed and associated equipment should be stated, the use to which the engine is to be put should be given and the parameters to be measured should be listed. If the project is of a more investigatory nature a similar analysis is required. For example, if it is concerned with an investigation into atmospheric pollution, the nature of the variables to be measured, the periods over which measurements are to be made, the factors likely to affect these variables and the uses which might be made of the information gained should be stated.

Practical Problems to be Solved
Having considered the project in outline you will be able to recognize the major practical problems which need to be overcome. These may be the design and manufacture of a piece of equipment or the design of experimental procedures, or both.

Possible Solutions
It should be possible at this stage to see your way to solving these major practical problems in order that success can be achieved. It is therefore important that you should offer likely solutions to these problems. It may be that one solution is so obviously the best that a lengthy consideration of alternative approaches is unnecessary. In most cases, however, a number of alternative solutions will occur to you or will arise as a result of consultation with your teacher or other people. The final choice of a solution will in most cases depend on further work and consultation, and the use of appropriate references. Your outline should give the main direction of your ideas at the time of submission.

Resources
The choice of the best solution will also depend upon the resources you have available. You should, therefore, list under the appropriate headings, equipment, manufacturing facilities, materials required, references, consultants, technical assistance available and the approximate cost involved. Such headings will not be equally important for all projects.

Timetable
You will now be in a position to draw up an approximate timetable of operation. It does not help to make wild guesses about the number of hours you will need; it is better to work in weeks available and then split the period into component parts. Do not forget to list the time necessary for writing the final report. In planning your time always assume that any task will take you much longer than you imagine on a first consideration. It is also important to allow a certain degree of flexibility; if you draw a time sequence diagram, allow for a fair amount of variation.

References
In submitting your project outline, list the books and articles you have read in connection with the planning and also the individuals whose advice you have sought.

Future Work
You are strongly advised to read the appropriate sections of the *Notes for the Guidance of Schools* at all stages of the project, particularly during the planning period. When the moderators have studied your outlines they will forward their comments to your teacher. You are strongly advised to follow any recommendations made by your teacher or the moderator.

The distributions of the marks are reasonably spread and consistent from one year to another. Such variations as occur do so at the top end of the scale. Perhaps the most interesting aspect of the evaluation relates to the differences between the marks of the teachers and moderators. Once again, consistency is reported. The teacher-assessors are more generous than the moderators in the application of the assessment criteria. This tendency is also observed when the teacher-assessor is a member of the moderating team: they are seen to be more severe than the other teacher-assessors. The average difference in scores is found to be of the order of 12% at the top end of the range and 7% at the bottom. In the view of the authors of the report this justified the standardizing procedure which the Board had adopted. The moderators took the view that the teacher-assessors could not be relied upon to place their own candidates in an acceptable rank order of performance with respect to the specific sets of criteria specified for engineering science, and this view was confirmed by their experience.

A detailed description of the whole examination is given in Chapter 13 and an analysis of other data provided. The ability to formulate a problem appears to be a crucial skill: it separates out those who can do projects from those who cannot. The fact that it does this consistently lends support to those like MacDonald (1969), who hold the view that problem-finding and problem-solving are different skills. Postgraduates, it seems also, find problem-definition difficult (Zuber-Skerrit and Knight, 1986), and the type of problem is likely to influence the approach to problem-definition adopted. For example, these engineering projects are essentially of the 'think-up' type, whereas the problems faced by a doctor arise from direct contact with a patient. Is medical problem-solving more akin to fault-finding in engineering (Morrison, 1985)?

Fredericksen (1981), of the Educational Testing Service, suggests that one of the chief blocks to developing a generalized problem-solving test is the fact that problem-solving seems to be highly subject matter-specific. If so, does cognitive style influence problem-solving? At least one study has shown that on the focusing as against scanning dimension (Bruner *et al.*, 1956), in a context-free fault-diagnosis task focusers show a superior diagnostic performance. Yet training did not improve the performance of either focusers or scanners.

A study of the first phase of problem-solving in medicine has questioned beliefs about the significance of pattern-recognition. The subjects in this study made immediate, active, interpretative or evaluative responses to initial items of clinical information elicited from 'patients' which could not be described as diagnostic hypotheses yet were, nevertheless, important operationally (Gale and Narsden, 1982).

Other authors have conceptualized the process as being cue-acquisition, hypothesis-generation, cue-interpretation, and hypothesis-evaluation (Elstein *et al.*, 1979). Clearly, there are important links between clinical memory and clinical strategy, but to what extent are the emotions involved? How important is the emotional element of surprise in cognition?

Scheffler (1977) writes:

> The constructive conquest of surprise is registered in the achievement of new explanatory structures, while cognitive application of these structures provokes surprise once more. Surprise is vanquished by theory, and theory is, in turn, overcome by surprise. Cognition is thus two-sided and has its own rhythm; it stabilizes and co-ordinates; it also unsettles and divides. It is responsible for shaping our patterned orientations to the future, but it must also be responsive to the insistent need to learn from the future. Establishing habits, it must stand ready to break them. Unlearning old ways of thought, it must also power the quest for new, and greater, expectations. These stringent demands upon our cognitive processes also constitute stringent demands upon our emotional capacities. The growth of cognition is thus, in fact, inseparable from the education of the emotions.

Another point arising from our evaluations of practical work is the failure to develop good performance in the critical review. Today we would call this 'self-assessment'. Students found it extremely difficult to go beyond the trivial. It seems that the advice given to teachers and students was insufficient. Related to this is the difficulty which students had in going beyond lists of errors to relative significance and calculation of magnitudes in the experimental investigations.

Finally, there is much debate about the role of projects in education. We have seen that they provide strong intrinsic motivation and many of us see this as its main justification. Content is not the point—skill is. Content should be marked for its correctness within the context used. To hope that projects will cause the student to acquire a wide range of content is to miss the point.

Recent work on intelligence theory by Sternberg (1985) throws a different light on the value of projects. He defines intelligence as the purposive adaptation to, and selection and shaping of, real-world environments relevant to one's life. Given this definition, it is possible to argue that projects contribute to the development of components which the curriculum does not otherwise do.

Sternberg argues that there are three components of intelligence which he also classifies by function and level of generality. These are *meta-components*, which are processes used in planning, monitoring and decision-making in task performance; *performance components*, which are the processes used in the execution of the task; and *knowledge-acquisition components*, used in learning new information. Each of these is characterized by three properties—duration, difficulty and probability of execution. They are, in principle, independent. It is evident that our project-assessment schemes and those of others are concerned with the evaluation of meta-components. Elsewhere he calls them 'executive processes'. We can see that a key difference between the project-planning exercises and the written subtest is the time element. The two situations require the student to use different information techniques. The written exercise is a different and 'new' domain of learning for which training is required. In order for the skill to become an 'old' domain a high level of automatization is required, so that the different processes in the meta-components are brought into play much more quickly. That is, at a certain level they have to become non-executive. The project and the written paper while demanding the same meta-components might be regarded as being at different levels in the experiential learning continuum (Figure 32). Some executive processing will always be required at the written paper level, and it is possible to argue that the task-performance and stress which it creates are a more accurate reflection of the everyday activities of executives than the substantive project.

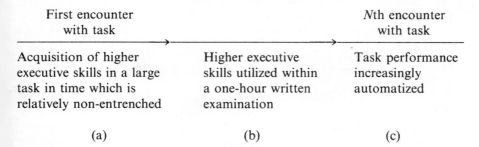

First encounter with task		Nth encounter with task
Acquisition of higher executive skills in a large task in time which is relatively non-entrenched	Higher executive skills utilized within a one-hour written examination	Task performance increasingly automatized
(a)	(b)	(c)

Figure 32. Sternberg's (1985) diagram of the course of experience with a task, modified to show the development of the higher executive processes in the Engineering Science project in relation to the (a) written one-hour examination requiring (b) these same skills

PROJECTS IN SUBJECTS OTHER THAN TECHNOLOGY AND SCIENCE

Project work has been done in many fields. One report from Griffith University in Australia suggests that explicit criteria developed for science have been taken up by departments in the humanities (Prosser and Oliver, 1983). In Table 52 the engineering science scheme has been adapted by history teachers. This was

Table 52. Marking Scheme for project work in history

		Mark *(max. 50)*
A.	*Historical information—located and recorded.*	
1.	In relation to the data collected the information is:	
	— inaccurate while the treatment of the topic is slight	1
	— accurate while the treatment of the topic is slight	2
	— accurate while the treatment of the topic is adequate	3
	— accurate while the treatment of the topic is excellent	4
2.	In respect of the available resources the candidate has made:	
	— poor use of the sources available	1
	— some use of the sources available	3
	— excellent use of the sources available	4
3.	Teachers may award two more marks to candidates who use primary sources	2
B.	*Comprehension*, i.e. the use the candidate makes of the historical information to construct a coherent pattern.	
4.	The student's understanding of the historical content:	
	— shows little or no relevance to the topic	1
	— shows some relevance to the topic	3
	— shows a clear grasp of the material	4
5.	The student's understanding of the historical content may be judged in part according to the degree to which he/she relies on direct transcription. This candidate:	
	— relies totally on unacknowledged transcription	1
	— uses some unacknowledged transcription but attempts to express the topic in his own words	3
	— has written the report in his own words, acknowledging sources where necessary	4
6.	The teacher may award two additional marks to a candidate whose total presentation shows a grasp of the historical setting of the topic (e.g. use of maps, diagrams, relevant illustrations, quotations)	2
C.	*Analysis and synthesis* (analysis is a preliminary step to arranging the material collected in a coherent pattern. It involves the selection of the most important and relevant points from the information assembled. Synthesis is the expression of the pattern that emerges from the analysis of the subject matter.)	

7. This candidate:
   — made no attempt at analysis — 0
   — fails to distinguish relevant from irrelevant
     material and issues and important from unimport-
     ant material and issues — 1
   — distinguishes some important issues arising from his topic — 3
   — has isolated the important issues, factors or
     questions arising from his topic — 4

8. This candidate:
   — shows little attempt to organize the material collected — 1
   — has organized his material into a coherent pattern — 3
   — has organized his material to answer questions
     or to describe issues, or to explain factors
     involved in the material — 4

9. Teachers may award two additional marks to candidates who have
   imposed an original structure on the material collected — 2

D. *Evaluation* (the student applies a standard of reasoning and judgement which leads him to assess causes and consequences and to
   distinguish between fact and opinion; history and legend. The project should have some form of conclusion in which the candidate is
   expected to explain his findings and/or opinions, having taken into
   account different viewpoints and values.)

10. This candidate:
    — made no attempt to distinguish fact from opinion;
      history from legend; causes from consequences — 0
    — fails to distinguish fact from opinion; history
      from legend; causes from consequences — 1
    — shows some ability to distinguish fact from opinion;
      history from legend; causes from consequences — 3
    — assesses causes and consequences; distinguishes
      fact from opinion and history from legend — 4

11. This candidate:
    — made no attempt to draw conclusion — 0
    — fails to come to any conclusion or judgement — 1
    — accepts received opinion and judgement
      without comment — 3
    — critically examines (questions) received opinions
      and judgements and forms his own independent
      judgement — 4

12. Teachers may award two additional marks to candidates who show
    a critical approach to the sources they have used — 2

E. *Presentation* (including the quality of illustrated material, list of
   contents, book list, references). — 10

developed over a period of two years after training. In the first round in which almost 1000 projects were completed the teachers came to reject the loosely structured scheme. After evaluation, and a year later, they redesigned the scheme along the lines of engineering science and tried it on about 400 projects. It was found that there was reasonable consistency between the teachers' marks and those of the moderators (Heywood, 1977; Heywood *et al.*, 1980).

Restraints

Departments in institutions of higher education do not have the assessor availability that is open to systems of public examination. However, in the scheme described by Black (1975) the monitoring is done by the supervisor and an independent assessor. The project report is first evaluated by the supervisor and, then with the assessor's critique it is passed to a panel of senior members of staff for grading. Carter and his colleagues report many similar practices in engineering departments in Britain. Nevertheless, a large number of projects will create supervisor problems.

In their paper Carter and his colleagues (1980) question whether such quality assessment should constitute a quantifiable and numerical component of a final degree classification, 'since different university departments are every bit as idiosyncratic as the individual staff and the students within them'.

There is a very simple answer to this question. It is that since, in Britain at least, students have to be classified into honours then any substantial activity should contribute to that classification. There is no reason why a group of university departments could not operate a cross-moderation scheme of the kind operated for Engineering Science at A level. Some formalized training would be necessary. Another way forward would be to involve students in their own assessment.

PROFILES

Project schemes of the kind described are in effect profiles of student performance. The term 'profile' is used fairly loosely in education, and in this section a distinction will be made between grade, criterion and learning profiles. A profile is a 'portrayal' of the characteristics of a person or institutions in relation to some kind of activity or another. Profiling is the task of drawing up a profile, and these have been used in industry for many years for purposes of staff appraisal (Fleishman, 1967). Within the last 20 years profiles have acquired some importance in education, especially in the school and further education sectors in Britain (FESC, 1981; FEU, 1984). A major study of the potential of profiles in schools was carried out by Scottish headteachers and their report is a classic (SHTA, 1977).

As has been shown repeatedly in this book and more especially in the references to Aptitude Treatment interaction, many factors contribute to achievement. Success is obtained in different ways. For this reason, a single grade as a measure of a person's overall performance is regarded as unsatisfactory or, to use Jackson's (1985) term, 'hazardous'. Profiles may therefore provided a means for overcoming this difficulty, and may also be used to give information about personal qualities and interests. In the case of low-achievers a profile may be presented in the form of a record of achievement, and much interest has centred on this aspect.

Profiles are described in specific criteria; for example:

Communication:
(1) The candidate is able to list, select and organize information using alphabetical order;
(2) Use accurate spelling and punctuation; etc.

Sometimes they are scaled; for example:

(1) Can make sensible replies when spoken;
(2) Can hold conversations and take messages;
(3) Can follow and give simple descriptions and explanations;
(4) Can communicate effectively with a range of people in a variety of situations;
(5) Can present a logical and effective argument; can analyse others' arguments.

It will be seen one again that these are behavioural descriptions derived from lists like those presented in Chapter 6. It will also be seen that they are very similar to the project-grading schemes in engineering science and history. Hundreds of profiles have been produced but there seems to have been little evaluation of their reliability and validity. The reader is referred to *Uses and Abuses of Profiling* by Law (1984) for details of the very many types of profile in use.

Grade Profiles

These relate to examinations. Many examinations at GCE A level and in universities are split into a number of subtests. It has been argued that a better description of the candidate would be given if the results of the individual subtests were included in the score. In the 1970s this possibility was examined for GCE Engineering Science at A level, and it was concluded that it would cause more confusion than the single grade. The analysis of the examination which is given in Chapter 13 shows just how complicated the problem is.

Criterion Profiles

These have long been used in technical and professional education (Gibney and Viersma, 1986). The licences of ships' officers and airline pilots are statements

Table 53. Nine criterion measures for the assessment of trainee general practitioners. (Reproduced by kind permission of Freeman and Byrne, 1976)

Criterion 1: Information gathering

This criterion is concerned with the trainee's willingness, ability and skill in gathering information necessary for diagnosis and/or decisions.

Behavioural objectives

The unacceptable trainee:	The acceptable trainee:
1. Follows no routine of history taking;	1. Takes a comprehensive history, when appropriate, including clinical, psychological and social factors;
2. Fails to identify or does not bother to develop salient leads;	2. Records his information carefully;
3. Will not pursue alternative hypotheses;	3. Uses previous and continuing records intelligently;
4. Does not seek information on clinical, psychological and social factors;	4. Plans investigations and uses diagnostic services intelligently.
5. Recording is sketchy and not systematic;	
6. Tends to use investigations in a 'blunderbuss' fashion.	

Criterion 2: Problem-solving

This criterion is concerned with the trainee's ability and skill in using information gained to develop diagnosis and support clinical activity.

Behavioural objectives

The unacceptable trainee:	The acceptable trainee:
1. Does not fully realize the implications of the data which he collects;	1. Realizes the importance of unexpected findings and seeks to interpret them;
2. Is unable to interpret the unexpected result which he may often ignore;	2. Understands the nature of probability and uses this to assist his diagnosis and decision-making;
3. His thinking tends to be rigid and unimaginative and impedes his recognition of associated problems;	3. Takes all data into account before making a decision and routinely tests alternative hypotheses
4. His general shortcomings—rigidity of thought and lack of capacity to range round flexibly, i.e. 'diverge' when thinking over a particular problem—have an inhibiting effect on his problem-solving skills.	4. Thinks effectively—he has the capacity to range flexibly, or 'diverge', in the search for relevant factors in connection with the particular problem in hand, and he has also the capacity to focus, or 'converge', in his thinking on whatever factors have been decided upon as relevant.

Criterion 3: Clinical judgement

This criterion is concerned with the trainee's ability to use sound judgement in planning for and carrying out treatment, and conveying his advice and opinion to patients.

Behavioural objectives

The unacceptable trainee:

1. Is concerned more with treatment than the overall welfare of his patient;

2. Plans treatment when not familiar with the procedures or therapy selected;

3. Choice of treatment is rigid;

4. Tends to use set routine or 'favourite' prescriptions, whether appropriate to a particular patient or not;

5. Does not explain his proposals in terms understood by the patient.

The acceptable trainee:

1. Is familiar with the uses and limitations of the treatment he selected. He recognizes his or her own limitations;

2. Considers simple therapy or expectant measures first;

3. Shows regard for the individual patient's needs, wishes and total circumstances;

4. Is flexible and will modify treatment or decisions immediately the clinical situation requires he should do so;

5. Takes patient into his confidence and explains his proposals in terms appropriate to the individual patient.

Criterion 4: Relationship to patients

This criterion is concerned with the trainee's effectiveness in working with patients.

Behavioural objectives

The unacceptable trainee:

1. Does not relate well to patients either through aloofness, discourtesy, indifference or pressures of work;

2. Has difficulty in understanding his patients' needs;

3. Is unable to give patients confidence and may even unnecessarily alarm them;

4. Reacts poorly to a patient's hostile or emotional behaviour;

5. Does not exhibit sympathy nor compassion in dealing with patients.

The acceptable trainee:

1. Gives patients confidence, affords co-operation and relieves their anxiety;

2. While patients appreciate his interest in their well-being he does not become emotionally involved;

3. Is honest with the patient and his or her family;

4. Patients like the trainee and feel he is an easy person of whom to ask questions or with whom they may discuss problems.

Criterion 5: Continuing responsibility

This criterion is concerned with the trainee's willingness to accept and fulfil the responsibility for long-term patient care.

Behavioural objectives

The unacceptable trainee:

1. Either loses interest after initial treatment or does not spend time on follow-up care;
2. Becomes discouraged with slow progress and cannot cope with a poor prognosis;
3. Is unable to communicate hard facts to a patient or his relatives;
4. Uses ancillary personnel inadequately or demands greater assistance than they are competent to give him;
5. Fails to review a patient's case at suitable intervals.

The acceptable trainee:

1. Encourages patients to work for their own rehabilitation and shows that he too has the same objective;
2. Observes patient's progress and alters management and therapy as required;
3. Understands the roles of ancillary personnel and makes maximum effective use of their help;
4. Maintains a positive and persistent attitude to health and under proper circumstances to recovery.

Criterion 6: Emergency care

This criterion is concerned with the trainee's ability to act effectively in emergency situations.

Behavioural objectives

The unacceptable trainee:

1. Panics easily and loses valuable time by ineffective action;
2. Becomes confused under pressure and has difficulty in establishing priorities;
3. Is unable to delegate appropriate aspects of care to others;
4. Is unable or unwilling to make and sustain decisions alone.

The acceptable trainee:

1. Quickly assesses a situation and establishes priorities with full regard to life-saving procedures;
2. Is aware of the consequences of delay;
3. Is able to obtain and organize the assistance of others;
4. Is able and willing to make and sustain decisions alone if necessary.

Criterion 7: Relationship with colleagues

This criterion is concerned with the trainee's ability to work effectively with his colleagues and members of the health team.

Behavioural objectives

The unacceptable trainee:

1. Has difficulty in personal relationships and lacks the ability to give and take instruction gracefully;

The acceptable trainee:

1. Gets on well with other people. He is conscious of the need for team-work and fits in well as a member or, on occasion, as leader of a team;

2. Tends to be tactless or inconsiderate;

3. Is unable to inspire the confidence or co-operation of those with whom he works;

4. Is unwilling to make referrals or seek consultation. Does not support colleagues in their contacts with patients.

2. Seeks consultation when appropriate and respects the views of others;

3. Acknowledges the contributions of others;

4. Creates an atmosphere of 'working with' not 'working for' in other people. Demonstrates self-control.

Criterion 8: Professional values

This criterion is concerned with the trainee's attitudes and standards as an individual member of the medical profession.

Behavioural objectives

The unacceptable trainee:

. Attempts to cover up his errors from his colleagues;

. Is difficult to locate in emergencies and absent when required without making deputizing arrangements;

. Discusses medical mis-management with patients.

The acceptable trainee:

1. Is kind, courteous, honest and humble. Reports accurately, including his own errors;

2. Respects the confidences of colleagues and patients;

3. Places patient care above personal considerations;

4. Recognizes his own professional capabilities and limitations.

Criterion 9: Overall competence

This criterion is concerned with the trainee's willingness, ability and skill in gathering information necessary for diagnosis and/or decisions.

---

of what they can do. In certain areas they must be able to do 'something', and failure to do it in the test will mean that they cannot get the appropriate licence. Sometimes quite specific definitions are given of the allowable error.

The scores allocated in each section of engineering science and history would, if published in that form, present a profile. As it is, they are summated into the single grade of the examination. Carter and his colleagues (1980) seem to think that there might be some value in providing the students with a profile of that kind, independently of the grade. A detailed list of descriptive statements designed to achieve this goal has been proposed by Hazeltine (1976) of Brown University. Such a proposition is open to measurement. If the correlation between the project and the written examinations is high there is little advantage to be gained from a separate mark provided that the score for the project contributes a reasonable grade to that score. An employer needs to know that a person has been properly assessed in the criterion areas. Employers are likely to be bemused by a profile and this might be an advantage, since it would be reasonable to expect an employer who used profiles to have an intimate understanding of what is done in particular universities and colleges. The problem is that a profile can provide as much noise as information.

One of the intentions of the school profiles mentioned above is that they should record progress. In that sense they are diagnostic. Given that teacher-remarks on essays have little meaning, essay schedules might help them to provide meaningful information to students in such a way that they can see realistic hurdles which have to be jumped if they are going to improve their performance.

Criterion profiles have been developed for use in the evaluation of medicine, although there is very little discussion of their validity and reliability in the literature. They have their origins in the work of Christine McGuire in orthopaedic surgery (Levine and McGuire, 1971). Freeman and Byrne modified her format for the assessment of general practice, and this scheme is shown in Table 53. It, in turn, created similar profiles for occupational therapy, teachers in training, and school pupils (Murphy, 1974). No evaluation of these forms seems to have been reported, apart from Freeman, who has found them to be valid (see Chapter 13).

A disadvantage of this form of profile is that it is scaled, and, as soon as that happens, the subjective view of the examiners comes into play. This suggests that anyone who is being assessed with forms of this kind should be assessed by two examiners at least, who should then agree the final score. Criterion profiles of this kind are not used by themselves in medicine: they are but one of a number of instruments of assessment.

One advantage of attempting to draw up such profiles is that it helps focus a teaching team's collective mind on the essential aims and objectives to be achieved in the course.

Some years ago D. Hinton, of the Birmingham School of Architecture, encouraged the development of a graduate profile. At that time (1974) the university did not require honours degrees in architecture to be classified. As an alternative the school prepared a graduate profile which was used to record aspects of the students' work in which he or she showed special interest and above-average ability. Ticks opposite the headings shown below indicated a student's distinctive characteristics.

This was essentially an internal record and was not released outside the school without the written agreement of the graduate. Each graduate received a copy of his or her own profile document. The recorded information was a tutorial consensus based chiefly on the part 2 course leading to graduation.

The profile does not claim to be predictive nor to mark the limits of a graduate's potential. Since all honours graduates are required to reach a good level of achievement in all fields, a blacked-out square does not indicate a poor standard. The categories in the profile are:

In academic work: Compass of knowledge; skill in reasoning; aptitude in research.

Subject bias: Success in specialized optional studies and/or general academic work; aesthetic theory; technology; applied science/maths; social sciences; management; planning landscapes.

In problem-solving: Displays originality, sensitivity, practicality. Works best as an individual, as a leader of team, as an active member of a team.

In general: Drive and determination; concentration; precision communication—oral, written, visual.

Attempts to produce profiles such as these formalize the procedures for which testimonials are obtained.

In Table 54 a set of domain areas devised by a staff–student seminar on assessment in higher education which could be developed into a profile are given. Surveys of students, staff and employers of chemist graduates have shown that profiling is a feasible supplement to conventional grades (Kempa and Ongley, 1979).

Table 54. Objectives of examinations in universities described by an informal staff/student group for purposes of surveying the first graduates from a new university

(a)	Creativity:	(imagination, originality, ingenuity)
(b)	Objectivity:	(open-mindedness, recognition of subject bias)
(c)	Perception:	(depth of understanding, assimilation of compiled data, critical observations)
(d)	Knowledge:	(recall of facts, of sources)
(e)	Integration:	(co-ordination, synthesis, ability to connect)
(f)	Application:	(concentration, diligence, persistence)
(g)	Utilization:	(ability to conclude, transferability of method, grasp of objective)
(h)	Communication:	(clarity, fluency, articulacy)
(i)	Motivation:	(interest, intellectual curiosity)
(j)	Behaviour:	(ability to work alone, with others, to react favourably under stress)

Learning Profiles

The term 'learning profiles' is taken from the work of Brewer and Tomlinson (1981). Within the Department of Anatomy at the University of Sydney they devised a nine-week course using two complementary teaching techniques (self-instruction and group interaction). During the course at the end of each seven modules (7 weeks) the students were given tests which measured recall, comprehension, application, and short-chain problem-solving. At the end of the course there was a summative examination designed to test the capacity to solve long-chain multi-step problems. Evaluations of this programme were made over a four-year period (1975–8).

The test results (seven per student) represent a measure of performance or learning curve which the authors call *learning profiles*. These were collected for each student in each of the four behavioural domains and regression curves were obtained for the group as a whole. In addition, general ability, age and interest data were obtained. An anxiety test was administered as well as the Banks Learning Styles test during the first and seventh week of the course.

The analyses revealed five distinct profiles of which two related to the same category. The Type I student started with a high level of performance on entry to the course in all the behavioural areas. There was little change in their performance throughout the course and the investigators suggest that these were the best students. The test items were not particularly discriminative for this group. If more items had been introduced they would have been too demanding for the rest of the group. Again, with Type II students there is relatively little change in performance with time. However, they differed from Type I students in that they started at a lower level of entry behaviour. Their examination results conformed with the predicted scores whereas the Type I students exceeded expectations. Type IIIA students showed a very substantial improvement in problem-solving but there was variation in their application. Examination performance was close to that predicted. Type IIIB shows an improvement in the combined skills profile. Even so, within this category other subtypes were distinguishable. Type IV deteriorated in all dimensions and never mastered the subject. The Type III students obtained the most benefit from the course. From the analyses it seems that Types I and III gained most from the method. The investigators suggest that students probably utilized deep processing whereas Types II and IIIB probably used a surface approach.

The construction of learning profiles of this kind should aid tutors to understand better what is happening in their courses. The technique also illustrates how studies of the effects of different kinds of coursework assessment may be made.

SELF- AND PEER- ASSESSMENT

The highest order skill in *The Taxonomy of Educational Objectives* is the skill of evaluation, or 'judgement' as it is sometimes called. We were particularly anxious that the A level Engineering Science students should develop this skill in practical work not only in regard to the projects but also in the experimental investigations. For this reason, in both assessment schedules one of the key items was evaluation, in which the student was asked to reflect on what had been achieved and look at how the task might be done better in the future. While answers to these questions depend to some extent on the characteristics of the investigation or topic there is no doubt that students found this task difficult. Experience suggests that, like design, it is a skill for which training can be given. It also seems to be one which is not readily transferable.

Since 1969 (when those items were included in the schedule) there has been increasing interest in the inclusion of self-assessment activities within the curriculum in higher education. It is one of the key competencies in the Alverno College curriculum, which is described in Chapter 13 (Loacker, 1987). Most recently Boud (1986) has summarized some of the work which has been done in this area by means of five case studies in architecture, law and engineering. He defines the concept of self-assessment as:

(1) Identifying standards and/or criteria to apply to their work; and
(2) Making judgements about the extent to which they have met these criteria and standards.

It will be seen that the questions in the Engineering Science schedule for the projects and the investigations satisfy these criteria. Indeed, they are inevitable outcomes of any project or practical activity which the students have to set for themselves. In the case study described by Boud (Boud *et al.*, 1986) the students went through the cycle of designing a pump. Before handing in their design they were given a self-assessment schedule to complete in relation to eleven criteria relevant to good design. Bonus marks were allocated for the conduct of the exercise. Over 70% of the students in each of three years felt that it was a worthwhile exercise. It would seem that the development of a schedule together with some examples of its use might have improved the submissions made by some of the Engineering Science candidates.

In an earlier study Boud and Holmes (1981) investigated the idea that third-year students should mark their own work in electronic circuits and that of one of their peers. The students were supplied with model answers with which to compare their solutions. After the examination each was randomly allocated the un-named paper of another student in the class to be marked in their own time against the model answers. They were required to mark in detail on the answer sheet where the other student had departed from the model and score each section on the scale provided. A week later they were given their own paper for scoring in the same way without knowledge of the marks awarded. The self- and peer-marks were then compared and if the percentage was within 10% then the student was awarded the self-mark. Where there was greater discrepancy the papers were re-marked by a member of the staff.

Such was the satisfaction of the staff and students with the technique that it has since become a permanent feature of the department's approach to assessment. In 82% of the cases the difference between self- and peer-marks did not exceed nine in magnitude. There was little evidence of mark inflation. Other studies have shown that peer-group ratings can be as reliable as those of trained observers. For example, Cheatham and Jordan (1979) have evaluated peer assessment of speech performance. They did not find significant attitudinal or achievement differences between the peer and instructor assessments.

Boud was, however, particularly interested in what happened when students could also determine their own goals. In the sense that the students determined what they wanted and would do in their practicals in engineering science there is no difference in aim. However, at Heriot-Watt University in Scotland the students set their own goals each week in civil engineering design (7 hours per week over one session). In lieu of examinations the learner prepared a self-assessment form containing a list of desired criterion goals, a description of the actual learning and a reconciliation of these in relation to an agreed benchmark which led to the choice of mark. Each stage was open to questioning and discussion. The report of this work which consists of a conversation between the student Helen Boyd and the teacher John Cowan (Boyd and Cowan, 1985) comes down heavily in favour of self-assessment. The analysis is presented in terms of attainment at the different levels of the Perry model together with depth and surface processing.

In the training of teachers of modern languages Devitt and Czak (1981) have reported on how the students keep journals of their experience of learning a new language which is taught in a variety of ways. These record experience undergone while they are in practice teaching so that they can relate their own experience to that of their pupils.

Boud points out that unless innovations of this kind are introduced with a great deal of care among staff and students they are likely to fail. Such innovations require changes in the role of staff and the expectations of students: 'Self-assessment must be practised if it is to be developed'. He argues that at this stage there is little research to help decide if marks should be included in the major grade or not. A first step might be to adopt the engineering science model. Here the questions are set to ensure that students assess their own work but the marks are given by a teacher.

CHAPTER 12

Objective Tests

INTRODUCTION

An objective test is one in which the testee selects one answer from a number of
alternatives which are either correct or incorrect. In Britain they are commonly
called multiple-choice tests and given the letters MCQ. These tests have been
used for a major part of this century in the United States, and not just in
schools. They are in everday use in higher education both for classroom quizzes
and tests which contribute to a student's Grade-Point-Average. Probably the
best-known test is the Scholastic Aptitude Test (SAT) of the Educational
Testing Program (ACT) which are important criteria in admissions to many US
Institutions of higher education. It is relative changes in the averages of these
tests which are used by politicians to determine similar changes in standards
over time in education in the United States. For example, they were used in
recent comparisons with the performance of Japanese high-school students
(Austin and Garber, 1981) and, more specifically, the work undertaken by
Adelman (1983) for the study group on the conditions of excellence in
American higher education, which examined the changes in standardized test
scores of college graduates between 1964 and 1982. Of the 23 examinations
evaluated, performance declined in 15, remained stable on four, and advanced
on the remaining four. The greatest decline occurred in subjects requiring high
verbal skills.

A British authority (Nuttall, 1986) has argued that the measurement of
change in educational systems is impossible, because it is not feasible to
establish an unchanging measuring instrument for any long period of time. In
any case, such an instrument would impede any change which was sought (see
also Messick et al., (1983) for an American viewpoint). No wonder that
objective tests have had, and continue to have, their critics.

Hoffman's (1982) book was a powerful indictment of this form of testing and
criticisms of their use in higher education continue in the United States. The
most balanced comment on American approaches to testing is to be found in
the two-volume report on ability testing of the National Research Council,
which discusses the issues associated with these tests in great detail (Wigdor and
Garner, 1982). Nevertheless, testing is big business in higher and secondary
education, and much of it is done with objective tests. There is a very large
literature on the topic.

There is even more scepticism about objective tests in Britain and Ireland. In several instances in Ireland teachers have told their children to guess the answers to objective items in public examinations: 'Just put the tick in one of the boxes.' They argue that this stance is justified, because these particular tests are not properly designed and evaluated. During the 1970s objective tests were introduced into some GCE A level examinations, and these compare favourably with well-designed tests in the same subject areas in the United States. Objective tests are used throughout the world by medical educators. Scientists and technologists also employ them but few would be used in final examinations. In sum, their use in higher education in Britain and Ireland is very sporadic. So do they have a role to play in higher education?

The purpose of this chapter are to show how these tests are analysed, to consider some of the criticisms which are made about them, and to indicate trends in their development, more especially in the United States. Another purpose of this chapter is to evaluate the role of traditional approaches to objective testing in higher education, since many teachers remain unconvinced as to their value. I have excluded discussion of Cronbach's (1976) alpha–beta technique as well as latent-trait test theory in which there has been continuing interest in the United States, although a summary of American and British views on latent-trait theory is included as a note to this chapter.

THE LANGUAGE OF OBJECTIVE TESTING

The most commonly used form is the so-called multiple-choice question, in which the candidate is asked to choose from among four or five responses. Other types are multiple-completion and assertion–reason. Examples of these different types of question are shown in Tables 55 and 56. The terminology associated with objective items is shown in Table 55. The questions are designed so that they each can be answered within a period of a minute or so. True/false items are also used quite widely. The term 'item' is more generally used than 'question', although MCQ is often used in medical education. Gibbs and his colleagues (1986) say that it is difficult to write best-answer questions, and that the most useful approach is to devise correct but poor answers for the distractors. One study has reported that high-school students in the United States preferred matching items to multiple-choice. They showed less test anxiety and scored better on them (Shaha, 1984).

Agutter (1979) has designed a precision test in which a student has to identify correct, imprecise and incorrect biochemistry statements which can be compiled from lectures (type 1), the student's own previous work (type 2), and the work of another student (type 3). He found that the greatest improvement in examination performance came when all three types were used in the order types 1, 2 and 3.

MACHINE MARKING AND COMPUTATION

A major attraction of objective tests is that they are easy to mark. Both large

Table 55. A multiple-choice question illustrating the terminology used for objective items

---

Which of the following graphs represents a Normal (or Gaussian) distribution?

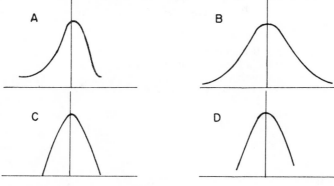

(A)...... (B)...... (C)...... (D)......

(An equally objective approach would be to request the candidates to label the diagrams.)

Terminology of objective items

Initial statement (stem)
A, B, C, and D (options)
Correct answer (Key (in this case, B))
Options other than correct answer (distractors)
Multiple-choice question (MCQ)

---

and small optical mark-readers are available for machine scoring. The small ones are relatively inexpensive and well worth their purchase, particularly if there are several users in an institution of higher education. The ease with which they can be interfaced with microprocessors eliminates the need for item analysis by hand and also enables the construction of item banks (Heywood *et al.*, 1980; Leuba, 1986; TDR, 1976). A typical approach to item analysis follows in the next section. There are other applications (Gibbs, 1986). For example, computer-assisted tests are being developed and an evaluation industry is beginning. An important issue is whether the mode of administration influences performance. Among 300 military recruits aged 18–25 it was found that those assigned to the computer mode from a random sample obtained lower mean scores in a test of arithmetic reasoning than those assigned to the traditional paper and pencil mode (Lee *et al.*, 1986) However, among a group of undergraduate students Lee (1986) showed that past computer experience significantly affected performance on a computerized test. Computerized testing may therefore discriminate against those who have not had experience of that kind of testing for which reason test administrators need to take into account the candidates' previous test experience.

Some interest has centred on the design of score sheets, and in one experiment optical mark scores were compared with optical character ones. School pupils had no difficulty with either, and the advantages of the optical

Table 56. Examples of objective items. (C and D are reproduced from Gibbs *et al.*, 1986 with the kind permission of the authors)

(A) *Example of a multiple-completion item*
Which two of the following were grievances of the American colonists in the eighteenth century:

A. The presence of British troops;
B. The laws restricting the importation of tea;
C. The threat to abolish slavery;
D. The debts of the British East India Company.

1. A and D only
2. A and C only
3. B and D only
4. A and B only

(B) *Example of a matching pairs item*
Which person in column 1 is correctly matched with the statement opposite his name in column 2?

1	2
A. Brunelleschi	wrote of his ideal state in a book called *Utopia*
B. Michelangelo	designed the dome of the cathedral in Florence
C. Thomas More	sculptured the *Pieta* in St Peter's Rome.
D. Harvey	discovered the circulation of blood

(C) *Example of a best-answer item*

A manual for an aptitude test reports a Kuder–Richardson reliability of $+0.95$ for 25,000 children. Which of the following conclusions about the test is most appropriate?

A   It is highly reliable
B   It is highly valid
C   It is highly internally consistent
D   It is suitable for selection purposes

(D) *Example of an assertion–reason item*

Assertion	Reason
The monarch rules Britain	The law assumes that the monarch can do no wrong

A   The assertion and reason are correct statements *and* the reason correctly explains the assertion.
B   The assertion and reason are correct statements *but* the reason does not explain the assertion.
C   The assertion is correct *but* the reason in incorrect.
D   The assertion is incorrect *but* the reason is correct.
E   *Both* the assertion and reason are incorrect.

character reader were made apparent (Heywood *et al.*, 1980). Other studies have suggested that answer formats do not influence results. There was, it seemed, among teachers, a general tendency to underestimate the adaptability of young people.

ANALYSING OBJECTIVE TESTS

Two methods of analysing objective tests suitable for use by teachers in higher education are discussed in this section. The first is the biserial method of classical test theory and the second a simple technique for classroom analysis. The illustrations which follow all refer to items which have four options (A–D), the correct option in each table being placed within a square. In Table 57 the top line (headed Facility) gives the percentage response to each option: 3.8% did not attempt an answer; 51.75% (or half the population) got the question right, i.e. answered B. The group is then split into three subgroups according to the total scores which they obtained on the test. Subgroup I is therefore the 'good' subgroup; II the 'average', and III the poor or low-achieving subgroup. In this test the maximum score was 39. Those in the 'good' subgroup scored in the range 18–31, those in the 'average' 13–17, and those in the 'poor' subgroup 2–12. Since the highest score was of the order 31, it is apparent that the test was difficult. The item analysis asks the question, How many in each subgroup obtained the correct answer? It calculates this as a proportion of the subgroup. Thus 75% of the 'good' subgroup got the answer right, 47% of the 'average', and 21% of the 'poor' subgroup. The item is said to discriminate well. More of the first subgroup as a proportion of that group got the answer right than the proportion of the third. Contrast this with the analysis of the item in Table 58, where there is very little discrimination between Groups I and II. Approximately the same proportion in each subgroup gets the answer right. There is some discrimination between the second and third subgroups. Some analysts prefer to have more subgroups. There is some value in such an approach when the population being tested is large.

Table 57. Item analysis of a 'good' multiple-choice question

Facility (%)			A	B	C	D	Omits
			19.01	51.75	13.45	11.99	3.8
Group		*Number*		*Number Correct*		*Proportion correct*	
I		129		97		0.7519	
II		133		63		0.4737	
III		80		17		0.2125	
Options	A		B		C		D
I	12		97		7		11
II	27		63		19		19
III	26		17		20		11

Point biserial correlation—0.4602.   Biserial correlation—0.6590

Table 58. Item analysis of a 'poor' multiple-choice question

Facility (%)			A	B	C	D	Omits
			8.48	24.57	28.7	38.96	1.3
Group		*Number*		*Number Correct*		*Proportion correct*	
I		143		45		0.3147	
II		181		55		0.3039	
III		136		13		0.0956	
Options	A		B		C		D
I	2		45		46		50
II	12		55		56		55
III	25		13		30		65

Point biserial correlation—0.1029.   Biserial correlation—0.1144

The measure of discrimination between the groups is the shape of the curve which plots the proportion. This can be expressed as a biserial correlation (r), the equation for which is given below. Since it is a calculation that can only be satisfactorily obtained with a computer, the non-statistically minded need only bother with its interpretation. In any case, that is all the information an examiner will receive. Most item analyses give the examiner the result of the biserial calculation from the formula:

$$\text{Biserial } r = \frac{Mr - Mw}{St} \times \frac{Pc\,(1 - Pc)}{y}$$

where

Mr = mean score on the test as a whole for students who choose the correct answer to the item,

Mw = mean score on the test as a whole for students who choose an incorrect answer to the item,

St = standard deviation of the total test scores for all students

Pc = proportion of students choosing the right answer,

$(1 - Pc)$ = the proportion of students choosing the wrong answer,

y = ordinate in the unit normal distribution, which divides the area under the curve in the proportions P and $1 - P$.

There is another refinement called 'point biserial r', which is sometimes given. All that is necessary for an examiner to know is that it is common practice not to accept items which give a value below 0.28 for biserial r. This value is a function of sample size. Some latitude is allowable as the sample falls in numbers. It is also possible to show that point biserial r should be separated from biserial r on the lower side by about one-quarter of the value of biserial r when the facility of the item is around 50%. The proportional difference between the two decreases when the facility (the number giving the correct response) decreases well below 50% and increases when it is well above 50%.

Of the criteria so far described, the item in Table 58 would be rejected whereas that in Table 57 is very acceptable. We can learn more from such tabulations.

Item writers try to design the question so that each of the distractors appears to be a reasonable answer. If it is 'way out' the student will not give it second consideration. If it appears reasonably correct then some students should respond to each option. In Table 57 some students have been attracted to each option, and given all the data, this must be regarded as a good item, especially as the most reliable tests are constructed of items with similar characteristics. The item in Table 58 is deceptive: at first sight, the options would appear to be working well. Closer inspection shows that the item was very difficult even for the best group. In these circumstances it is possible that there was a lot of guessing, a view which is supported by the large numbers opting for the distractors C and D.

It will be appreciated that when many students give only the correct answer the item is very easy. It would not be used in a test which seeks to differentiate between students, although it might be appropriate in mastery-learning. An item in which three of the options are used while the fourth is left alone is equally unsatisfactory, and will pull the biserial below the level considered acceptable. A very difficult item will discriminate badly and, in all probability, cause guessing. An alternative method of presentation is shown in Figure 33.

A Simple Technique for the Item Analysis of a Small Group of Students

The technique which follows is suitable for use in the classroom. The class is divided into two subgroups (i.e. above and below average) and their performance compared. If the number of correct responses in the top 27% of the pupils is denoted H and that of correct responses in the bottom 27% of the pupils L then:

$$\text{Discrimination } (D) = \frac{H - L}{M}$$

Where M is the number of candidates in each of the subgroups, i.e. those who make up 27%. Fraser and Gillam (1972) suggest that the value of D should not fall below 0.3.

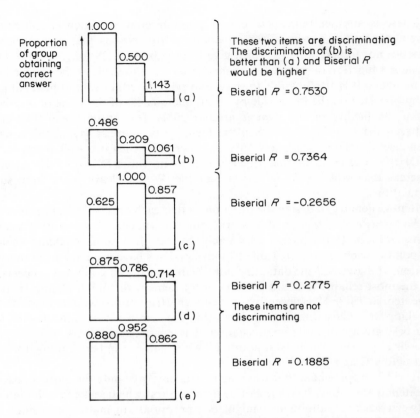

Figure 33. An alternative method for the presentation of an item analysis

RELIABILITY OF OBJECTIVE TESTS

The problem of error in the marking of essay examinations has been discussed, and it was shown that individual scores are not 'absolute' values. This is as true of an objective test as it is of an essay. In all scores there is error, and teachers often ascribe this error to guessing. However, the contributory factors to error even in an objective test are complex. Diederich (1960) has calculated the standard error for multiple-choice items, and has found it to be 3 for between 24 and 47 items and 4 for between 48 and 89.

The definition (or, more correctly, description) of reliability as commonly applied to objective tests differs from that given in Chapter 10. The measurement is usually undertaken on one administration of objective tests and not on comparisons of the test taken on a different number of occasions. It stems from the assumption that the candidate's behaviour in responding to the test should be similar in respect of each item. For example, if the test were to be divided into two halves we would expect the candidate to perform equally well in both.

If the candidate performs badly on the second half of the test but well on the first then the test is not reliable if all the items are of equal difficulty and measuring the same thing. A better measure would be to compare a candidate's performance on the odd-numbered items with his responses to the even-numbered ones. The measure of reliability is the coefficient of correlation between the two halves of the test.

Unfortunately, there could be bias in the items in each half. For this reason, the equation commonly used for reliability is the Kuder–Richardson:

$$r_n = \frac{n}{n-1} \left[\frac{s^2 + \Sigma p_i q_i}{s^2} \right]$$

where n = number of items in the test,
s = standard deviation of the test,
p_i = proportion of candidates responding correctly to item i,
$q_i = 1 - p_i$

This equation looks at every possible split in the arrangement of the items and is therefore a better measure of the *internal consistency*, as reliability is sometimes called.

The assumptions on which this measure is based are first, that all the items in the test measure the same thing, and second, that maximum reliability is obtained when all the items in the test are of average difficulty. Inspection of the formula shows that it depends on the number of candidates with correct responses and those with incorrect ones (i.e. P_i and Q_i). Moreover, it depends on the product of P_i and Q_i. The maximum value of this product occurs when half the candidates get the item wrong and half get it right (i.e. $0.5 \times 0.5 = 0.25$). Any other proportion produces a lower product, as, for example, when three quarters get the item right and one quarter get it wrong (i.e. $0.72 \times 0.25 = 0.1875$, which is much less than 0.25). This is a major reason for the view that tests should be constructed of discriminating items which have a facility of around 50%. It is also clear that the longer the test, the greater will be its reliability. Similarly, the more difficult the test, the less its reliability. Thus reliability depends on the range of scores in the group tested.

To summarize: reliability explains the proportion of variance in the test which is non-error variance. It depends on the spread of scores and is a function of test length.

TEST LENGTH AND TEST STRUCTURE

Such are the objections (fears, perhaps) of those involved in public examinations in the British Isles to objective tests that odd stratagems are often adopted. Many examinations incorporate short- and long-answer questions together with objective items. One test I have seen began with 15 items and then changed to short answers, after which it was completed by another 15 objective items. It is difficult to object to the separation of the tests on the grounds that they are 'separate' tests. Since they are incorporated into the same examination there are parts of a test for which overall test reliability could be calculated. However, it is possible that the separation of the 15 items might lead to less reliability than when they are taken together. Of course, if the two sections are meant to measure different things then the argument changes, because the reliability equation assumes that all the items measure the same thing. The National Foundation for Educational Research claims correlation coefficients of 0.95 with well-evaluated 50-item tests. My own work with teacher-made tests suggests that the comparisons we should make should be with a value around 0.8.

It is held to be important to maintain rhythm, although there is very little research on personal tempo (Nevo and Spector, 1979). This means retaining the same technique for a reasonable period of test time. General Studies at A level is primarily an objective test, but essay answers are required and, comprehension exercises are included.

Table 59. Structure of an experimental test in mathematics designed to assess four different skills

Knowledge	Mean score	3.26313
(9 items)	Standard deviation	1.58605
	Range	0 to 8
	Reliability	0.257 (0.58)
Analysis	Mean score	3.92398
(10 items)	Standard deviation	1.86223
	Range	0 to 9
	Reliability	0.38657 (0.72)
Comprehension	Mean score	4.16959
(10 items)	Standard deviation	2.09019
	Range	0 to 10
	Reliability	0.54759 (0.83)
Application	Mean score	4.12573
(10 items)	Standard deviation	2.04167
	Range	0 to 10
	Reliability	0.54987 (0.83)
Total test:	Mean score	15.48
	Standard deviation	5.42
	Range	2–31
	Reliability	0.73

Figures in parentheses are for the reliability upgraded to 40 items by means of the Spearman–Brown formula (see text).

Table 59 shows the analysis of a 40-item experimental test in mathematics in which the items were grouped into four sections. Each section was intended to test the specific skill indicated. It was administered under the worst possible conditions, since at the end of each subtest the students were asked to rate each item for things such as difficulty and guessing (see below). Because it had to be administered in class, it generally took two sessions to complete the test. The really surprising thing about this test is that it attained an overall reliability of 0.73.

The significance of test length is, nevertheless, illustrated, since the subtest reliabilities range from 0.257 to 0.54987. The first subtest has very low reliability. In part, this was due to the fact that the fifth item had to be excluded because it was found to have two answers! This meant that the calculations had to be for nine items. Inspection of the item parameters showed that this subtest was very difficult. The subtest for application had a much higher reliability. Given that the tests were measuring different things, the more correct analysis is to separate the subtests. This has the effect of producing higher biserial correlations.

Although this particular test clearly demonstrates the relationship between length and reliability it does not answer the question, Is it sensible to offer a small number of items as part of an examination? We can approach the answer to this by submitting the reliability obtained from a short test to the Spearman–Brown formula. This tells what the reliability of a longer test would be if it were composed of items similar to those in the test for which the reliability has been obtained: i.e.

$$r_{tt} = \frac{nr_{it}^{-2}}{1 + (n - 1)r_{it}^{-2}}$$

where n is the number of items in the test,
r_{it} is the original reliability, and
r_{tt} is the reliability of the test n times as long.

In order to predict the reliability of a test which has 20 items to replace the 10-item subtest of knowledge in the test shown in Table 59 let us substitute 2 for n. The calculation is then for a test twice as long; for a test which is six times as long (i.e. 60 items) let us substitute 6 for n. In Table 59 the figures in parentheses show the substitutions for 40 items (i.e. four times as long). The subtests for comprehension and application would appear to be reliable, whereas those for analysis and (especially) knowledge do not meet the criteria suggested above. Since some of the items in these subtests are bad, the obvious thing to do is to replace them with different items. This should bring the overall test reliability into the region of 0.8.

However, what about the examination which includes 10 or 15 items as part of a test in which there are both long and short answers? While it is possible to calculate the reliability of the different components it is nevertheless difficult. We calculated the biserial, facility and reliability of a 10-item objective test which was included as part of a sample paper for a public examination, and found it to be 0.39, which, when recalculated, came to 0.72 for 40 items. This value is below that required for public examination. In general, the biserial correlations were reasonable, and this suggested that if some of the items were improved this short test would have had a better fit (Heywood, 1977).

Criticisms of this test rest rather more on examination structure than on length. In this particular examination the objective items followed a series of short answers, and this meant that the candidate had to change his or her response style. Having got used to one style of answering he or she had to make a sudden change to another.

In general, final test-design will be the result of a series of compromises. It would, for example, be impossible to extend the items in each of the subtests in the experimental mathematics examination to 40 items. This would mean 4 hours of testing, which would inevitably rule out other forms of testing (for example, essays). As Cronbach and Gleser (1965) have pointed out, it is the degree of risk that can be tolerated which has to be ascertained. For example, in the classroom situation where one wishes to identify those who are below and above average a reliability of 0.5 will suffice. The second of the subtests in Table 59 would meet this need.

The objective test seems to work best in these particular testing situations when it is used with between 40 and 80 items. (There is a limit beyond which large increases in the number of items contribute any significant increase in reliability.) Sometimes an objective test could replace short-answer questions requiring at least a sentence for their completion. For example, in the same sample test in which the 10-item objective test occurred there were a number of short-answer questions. A group of teachers was asked to turn these into objective items and wrote 32 items in all. We had to reject items 23–32 from the analysis because many of the students had not covered that part of the syllabus. The 'poor' group ruled themselves out of the analysis. Six of the items would have been rejected on grounds of poor biserial correlations; seven were too difficult; eleven would have been rejected if strict criteria were used on these grounds. The reliability was relatively good, given the other parameters.

This is not to argue that short answers involving sentences have no role. In engineering science we found it easier to design comprehension exercises with short-sentence answer questions than we did with multiple-choice items when testing the understanding of material in a technical item. The short-sentence technique has been retained since 1969 (Carter et al., 1986) (see Chapter 13). It has also been preferred in medical examinations for the assessment of clinical competence where multiple-choice questions have also been tried (Fabb and Marshall, 1983).

In medicine it is not uncommon to use tests of more than 200 items. Several hundred are necessarily required in any form of computer-assisted instruction and many other tests use up to 100 items. I have a preference for 40 problem-solving items designed to take an hour, as this leaves room for other types of assessment in a comprehensive examination.

UNUSUAL RESPONSES: GUESSING

If there is one thing which unites critics of objective tests it is guessing. They conveniently forget that it can be argued with some confidence that it is the 'fudge factor' in essays which leads to the low inter-marker reliabilities so often reported. For some reason, examiners find it difficult to accept that the proportion of questions in an objective test which a candidate can answer correctly by blind guesswork is very unlikely to exceed 20–30%, for which score in an essay examination, wrote Iliffe (1966) 'many examiners are prepared to give by impressionistic marking to an answer composed largely of indifferent ideas and irrelevant material'

Nevertheless, much interest is centred on the equation used to correct a test score for guessing:

$$\text{Score corrected for guessing} \quad = \quad R - \frac{W}{(K - 1)}$$

where R = number of correct responses,
  W = number of incorrect responses, and
  K = number of choices offered in the item.

This equation illustrates the point that, as the number of options increase (for example, from four to five), the effects of guessing decrease. This is why many examiners prefer to write five options. However, all the items in my experimental examinations were written with four because we found it difficult to write sensible fifth options, and preferred to include a realistic one rather than 'none of these'. This does not mean that the total test score could be made up of 25% guessing because there is a one in four chance of correctly guessing in a single item. The assumption made by those who criticize objective tests is that students can randomize their guessing, but this is a highly sophisticated operation which would be beyond most students in the time allowed.

Lord and Novick (1968), two of the pioneers of latent-trait theory, wrote:

> Examinees who have *partial information* about an item do not respond at random nor do examinees with *misinformation* about that item. In these situations wrong answers cannot be equally attractive to the examinee.
> No simple correction formula is appropriate in these cases.... and elsewhere....
> The simple knowledge or random guessing model is used extensively despite its several weaknesses. One such weakness is that it ignores possible day-to-day variations in examinee performance.... which experience has taught us cannot be neglected. An equally serious weakness is that the model assumes that if the examinee is unable to pin-point the correct response then he is completely ignorant in this situation and has no basis for choosing among the possible responses. This second assumption can seldom be seriously entertained.

298

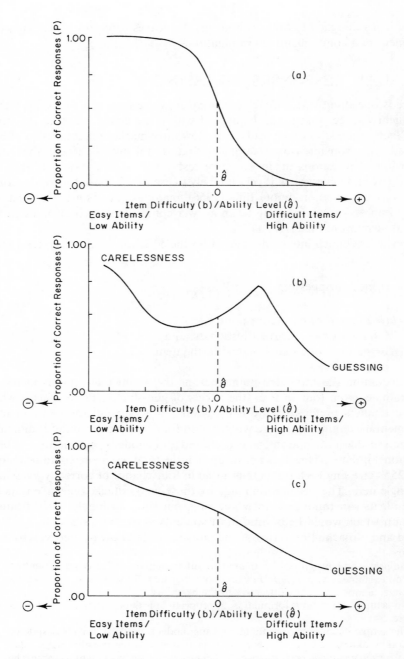

Figure 34. Three person–response curves for the individuals with the same ability level ($\hat{\theta} = 0$). (Adapted from Trabin, T. E. and Weiss, D. J. (1983). The person–response curve: fitting individuals to item–response theory models. In Weiss, D. J. (ed.), *New Horizons in Testing*, New York: Academic Press)

That unusual events are not just due to guessing may be illustrated by the person-response curves in Figure 34, the idea for which comes from Trabin and Weiss (1983). In Figure 34(a) the response of a candidate to a particular set of items is shown: 50% of the items were answered correctly. The steep slope of the curve suggests that the candidate was answering the test in the way that would be predicted for a person of average ability. A good performance was returned on the relatively easy items whereas a poor one was seen on the relatively difficult.

Figure 34(b) shows another candidate who took the same test whose performance was uneven across the range of items to the point that some more difficult items were answered well. Given that the candidate was also of average ability, we conclude that there is more error in the final score of 50% obtained by the testee. The same is true of the candidate in Figure 34(c), who also obtained 50% from the same test. Since these two candidates obtained correct answers to some very difficult questions whereas the first candidate did not, it is probable that these candidates were guessing. The lower performance of these two candidates on the easy items suggests that they might have been careless, and the peak in the response to the more difficult items by the second candidate implies that the examiner might have had some special knowledge with which to improve his or her performance.

Single summated scores do not give us any information about the way in which the examinee approached the test. The paradox is that while we know this to be the case and while we accept that anxiety, motivation and prior knowledge all influence performance, we tend only to correct norm-referenced tests for guessing.

A major problem with the guessing equation is that it overcorrects for guessing when the distractors in the item do not prove attractive to weak students and undercorrects when students are able to eliminate the distractors with ease. It may be concluded that the extent to which students resort to guessing largely depends on the quality of the item-writing. While most able students should choose the correct response, distractors incorporating popular errors or fallacies should appear correct to students with misinformation, while others should appear superficially correct to students with little information or skill relevant to the item. Indeed, the purpose of carrying out an item analysis is to ensure that items do discriminate between better and weaker students, and that distractors are plausible to poorer ones.

As Iliffe has pointed out, guessing can be further eliminated by more complex item design. In Iliffe's first example the stem begins: 'Tick any one of the following statements' Since there are five options there are 32 possible answers. A further example takes the form:

Check three of the statements below which express best the function which education should serve in our society.

1 ...
2 ...

```
3 ...
4 ...
5 ...
6 ...
7 ...
8 ...
```

In this case there are 56 different possible answers: if credit is given only for choosing the three correct statements, the probability of gaining a mark by guessing is less than 0.2. Gulliksen (1950) makes the point that when there is a sufficiently long list of choices at the beginning of a test section the task of item writing is made easier.

Another method which has been used with students of approximately freshman level in England employs a complex statement about a given subject in the stem. A series of questions is then asked about the statement which demand one of the following responses against each item:

A is true;
B is possibly true;
C contains insufficient evidence to justify itself;
D is false.

STRATEGIES IN SOLVING OBJECTIVE ITEMS

Even with all the work which has been done on testing, very little effort has been made to discover what students do when they answer objective items. As part of another investigation, Heywood and Youngman (1981) included a rating scale for students to answer at the same time as they responded to the 40-item test in mathematics, the details of which were given above. In respect of each item they were asked to respond to the following scales:

(1) *Difficulty*: I found this question very difficult/fairly difficult/easy/very easy.
(2) *Interest*: I found this question very interesting/fairly interesting/neither interesting nor uninteresting.
(3) *Calculation*: I worked out the answer to this question completely/partly/not at all.
(4) *Recall*: I recalled the answer to this question completely/partly/not at all.
(5) *Guessing*: I guessed the answer to this question completely/partly/not at all.
(6) *Prediction of answer*: I am very certain/fairly certain/uncertain that my answer is correct.

In addition to the test the students were given a multiple-aptitude test and a personality inventory. The former included tests for vocabulary, general information, arithmetic, number series, figure classification, mechanical comprehension, word recognition, scrambled letters, checking and paper formboard. The latter was intended to evaluate extroversion and neuroticism.

Cluster analysis was used to evaluate the data and five clusters were revealed.

Cluster 1 defined a group of pupils who *guess*. They had some difficulty in answering the items and relied on recall. In addition to making a wrong prediction about the correctness of their answers they also failed to guess correctly. On the criterion measures they performed significantly badly on the number-series subtest.

Cluster 2 showed a group who performed very badly on the test. In addition to being *incapable they were also uninterested*. They did not attempt to work out the answers, neither did they bother to use their facility for recall. Inspection of the criterion measures shows that they did significantly badly on the arithmetic subtest.

Cluster 3 described a group of pupils who were *successful* in the test. They tended to work out the answers to the question and make correct predictions of their answers. In the criterion tests they performed significantly well on General Information, Arithmetic and Number Series, in which they performed best.

Cluster 4 is perhaps the most interesting of the groups for it showed a group of *highly interested pupils who nevertheless found the test difficult*. Although they guessed some of the items they did not resort to recall. They were not, as might be expected, successful at predicting their performance. They did not perform significantly well or badly in the criterion measures.

Cluster 5 described those pupils who *overestimated their performance*. They did not believe that the items were difficult and showed a high level of interest. While they believed in their use of recall they had a strong tendency to work out the answers. They often thought the answer was correct when it was wrong. The only criterion measure which was significant for this group was the checking test.

This investigation was completed with a sample of 300 students. It suggests that the guessing issue is much more complicated than has been previously thought. There are, it seems, groups of students who guess and groups who do not.

There may have been some misunderstanding of the meaning of recall because while a number of students said that they recalled the answer it is difficult to believe that the items did not involve them in some calculation. There is very little in mathematics which can be remembered when solutions to problems are required. The students must therefore have been referring to components of the problem-solving exercise which are recalled (for example, the 'tables'). If this is the case it makes a further distinction between the able and successful group and the others. Since the former does not regard recall as important it would seem that their perception of problem-solving in mathematics is different to that of the students in the other groups.

Perhaps the most important result for further investigation among larger samples is the finding that the guessers guess wrongly. This supports the view of those authorities who do not feel there is any need to make a correction for guessing in the objective tests, but it also throws some light on the dispositions (response) sets of testees. Further studies in the general area of personality might help with the problem of person fit. Because the population was so small this investigation can only be the beginning of such work.

There are many other problems which need to be solved. Wigdor and Garner (1982), in their report to the National Research Council in the United States, point out that test developers have not made much of an effort to study the effect of test items on internal mental processes. As we have seen above, it would be useful to know much more about the problem-solving skills which students bring to the solution of problems set in the objective format. For example, in Table 60 an objective item is shown together with the thought process which the item-writer believed the student would operate. Is this the case, or do students use different methods? Are there some students who work backwards from the answers, and, in any case, does this matter? If they do, is their understanding of mathematics adequate?

One promising way forward would be to see how the solving of objective items helps develop skills in semi-automatization (see Chapter 11). Many of the tasks which examinees have to undertake are executive skills which have a long-time duration. Yet much of life is concerned with semi-automatized problem-solving. Problem-solving objective items might contribute significantly to the development of information-processing skills. There are many examples which testify to the fact that they can be set in the sciences (Leuba, 1986).

Table 60. An item-writer's view of the thought process involved in solving a multiple-choice item

---

The length of a rectangular playing pitch is twice its width and the area of the pitch is 7200 m². If the width of the goal is one-twentieth the width of the pitch which of the following is the width of the goal:

A. 2.1 m
B. 3 m
C. 4.2 m
D. 6 m

Thought process
(a) If the length of the pitch is twice the width then the area of half the pitch is a square.
(b) The area of this square is 3600 m² therefore the length of one side is the square root of 3600 = 60 m.
(c) The width of the goal is one-twentieth of this side = 3 m

or let x_m = length of shortest side. Then area of pitch = $x_m \times 2_{xm}$

$2x^2 = 7200$ m²; $x^2 = 3600$ m²; $x = 60$ m.

Width of goal = $\frac{1}{20} 2x_m$ (60 m) = 3 m

INTELLIGENT GUESSING

In real life we are often called upon to guess, and there is a substantial case to be made for tests which develop the ability of 'intelligent guessing'. Billing (1973) has attempted this task. The rubric which precedes the item is self-explanatory:

> Four suggested answers are provided for each question below. Cross out those answers which you *know* or can *deduce* to be incorrect. In crossing out incorrect answers *do not* guess—there will be a penalty for this. Then indicate the *correct* answer by writing A, B, C or D against the question number in the right hand margin. If you don't know or cannot deduce the correct answer, use an intelligent guess. There will be no penalty for incorrect answers, so answer all questions. This system allows the paper to be marked in *two* ways. Firstly, a score is assigned on the basis of incorrect answers crossed out. Secondly, a score is given by the correct answer in the right hand margin. Your overall mark for the test will be the *higher* of the two scores.

Table 61 shows the method of scoring and Billing's text has been abbreviated in the last two columns. The only codes used in the actual assessment were 1 and 4. Score 3 is a prediction of what score 5 would be in the absence of intelligent guessing. As predicted from previous work on guessing, a very high correlation was obtained between the conventional scores 4 and 5. The correlation between 3 and 4 was much lower, i.e. 0.68 (on Test 1) compared with 0.96 (on Test 2). Billing concluded that 'one reason for the imperfect correlation revealed above between scores 3 and 4 could therefore be that "knowledge" and "intelligent guessing" are two separate abilities which do not correlate well; score 3 depends on knowledge, while score 4 depends on both the knowledge and the intelligent guessing abilities'.

He supported this argument for an alternative approach to the separation of these abilities thus:

> When objective tests are used conventionally, the two abilities are arbitrarily conflated and potential information about the student's performance is lost. The results lead to the belief that instruments better than the tests could be constructed which would allow measurement of the two abilities of 'knowledge' and 'intelligent guessing'. Both of these abilities may well be considered to be useful and therefore worth developing and assessing. Knowledge, and the other usually quoted cognitive abilities, are not the only basis for the student's education. After graduation, he is likely to be called upon to venture opinions and interpretations, make decisions and carry out designs on the basis of incomplete information. One aid to success in such situations could well be an ability to make intelligent 'guesses' and this factor should not perhaps be regarded as a superfluous and undesirable feature which merely complicates the interpretation of test results.

Bligh (1973), in a more simple procedure, introduced a 'don't know' category into the True/False test and scaled thus;

Correct	Don't know	Incorrect
2	1	0

Table 61. Marking strategy to allow for intelligent guessing. (Designed by David Billing and reproduced with his permission)

Code	Description	Strategy	Student response	Assumptions and information
1.	Penalized	Each incorrect answer eliminated = +1		Accurate knowledge without guessing
	Knowledge	Each answer incorrectly eliminated = −3		
2.	Unpenalized	Each correct answer eliminated = +1	Crosses out answers	Informed that score would not apply
	Knowledge	Each answer incorrectly eliminated = 0		
3.	Penalized	One remaining answer is correct = +3		Estimate assuming that the student had been told that errors would be penalized and had abstained from guessing
	Guessing	One remaining answer is incorrect = −1		
	Predicted	Several remaining answers = 0		
4.	Unpenalized	Each correct answer in right hand margin = +3	Enters answers in (conventional scoring)	Obtains most points for guessing behaviour
	Guessing	Each incorrect answer in right hand margin = 0		(conventional scoring)
5.	Penalized	Each correct answer in right hand margin = +3		Informed that score would not apply
	Guessing	Each incorrect answer in right hand margin = −1		

His purpose in developing what he called *truth-functional* tests was to...

... objectively assess students' thought processes during lectures or other presentation methods of teaching... Truth-functional tests are tests in which the student is asked to agree, disagree, or say he does not know whether a certain statement is true.

Bligh's particular tests were designed to exemplify the categories in *The Taxonomy of Educational Objectives*. He claimed that these tests are a direct measure of teaching effectiveness in terms of objectives achieved, that they have high reliability and construct validity, and that guessing can be correct.

In medical education Essex (1976) has found that a partial-credit scoring schema was favoured by students when compared with a dichotomous approach. The variance of the dichotomously scored scheme was greater but not significantly more so than the partial credit scheme. He suggests that partial-credit schemes are useful if it is thought important to reward partial knowledge.

Ebel (1958) has gone so far as to argue that

> True/false questions can be thought provoking, unambiguous, and highly discriminating. That they are often not is more the fault of the writer of the item than of the form of the item.

At school level it has been shown that the introduction of deliberately flawed items has little effect on validity and reliability, although the items become easier for the students (McMorris, 1972). However, another experiment among political science students found that the concurrent validity and internal consistency were weakened by flawed items although the item difficulty was not flawed (Board and Whitney, 1972).

The more items depart from knowledge of recall and concept testing toward application and problem-solving, the more difficult I have found it to write the fourth option. In a very carefully designed experiment among first-year educational psychology students Owen and Freeman (1987) compared the efficacy of three- and five-option objective items. They did not find any significant difference between them, the major variation being in the time spent per item. The students preferred the shorter items and 97% balloted for three-option item tests. Their findings supported previous work in Australia (Straton and Catts, 1980) and the United States (Tversky, 1964).

In respect of the 'blanket' option Tollefson (1987) evaluated the use of three formats (each written for 12 items), (1) one correct answer, (2) none of the above as a foil, and (3) none of the above as correct answers, in a college statistics examination. Students found that (3) was the most difficult of the formats, although no consistent differences in the item discriminations statistics were found. The most reliable test was the multiple-choice with one correct answer. The use of none of the above did not increase discriminations, as some authorities held it might do. A similar study by Oosterhof and Coats (1984) in a different content area supports these findings.

THE QUESTION OF TRIVIALITY

Apart from the issue of guessing, the most often-used objection to objective items is that they only test recall of knowledge. To put it in another more cogent way, they do not test reasoning. If this is the case, it is argued, they have no potential in higher education because higher education is concerned with the development of reason.

Ebel (1965), an American authority on objective tests, considered the differences between factual and reasoning questions thus:

> There are several important differences between factual and reasonaing questions. Factual questions tend to be simpler to state, easier to answer, and less controversial when correct answers are announced. Reasoning questions, since they are designed to provoke thought, sometimes also provoke arguments. Critics of objective tests, including students who have just taken one, frequently find flaws such as these: (a) the best answer is not a completely correct answer; (b) some of the distractors provoke answers just as good as the 'correct answer'; (c) the problem situation is not described fully enough to prevent diverse interpretations leading to different answers.
>
> The best answer to these criticisms is to present evidence that competent experts have agreed that the correct answer is clearly better than any other alternative offered, and that when the item is scored with this as the correct answer it discriminates clearly between students of high and low achievement. This evidence should not be used by a writer of test items as grounds for opposing changes in wording which improves the item by making the problem situation clearer, the best answer more nearly correct, or the distractors more clearly wrong—without destroying the ability of the item to discriminate. But this evidence can be used to defend thought-provoking items which require the examinee to make reasonable inferences about complex but concisely described problem situations. Loopholes for unwarranted assumptions and unconventional interpretations exist in almost all reasoning items. It is practically impossible to eliminate them without making the item excessively verbose. So long as experts can agree on a best answer, and so long as the item discriminates well between good and poor students, these alleged flaws in reasoning items need not be regarded as serious. They make the item somewhat less objective but more valid as an indication of important achievement. Objectivity is highly desirable, but it is not the most important quality of a test item. Validity should never be sacrificed to gain objectivity.

Assertion–reason and multiple-completion items have the positive value of being able to tolerate ambiguity. In England, Iliffe (1966) attempted to dispel the fear that objective tests will encourage students only to amass isolated scraps of knowledge with two examples. The first said:

> Tick any of the following statements which are not held to be true by Plato:
> A. The soul survives the body.
> B. All knowledge of 'right' and 'wrong' comes through the soul's encounter with the absolute.
> C. The world of the senses is a hindrance to the philosopher.
> D. The mind at birth is blank, and all ideas come from experience.
> E. Suicide is immoral.

According to Iliffe:

> Clearly this question will be answered correctly only by a student who has studied and understood Plato's philosophy with some thoroughness. The form of the question requires a candidate to look carefully at each of the five statements and

to make a separate decision in each case; it is not enough to spot one of the five statements which fits the instructions and to ignore the rest.

In the next example the correct answer can be identified only by a candidate who is capable of making careful distinctions and of ranging in his mind over a number of instances of a constitution:

Which of these statements most adequately defines a constitution?
A. All of the laws and customs of a people.
B. That portion of the pattern of government which is legal rather than customary or political in nature.
C. The formal written document under which a government functions.
D. The basic functional pattern and powers of government, whatever their derivation.

In regard to the teaching of English Literature Iliffe wrote that 'the cry which commonly goes up from teachers of literature is that these tests cannot tell us what we want to know about our students' cannot be answered in any way until the teachers are prepared to say clearly what it is they want to know about their students. Once that is done, it is possible that some of the qualities or achievements with which they are concerned can be assessed by objective tests while others cannot. In the first category falls the ability to describe a work of literature in terms of its content, structure, form, style, etc.; also the ability to assess its place in the larger phenomenon called literature. In the second category (not susceptible to objective testing) must fall the students' own responses to the work of its characters, the way in which they relate what they have read to their own experiences, and whether they interpret the work in such terms as mimetic, symbolic or moral. Purves (1961), in a careful analysis of this issue, concluded that good objective questions can be devised to deal with interpretation and evaluation, but they measure 'the ability to reason about a work of literature more than they do a strictly literary skill; they measure the ability to justify conclusions from the evidence given'.

The position has not changed since the 1960s. The problem is solved to the extent that the item writer can write appropriate items. Whether it is worth solving the problem in a particular assessment context is another matter, but that reasoning items in the humanities cannot be produced for particular groups of students is not confirmed by the evidence.

It is much easier to see that problem-solving skills are used in objective tests in mathematics, science and technology, and this has been demonstrated repeatedly, even with respect to the construction of true–false tests (Avital and Shettleworth, 1968).

Hoare and Revans (1969) designed questions to test the skills of knowledge comprehension and application after students had read instructional programmes in chemistry for their first medical examinations. The programmes were pre- and post-tested with published tests for the programmes. The improvement on the published tests was better than that of the tests designed from educational objectives. Nevertheless, consistent differences between students suggested that the knowledge and application questions were testing different abilities. The authors claimed that the investigation showed that programmed learning teaches students to apply, as well as remember, facts, theories, and formulae. This study emphasized the importance of question design and the significance in obtaining a match between the materials and learning experiences and the assessment procedures.

Having said all this, it is important not to underestimate the value of recall in objective tests. Many professionals (for example, doctors and engineers) have to have a very wide range of knowledge at their disposal. Success in objective tests at what we suppose might be the level of recall might give weak students confidence. What they and we perceive to be recall may involve two different skills.

LOTTERY TECHNIQUES

Diagnosis is clearly a skill which requires more than knowledge of recall. I have shown elsewhere how objective items can be used to test this skill but my items might take up to 15 minutes to answer (Heywood, 1976). Objective tests can be used to test this skill in a series format which leads the respondent through a case history. It is a challenge to design such tests. One formula which has been adopted might be called the lottery technique. For example, in the 1950s the cost of providing radio and television receivers for practical examinations proved very expensive in England. Therefore the Radio Trades Examination Board borrowed a written technique from the armed forces. A circuit diagram of a radio or television receiver was presented to the candidate and a fault was stated. At certain points on the diagram information was given which would lead to a solution of the fault but this information was covered up and had to be rubbed away, as on a lottery ticket. It was so arranged that the assessor could follow the path taken by the candidate to solve the problem.

A similar technique was devised for medicine by Barber Mueller. The answers (correct or incorrect) are given with each option but are covered up. As in the previous case, the candidate uncovers the information in the boxes and continues doing this until the answer is obtained. If the questions are set as simple multiple-choice items in which there is only one right answer then in a 40-item test with four options there will be a possibility of 120 (3×40) negative answers. The score is the number of negative choices and the maximum score is zero negative marks, in which case the candidate will have scored all the items correctly. The least score is -120 and so on. Fabb and Marshall (1983) suggest that items regarded as important could be given a high weighting whereas those of least importance could be given a low weight. Such tests are now easily administered with the aid of microcomputers.

ITEM AND TEST CONSTRUCTION

If, then, objective tests are to work well the evidence is that the items have to be well designed. This applies as much to classroom tests as it does to standardized tests. The rules are very simple, and of these the two most important are

(1) To remember that what you think the examinee sees (reads into) the question may not in fact to be what he or she actually reads and sees;
(2) Write the items so that they are easy to read and, to achieve this, make sure they have rhythm.

It follows from these two principles that an item or series of items should be related to the objectives of the course. As we have seen, the majority of questions should be set at the difficulty level experienced by the average student. In order to obtain rhythm ensure that the stem and the options are grammatically correct. Do not bring the rhythm to a halt by the use of unnecessary subordinate phrases or double negatives, even when substantial time is allowed for the answer. The distractors should appear to be potentially real answers. In many instances their order is important. In 'number or equivalent questions' the numbers should be presented in descending or ascending order of magnitude. The terminology used in items should always be precise.

One of the great advantages of objective tests is that they can be pre-tested even in the classroom, although some would argue that appropriate sample populations among university students do not exist (Holme, 1976). Over a period of time a pool of items can be established (Wood and Skurnik, 1969) and this can be done relatively cheaply by groups of universities (Chelvu and Elton, 1977).

In pre-tests, which I have used to test knowledge and simple problem-solving skills, I began the test with one or two easy items. I then followed these with one or two of average difficulty and sometimes concluded the bank with a very difficult one. Constructing the test in this way ensured that through the backwash effect of post-inspection by the students when preparing for their examination, they would, in later years, attempt to study the range of the syllabus. It also ensured that particular principles would be studied, for this was the reason for including the very difficult item in the test. In other words, we felt that the pre-test sample ought to have been able to do the item. With these provisions it was not unreasonable to begin each test with an easy item. It should be noted that Leary and Dorans (1982), of the Educational Testing Service, have shown that in time-limited tests students usually score more highly if the items are arranged with the easier at the beginning and the most difficult at the end. Correlations of our paper with others in the same examination were reasonably high. However, if the items are measuring different things, as has been shown to be the case in other similar science examinations, this might not be the appropriate procedure, as the selection of items on this basis might also distort the distribution.

Lane et al. (1987) came to the conclusion that the idea of beginning tests with easy items was over-simplified. The performance of students was shown to be highest when statistical and cognitive difficulty (as measured by the categories of The Taxononmy of Educational Objectives) increased together and least when statistical and cognitive item difficulty changed in opposite directions. Since labelling affected performance positively it could be that it negates the effects of item order. The use of labels may cause students to employ more appropriate response sets.

Ebel (1965) devised three tests, each of 16 items, which were taken from another test of 61 items. In the first he chose items with difficulty values around the middle of the distribution of all the items. A mean score of 9.22 was obtained with a reliability of 0.485. When the level of difficulty of items was distributed across the whole range of difficulty values the mean mark fell to 8.02 and the reliability to 0.416. Both distributions were reasonably bell-shaped, with the peak of the former above the median mark for the test (i.e. 8) and that of the latter below. The range of the latter was reduced. When he set a third test which included the eight most difficult items and the eight easiest from the 61, a sharp cut-off on either side of the median was produced. The mean score was 8.01 and most of the candidates were grouped in the band 6–9, the range being considerably reduced even when compared with the second test. The reliability fell to 0.13.

There is no compelling reason why all the test score distributions should approximate to the normal curve. Rummel, working with a college-level mathematics test used to exempt some entering freshmen (about 50%) from a course in basic mathematical skills. He found that item revisions which flattened the distribution of scores also reduced the errors made in exempting some freshmen and not others (quoted by Ebel, 1965).

The rule would seem to be that in the absence of detailed information about the students or the characteristics of the subject (for example, mathematics) the examiner should try to produce a normal distribution; that is, spread the results evenly and not bias the marking towards either end of the distribution.

The safest approach, therefore, is to begin by selecting items in the middle range of difficulty and check these for discrimination, content and skill. A detailed knowledge of the candidates will give some idea of the degree of flexibility with which the teacher can approach this task.

Some of the difficulties in accommodating both weak and poor students might be overcome by using different examination structures. One of these is the *partly tailored examination*, a term which is apparently due to Bedard (1974).[2] He describes it as an examination in which there is both a compulsory and choice component. This is normal in many examinations in Britain and Ireland, where the facility to choose questions is part of the philosophy of examining. However, the structure of partly tailored tests is very different and more reliable and systematic. The design of Bedard's partly tailored examination is shown in Figure 35.

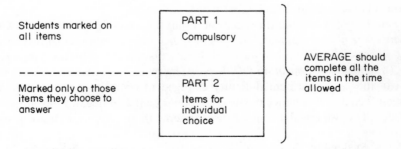

Figure 35. Structure of a partly tailored examination

The maximum number of marks a student obtains is determined by the number of questions answered. The student's score is the ratio of marks he would have obtained if he had answered all the questions correctly plus the 'free' ones he chose to answer. Bedard's goals were:

(1) To try to provide an examination in the category of power tests for all examiners;
(2) To allow the examinee to adjust the examination to his individual differences;
(3) To keep the testing duties of teachers to a minimum.

He experimented with control groups taking examinations in algebra and calculus at secondary grade 12. He claimed that students benefited from this type of examination, particularly in respect of short-answer questions, and he felt that they offered opportunities for increasing the class average.

TEST-WISENESS AND TEST PREPARATION

Sarnacki (1979) defined test-wiseness as a cognitive ability or set of skills which a test-taker can use to improve a test score independently of the content area of the test. For example, Smith (1982) devised a strategy which involved the student in examining the relationship of the four options to each other and found that when the testees were trained in this technique not only did they improve their test scores but they also acquired more self-confidence. Using the same strategy, Dolly and Williams (1983) were unable to detect a significant difference between undergraduates in an experimental group and a control group both taking classroom tests. However, in a subsequent investigation with 54 undergraduate education students they used four strategies. These included training students in how to maximize the chance of selecting a correct option when the test-taker was forced to guess because of a lack of information concerning the content of an item. This time, on all measures of test-wiseness they found that the experimental group did better than the control one. There was no significant difference between the experimental and control groups on the non-susceptible items. The training strategy, based on the view that test-wiseness is not a transferable skill but cue-specific (Diamond and Evans, 1972), was also investigated. The subjects were taught to respond to cues of length of option, middle value, similarity or oppositeness of options and cues from stem to option (deduction). Both groups produced similar performances when the cues were not present but the experimentals did better when they were. Dolly and Williams (1986) concluded that an efficient programme for test-wiseness would increase the accuracy of academic skills measurement and in support of this, like so many others, they referred to Ebel (1965), who had written: 'More error in measurement is likely to originate from students who have too little, rather than too much, skill in test taking'.

Related to this is the problem of test preparation. Does it help or hinder the learner? Should the tests used in public examinations be published?

The JMB has always published its tests. It is now a legal requirement in New York State that students taking the SAT have a right to a copy of the questions. Lockheed *et al.*, (1982) found that out of 113 000 students only about 5000 asked for the questions. It was found that the more able and ambitious students from wealthier, better educated families applied. Once again the power of tests to influence learning is shown.

OBJECTIVE TESTS IN HIGHER EDUCATION

As we have seen, objective tests are utilized widely in higher education. Sometimes they are used as quizzes, at others in terminal examinations. It is very often a matter for the subject teacher as to whether they are used or not. Their widespread use in American higher eduation was severely criticized at the 1987 conference on Assessment in Higher Education of the American Association for Higher Education. As in Britain, there is a move toward multiple-strategy assessment in which objective tests will have a less significant role.

In respect of Britain (and this would seem to apply to other countries) Carter and Lee (1974) have pointed out how they could be used to reduce costs if all the universities with first-year electrical engineering courses examined those courses by means of an objective test, and showed that the syllabuses used by the different universities offering these programmes were very similar. They proposed that the teachers from these universities should come together and create a pool of items from which universities could draw their own sample. Apart from anything else, this would provide an important shared experience and might lead to development in computer-assisted instruction.

Objective tests of one kind or another have an important role to play in the classroom. Not only can they be used to assess achievement but they can assist the development of other skills (Clark, 1974). I have used them as a form of programmed instruction to prepare students to accommodate areas in a course which in their future study might prove difficult. In our attempt to teach science to arts students we found that the development of elementary knowledge in mathematics and confidence in its use could be achieved by a self-programmed instruction provided that the goals were clearly defined (Heywood and Montagu-Pollock, 1976). Programmed learning is, of course, a form of self-testing (Rawls *et al.*, 1966). In order to motivate these same students we gave not only instructions for set reading but also tests on this reading immediately prior to the beginning of each section of the course, which attempted to ensure that the reading was done as well as to assess the degree of understanding of principles. We resorted to a technique used in verbal reasoning. The students had to fill in missing words which were chosen for the possibilities they offered in testing whether or not the principle had been understood. We did not use short answers, since if they required interpretation they would suffer from the same disadvantages as the essay.

One of the most interesting and unusual approaches to learning using examination questions was described by W. K. Viertel in a letter to *Engineering Education*:

> An experiment in getting students to submit possible test questions for current courses has been, I believe, quite successful. For years I had solicited such suggestions from most of my classes, and got little or no response. One day after a 'pop-quiz' on the current work in mathematics which I had thought fair, but on which the results were especially poor, I required the class to prepare as a homework assignment what they thought would be a fair question on that topic. Later I required further questions on the term's work. To my pleasant surprise, I got some useful ideas, and the variety of problems was such that most or all were clearly the students' own work. But more important, it seems to me, was that the students' ego became involved and I believe that they saw better the instructor's point of view as a result.
>
> This same idea has been useful also in the physics laboratory where I have found it a good practice to test each week on one of the basic ideas of the previous week's experiment. Occasionally, I could not think of a question or problem that I was satisfied with, so the test read: 'Think up a suitable question or problem on last week's experiment of about the right length and degree of difficulty and submit it with the correct answer'. The results here are also very interesting, revealing as they did what the students considered most significant about the experiment.
>
> In all these cases, the basis for evaluation of the items submitted was their suitability for further use as test questions. It should surprise no one that there was good correlation between the grades obtained in this way and those previously obtained by more conventional testing.

I have subsequently tried this approach with children with some success (Heywood, 1977). Ultimately procedures of this kind take us toward the kind of negotiated curriculum offered by Alverno College.

From the above we may safely conclude that there is much scope for objective testing in higher education.

Notes

1. The discussion of objective testing in this chapter has been confined to the classical approach which uses the biserial r. During the last 20 years interest in the United States has focused particularly on latent-trait theory (Lord and Novick, 1968; Messick *et al.*, 1983; Weiss, 1983).

   It is claimed that this approach gets over some of the objections to classical theory. Smith (1986) has described how this development came about with a general concern for 'person fit':

   > Whether recognized or not, most people have a standard reasonableness for their measurements. It requires that the results of a test provide an ability estimate such that performance on each item and subset of items is consistent with the overall ability estimate. This standard is usually unexpressed, sometimes even unrecognized, but it is implied when a single score is reported. . . if the notion of easy and hard items is to have any meaning then persons taking this test must be expected to pass the easy items more often than the hard items. Patterns which contradict this expectation violate this standard of reasonableness.

Smith describes a number of response patterns to illustrate the problem. Why, for example, does one candidate pass the hardest item yet fail the easiest? Why does another pass all the broadest items and fail the easiest? Person-fit statistics are indications of the believability of a pattern of responses.

In traditional theory a pattern of lucky guesses is treated in the same way as a pattern of silly mistakes. Only when the relative difficulties of all the items are considered is it possible to say in which way the score should be amended.

Smith's article considers four major themes in the history of attempts to solve this problem. Of these, two are of particular interest. Cronbach (1946) developed the idea of a response set. i.e. any tendency causing a person consistently to give different responses to test items than he would when the same content is presented in a different form. He thought there were six types of response sets applicable to educational tests: (1) tendency to gamble, (2) definition of judgement categories, (3) inclusiveness, (4) bias, (5) speed versus accuracy, and (6) miscellaneous. His suggestions to overcome these problems relate to the administration and design of tests. The study reported by Youngman and myself (1981) suggests that there are other kinds of response set, although the measurements we made did not wholly embrace personality. Lumsden (1977, 1978) also comes near to regarding the affective domain as an influence, on a candidate's response. He suggests that three types of change can influence a person's ability:

(1) Trends: growth curves representing long-term development;
(2) Swells: temporary fluctuations of ability lasting several hours or days;
(3) Tremors: momentary fluctuations in ability which can be thought of as random errors.

It will be seen that belief that this is the case underpinned the movement to coursework assessment in Britain. Lumsden argues that all the reliability (unreliability) of a score is due to the person. Test score unreliability results from the swells and tremors experienced by a person during the test. Given that this axiom is correct, then, by definition, all tests are reliable. What we need to know is not the summed reliability of a test but how a person 'fits' the population within which they are tested.

To achieve this goal a graph (model) may be constructed which gives the person's probability of responding correctly to items having a wide range of difficulties so as to express the dispersion of the attribute locations resulting from tremors. The flatter this curve, the more likely the person is to have been affected by tremors.

When a person is tested within a group the 'average slope' for the group is found and the person's slope is compared with the average for the group. If the person does not fit that curve then that person is unmeasureable. The general idea may be obtained from consideration of the curves in Figure 34. To put it in another way, the average person–characteristic curve defines what might be reasonably expected, i.e. the proportion of correct responses for the range of item difficulties on the test. The person's reliability is quantified as the degree of departure from the expected on an item-by-item analysis.

Smith draws attention to the many similarities (and some differences) between Lumsden's model and latent-trait theory. In the latter (commonly called 'item response theory') a 'trait level' which is the equivalent of the true score is derived from the candidate's performance. The candidate's ability is assumed to be constant: it is the error which varies and causes the responses to vary about the true ability or trait level. The models (curves) attempt to describe the relationship between the observed responses and the latent-trait level as a function of the characteristics of the test items. The models deal with items rather than test scores. The ability of an individual's responses to the items can be predicted. Computers enable simulations to be made of model.

The Graduate Record Examinations Board has tested the feasibility of using item response theory as a psychometric model for the GRE aptitude test. Kingston and Dorans (1982) concluded that the ITM response theory model (several models are possible) as well as another involving the pre-calibration of data appeared to be applicable to the verbal section of the test but not to the quantitative, although they felt that, with modification, those models would be applicable to that section.

The Rasch model is a special case of latent-trait theory the person-fit statistics of which are considered by Smith. A one-parameter model, it is named after its Danish originator, Rasch. Much work has been done by Wright (1979) on this model (Willmot and Fowles, 1974) and three aspects have been of interest. These were its use in item writing, the contribution it could make to the development of item banks, and its potential in the measurement of educational change. As in the United States with the National Assessment of Educational Progress, so the Assessment of Performance Unit in Britain wanted to measure change over time, and this accounted for its interest in the Rasch model.

In Britain the experts were critical of the model on both technical and educational grounds (Goldstein, 1986; Nuttall, 1986). The latter was held to be the more serious. The problem with the Rasch model is that the principal parameters are invariant. The items are always set to have the same difficulty so that they cannot be used to compare groups which have received different kinds of teaching and different components of the syllabus. This would mean that tests would have to be analysed item by item.

The British view is summarized by Nuttall (1986), who argues that the Educational Testing Service which is responsible for the National Assessment of Educational Progress has remained silent on the educational criticisms although the technical criticisms seem to have been met. The Educational Testing Service does, however, intend to use other approaches.

My interest in the Rasch model arose from the fact that tests which were supposedly designed to test different abilities/behaviours when factored yielded (as is often the case) a rather large single factor. There were four tests each of 50 items designed to assess terminology, specific information, generalization, interpretation and analysis. There were ten items for each educational behav-

316

iour (objective) in each test. This meant that there were a total of 40 items representative of each behaviour in the subtests. When the Rasch model was applied to each group of subtest it extracted 20, 23, 18, 18 and 17 items from each group of 40. The advantage of the technique in these circumstances was that it enabled the item-writers to compare the items for their similarities and dissimilarities and provided a complementary tool to factor analysis in the understanding of what was happening. We also evaluated the items in an engineering science examination in the same way and found that 38 out of 40 fitted the model (Heywood, 1977).

The latent-trait method of selecting items for mastery tests which assumes a well-defined cut-off is complex, and so some interest has centred on producing a simpler method for use in the classroom (Harris and Subkoviak, 1986).

The relative merits of alpha–beta, biserial and Rasch methods of items analysis have been compared by Youngman (1980). Alpha–beta is Youngman's modification of Cronbach's method. He claims simplicity for this technique and maintains that it is more than adequate when both reliability and validity are considered.

2. This is not the same as a tailored test, which requires that each candidate is presented with items of 50% difficulty for them (i.e. they should get one out of every two items correct). Wood (1986) does not believe that tailored tests of this kind would be optimal for the student psychologically because we do not know how motivation, task difficulty and immediate past experience work on each other.

CHAPTER 13

Toward Multiple-strategy Assessment

RETROSPECT AND PROSPECT

In Chapter 1 a broad resumé of developments in and problems associated with assessment in higher education was given. We saw that 'Assessment', to quote Hartle (1986) about the American scene, 'appears to have become in higher education a catch-all phrase that refers to a wide range of efforts to improve educational quality.' As if to demonstrate the validity of this view the Governors of the States, through their task force on higher education, emphasized the need for assessment to improve quality which had many dimensions. They called it multiple-strategy assessment (NGA, 1986).

The range of meanings applied to assessment was not only illustrated by Hartle but by other articles in the same report (Adelman, 1986). In that report. which was published by the US Department of Education, as well as in the Report of the Governors and the 1987 Conference of the American Association of Higher Education, considerable attention was paid to a small number of colleges and universities which were thought to be meeting the goals of assessment as perceived by those judges and the authors whose task was to review such developments. Among them were Alverno College in Milwaukee, the University of Tennessee at Knoxville, and North-east Missouri State University. Many other examples were cited. In this chapter the focus will be on the Alverno programme which, Hartle says, is the best and perhaps only comprehensive example of a multiple-measure programme in which observers track intellectual and personal growth over an extended period of time. During a four-year career the typical student will undergo more than a hundred performance assessments. It is a scheme built around the view that properly designed assessments create and enhance the conditions for effective learning. It was that axiom which led to the first edition of this book, where it was argued that a multiple-objective approach is required for the design of assessment; that assessment is an integral part of learning; that instructional procedures have to be designed to obtain the goals of assessment; and that the processes of assessment and curriculum design are one.

The consequences of this were a particular systems approach to the curriculum in which the syllabus is the outcome of a complex activity involving the selection of 'significant' objectives, the design of instructional and assessment procedures to meet those objectives, and their summation into the syllabus. A visual picture of this model is given in Figure 3 of Chapter 1. Content derives from the key concepts of the curriculum, and these key concepts are as much objectives as learning skills, for it is the function of learning skills to ensure that the concepts are met. Assessment and evaluation in this model imply feedback to the institution, its faculty, and its students.

The selection of objectives is not a simple activity involving the incorporation of a list of objectives like *The Taxonomy of Educational Objectives*, however useful that may be. It involves an understanding of institutional and societal goals, on the one hand, and student learning, on the other. The skills of learning are objective in just the same way as key concepts. Faculties have to know about their students and this is illustrated by the entering characteristics in Figure 4. Equally, they have to know about their institution (Figure 5).

My model arose from the work which I had done on the education of technologists (Heywood *et al.*, 1966; Heywood, 1969), the teaching of science to arts students in a university (Heywood and Montagu-Pollock, 1976), and the development of a GCE A level examination in engineering science (Carter *et al.*, 1986). Other studies of history and mathematics at school level supported these findings (Heywood *et al.*, 1980).

In the first edition of this book both the work on engineering science then in progress and the study of teaching science to arts students were reported. The purpose of the former was to demonstrate the validity of the multiple-objective approach to assessment while that of the latter was to demonstrate the role of the teacher as an evaluator and to promote the concept of illuminative evaluation. I have not repeated that case study in this edition since it should be clear that a multiple-strategy approach to assessment demands much more of the teacher in higher education than in the past. Teachers have to become designers and evaluators, experimenters and analysts if they are to be truly professional. Eisner's concept of connoisseurship is little different to the concept of the teacher as an illuminative evaluator.

As Cross (1986) says,

'if college teachers were to practise their profession at a more sophisticated level, they would discover that the classroom is, or should be, a challenging research laboratory, with questions to be pursued, data to be collected, analyses to be made, and improvements to be tried and collected'.

The question is, how far do institutions and their faculty have to go to meet the requirements of multiple-strategy assessment?

In this book I have attempted to set down a framework in which answers to this question can be sought. The three case studies below (which are descriptive rather than critical) describe three different responses to the model which involve institutions and their faculty in different approaches and types of activity.

It is important at this stage to enter the caveat that it is not possible to do justice to any of the three developments described. I can only hope that the selections will lead the reader to look at the documentation on these developments, which is considerable.

FROM COMPREHENSIVE TO MULTIPLE-OBJECTIVE EXAMINATIONS

In their background paper for the AAHE Second National Conference on Assessment in Higher Education (1987) Resnick and Goulden ventured four very general observations about assessment in the United States which were based on an analysis of survey data. These were to the effect that:

(1) Assessment of entering student performance for purposes of placement is common in American colleges and universities.
(2) Assessment of learning during the college years, through devices other than course exams, is not common but is likely to grow in coming years.
(3) Devices like comprehensive examinations in the major field will become more important, focusing attention on both student learning and the quality of undergraduate programmes.
(4) Four-year colleges will be actors of increasing importance in the assessment movement.

The first case study illustrates the second point, and it would come within the category of aptitude treatment interaction, about which reference was made in Chapter 4. This is about the assessment of doctors who have qualified but have to do postgraduate training for general practice. The total programme would seem to be as comprehensive as that envisaged by the Governors of the United States for multiple-strategy assessment. The same seems to be true of the third case study, which describes the approach of Alverno College. The focus of both these studies is on the assessment of students, but, as they show, their ramifications have implications for the institution as well as for teachers. The second case study relates to the third of Resnick and Goulden's points and describes the development of a comprehensive examination in which the subtests focus on precisely stated domain criteria. It would seem to represent a midpoint in development towards the kind of system operated at Alverno College. As such, it might prove attractive to teachers and institutions who, in the course of such a development, could introduce additional investigations of the kind undertaken in the first case study in the personality and value domains.

CASE STUDIES

1: The Assessment of General Practice

The work described in this case study was undertaken in the Department of General Practice in the University of Manchester. The senior research worker involved in all of the studies was Dr James Freeman, and it is to him that the references are made in this section.

The first and second of the studies were reported in 1973 and 1976. In the first of these Freeman and Byrne described how they had developed a multiple-strategy approach to the assessment of doctors training to be general practitioners in a postgraduate course specifically devised for this purpose. This strategy included instruments which would not only test knowledge and patient planning skills (MCQs and MEQs) but measures of non-verbal (Raven's matrices) high-grade (AH5) and adult (Wechsler) intelligence. These were accompanied by a test of abstract/concrete performance based on the work of Guilford, Hudson and Vygotsky, and a convergent/divergent test based on Guilford's approach to creativity. In parallel with these 'cognitive' measurements assessments were also obtained of student interests (the Strong Vocational Interest Blank) as well as of their biographical and academic interests. During the course evaluations were also obtained from both interviews and group discussions with the trainees as well as ratings of students' attitudes and performance by their tutors. The attitude ratings sought information about their attitudes to the quality of primary care, professional values, teamwork, appointment systems and long-term care as they saw them in operation during the course. The study embraced both evaluation and assessment. The tutors rated performance using the profile which was described at the end of Chapter 11 (Manchester Trainee Evaluation Scale).

Subsequent reports from Freeman and his colleagues describe the results and the changes which were made as the study progressed. The second report (Freeman and Byrne, 1976) is a second edition of the first which gives the results of pre- and post-testing. It includes the description of the principles of the investigation given in the first edition.

The third report (1981) contains a brief summary of the first study and then goes on to describe how they gave the same tests not only to the teachers but also the trainees. They made some important amendments and additions to the instruments used. First, they changed the high-grade intelligence test from AH5 to AH6, which had been developed with the help of students at the University of Cambridge. Second, they substituted a divergent thinking hypothesis test developed by Pole (1969) for the original convergent/divergent thinking measure.

Within the domain of personality the Eysenck personality inventory of extroversion/introversion was used together with assessments for convergent and divergent thinking and, introversion-rigidity developed by Freeman and McComisky as well as a self- and peer-rating derived from work by the US Office of Strategic Services (1948).

A fourth report looked at the correlations between the techniques of assessment, and describes in particular the work of Dr Gerard Keele, who was able to observe the trainers at work (Freeman et al., 1981; Keele, 1982).

The origins of the study describe how from a review of the literature they derived objectives which courses of general practice should obtain. The work of Christine McGuire and George Miller in the United States was a considerable influence on the design of the investigation. These objectives not only showed the importance of knowledge and technical skills in patient management but highlighted the personal qualities required by doctors in that very sensitive relationship between practitioner and patient. It seemed that training should be provided and assessed in both areas. It will be seen in the third case study that Alverno College takes the view that interpersonal competence is a skill which should be developed and assessed in any programme of liberal education. Freeman and Byrne's strategy might be described as a frontal attack on this problem. There is, it will be seen, a clear relationship between the instruments of assessment used and the objectives of the programme. This relationship is perhaps best observed in the performance rating profile which describes the expected performance of good and poor practitioners in nine domains (see Table 53). As the investigation progressed, so the element of evaluation became stronger. The medical trainers agreed to take the knowledge skill tests and also to be observed at work. This is the most unique feature of the study, and is an attempt to evaluate the influence of the teacher on the trainee in one-to-one tutorials as well as practice classes.

Eighty trainees and 80 teachers participated in the first study and 76 of each in the second.

A summary of the first study at the beginning of the second (1982) records that there were statistically significant increases in knowledge and patient management skills as measured by the tests. It will be appreciated that this does considerable injustice to the scope of the work as described above, particularly the comparative assessments which they made with other groups of students.

For example, in the first study they found that in terms of level of performance (general abilities/intelligence) there were no significant differences between the trainees and students in other subjects (architecture, economics and social science). However, like other studies, it did show that there was a significant difference in the bias of the different groups of students. In contrast to the social science students, the trainees were stronger diagrammatically than verbally on the measure of intelligence. This might be expected from persons with an essentially scientific training from the age of 16. Similarly, the architectural students scored more highly on the abstract/concrete test, a result which is equally consistent with type of training. The trainee practitioners also obtained higher scores than the social scientists and tend to convergence, whereas the economists and social scientists are all-rounders. It should be remembered, however, that convergent/divergent tests are strongly verbal and, as such, operate against the performance of those whose training has been biased toward the scientific from an early age. In this study the trainees' learning skills were strongly reinforced by the multiple-choice testing of knowledge, which would not be the case with the other students in the sample. Freeman suggests that it is not so much the verbal nature of the creativity tests but their open-endedness which is the cause of the problem. However, this is consistent with the view that prior training which does not emphasize open-ended problem-solving will act as an impediment in such tests. One of the reasons for the application and analysis papers in engineering science at A level described in the next case study was to encourage more open-ended problem-solving, particularly in relation to the economic and social context of engineering.

In contrast, the trainee medical practitioners were much more facile with the spoken word than were the economists or social scientists. This is of some interest, since Resnick and Goulden make particular mention of oral tests in the comprehensive examinations in the United States. Clearly, they test an important and different skill, and have considerable value if they can be conducted so as to have high reliability.

It was found that the trainee practitioners tended to demonstrate technical and scientific interests, whereas the economists and social scientists expressed cultural and social ones, as might be expected. Less expected was the fact that there was an expression of religious values among the trainee practitioners.

Freeman and Byrne found that when the profile ratings of the same trainees were compared for different tutors there was a high degree of correlation among the tutors about the performance of the best trainees. However, discrepancies occurred in the middle of the range of performance as well as among the tutors in the ratings they gave to the poorest students. The poorest assessments were given for performances that were above those which would normally be regarded as a failure.

In response to questions about their reasons for taking up the course it was found that the best trainees had clearly defined goals in respect of the course, whereas the poorest did not. An example of the trainee who had entered the course 'because he wished to learn about the interview in general practice' is given as a positive goal.

Freeman correlated the personality ratings with the tutor ratings on the coursework assessment schedule to obtain a picture of the best and poorest trainees. When the best trainees were compared with the worst it was found that they were less rigid and authoritarian. As a group the best were also much more confident. In so far as personal relationships are concerned, the best had balanced scores on the extroversion/introversion dimension.

Finally, from among the many findings of the first investigation mention should be made of the conclusion that some training in interviewing of the kind done in the business schools was desirable. Such training would facilitate the development of some of the professional skills and abilities of the general practitioner (for example, in the area of history-taking and managing patients). The trainees had given the impression that in interviews they sometimes lacked a positive manner and, to a less extent, intellectual force.

While the second study is as impressive as the first it is not possible to describe it in detail. I have chosen to concentrate on the relationship between the relative performances of trainees and teachers, since it is important in such studies to evaluate the influence of the teachers on trainees.

As a matter of general report, while the teachers did very much better than the trainees at the beginning of the course (mean scores of 60.5 and 54.3 on the MCQ and 79.06 and 62.43 on the MEQ), the trainees levelled with the teachers on the post-course MCQ (61.6) and came near to them on the MEQ (76.1). The increase in the MEQ scores of the trainees was significantly greater than that in the MCQ scores.

When the scattergrams were drawn it was found that the highest-scoring trainees (pre-course) scored considerably higher than the lowest-scoring teachers. The problem which the investigators had to solve was whether the increase in an MCQ score was due to training, when at entry the trainee had a higher MCQ score than that of the teachers to whom he or she was attached. Answers to this question can be inferred from correlations of the changes in scores.

The correlations of the changes in pre- and post-test scores with those of the teachers show a significant positive relationship. The individual scores show that the trainees with high entry scores who were attached to high-scoring teachers obtained higher post-test scores than similar pre-entry scoring trainees attached to low-scoring ones. Thus it is inferred that teachers do have an influence on trainees. Freeman goes so far as to suggest that in circumstances where teachers can be selected their MCQ rating is a focal point for vocational training schemes of this kind. Not surprisingly, such things as the time spent in preparing tutorials, the number and variety of journals read and enthusiasm were found to be important for effective teaching.

Freeman, in response to criticisms by Mrozik (1984) who had suggested that such measurements were rather crude, pointed out that the questionnaires were supported by interview. He also said that one group of trainees was more able than the other to name and discuss articles which it had recently read. However, Freeman was more concerned to refute the criticism that the experimental design was at fault, particularly as it related to the comparison of pre- and post-course performance. Mrozik claimed that the statistical measures were inadequate. Freeman replied that what was being reached for was the concept of covariance, although this was not wholly achieved. Thus the analysis of variance conducted on the post-course scores is corrected for the pre-test ones, which are the covariates. In this way it is possible to highlight the significance of the training given.

Studies of this kind are always open to criticism, as the example of the second case study will show. Nevertheless, they do provide indicators and point to issues which may need to be examined further. One finding which drew the wrath of Marinker (1984) related to the personality characteristics of the teachers and their trainees. A significant relationship between the personality variables of the 25 trainees showing the greatest scores in the MCQ and the personalities of their teachers was found. However, no such relationship was found for the 25 trainees with the least improvement in their pre- and post-test MCQ scores.

The better trainees tended to produce more balanced scores. For example, excellent students were just below average on the rigidity scale whereas the marginal trainees demonstrated high rigidity. Similarly, the excellent trainees showed much more self-confidence. Balanced scores, suggests Freeman, may correlate with acceptable and social behaviour. Some psychologists, he reminds us, have gone so far as to argue that many introversion/extroversion scales are, in fact, indicators of social adjustment.

Freeman goes on to suggest that, since consonance between the personality variables and cognitive styles of teachers and trainees is likely to help the learning process, in the one-to-one situation of postgraduate medical training it should be possible to devise a system of matching teachers to trainers, although this point has been challenged. Marinker (1984) argued that there was great potential for intellectual and emotional growth of the trainee in the very conflicts of personality and cognitive styles against which Freeman warns. However, this is to ignore the problem of cognitive dissonance, which shows that the outcome of such conflicts is likely to depend on the values of tutor and trainee. Most teachers in higher education can recount stories of arguments between students and tutors which have led to learning withdrawal on the part of the student. Marinker also argues that the goals of vocational training have nothing to do with ability to perform in written tests. This cannot be wholly correct, for knowledge and skills in planning are surely essential to good practice, as is the training of the memory. In any case, the programme included the criterion measures shown in Table 53, which were based on what practitioners do. The most convincing refutation of this point is a subsequent study by Keele (1982) of practitioners at work, which is now described.

In a separate study an assessment of the clinical competence of 65 of the general practitioner teachers was made by direct observation of their clinical performance. Keele, the observer, carried out three days of observation (or the equivalent number of surgery sessions) of each trainer. These sessions were split in the ratio of 2 days to 1 day, and a period 3–6 months elapsed between the two observations. Competence was assessed for information-gathering, problem-solving, clinical judgement, relating to the patient, continuing care, and organization of the practice.

In order to develop observer reliability the observer sat in with 25 doctors for varying lengths of time during the period of a year. The criteria as well as the techniques of observation were refined. At the end of the pilot study the observer was set a practical observation test in the presence of two other observers. The clinicians who were observed were also questioned about their reactions to the observer. It was found that their performance tended to be constant, which suggested that the observer had little influence over their behaviour.

Because two observations were made it was possible to calculate the consistency (reliability) of the ratings. The mean consistency coefficient was 0.84, suggesting a high level of reliability.

When the observer's ratings were correlated with tests taken by the teachers it was found that there were considerable variations in the criteria assessed by the observer and the MCQ and MEQ scores of the doctors. A traditional type of essay paper was also set in this particular investigation and it was found that the correlation of this paper with the observer's ratings showed more consistency than those obtained from the other measures. None of these instruments correlated with the doctors' behaviour in the surgery, particularly in regard to the criterion relating to the patient. This highlights the limitation of written examinations as predictors of performance in activity-based contexts.

The analysis (which included analysis of variance, ANOVA) showed, among several other things, that a well-constructed MCQ can test the knowledge involved in the selection and use of drugs, which is a major aspect of patient management. It also supported the view expressed earlier (Chapter 6) that problem-solving is a category which needs to be defined within specific contexts, a fact which is consistent with other researches reported in previous chapters. There is a need for definition and precision in this area. The observer had to rely on the doctor's elucidation and exploration of the processes involved in gathering information on a wide range of matters. It was found that the observer's assessments yielded similar correlations for the criterion concerned with information.

Keele found that advice on the potential side-effects of drugs was given in only a third of instances when a psycho-active preparation was prescribed for a new episode of illness. The doctors who gave this advice were those who achieved high scores in a range of problems associated with patient management in the MEQ paper. He was led to argue that because medical education had concentrated on clinical problem-solving it had neglected the 'executive' end of the consultation, i.e. the proper use of drugs and advice given to the patient. He and Freeman (1982) drew attention to the need to develop listening behaviour and attitudes in emergency care. The fact that a doctor's score on one MEQ (which was the written source for problem-solving) did not correlate with the responses to other MEQs indicated (as previously reported in Chapter 10) the need for a substantial number of MEQs in any MEQ paper if the technique is to have validity.

Multiple-strategy assessments of this kind undoubtedly pose problems from which course designers cannot escape. In this instance it has led to a revision of the Manchester Trainee Evaluation Scales, but it also points to the need for training of trainers. As far as one of the central themes of this book is concerned, the study calls for precision and clear definition in vocational training of this kind. It illustrates the need for clear objectives based on detailed analysis of the tasks undertaken. Together, the three investigations briefly described show how objectives are informed not only by the task analysis but by the learner and the ways through which learners learn. In medical practice there can be no divorce between the cognitive and affective, and both must be assessed if potential performance in practice is to be adequately predicted. The third case study demonstrates this to be as true for liberal/general education as it is for vocational/professional study.

The design of comprehensive examinations whose subtests focus on well-defined domains should help teachers to break the mould of traditional thinking about assessment and point them in the direction taken by teachers in the first and third case studies. The second case study, therefore, describes the development of a comprehensive examination in England.

2: A Multiple-Strategy Examination

Background The development and evaluation of engineering science at GCE A level over a 16-year period has been told in detail elsewhere (Carter *et al.*, 1986) and the coursework was described in Chapter 11. This section, therefore, is concerned only with those features which bear on the design of multiple-strategy assessment.

The syllabus for engineering science was developed by the JMB in response to the view that the perceived shortage of professional engineers in Britain was due in part to the fact that able students in schools did not come into contact with the applications of science, which was what engineering was about. The syllabus was designed to be equivalent to physics at A level but at the same time to concentrate on the applications of physical science to practical problems. At the time of the Board's approval of the syllabus in 1967 it was thought that the most important study from the point of view of the design of comprehensive examinations was that of engineering examinations by Furneaux (1962), to which reference has already been made. Apart from the relationship to personality (discussed in Chapter 4), Furneaux also examined the correlations between assessments in years 1 and 2 as well as those between the individual papers which comprised the Part 1 examination.

First, he found that there was no direct correlation between performance in the subjects studied in the first year and their equivalents in the second. This led him to ask why it was necessary for those who had a near-miss in the June examination to have to repeat it in September. Given the poor correlations between years 1 and 2, why not allow such a student to proceed to year 2 without the bother of a repeat?

The second (and more significant of his findings from the point of view of engineering science) was that a factorial analysis of the separate written papers (mathematics, aerodynamics, thermodynamics, etc.) showed that they all tested the same thing. He called this factor 'examination-passing ability'. As we saw in Chapter 4, there was an exception—engineering drawing. Why set all these examinations to test the same skill? he asked. I later defined this skill as engineering analysis using particular mathematical techniques (Heywood, 1968). In a typical university examination a student might take as many as seven such examinations at the end of each year, and the time taken in sitting these might range between 12 and 21 hours.

The syllabus for GCE A level was in eight sections which mirrored college courses in engineering science. The time available for written examinations was 6 hours and an additional component was available for coursework. The question for the working party was, should it depart from the traditional A level structure in physics in which candidates attempted five or six problem-solving exercises in each of the two papers? It was assumed that the traditional approach in physics would lead to the testing of knowledge and analysis as defined in *The Taxonomy of Educational Objectives* (see Chapters 5 and 6).

The working party which designed the assessment procedures thought that it should not, and, as was explained in Chapter 11 which described the coursework for the examination, attempted to design assessments based on the skills it was believed were essential to the engineering scientist at work.

The Structure of the Examination The clue as to how to structure such an examination came from the JMB A level examination in General Studies. This used several strategies to test the categories of *The Taxonomy of Educational Objectives*. In the particular examination papers which we saw there was a comprehension test related to scientific literacy. A substantial passage from a quality newspaper article was given, the understanding of which was tested by multiple-choice questions. This led to the decision to include such a test in the examination. The other decisions which were arrived at, after a trial test on students who had started the course, included a series of multiple-choice questions to test knowledge and short-term (chain) problem-solving, a paper to test skills in project design and planning, one to test the applications of science within both their scientific and economic contexts, assessment of practical work by means of experimental discovery exercises and a project undertaken during the course. The structure of the examination up to 1974 is shown in Table 62.

Evaluation The system of assessment for the coursework which was semi-criterion referenced was discussed in detail in Chapter 11. The analyses which we made showed both the limitations and potential of project work. The same would seem to be true of the analyses which were also made of the written examinations which are the subject of the paragraphs which follow.

Table 62. Structure of the examination in engineering science

	Objective and technique of assessment	Percentage of total score
Paper I	Knowledge and short-chain problem-solving (1 hour—objective test, 40 items)	$13\frac{1}{2}$
Paper IIA	Comprehension exercise (1 hour—short answers)	$13\frac{1}{2}$
B	Project planning and design (1 hour—as required by the student)	$13\frac{1}{2}$
Paper IIIA	Applications of engineering science (analysis and application) ($1\frac{1}{2}$ hours. Six out of 9 questions)	20
Paper IIIB	Applications of engineering science. ($1\frac{1}{2}$ hours. Three from 6 questions)	20

Papers IIA and B and Papers IIIA and B are set at the same sittings.
Coursework accounts for 20% of the total mark.

In traditional test theory it should be possible to demonstrate that each of the subtests tested something which was different to that examined in the other subtests by factorial analysis. In theory, each of the subtests in the engineering science examination was designed to test knowledge of engineering science together with something else, which was thought to be a skill in handling that particular knowledge. An analysis of the test scores should therefore show a communality between them as well as something specific which the test does that is different to the others. Intercorrelations were obtained and factorial analyses undertaken to see if this was the case.

It was found that the pattern of results was remarkably stable over the years, which is of some significance to small-scale research because the numbers in the total population were small. It does mean that this kind of analysis can be done with student numbers of the order of 100 provided that the testing conditions are relatively standardized over several years. That is, in circumstances of small numbers where the population has the same kind of homogeneity (in terms of admission scores, prior study in the subject, etc.), an examiner might expect to replicate his or her results from one year to another.

However, of most interest to the test designer was the difference between the results obtained by Furneaux and those given by this particular examination.

Whereas Furneaux found that all the written examinations were dominated by one factor, this particular technique of factorial analysis showed that there was a component in each subtest in engineering science which was specific to the test. The variance between the subtests on the unrotated factor matrix was 52%. The remaining 47% of the variance could be accounted by specific factors. This was established by extracting all the factors that each variable loaded highly on particular factors, and since we obtained the same results every year we took the view that there were highly specific factors which contributed to each variable and which therefore related to the subtests. This led me to use the term 'multiple-objective examination' to describe this kind of test.

'Domain' and 'Focusing' Objectives My reasons for using the term 'multiple-objective' were as follows. Although we did not design a paper to meet the main categories of *The Taxonomy of Educational Objectives* except with respect to comprehension, we did have clear domain objectives in mind which stemmed from the general aim of developing skills in the applications of science to engineering, and this to embrace engineering design. To achieve this goal the subtests were constructed around two focal points. On the one hand, there were the knowledge requirements related to skills in short-chain problem-solving, and on the other, there were the executive skills involved in the planning, implementation and evaluation of practical activities which were described in detail in Chapter 11. Thus each subtest had a principal focus. In this book I have called these 'focusing objectives' or 'domain objectives'. 'Focusing objectives' describe an area which the course designers feel should be given prominence. In any one course it is only possible for there to be a limited number of these. Each of them will embrace a domain of 'lower-order

objectives' which may or may not be obtained as a function of teaching, learning and assessment. I have also used the term 'domain' in this sense, i.e. to encompass the minor objectives from which the domain is constructed.

In the engineering science programme the minor objectives which contribute to a domain are only listed in respect of the coursework projects and experimental investigations. Even here, the number of subcategories considered is very small. It might be argued that the same approach to the design of the written examination should have been taken by the course designers, who instead concentrated on writing questions for the subtests which had high face validity. In the circumstances this was justifiable, since within the system of public examinations it was held that the examinations should not dictate teaching.

Supporting Evidence When we undertook the investigations into the public system of school examining in Ireland we decided to adapt the engineering science model for the examinations set at 15-plus years of age in history and mathematics (Heywood *et al.*, 1980). Domain objective subtests were designed by teachers for both experimental examinations. Factorial analyses separated out specific factors related to the general domain categories but went no further. Key subcategories in the mathematics test were not isolated. We might have revealed more had we used discriminant analysis. Nevertheless, the data lent support to the model. Perhaps the most important outcome of the investigation, since it relates to the debate about reliability and validity, was the fact that the teachers preferred the experimental examinations to the public ones because they perceived them to have higher face validity.

Nevertheless, we should be cautious in our interpretation of face validity data, as our experience of the experimental examination in history shows. In one of the subtests we designed we claimed to be testing the skill of evaluation. Students were asked to evaluate the objectivity of two accounts of the same event. Critics of this test have argued that what was tested was skill in handling statistics and not evaluation within a historical context, even though the events described took place in the 1800s. My own view is that reliability and validity go hand in hand; measurement can throw up questions which lead to important insights, and this is demonstrated by the poor correlation which we found between coursework and the written paper designed to test skills in the same area in engineering science (see below).

The Interpretation of Multiple-Strategy Assessments Our work shows in particular just how difficult it is to analyse tests for their validity. There is a very real danger that too much will be expected from the measurements, and that when they do not fit preconceived models they will be discarded without further action.

There are many case studies which highlight the value of such work. For example, in an introductory course in psychology in the University of Sydney, 15 components are assessed: five are aspects of classwork; nine are examinations, and one is a mark given for participation in experimental work conducted within the department. Johnson (1985) describes how these courses in his department are taught for nine weeks and examined one week later. The classwork and the examination marks are intended to provide students with continuous feedback which, it is held, is less stressful. They can also modify their study or writing techniques as the year progresses. At the end of the year a summative collation is made. In this introductory course three content areas are taught per term. They are assessed in one 2-hour period either by one long essay, two short essays, 30 multiple-choice items, or a short essay together with 15 multiple-choice items. These examinations account for 60% of the final mark. The classwork consists of two essays and three quizzes using factorial analysis. Johnson found that four factors contributed to the variance: 27.7% related to the multiple-choice examination, 18.24% to a factor related to classroom, 12.3% to an essay examination factor and the fourth (but very unimportant) factor (4.57%) related to the student's endurance, i.e the experimental (time) work on the course. In spite of its apparent unimportance, this was retained in the programme because that part of the course allows the students to experience research from the student's perspective. Such decisions illustrate the role of measurement technique in assessment. The course designer does not necessarily abandon a course section because it does not yield a strong factor. Face validity and desirability judgements have an important role to play.

Similarly, even though the multiple-choice tests were found to be the best predictor of subsequent performance, the essay was not abandoned because apart from the fact that it was considered to be an important technique it was also shown that there was an improvement in essay writing. The later essays were found to be better predictors of subsequent performance than the earlier ones, a result which confirms the work of Hounsell and Gibbs reported in Chapter 10. It is also a reminder that school and university essay performance are different things, and that many students do not appreciate this unless they are told. It is interesting to note that the tutorial quizzes served as an incentive to attend tutorials. It would be interesting to know what students thought about the system and the way they perceived it to influence their approaches to learning.

The Systems Model and Other Issues Perhaps the most interesting finding of the engineering science study was the fact that the coursework did not correlate with the written subtest with which it was supposed to have a high correlation (i.e. Paper II b: Project Planning and Design). Illuminative evaluation suggested that this was due to the fact that teachers thought that there was a transfer of skill between the preparation of the project outline and the project planning exercise in the written examination. Because of this, they did not provide specific training for this written paper. This broke the system, for instruction and learning were not focused on the domain objective: formal teaching in the design method was required. While the Board accepted this view, it did not make such teaching a formal requirement. That there should be formal instruction is reinforced by the view (implicit in my opinion) in Sternberg's work (see Chapter 11) to the effect that the time restraints in the two situations are so different as to cause the utilization of different problem-solving skills.

We also found this to be true of the experimental mathematics examination. Despite the fact that the teachers wanted a subtest on problem-solving, the paper was badly done. It was clear that the students received no training in this area of mathematics. As investigators, we were not allowed to ask teachers to intervene in the teaching process, so the experimental examination was not directly related to the objectives. Satisfactory results are only likely to be obtained when the two are aligned.

These studies illustrate several problems in the construction of examination papers to test high-level skills. First, there is the suggestion that problem-solving and the *Taxonomy* category of analysis might be the same thing in science subjects, particularly where the solution to a scientific problem depends on a particular mathematical technique. In contrast is the idea that it is the way the questions are constructed which leads to the problem-solving technique adopted.

Frederiksen and Ward (1978) in the United States have suggested that their Test of Scientific Thinking for candidates seeking admission to graduate school in psychology had some correlation with the Graduate Record Examination, but that the number of unusual ideas which was a key feature of the test was unrelated to conventional tests. Their work, which was somewhat more sophisticated than ours, did not produce any evidence of a generalized ability to produce ideas which are either numerous or good. It also showed that the number of unusual responses appeared to be a direct consequence of the rate at which the more obvious possibilities were exhausted, and this would seem to confirm the views put forward previously about the influence of experience on perception. Might it be that the more a candidate is trained to cope with such tests, the higher the correlation will be? If examinations are to influence learning this is how it should be, but it does make for more measurement difficulty.

We tried to design questions which would test skills in design, and came to the conclusion that what we were testing was skill in the analysis of design. If an examiner wanted to test creative design the only thing that he or she could do was what no examiner would be prepared to do, i.e. give the candidates a blank sheet of paper with the instruction—DESIGN!

Pencil and paper tests are no substitute for practical work in subjects like engineering. Generally speaking, an 'equivalent skill' is likely to be better tested by a substantive exercise during the course than by a simple paper and pencil test. As we have seen, despite much confusion this is the way in which comprehensive examining has moved in Britain during the last decade.

3: Assessment in Liberal and Professional Education

Included in Adelman's (1984) report of many promising approaches to assessment in American higher education is that used by Alverno College,

Milwaukee. Their approach involves every member of faculty in the college. As a result, a very small college has found itself in the centre of the national debate about assessment. It is the only one which I know where the general philosophy stems from 'what is to be assessed?' rather than from 'what is to be taught?' This is not to say that content and its preparation are held to be unimportant but that there is an acceptance of the systems model described in Chapter 1. Internally published material for students shows that a great deal of attention is paid to content. Recent publications on critical thinking in liberal arts and psychology (to which reference has already been made) do, to some extent, rectify the balance in the published reports from this institution (Cromwell, 1986; Halonen, 1986).

Alverno College is a small liberal arts college for female students founded by the Franciscans. In the early 1970s the College, under the leadership of Sr Joel Read, began to rethink its mission. She put to the staff four questions fundamental to any institutional evaluation, which led in turn to the questions for research of the kind listed in Figure 36, column (a). As will be evident from the first case study, they apply equally to professional and liberal (general) education if, in the end-product, there should be any difference! It is of interest to note that Alverno College has particular professional and vocational strengths in business and management as well as in nursing. It also provides an engineering degree, although some of the teaching in engineering *per se* is done in another university.

The answers which the College gave to these issues led to a fundamental change in direction in curriculum and teaching. First it was a change from teacher- to learner-centred education. The consequence of this position meant that the 'grade' had to 'say' something about how the students used their talents and grew towards their potential. In other words, students would have to have a different kind of credential. At the same time, the faculty would have to obtain this information, and this meant that stratagems different to those in traditional testing would have to be used. Moreover, their criteria would have to lead to well-defined judgements about each individual learner in action. The implications of this for the design of the curriculum will be apparent from column (b) of Figure 36.

It is recorded that the staff spent a whole week in rigorous thought and discussion to answer the question 'What are the outcomes for the student, rather than input by the faculty, in terms of the meaning and purpose of liberal education?' (Alverno, 1981). At the end of that period four goals were defined which, over a period of a year, were developed and described in detail. Eight outcomes were fully developed over a period of 3 years, which seems from other research to be the amount of time necessary for members of an institution to obtain commitment to a substantial change of direction (Murphy, 1976).

In arriving at these goals the faculty was aware that the College's heritage would condition some of their thinking. For example, 'it was quite natural', given the commitment to a women's college, 'that one of the four "goals"

(a)   (b)

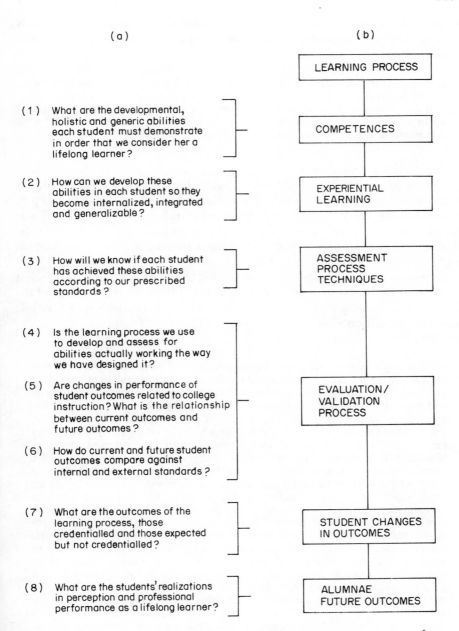

(1) What are the developmental,
       holistic and generic abilities
       each student must demonstrate
       in order that we consider her a
       lifelong learner ?

(2) How can we develop these
       abilities in each student so they
       become internalized, integrated
       and generalizable ?

(3) How will we know if each student
       has achieved these abilities
       according to our prescribed
       standards ?

(4) Is the learning process we use
       to develop and assess for
       abilities actually working the way
       we have designed it ?

(5) Are changes in performance of
       student outcomes related to college
       instruction ? What is the relationship
       between current outcomes and
       future outcomes ?

(6) How do current and future student
       outcomes compare against
       internal and external standards ?

(7) What are the outcomes of the
       learning process, those
       credentialled and those expected
       but not credentialled ?

(8) What are the students' realizations
       in perception and professional
       performance as a lifelong learner ?

LEARNING PROCESS

COMPETENCES

EXPERIENTIAL
LEARNING

ASSESSMENT
PROCESS
TECHNIQUES

EVALUATION/
VALIDATION
PROCESS

STUDENT CHANGES
IN OUTCOMES

ALUMNAE
FUTURE OUTCOMES

Figure 36. Faculty questions and Alverno learning process components. (Slightly adapted from Mentkowski, M. and Doherty, A. (1984). *Careering after College: Establishing the Validity of Abilities Learned in College for later Careering and Professional Performance*, Milwaukee: Alverno College Productions, and reproduced by permission of the authors)

we first identified was involvement ... it became clear that involvement was more a quality of the whole person than specific skill' (Alverno, 1981). They recorded that

> working this through was one of many experiences that helped us to discover the notion of *competence* as a characteristic of the individual person, rather than a skill or an enumeration of tasks. A competent student demonstrates certain abilities; she is also committed to using them. Not only can she analyse or communicate effectively, she habitually does so (Alverno, 1981).

Thus what emerged was a competency-based programme. Eight major categories of competence were defined, and within each competence six levels were hierarchically ordered which, it was believed, involved the whole person, were teachable, could be assessed, and would transfer across seminars. It was also agreed that the programme should be continually evaluated and that the competencies would be redefined as required. One version of the competencies and their categories is shown in Table 63.

Inspection of these competencies shows that they embrace the goals of what is called liberal education in the United States. Given the Catholic nature of the College, it is of substance to compare them with the outcomes of a Catholic university education such as that outlined by Cardinal Newman in his lectures on *The Idea of a University*:

> A university training is the great ordinary means to a great but ordinary end; it aims at raising the intellectual tone of society, at cultivating the public mind, at purifying the national taste, at supplying true principles to popular enthusiasm and fixed aims to popular aspiration, at giving enlargement and sobriety to the ideas of the age, at facilitating the exercise of popular power, and refining the intercourse of private life. It is the education which gives a man a clear conscious view of his own opinions and judgements, a truth in developing them, an eloquence in expressing them, and a force in urging them. It teaches him to see things as they are, to go right to the point, to disentangle a skein of thought, to detect what is sophistical, and to discard what is irrelevant. It prepares him to fill any post with credit, and to master any subject with facility. It shows him how to accommodate himself to others, how to throw himself into their frame of mind, how to bring before them his own, how to influence them, how to come to an understanding with them, how to bear with them. He is at home in any society, he knows when to speak and when to be silent; he is able to converse, he is able to listen, he can ask a question pertinently, and gain a lesson seasonably, when he has nothing to impart himself; he is ever ready, yet never in the way; he is a pleasant companion, and a comrade you can depend upon; he knows when to be serious and when to trifle, and he has a sure tract which enables him to trifle with gracefulness and to be serious with effect. He has the repose of a mind which lives in itself, and which has the resources for its happiness at home when it cannot go abroad [we think here of all that is said today about 'education for leisure']. He has a gift which serves him in public, and supports him in retirement, without which good fortune is but vulgar and with which failure and disappointment have a charm. The art which tends to make a man use all this, is in the object which it pursues as useful as the art of wealth or the art of health, though it is less susceptible of method, and less tangible, less certain, less complete in its result.

Newman's view is holistic. It assumes that this is what will happen to a student if the university arranges appropriate experiences. It is for this reason that halls of residence are important vehicles for the induction of student conversation and argument.

The Alverno view is not dissimilar, but it goes further. It says that if you want a student to utilize the skills and have a commitment to the values inherent in being an educated person you have to do something about it quite formally in the curriculum. It is not sufficient to leave it to a hall of residence (college). If you do something about it, then a quite different approach to teaching and assessment will emerge. In both cases the aim is the development of the whole person, and the teachers at Alverno would argue that their programme is holistic, since the competences they wish to develop are inseparable parts of the whole person they, as educators, seek to develop. This view is no different to those who designed the assessment schedule for the coursework of A level in engineering science in the second case study.

The system operates as follows. Students are required during their degree programme to develop the first four levels of competency within each of the competency domains. The other two (levels 5 and 6) are pursued within the student's area of specialization, which corresponds to academic or professional major(s). These take more time and effort to achieve than those at the general level. The basic 32 units are usually completed during the first two years of the four-year programme.

Each teacher who is responsible for a course has to state the competence levels available, the teaching strategies which will be used and the techniques of assessment. Because competencies are sought, performance modes of assessment such as essay, group discussion, oral presentation, interview and in-basket tend to be preferred to passive modes, which are more artificial.

When a student has demonstrated achievement in any one of these levels she receives one competence level unit. An Associate Arts degree in General Studies is awarded when the first four levels of each of the eight competency domains have been demonstrated. To obtain a Bachelor's degree another eight units must be obtained, one of which must be at level 6. Thus a student collects competencies rather than grades, and what is being assessed is a profile of performance. It will be seen that several of the levels relate directly to the scheme used in engineering science at A level (see Chapter 11).

It is clear that any major innovation of this kind requires both support and commitment to the innovation throughout the organization. This it had, and has both in terms of organizational structure and supporting services. For this purpose a matrix organization has been developed. The faculty serves in six discipline divisions and also volunteers to serve in a competence division. Although there were eight competence divisions it now collaborates in pairs or groups on central or overlapping themes.

A crucial dimension of the assessment philosophy is what is called 'externality'. This term has several meanings, depending on the context in which it is used. First, it refers to the 'distance within the learning situation between the

Table 63. Extract from *Competence-based Learning Program: Competences and Developmental Levels* (1984). (Reproduced by kind permission of Dr. G. Loacker and Alverno College Productions, Milwaukee.) (Following definitions given previously, I have introduced the term domain into the competence category titles)

Competence domain 1: Develop communications ability (effectively send and respond to communications for varied audiences and purposes)

Level 1— Identify own strengths and weaknesses as communicator

Level 2— Show analytic approach to effective communicating

Level 3— Communicate effectively

Level 4— Communicate effectively making relationships out of explicit frameworks from at least three major areas of knowledge

Level 5— Communicate effectively, with application of communications theory

Level 6— Communicate with habitual effectiveness and application of theory, through co-ordinated use of different media that represent contemporary technological advancement in the communications field

These to be developed in writing, speaking, listening, using media quantified data, and the computer.

Competence domain 2: Develop analytical capabilities

Level 1— Show observational skills

Level 2— Draw reasonable inferences from observations

Level 3— Perceive and make relationships

Level 4— Analyse structure and organization

Level 5— Establish ability to employ frameworks from area of concentration or support area discipline in order to analyse

Level 6— Master ability to employ independently the frameworks from area of concentration or support area discipline in order to analyse

Competence domain 3: Develop workable problem-solving skill

Level 1— Identify the process, assumptions, and limitations involved in problem-solving approaches

Level 2— Recognize, analyse and state a problem to be solved

Level 3— Apply a problem-solving process to a problem

Level 4— Compare processes and evaluate own approach in solving problems

Level 5— Design and implement a process for resolving a problem which requires collaboration with others

Level 6— Demonstrate facility in solving problems in a variety of situations

Competence domain 4: Develop facility in making value judgements and independent decisions

Level 1— Identify own values

Level 2— Infer and analyse values in artistic and humanistic works

Level 3— Relate values to scientific and technological developments

Level 4— Engage in valuing in decision-making in multiple contexts

Level 5— Analyse and formulate the value foundation/framework of a specific area of knowledge, in its theory and practice

Level 6— Apply own theory of value and the value foundation of an area of knowledge in a professional context

Competence domain 5: Develop facility for social interaction
Level 1— Identify own interaction behaviours utilized in a group problem-solving situation
Level 2— Analyse behaviour of others within two theoretical frameworks
Level 3— Evaluate behaviour of self within two theoretical frameworks
Level 4— Demonstrate effective social interaction behaviour in a variety of situations and circumstances
Level 5— Demonstrate effective interpersonal and intergroup behaviours in cross-cultural interactions
Level 6— Facilitate effective interpersonal and intergroup relationships in one's professional situation

Competence domain 6: Develop responsibility for the environment
Level 1— Perceive and describe the complex relationships within the environment
Level 2— Observe and explain how the behaviour of individuals and groups has an impact on the environment
Level 3— Observe and explain how the environment has an impact on the behaviour of individuals and groups
Level 4— Respond holistically to environmental issues and evaluate the response of others
Level 5— Identify a researchable environmental problem and independently develop responsible alternative solutions
Level 6— Select and rigorously support a responsible solution to an environmental problem with an implementation strategy

Competence domain 7: Develop awareness and understanding of the world in which the individual lives
Level 1— Demonstrate awareness, perception and knowledge of observable events in the contemporary world
Level 2— Analyse contemporary events in their historical context
Level 3— Analyse interrelationships of contemporary events and conditions
Level 4— Demonstrate understanding of the world as a global unit by analysing the impact of events of one society upon another
Level 5— Demonstrate understanding of professional responsibility in the contemporary world
Level 6— Take personal position regarding implications of contemporary events

Competence domain 8: Develop aesthetic responsiveness to the arts
Level 1— Express response to selected arts in terms of their formal elements and personal background
Level 2— Distinguish among artistic forms in terms of their elements and personal response to selected art works
Level 3— Relate artistic works to the contexts from which they emerge
Level 4— Make and defend judgements about the quality of selected artistic expressions
Level 5— Choose and discuss artistic works which reflect personal vision of what it means to be human
Level 6— Demonstrate the impact of the arts on your life to this point and project their role in personal future

student and the assessor'. If teachers are to be successful judges they must be able to stand back, i.e. distance themselves from the student if the judgements are to be 'objective'. Students are also expected to develop this skill in their own self-assessment. In this sense 'externality' is a competency of the same order as those others stated by the College. It has dimensions similar to the evaluation category in *The Taxonomy of Educational Objectives*. To obtain externality, students are often assessed by faculty other than those who teach them as well as by external assessors brought in from the world outside. Integrated assessments which cut across the disciplines also contribute to externality and may be assessed by a team of faculty or the external assessors. An Assessment Center (i.e. as an organization) co-ordinates administration, assessment and feedback. Responsibility for assessment is vested in an Assessment Council.

External assessors, new teachers and students are trained for this work by the staff of the Assessment Center. Before students begin their first year they attend college for a day and participate in assessment exercises. They provide the College with a diagnostic profile and introduce students to the idea of self-assessment. These assessments are in the areas of writing, speaking, listening, reading, quantitative, and computer literacy. Assessments in the Assessment Center are made throughout the course and contribute to externality. The Center also makes provision for remediation. Each student has to demonstrate competence in a variety of contexts in order to obtain one of the levels in the competence domain. In this way it is hoped that transferability of competence to other areas of human endeavour is achieved.

The College uses the term 'expansive' to describe the possibility of developing abilities beyond those where the student is seeking validation:

> We attempt to elicit from the student the most advanced performance of which she is capable. For example, while keeping a journal to find and make explicit what her values are (level 1 of valuing), a student is likely to explore her actions, her aesthetic experiences, or her religious heritage. She might record reflections on various products of our technological age, from modern medicine to transistor radios. Her instructor would examine the journal according to the criteria for level 1. In addition, the instructor would point out where the student discerns expressed values in artistic and cultural works (level 2) or infers values problems implicit in technology (level 3). The feedback would thus show her where she is already developing abilities beyond those for which she is seeking validation.

As the student develops so the College determines that the competence should become more integrated, i.e. a range of abilities acting together. For example:

> An English student seeking validation at levels 5 and 6 would be given a week-long simulation exercise. At this level she must be able to analyse, respond to, and evaluate complex literature that represents a variety of writers and historical periods. She must also be able to extend to human experience in general the understanding of the multiplicity of points of view that she has developed in the context of literature.
>
> Working two to three hours a day with several peers as the staff of a fictitious community cultural center, she handles a variety of problems. While planning an

upcoming literary festival, she might be asked to step in as emergency substitute teacher in an adult class on Elizabethan plays. She may have to deal personally, in a videotaped interaction and in writing, with a benefactor's repeated attempts to influence the poetry selections for a festival. On short notice, she may appear on a radio talk show (also videotaped) to respond to citizens of varied perspectives who call in to criticize city plans for razing a block of tenements in order to expand the center.

In a variety of ways, she is called on to apply her literary knowledge, her ability to define and defend criteria for judging works, and her understanding of the impact of literary art on its audience (aesthetic response). At the same time she must frame and deliver complex messages to varying audiences using several media (communications). And she must repeatedly draw together a variety of works in terms of their commonalities and contrasts (analysis). The written, soundtaped, and videotaped records of her week's work thus provide an ample basis for assessing the student's abilities in three different competence areas.

It will be seen that the procedures adopted owe much to the translation of the Assessment Center's technique from industry into the teaching milieu, and the College acknowledges this to be the case.

For those interested in higher education research the most interesting feature of the development was the establishment of an office of research and evaluation, which had the objective of answering the question 'Are we achieving what we set out to achieve?' Many of its studies were supported by the National Institute of Education. It differed from those research units which appeared and disappeared in Britain in the 1960s and 1970s in that it received an institutional commitment which was not given to the British units, whether they were doing research on institutions, teaching methods or assessment.[1]

The questions which the college seeks to answer relate to the effect that college had on students in respect of the goals sought. They are the questions shown in Figure 36 with which this case study began. The implications of them for the strategies of institutional evaluation are shown in Figure 37. From 1976 they undertook a number of studies which were financed by the National Institute of Education. These included investigations of the career patterns of their students (Mentkowski and Doherty, 1984) and of the work done by nurses and managers in order to determine the competences which should be in a programme of professional education (Mentkowski et al., 1980, 1982). Of particular interest is their attempt to measure change among both weekday and weekend students across the age range so as to try to account for the effects of maturation independently of college experience. Like other studies, and in particular those of Freeman and his colleagues, they used a multiple-strategy approach. It did not include content since they were concerned with change per se, a fact which is reflected in the particular instruments chosen.

Since the College had focused on assessment, the measures used both production and recognition type measures (called 'operant' and 'respondent' by McClelland, 1980). This choice was due to the fact that the response to a test is likely to be a poor predictor of future behaviour when the tester is not asked to create but to recognize a response. As we have seen, this was a fundamental problem in the design/creativity element of the engineering science examination in the second case study.

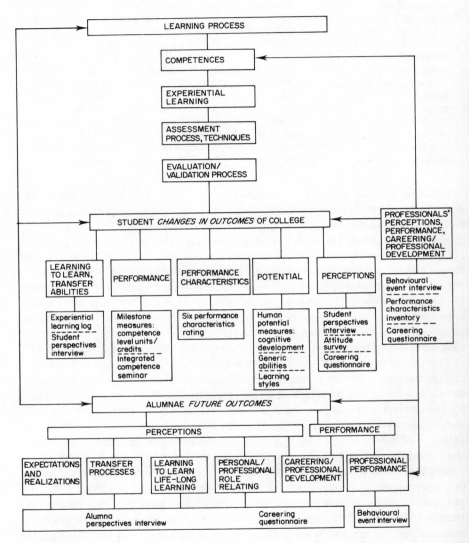

Figure 37. Components of a validation model for the Alverno Learning Process with external validation instruments. (From Mentkowski and Doherty (1984), *op. cit.*, and reproduced by permission of the authors)

The College had also been much influenced by cognitive development psychology and had embraced the ideas of Kohlberg, Perry and Piaget in its thinking on the grounds that performance in every component has a developmental dimension. Tests were included for these differing components of development. Their approach to the assessment of personality was to use a measure of ego-development which had been shown to be related to a range of cognitive development theories (Loevinger and Wessler, 1970). The milestones of ego development in this measure are pre-social, symbiotic, impulsive, self-protective, conformist, conscientious, autonomous and integrated. The relationship between these and Perry's development theory is evident. Coping with relativistic data (which the higher levels of development call for in his theory) requires autonomy and integration.

Allied to this test of ego-development was a Picture Story Exercise, taken from the Cognitive Competence Assessment Battery (Winter *et al.*, 1981). This is intended to evaluate adaptation in a matrix which contains the receptive, autonomous, assertive and integrative dimension on one axis and attitude towards authority, relations with others, feeling and orientation on the other. Again, the relationship to the Alverno competencies is clear. The choice of Kohlberg's moral development instrument is similarly related. It was chosen before the criticisms of Kohlberg's theory in respect of women were published and it is interesting to conjecture what might have happened had they used the alternative paradigm.

Also included in the tests were Kolb's learning style inventory and tests of critical thinking (thematic analysis: Winter and McClelland, 1978; analysis of argument: Stewart, 1977a,b; and the Watson–Glaser critical thinking appraisal). A test designed to measure human relations ability was included in the battery even though it was in an early stage of development (Klemp and Connelly, 1977).

Cross-sectional and longitudinal studies were carried out with this battery of instruments among day students as well as those attending weekend college. This design gave an age range (17–55) as well as a subject one. The cross-sectional study investigated entering and graduating students, while the longitudinal one followed two consecutive entering classes at entry and two and three and a half years after entry. The cross-sectional study is very similar in approach to that used by the American Assembly of Collegiate Schools of Business (see Chapter 6).

It is difficult to summarize the considerable amount of data yielded. Some idea of the approach can be gained from inspection of Table 64, which is a summary of the significant differences between groups in the cross-sectional study. Age was only found to be a significant covariate on the measure of moral development, while high-school grade was a significant variable with two subtests of critical thinking appraisal. The test of cognitive development did not work in the way they had expected, i.e. as a developmental measure, for it was related significantly to high-school grades.

In both the cross-sectional and longitudinal studies there were more instances of significant differences between groups or more significant change over time, respectively, on measures designed to test aspects of general cognitive development than there were on measures designed to test generic abilities, particularly analytic ability. This is in line with the view that critical

Table 64. Significant differences between groups for the cross-sectional study. (Reproduced by kind permission of the authors Mentkowski and Doherty (1984))

			Covariate	Group having significantly higher mean score
P	Measure of vocational, educational, and personal issues (Mines, 1982)	'Best class' essay		
		'Decision' essay		Graduating
		'Career' essay		Graduating
P	Sentence-completion test (Loevinger, 1976)			Graduating
P	Moral judgement instrument (Colby *et al.*)		Age	
R	Defining issues test (Rest, 1975)	P% Score	Age	Graduating
		D Score	Age	Graduating
R	Test of cognitive development (Renner *et al.*, 1976)		GPA (high school)	
P	Picture story exercise	Stages of adaptation (Stewart, 1977)		
		Receptive		
		Autonomous		
		Assertive		
		Integrative		Entering
		Self-definition (Stewart and Winter, 1974)		Entering?
		Achievement motive (McClelland, 1953)		Entering
		Affiliation motive (Atkinson, 1958)		
		Power motive (McClelland, 1975)		Graduating?
R	Learning style inventory (Kolb, 1976, 1978)	Concrete experience		
		Reflective observation		Entering
		Abstract conceptualization		Graduating
		Active experimentation		
		Abstract/concrete Learning orientation		Graduating
		Active/reflective Learning orientation		Graduating
P	Test of thematic analysis (Winter and McClelland, 1978)			
P	Analysis of argument (Stewart, 1977)	Attack		
		Defence		Graduating

| R | Critical thinking appraisal (Watson–Glaser, 1964) | Inference Recognition Deduction | GPA (high school) GPA (high school) |

---

thinking skills have to be developed within the framework of specific subject content and are not easily transferable and it is also in keeping with the findings on problem-solving in the clinical setting described in the first case study. Nevertheless, if logical thought is the same thing then there was more change in logical thought (or intellectual development) than socio-emotional development. Mentkowski and Doherty (1984) suggest that the tasks in the analysis tests could have been more difficult than those in the cognitive development measures. They point out that the investigation did not set out specifically to relate analysis to the levels of competence in this skill as defined by the Alverno faculty. The extent to which skills in this area are content-dependent continues to be a problem for both education and research.

Although the longitudinal study shows that the most significant changes take place in the first two years of college (and this might be expected as part of the normal pattern of growth), it also suggests that change in the final two years is more likely to be a function of college performance than not. The results suggest that those students who changed little in the first two years suffered negative changes in their second two. Mentkowski and Doherty argue that because more change is shown with the recognition measures than with the production measures (defining issues test; learning style inventory) this finding cannot be used to suggest that the small indications of change on the production measures will not be found to be greater in their long-term effects on career performance. This point is confirmed by the fact that students found it much more difficult to understand learning processes and roles in the first two years than in the last two. Of particular interest is the fact that students appear to develop high-order decision-making skills during the first two years of the course, after which they decline to the low level of sophistication at which they were in the beginning.

To explain these variations in growth, Mentkowski (1988) is led to a complex model of the student. It is similar to that offered by myself in terms of Whitehead's rhythmic theory of learning and is intended to explain the contextual elements which dictate approaches to learning new topics (Heywood, 1984). All learning begins with romance, for it is interest which drives us forward. It is the inability to cope with the circumstances we find which drives us away from learning. We continually enter into stages of romance, and sometimes we pursue them through precision to generalization. The subject discipline belongs to the stage of precision. It is the grammar of the subject. We approach all new topics in this way. To grasp the grammar of the subject the student has to constrain his or her mode of thinking in order to take the material forward in depth. Mentkowski gives the rather apt title of 'recycling' to the process. She draws attention to the fact that Piaget had noticed that learners can only cope with new challenges if they revert to an earlier cognitive strategy. Alternatively, they may always approach problems from the concrete. This has implications for the design of instruction and assessment in subjects of which students have no previous experience. Another finding of the enquiry which has equally profound implications for teaching is that it seems that the dimensions of intellectual ability and emotional maturity merge harmoniously as the experience of college lengthens. The stimulation of this integration demands that the experience of college should not cater exclusively for one or the other.

I have chosen this particular investigation from among several others to illustrate the multiple-strategy approach used by the College to evaluation which included systematic and substantial interviewing of students. During their course at Alverno the students receive over a hundred assessments. At first sight, this seems excessive. However, on closer inspection it is little more than three assessments per course, which corresponds with what happens in many subjects in Britain. I doubt if the time taken is any more or any less than that which is taken by a combination of comprehensive examination and course-work in Britain. For our one-year diploma for teachers the comprehensive examination amounts to $13\frac{1}{2}$ hours, coupled to which is a dissertation, three major assignments, six evaluated lesson plans and five evaluated lessons. The difference between what happens with us and what happens in Alverno are first, that the Alverno effort is a team one designed to achieve goals which cut across the subject boundaries. This means that each member of staff has to work in a team and have a commitment to that team. To achieve this goal, Alverno is organized, as we have seen, into a matrix. In the vertical axes lie the subject disciplines. Across these are a series of committees which deal with the competencies. In the research university the goals are seldom expressed, and there is little attempt to define them for purposes of evaluation. Such universities cannot escape the criticism that it is very easy to pass a degree at a minimal level of knowledge, and the question arises as to whether the many students who just pass would not have gained more from a competency-based curriculum. To be fair to my colleagues, within our own methodological courses we do aim for a high level of competence. One important difference between Alverno and ourselves is class size. In some of our courses it would be impossible for the tutor to operate a competency-based curriculum because of numbers. Time would prevent the implementation of such an exercise, which would, in any event, require the back-up of an assessment centre. For those concerned with the efficiency of learning in universities the Alverno experience poses a major problem, for if more time is to be devoted to teaching and a great deal of time has to be spent in preparation it may mean more, rather than fewer, teachers. It would also demand new commitments to departmental and collegiate goals which could not be obtained without some knowledge of learning, for which training would be required. Support services in the form of an assessment centre or a centre for learning in higher education which helped both staff and students would seem to be an imperative.

It is clear that there is a real attempt to complete the system in the assessment curriculum model shown in Chapter 1. It is not just a matter of assessment. The course notes which are available in the shop not only state the objectives but show how they will be assessed, what the students have to do, and what the instruction will contribute. There was clear evidence of focus on key concepts in those sets of notes which I inspected, and in the few classes that I attended I found a correspondence with the 'what' and 'how' of my fourth-year undergraduate educational administration class. There was little evidence of any difference in content levels. The pacing seemed to be appropriate to the objectives. Students believed (and this was reinforced by one or two students who had transferred from other universities) that whereas other universities concentrated on memory work this was not the case with Alverno, and they preferred its approach for that reason. Ultimately, the evaluations which tell are not the course-independent measures of the kind described but the course-dependent assessments, for it is those which condition learning and it is those that are the judgements of the effectiveness of instruction, not simple ratings of whether a lecturer's performance is perceived to be good, bad or indifferent.[1]

CONCLUSIONS

As Ted Marchese (1985), Vice President of the American Association for Higher Education, said, assessment is with us. We might add that it is here today. There is no doubt that there will be an increase in the variety of techniques and structures used in courses. The central theme of this book has been that if assessments are to be valid, a systems approach to the design of the curriculum and its assessments (in which objectives are clearly specified and instructional strategies designed to obtain those objectives) is necessary. It is my contention that these case studies reinforce this view, the consequences of which, for teachers in higher education, are profound.

Note

1. The ten studies supported by the National Institute of Education were re-evaluated in a final report published in 1983 and revised in 1984 (Mentkowski and Doherty, 1984). It will be seen that the college conducts both institutional and program research. The latter is the responsibility of the Office of Research. The most recent studies are Mentkowski (1988) and Mentkowski, M. and Loacker, G., Assessing and Validity: The Outcomes of College in P. T. Ewell (1985) *Assessing Educational Outcomes*. New Directions for Institutional Research No. **47**. San Francisco: Jossey-Bass.

Glossary

Ability   How one performs as opposed to aptitude: the potential to perform, although aptitudes and abilities are often used to describe the same tests. Psychometric theories of intelligence attempt to study the difference between individuals in terms of a set of underlying abilities: for example, verbal, numerical, reasoning, mechanical, spatial. In instruction the term is used to describe what the student will be able to do at the end of a class or a course of instruction. (See also *Achievement test* and *Aptitude*.)

Accreditation   Used in the United States to describe the process by which an institution obtains external recognition for its qualifications from an external authority. Its purposes are to certify the quality of the educational institution and to assist in the improvement of the institution. These are similar to the purposes of the CNAA and BTEC in Britain, who use the term 'validation' for their work. In the United States it is voluntary.

Accrediting agencies (US)   There are six regional associations of schools and colleges and several associations which limit their scope to particular kinds of institutions and subjects (for example, business, engineering, medicine). See *A Handbook of Accreditation (1985–1986)*, Commission on Institutions of Higher Education, 159 North Dearborn Street, Chicago, Illinois 6061, USA.)

Achievement test   Measures what a student has achieved in a particular field of study. Teachers often speak of low- and high-ability students. Nowadays, however, it is more common to say high- and under-achieving students.

Aims   Associated with statements of educational purposes. Often given the same meaning as goals and objectives, but seldom confused with specific behavioural objectives or competencies. (See Chapter 1.)

Appraisal   Not used until recently in educational settings. In industry it is employed to describe the formative (annual) assessment of personnel. Sometimes called performance appraisal. It usually involves the person and his or her managers establishing objectives for the future as well as evaluating performance in the past. The term is also used of departments and institutions, and in this sense is similar to evaluation. The appraisal of students using similar approaches which involve the students is likely to become important. (See Anstey, E., *et al.* (1976). *Staff Appraisal and Development*, London: Allen and Unwin: Colling, C. (ed.) (1986). *Models of Appraisal* 1, Occasional Paper 33, Standing Conference on Educational Development Services in Polytechnics, Birmingham Polytechnic: Main, A. (1985). *Educational Staff Development*, Beckenham: Croom Helm.

Aptitude   The potential to perform. The term is often confused with 'ability'. Batteries of standardized ability and aptitude tests, in addition to measuring specific abilities, also measure overall learning ability. A test like the Wechsler measures performance in specific abilities which, taken together, are also indications of future potential.

Arithmetic mean (average)   The result of adding all the scores together and dividing by the number of cases.

Assessment   Used in a variety of ways in educational settings (see Chapter 1). Invariably used of people and competencies they may or may not possess which can be specified in relatively precise terms. Assessments may be formative, summative, or both.

Assessment centre   'An assessment centre is a comprehensive, standardized procedure in which multiple performance exercises (i.e. discussion groups, reports and presentations) are used to evaluate individuals for various purposes. A number of trained evaluators, who are not in direct supervisory capacity over the participants, conduct the assessment and make recommendations' (W. C. Byham Development Dimensions International, Pittsburgh, Pennsylvania, at June 1987 American Association for Higher Education Conference on Higher Education: see Alverno College, p. 000). The technique has been used at Moray House College of Education, Edinburgh, by J. D. Wilson for the selection of teachers.

Assessment objectives   A term used by some examining and test agencies and teachers to describe the specific objectives which are to be tested in an examination or test. Sometimes the syllabus may show the marks which would be awarded for performance in each of these objectives.

Average   See *Arithmetic mean.*

Backwash effect   Used to describe the effect of an examination or test on both learning and teaching.

Borderline review   Used to describe the procedure employed by test agencies or examiners to review the performance of those candidates who are a mark or so on either side of borderline between two grades.

Business and Technician Education Council (BTEC) (UK)   Established by Royal Charter to make awards at the technician level in Britain in the areas of business and technical/engineering studies. Like the CNAA, is concerned with validation.

Bunching   Description of a cluster of marks which has a low standard deviation and are clustered within a limited range. This shows that the examination is not discriminating. In mastery tests scores should bunch around the mastery level.

Chi-squared test   A test of significance. Its purpose is to determine if the observed frequencies (for example, of a test or survey) differ from expected or theoretically predicted frequencies:

$$\chi^2 = \Sigma \frac{(O - E)^2}{E}$$

where O = observed frequencies and E = expected frequencies. When $\chi^2 = 0$ the observed and expected frequencies agree exactly: when $\chi^2 > 0$ they do not agree and the larger the value, the greater the discrepancy. χ^2 tables are available for various levels of significance, particularly for 5% and 1%. They are tabulated against degrees of freedom. The degrees of freedom are one less than the number of items in the sample. The chi-squared test should not be used when the expected frequency of a cell is less than 5.

Comparability   Used in Britain by the school examining agencies to describe the extent to which the same grades in the same subject but set by different agencies are validly equivalent in terms of the same requirements for performance. In higher education external examiners offer advice on the standards of assessment in order to achieve comparability between the institutions which teach their subject (see Chapters 2 and 3).

Competency-based testing   Designed to test particular competencies. A level of mastery is required and the purpose of the test is to check that the student has mastered the competency required. Such tests are important in medicine, flying, etc. Contrast with norm-referenced testing. (See Chapter 13.)

Confidence limits   These limits reflect the accuracy or inaccuracy of tets scores. They are expressed as a percentage (for example, we may be 95% confident that a candidate's score does not vary above x or below y). There are various methods for calculating confidence limits (Glutting *et al.*, 1987), of which the standard error of measurement is the best known. (See below and Chapter 3.)

Council for National Academic Awards (CNAA) (UK)   Organization established by Royal Charter to recognize the work done in institutions of higher education in the public (as opposed to university) sector. The process of recognition is called 'validation', and it has the same objectives as accreditation in the United States. The degrees (Bachelor's, Master's and Doctor's) awarded are those of the CNAA. (See *Validation*)

Correlation   The coefficient of correlation expresses the degree of relationship either for the same group of individuals or for paired individuals such as twins. Correlations supply evidence of a statistical association between variables. Two measures of correlation are commonly used in educational measurement.

(1) *Spearman–Rank Difference Coefficient of Correlation.* This expresses the relationship between rank orders of individuals as, for example, when a group of candidates take two tests. In Example 1 there is little or no correlation, whereas in Example 2 there is a one-to-one correlation.

	EXAMPLE 1			EXAMPLE 2			EXAMPLE 3	
	Test A	Test B		Test A	Test B		Test A	Test B
	1	10		1	1		1	2
	2	9		2	2		4	6
	3	8		3	3		6	3
Candidate's	4	7	Candidate's	4	4	Candidate's	3	1
number in	5	6	number in	5	5	number in	2	4
rank order	6	5	rank order	6	6	rank order	7	7
of scores	7	4	of scores	7	7	of scores	8	5
	8	3		8	8		9	6
	9	2		9	9			9
	10	1		10	10		10	10

The more interesting cases are those of the kind shown in Example 3. The formula for the coefficient is:

$$r = 1 - \frac{6(\Sigma d^2)}{n(n^2 - 1)}$$

where d = difference between a pair of ranks and n = number of ranks.

(2) *Pearson Product Moment Correlation Coefficient.* This coefficient expresses the correlation between scores as opposed to ranks:

$$r = \frac{\Sigma Z x Z y}{n}$$

where Σ = sum of
Zx = any individual score expressed in standard form,
Zy = any individual's score on the related measure also
        expressed in standard form,
  n = number of individuals.

Criterion error   The error in judgements made by different examiners about the criteria in an examinee's script.

Criterion-referenced grading   Grades are awarded for specified performance in which the criteria are described in detail in mastery terms. (See *Criterion referenced testing*.)

Criterion-referenced testing   Tests designed to check that a student has obtained mastery in an area of knowledge or skill. Formative assessment is based on criterion- rather than norm-referenced tests.

Decile   (See *Quantile*.)

Degrees of freedom   (See *Chi-squared test*.)

Departmental review   Review is a substitute for appraisal or evaluation sometimes used by schools. It has come to be used in higher education in preference to either of these terms when the work of a department is under consideration. (See McDonald, R. and Roe, E. (1984)). *Reviewing Departments*, Higher Education Research and Devlopment Society of Australasia, University of New South Wales, Australia.

Discriminant analysis   A statistical technique which enables the differences between two or more groups of objects with respect to several variables to be studied simultaneously. (See Klecka, W. R. (1980). *Discriminant Analysis*, Beverley Hills: Sage.)

Discrimination index (D)   For choice type essay and problem-solving type tests. D is the product-moment correlation between the marks for a question and the corresponding total marks gained by the candidates on the other questions. When a candidate's mark is x_q on a question and x_t is his or her total mark the discrimination index is given by the product-moment correlation between x_q and $(x_t - x_q)$. Morrison (1974) says that D should preferably be greater than 0.4.

Evaluation   Used in educational settings in a variety of ways. Generally refers to courses, departments, or institutions. Evaluation seeks to determine if goals have been achieved, and in this sense is similar to validation. It is usually broader in concept than the determination of goals by examinations and tests. At course level it may take into account student attitudes and the effects of the institution. A teacher 'evaluates' his or her course. The paradigm is the same for assessment, whether it be course, departmental, or institutional evaluation (see Chapter 1). It may be formative, summative or, both. (See *Departmental review*.) Research in evaluation has been dogged by numerous methodological and administrative problems. (for a short review see Easterby Smith, M. (1986). *Evaluation of Management Education: Training and Development*, Aldershot: Gower, See also Gibbs, G. and Haigh, M. (1984). *A Compendium of Course Evaluation Questionnaires*, Occasional Paper 13, and Gibbs, G. and Haigh, M. (1983). *Alternative Models of Course Evaluation* (Examples from Oxford Polytechnic), Occasional Paper 17, both from Standing Conference on Educational Development Services in Polytechnics, Birmingham Polytechnic, Birmingham.

Facility index (F)   For choice type essay and problem-solving type tests:

$$F = 50 + (M_q - M_t)\%$$

where M_q is the mean percentage mark obtained for the question and M_t the mean total percentage mark obtained in the test for the subgroup answering the question (i.e. mean ability index). Morrison (1974) states that $(M_q - M_t)$ is reasonably independent of the leniency or severity of marking, and that M is a close approximation to the ability of the subgroup answering the question.

Factorial analysis   A method of testing hypotheses about the relationship between variables which are correlated. In educational and psychological testing it seeks to establish what is common between two or more tests (communality) and what is specific to each (specificity). The presence of specific components in tests reduces the correlation between them. The factors produced by factorial analysis are not 'actual' factors of the mind because test scores derive from complex mental processes. They are categories which aid the classification of the abilities (aptitudes–skills) tested, and as such contribute to the evaluation of test validity. The results of factor analysis are often difficult to interpret. They are greatly influenced by the size of the sample as well as its heterogeneity or homogeneity. Curvilinear relationships between variables should be treated with caution. Factor analysis is closely related to the concept of variance. Thus communality is related to the common variance between tests and unique variance to the specificity. The unique variance contains two components, one due to error and the other to the specific component. There are two kinds of common factor, i.e. general factors, which 'load' significantly on all the tests in the analysis, and group ones, which load on a few of the tests in the same factor. There are several techniques of factor analysis, and the one adopted influences the interpretation made. (See Child, D. (1970). *The Essentials of Factor Analysis*, London: Holt, Rinehart and Winston: Kim Jae-On and Mueller C. W. (1978). *Introduction to Factor Analysis*, Beverley Hills: Sage: Vernon, P. E. (1956). *The Measurement of Abilities* London: University of London Press. (See also *Scattergram*.)

Formative   Used in respect of assessment and evaluation and in contrast to summative. Takes place while a course is in progress and has as its objective the improvement of teaching and learning from the data obtained. Coursework assessments are only formative when they are used for this purpose.

Grade description   A term used by the Secondary Examinations Council in England to describe the expected attainment of candidates in the grades of the General Certificate of Secondary Education. Descriptions are required for Grades 3 and 6 in every subject. The term is equally applicable to competency-based systems in higher education (for example, the levels within the eight major competencies of the curriculum of Alverno College). (See Chapter 13.)

Goals   Associated with statements of educational purposes. These may relate to the general areas of education as seen by society or the purposes of institution or curriculum. Often used in place of aims. (See Chapter 1, and *Aims*).

Hurdle   A component of assessment which has to be passed before either the next section of a course can be begun (for example, in mastery learning) or the next component of an examination or test marked. For example, in the Engineering Science Examination described in Chapter 13 a pass in coursework is required if the candidate is to pass his or her examination.

Incline of difficulty   A term used to describe a series of items (questions) designed to become progressively more difficult.

Intelligence quotient   The IQ distribution of a large population is found to conform closely to the normal curve:

$$\text{Intelligence quotient} \atop \text{(Mental ratio)} = \frac{\text{Mental age}}{\text{Real age}} \times 100$$

(The mental age is obtained from the success rate of different age groups in respect of their performance in intelligence tests. The average performance of an age group gives the standard for that group. Performance away from the average is related to other age groups to find the intelligence quotient.)

Median   The middle score in a distribution or the point between two middle scores.

Moderation   Has the same meaning as scaling when two components of a test are brought into alignment. This may be achieved statistically or by an examiner who inspects samples of a candidate's work. In public examinations such persons are sometimes called moderators. They may or may not also vet the questions which are set in examinations.

Mode   The score made by the most number of persons.

Modes of examination   In Britain these are used to define types of examination offered by the school examination authorities:

Mode 1:   Examinations and syllabuses set and designed by the examining authority.

Mode 2:   Examinations conducted by an examining authority on syllabuses designed by a school or groups of schools.

Mode 3:   Examinations set and marked by a school or schools which are moderated by an examining authority.

Norm-referenced testing   Describes those tests which are used to discriminate between students, i.e. to show how particular students stand in relation to their peers. terminal tests and examinations in higher education are most often norm-referenced.

Objective items (questions)   Items which require no subjective judgement. (See Chapter 12.)

Percentiles—percentile score   Percentile rank: the *percentile score* is the percentage of persons who fall below a given raw score. The fortieth *percentile* is the point above which 60% of the scores fall and below which 40% fall. The ninetieth percentile is the point above which 10% of the scores fall and below which 90% fall. The *percentile rank* indicates the percentage of scores falling below a given score. Given a normal distribution, t scores and z scores can be converted to percentile ranks. (See *Quantile*.)

Probability

$$\frac{\text{Probability of an event}}{\text{occurring } (Pe)} = \frac{\text{Total number of favourable outcomes}}{\text{Total number of possible outcomes}}$$

When probability is determined by experiment:

$$(Pe) = \frac{\text{Number of trials with favourable outcomes}}{\text{Total number of trials}}$$

Total probability $= 1$

Profile reporting   Method of describing the performance of a candidate by reference to specified criteria. (See Chapter 11.)

Quantile   Generic term used to describe decile, percentile and quantile. Deciles divide a frequency distribution into ten parts, percentiles one hundred parts and quartiles four parts. The ninetieth percentile corresponds to 90% of the total frequency.

Quartile   See *Quantile*.

Range   The difference between the highest and lowest scores. It is an indication of variability. Unfortunately, it emphasizes extreme cases, for which reason the standard deviation is preferred.

Raw score   The unadjusted score obtained by a candidate on a test.

Regression analysis   A technique for discovering the nature of the association between variables. Given that sufficient information is known about one variable (the independent variable—x axis), it may be used to predict the dependent variable (y axis). The equation describes the line of best fit (regression line) through a series of points on a scattergram.

Reliability   An expression of the extent to which a test can be repeated on an identical population and obtain the same distribution. Usually expressed as a coefficient of correlation.

Methods of determining Reliability

(1) Split Halves Method. Normally it will not be possible to repeat a test. This method enables the internal consistency of a single test to be determined. Consider a multiple-choice test. Its reliability is calculated by correlating the results obtained by the candidates from the odd-numbered items with those of their scores from the even-numbered ones. The Spearman–Brown formula is used for this calculation:

$$r_{tt} = \frac{nr_{it}^{-2}}{1 + (n-1)r_{it}^{-2}}$$

where n is the number of items in the test r_{it} is the average item–test correlation in the test and r_{tt} is the reliability of the test (or part-test).

(2) Kuder–Richardson Method. In this method the test does not have to be split into two halves and restored for the calculation of the correlation coefficients. It assumes that all the items in the test measure the same ability, are of the same difficulty and that the correlations between them are equal. Following Thorndike's notation the formula is:

$$r_n = \frac{n}{n-1}\left[\frac{s^2 + \Sigma p_i q_i}{s^2}\right]$$

where n is the number of items in the test,

s is the standard deviation of the test,

p_i is the proportion of candidates responding correctly to item i

$$q_i = 1 - p_i$$

(3) Test–Retest. The same instrument is used on the same group of students in similar circumstances.

(4) Equivalent Forms. Equivalent forms of the same test are made as similar as possible in respect of content, mental processes, level of difficulty, etc. The two forms of the test are taken one after the other. For example in a recent experiment with Modern Mathematics, the Southern Regional Examinations Board rewrote an objective test into short answers. They obtained a higher reliability with the short answers.

The reliability of an objective test may be increased by increasing its length, although there is a limit where the practical increase in reliability does not justify an increase in the number of items. It will be clear that the standard error and the reliability are related and that in short tests the standard error proportionately more effect. Thus in tests (particularly public examinations) which are measuring achievement through a variety of measures the inclusion of a single set of measures among others (for example, an objective test among short and long responses) should be treated in terms of its effect on the total examination. The question is sometimes asked, how short can an objective test be to give good reliability? Because of the complexity of this subject the reader should refer to the treatise on this topic in the books listed above.

Scaling (See also *Standard score*).

One Procedure for Scaling

This particular example was derived by a group of teachers who were given several textbooks in which were contained a variety of procedures, and chose this particular method to illustrate the problem which they subsequently built into the script of a videotape.

(a) Inspection of Table 1 shows two tests and the distribution of scores.

(b) Purpose of exercise: to demonstrate that 8 out of 10 in Test One is the better mark.

(c) Obtain the Mean Mark for each Test

Test 1:

<pre>
1 received 2 = 2
4 received 2 = 12
6 received 4 = 24
8 received 5 = 40
6 received 6 = 36
7 received 4 = 28
8 received 1 = 8
</pre>

Total marks = 150

Mean = 150/30 = 5

TABLE 1

Test One		Test Two	
X	f	X	f
0	0	0	0
1	0	1	0
2	1	2	0
3	4	3	7
4	6	4	5
5	8	5	2
6	6	6	2
7	4	7	2
8	1	8	5
9	0	9	7
10	0	10	0

X = marks
f = frequency of a given score
awarded among two classes each
of thirty students in the same
subject taught and assessed by
different teachers.

Test 2:

Total marks = 180
Mean = 30/6 =

To establish how each student in Class 1 did in relation to the students, it is necessary to find out how each set of marks deviates from the mean.

$$X \quad M \quad d$$
$$0—5 = —5$$
$$1—5 = —4$$
$$2—5 = —3$$
$$3—5 = —3$$
$$4—5 = —1$$
$$5—5 = 5$$
$$6—5 = 5$$
$$7—5 = 2$$
$$8—5 = 3$$
$$9—5 = 4$$
$$10—5 = 5$$

(d = deviation of possible marks (X) from the mean for Test 1)

The next step is to establish how often each deviation occurs. Each deviation is multiplied by the number of times it appears thus:

$$
\begin{array}{rcl}
f & d & fd \\
0 & -5 = & 0 \\
0 & -4 = & 0 \\
1 & -3 = & -3 \\
4 & -2 = & -8 \\
6 & -1 = & -6 \\
8 & 0 = & 0 \\
6 & 1 = & 6 \\
4 & 2 = & 8 \\
1 & 3 = & 3 \\
0 & 4 = & 0 \\
0 & 4 = & 0 \\
\end{array}
$$

Next, the average deviation fd^2 is found:

$$
\begin{array}{rcl}
d & fd & \\
-5 & 0 = & 0 \\
-4 & 0 = & 0 \\
-3 & -3 = & 9 \\
-2 & -8 = & 16 \\
-1 & -6 = & -6 \\
0 & 0 = & 0 \\
1 & 6 = & 6 \\
2 & 8 = & 16 \\
3 & 3 = & 9 \\
4 & 0 = & 0 \\
5 & 0 = & 0 \\
\end{array}
$$

Next, calculate the standard deviation.

The standard deviation is then calculated for Test 2. It is 2.37.
(d) The z score (standard score) is now calculated. For example:

$$\frac{\text{Actual score} - \text{mean}}{\text{Standard deviation}} \quad \text{e.g.} \quad \frac{8-5}{1.4} = 2.1$$

(e) The standard scores are converted into t scores as follows:

Z scores $10 + 50$ or $t = 10\% + 50$

Therefore the scaled scores for the highest values in the two tests are:

Test 1: $t = 50 + 10\ (2.1)\ 50 + 21 = 71\%$

Test 2: $t = 50 + 10\ (1.3) = 50 + 13 = 63\%$

Therefore the eight out of ten score in Test 1 is better than the nine out of ten score in Test 2.

Scattergram   It is possible to get some idea of the degree of correlation between two measures from the scattergram of the scores. The candidate's scores are plotted for each test on the same graph, thus:

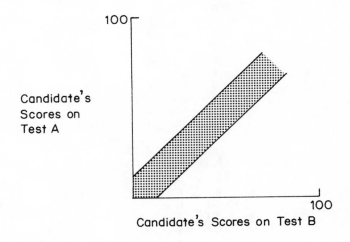

The plots below indicate when a relationship between the tests may be expected. Scores are distributed throughout each of the bands.

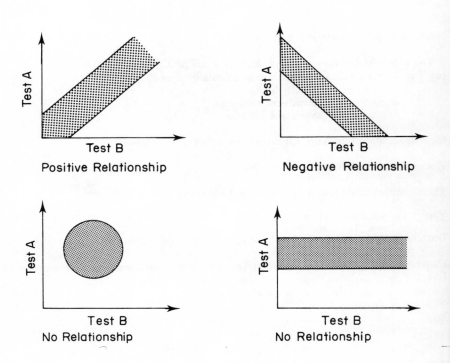

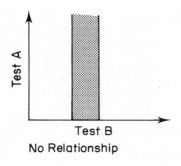

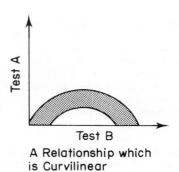

Test B
No Relationship

Test B
A Relationship which
is Curvilinear

The majority of scores lie within the shaded bands

Youngman has shown how simple correlation plotting can be used to provide a quick representation of variable intercorrelations, and thus provide an introduction to factor analysis. (Youngman, M. B. (1980). Correlation scatter plotting as a quick substitute for factor analysis. *Research in Education*, **25**, 13–18.)

Significance　　When it is assumed that data obtained by measurement should conform to the normal distribution departures from that distribution may or may not be significant. Statistical tests of significance compare the found distribution with the normal one. When a sample is taken from a known population assumptions are made about it which are expressed in the form of hypotheses. More often than not a null hypotheses (H_0) is formed which can be accepted or rejected.

For example, when setting a hurdle (pass level) for a test we may wish to relate the score to the proportion of candidates obtaining that score. So we test the assumption that the mean value of all the scores in a test is S_1. We reject that mean only if it is clearly rejected by the mean score of the sample.

$$\therefore H_0: \mu = S_1$$

The alternative hypothesis is

$$H_1: \mu \neq S_1$$

$$\mu \text{ (mean of population)} = \frac{\bar{x} - \mu}{\sigma/\sqrt{n}}$$

where n = sample size,
　　　　σ = standard deviation,
　　　　$\bar{x}$ = arithmetic mean.

The *level of significance* is the maximum probability with which we risk rejecting the null hypothesis. The two levels most commonly used are 0.05(5%) and 0.01(1%), which tell us the level of 'chance' by which a sample differs from a true distribution. A 'one-tailed test' of significance considers the critical region where a distribution might depart from the normal in the area of one of the tails of the normal curve. A 'two tailed test' takes account of both tails. (See also *Chi-squared test* and confidence limits.)

Spread　　See *Standard deviation* and *Variability*.

Standard deviation (SD.*s* σ)　　Very often we wish to compare the performance of a group of students on similar tests or two groups of students on the same test. The simplest way to do this would be to quote the *average* or mean marks of the group(s) on the different tests. The mean mark should be accompanied by some measure of the spread or scatter of the scores, i.e. the extent to which the individuals in the group depart from the mean. Thus the mean should be accompanied by a statement of the *range* (one plus the difference between highest and lowest scores of the group) of marks. Taken together, these two items give some idea of the variability between the groups. They are, however, unsatisfactory measures. The usual measure of variability is the standard deviation. This is the square root of the mean of the squared deviations of the scores from the arithmetic mean:

Standard deviation $= \Sigma x^2/N$

Where $\Sigma =$ the sum and $x =$ the deviation of each score from the arithmetic mean.

When the standard deviation is small the scores will be clustering about the mean. One standard deviation accounts for approximately 68% of the area under the normal curve (i.e. 34% on either side of the mean).

Standard error (of a score)

(1) Calculation:

$$\text{Standard error of a score} = \begin{matrix}\text{Standard deviation}\\\text{of the scores on}\\\text{the test}\end{matrix}\sqrt{\left(1-\begin{matrix}\text{Reliability}\\\text{coefficient}\\\text{of the test}\end{matrix}\right)}$$

(2) Diederich, P. B. (1960). *Short Cut Statistics for Teacher Made Tests*, Princeton: Educational Testing Service, gives the following table for objective tests (i.e. for answers which can be scored 1 or 0), which are intended to measure performance within a reasonably generous time limit. (Such tests are sometimes called *Power tests* as opposed to *Speed Tests*, in which the speed of response is considered an important variable.)

Number of items (e.g. multiple-choice questions) in the test	Standard error
Less than 24	2
24—47	3
48—89	4
90—109	5
110—29	6
130—50	7

Thus in objective tests of 60 items (which are increasingly common at GCE A and O levels) the score band for a candidate with a score of 30 would be within the range 26–34. As the test becomes longer the proportion of error becomes smaller (Lord, 1956). P. J. Mcvey, at a recent conference, reported an attempt to calculate the standard error of a problem-solving examination in engineering. He arrived at a standard error of about 8 for a typical 3 hour paper (see Chapters 3 and 12).

(3) Note that, in addition to the standard error of a score, there are many other standard errors (averages, differences, correlations, etc.). These are arrived at in different ways but all have the same meaning. The standard error of a single score is usually larger than that of an average. Similarly, the standard errors of each of two scores will be smaller than that of the difference between them. To be sure that two scores represent differences in ability the difference between them should be at least twice the standard error of that difference.

Standardization   Has two meanings. In the first it relates to standardized tests and is the process of administration. Standardization is to ensure that the tests are always administered in the same way. In the second it is the process of aligning the marks of a group of examiners responsible for the tests and examinations in a particular subject.

Standard score   See also *Scaling*. The standard score is derived from a raw score to enable the relative performance of a student in different subjects to be calculated. There are various methods used to achieve this goal.

(1) z scores: this is the method used in the illustration for sealing. A z score is the deviation of a score from the arithmetic mean in standard deviation units. They are useful in a simple situation where it is of interest to find out how well a candidate did in respect of two or more subjects.

For subject A $z = \dfrac{X - \bar{x}}{\sigma}$

For subject B $z = \dfrac{X_B - \bar{x}_B}{\sigma_B}$

Where $\bar{X}$ = the near mark of the subject under consideration,
$\quad\quad X$ = raw score of the subject under consideration,
Where σ = the standard deviation.

The standardized score indicates in which subject the candidate did best. Often it will not be that for which the highest raw mark was given.

(2) t scores: while z scores may be positive or negative, t scores are always positive, and for this reason are often used. They are adjusted to an arbitrary scale with a given mean standard deviation. These are often set at 50 and 10, respectively:

$$t = \bar{X} + \frac{\sigma A}{\sigma}\,(X - \bar{X})$$

where t = The score in the arbitrary scale,
σ = standard deviation in the original distribution,
σA = standard deviation in the arbitrary scale,
$\bar{X}$ = the arithmetic means in the original scale,
$\bar{X}A$ = the arithmetic means in the arbitrary scale,
X = the score in the original scale.

Structured items (questions)   Items requiring clear guidance on what is required (for example, when a series of subquestions are asked about the same topic). These can be in the form of sectionalized essays or data-response items.

Summative   That which takes place at the end. An examination or test which measures performance at the end of a course is a summative assessment. Its primary goal is the grading of students, but it also enables judgements about teachers to be made and comparisons of curricula to be undertaken. The term is also used in respect of evaluation. (Contrast with *Formative assessment* and *Evaluation*: see also *Criterion-referenced* and grading *Norm-referenced* testing.

Tariff items (questions)   A series of items of different difficulties for which the marks awarded are stated on the test paper and related to the relative difficulties of the items.

Validation   Used in a variety of contexts in educational settings. It may refer to the validation of the examinations of the examinations or tests of a course (see *Validity*) or to those procedures used by an institution to determine if a proposed course may be established or an existing course continue to run. The procedures of the Council for National Academic Awards in England are called 'validation'. In this usage the term differs little from that of accreditation as used in the United States (see Chapter 1). See Church, C. H. (ed.), 1983. Society for Research into Higher Education, Guildford.

Validity

(1) *Face validity*. The extent to which an examination or a test appears to be measuring the variable it is intended to test (for example, assessed by visual inspection of the items or questions).

(2) *Predictive validity.* The extent to which the test predicts future performance (for example, at work, in university).

(3) *Concurrent validity.* The extent to which a test accurately assesses present performance.

(4) *Content validity.* The extent to which a test measures the content it is intended to assess.

(5) *Construct validity.* The extent to which a test measures psychological qualities (for example, the extent to which mathematical aptitude depends on spatial ability).

Variability   Describes the distribution of a score. (See also *Range, Spread*, and *Standard deviation*.)

Variance   A central value for calculating the average deviation of a dispersion (range). It is the average of the square of the deviations:

$$\text{Variance} = \frac{\Sigma(x - \bar{x})^2}{n}$$

Because it is measured in units of the square of the deviations it is more usual to quote the standard deviation which is the square root of the deviations (see above). The concept of variance is very important in assessment since we often wish to known if the scores in a test can be explained by the action of another variable (for example, intelligence, personality trait, sex), i.e. we ask how much do the variations in x contribute to the variations in y? When several variables are involved a technique called *analysis of variance* (abbreviated to ANOVA) is used.

Weighting   Defines the contribution which a component or subtest makes to the total mark of the test.

References

AACSB (1980). Outcome Measurement Project Phase I Report. *AACSB Bulletin* (Winter), American Assembly of Collegiate Schools of Business, St Louis, Mo.

AACSB (1984). Outcome Measurement Project Phase II Report. American Assembly of Collegiate Schools of Business, St Louis, Mo.

AACSB (1987). Outcome Measurement Project. Phase III Report. American Assembly of Collegiate Schools of Business, St Louis, Mo.

Abercrombie, M. L. J. (1980). Changing basic assumptions about teaching and learning. In D. Boud (ed.), *Developing Student Autonomy in Learning*, London: Kegan Paul.

Adamson, H., P. Hughes, and A. Edgecombe (1979). Home experiments for first-year university students. *Journal of Biological Education*, **13**, (4), 297–302.

Adelman, C. (1983). *The Standardized Test-Scores of College Graduation 1964–1982*, Washington, DC: The National Institute of Education.

Adelman, C. (1984). *Starting with Students: Promising Approaches in American Higher Education*, Washington, DC: The National Institute of Education.

Adelman, C. (ed.) (1986). *Assessment in American Higher Education*, Washington, DC: US Department of Education.

AEB (1982). *Marking Procedures in Modern Languages at Ordinary Level*, Associated Examinations Board, Guildford.

AEB (1985). *How AEB Sets and Marks GCE Examinations*, Associated Examinations Board, Guildford.

Ager, M. and J. Weltman (1967). The present structure of examinations. *Universities Quarterly* **21**, (3), 272.

Agutter, P. S. (1979). Precision testing: A method for improving students' written work in biochemistry. *Journal of Biological Education*, **13**, (1), 25–31.

Ainsworth, C., and D. Maynard (1976). The impact of roommate personality on achievement: an exploratory study and model of analysis. *Research in Higher Education*, **4**, 291–301.

Alpert, R. and R. N. Haber (1960). The Achievement Anxiety Test. *Journal of Abnormal and Social Psychology*, **61**, 207–15.

Altmaier, E. M., and R. J. Rapaport (1984). An examination of the use of counselling service. *Journal of College Student Personnel*, **25**, 453–8.

Altricher, H. (1982). Austrian graduates in education and their jobs: an empirical analysis of occupational distribution of university graduates, *Higher Education*, **11**, 499–510.

Alverno College (1923) *Validating Assessment Techniques in an Outcome-centered Liberal Arts Curriculum: Six Performance Characteristic ratings* (NIE–6–77–0058), Milwaukee: Alverno Productions.

Alverno College (1981). *Liberal Learning at Alverno College*, Milwaukee: Alverno Productions.

Alverno College (1985). *Assessment at Alverno College*, Milwaukee: Alverno Productions.

Alwood, C. M., and H. Montgomery (1979). *The pedagogics of problem solving R and D for higher education*, Stockholm: National Board of Universities and Colleges.

362

Anderson, A. W. (1983). *Academic Staff Views on Criteria of Teaching Competence/ Excellence*, Paper 4, University of Western Australia, Research Unit in University Education, Perth.

Anderson, D. S. (1962). The person and the environment in first year medicine. *Melbourne Studies in Education*, 91–113.

Anderson, S. B., S. Ball, R. T. Murphy, and Associates (1975). *Encyclopedia of Educational Evaluation: Concepts and Techniques for Evaluating Education Training Programs*, San Francisco: Jossey-Bass.

Anisef, P. (1982). University graduates revisited: occupational mobility attainments and accessibility, *Interchange*, **13**, (2) 1–19.

Armstrong, M. and V. Shanker (1981). *Students' Experience of Research in their Honors Year*, Tertiary Education Research Centre, University of New South Wales.

ASEE (1986). Quality in Engineering Education. Final report, American Society for Engineering Education. *Engineering Education*, **77**, (1), 16–24, 49, 50.

Austin, G. R. and H. Garber (1981). *The Rise and Fall of National Test Scores*, New York: Academic Press.

Avital, S. M., and J. S. Shettleworth (1968). *Objectives for Mathematics Learning. Some Ideas for the Teacher, Bulletin No. 3*, Ontario Institute for Studies in Education, Ontario, Canada.

Baggaley, J., M. Ferguson, and P. Brooks (1980). *Psychology of the TV Image*, Aldershot: Gower.

Balaram, S., and K. S. Venkatakrishnan (1980). Identifying engineering, goals and priorities for the future: an experiment with the Delphi technique. *Higher Education*, **9**, (1), 53–67.

Bannister, D., and J. M. M. Mair (1968). *The Evaluation of Personal Constructs*, London: Academic Press.

Banta, T. W. and J. A. Schneider (1988). Using faculty-developed exit examinations to evaluate academic programs. *Journal of Higher Education* **59**, (1), 69–83.

Bardell, G. S., G. M. Forrest, and D. J. Shoesmith (1978). *Comparability in GCE: A Review of the Board's Studies, 1964–1977*, Manchester: Joint Matriculation Board.

Bare, A. C. (1980). The study of academic performance, *Research in Higher Education*, **12**, (1), 3–22.

Barger, G. W. (1982). Classroom testing procedures and classroom anxiety. *Improving College and University Teaching*, **31**, (1), 25–6.

Barker, D., and W. G. Hapkiewiez (1979). The effects of behavioural objectives on relevant and incidental learning at two levels of Bloom's Taxonomy. *Journal of Educational Research*, **72**, (6), 334–9.

Barnes, L. B. (1960). *Engineers and Organizational Groups*, Harvard Graduate School of Business Administration.

Baumgart, N. (1984). The student assessment project. *Assessment and Evaluation in Higher Education*, **9**, (1), 1–8.

Becker, H., E. Greer, and E. Hughes (1968). *Making the Grade: The Academic Side of College Life*, New York: Wiley.

Bedard, R. (1974). Partly tailored examinations. *Alberta Journal of Educational Research*, **20**, (1), 15–23.

Belbin, E., and R. M. Belbin (1972). *Problems in Adult Retraining*, London: Heinemann.

Bell, R. C. (1980). Problems in improving the reliability of essay marks. *Assessment and Evaluation in Higher Education*, **5**, (3), 254–63.

Benjamin, M., W. J. McKeachie, Y. G. Lin, and D. P. Holinger (1981). *Journal of Educational Psychology*, **73**, (6), 816–24.

Bennett, S. K. (1982). Students' perceptions of and expectations for male and female instructors: evidence relating to the question of gender bear on teaching evaluation. *Journal of Educational Psychology*, **74**, (2), 170–79.

Berdahl, R. (1982). Great Britain: cutting the budget: resetting priorities, *Change*, **14**, 38–43.

363

Berk, R. A. (1980). *Criterion Referenced Measurement. The state of the Art*, Johns Hopkins University, Baltimore.

Beveridge, G. S. G., and T. Mathews (1986). Case studies in chemical engineering education: their use and evaluation. *Assessment and Evaluation in Higher Education*, **11**, (3), 209–18.

Bey, C. (ed.) (1961). A Social Theory of Intellectual Development in N. Sanford *The American College* Wiley: New York.

Billing, D. E. (1973). The Effects of Guessing on the Results of Objective Tests; A novel Approach in Billing, D. E. (ed.) *Research into Tertiary Science Education*, Society for Research into Higher Education Guildford.

Bishop, J. M. *et al.* (1981). Competence of medical students in history taking during the clinical course. *Medical Education* **15**, 368–372.

Black, J. (1975). Allocation and assessment of project work in the final year of the engineering degree course at the University of Bath. *Assessment in Higher Education* **1**, (1), 35–53.

Blackburn, R., R. Armstrong, E. Conrad, C. Didham, and T. McKune (1976). *Changing Practices in Undergraduate Education.* Carnegie Council on Policy Studies in Higher Education: California, CA.

Blackburn, R., R. Armstrong, E. Conrad, C. Didham, and T. McKune (1976). *Changing Practices in Undergraduate Education.* Carnegie Council on Policy Studies in Higher Education: California, CA.

Blair, P. (1977). Cost and efficiency of self-paced education: an experiment with Keller P.S.I., *Engineering Education* **68**, (7), 763–764.

Blanc, R. A., L. E. De Buhr, and D. C. Martin (1982). Breaking the attrition cycle: the effects of supplemental instruction on undergraduate performance and attrition. *Journal of Higher Education*, **54**, (1), 80–90.

Bligh, D. (1973). Truth functional tests in D. E. Billing (ed.) *Research into Tertiary Science Education*, Society for Research into Higher Education: Guildford.

Blimling, G., and D. Hample (1979). Structuring pure environment in residence halls to increase performance in average ability students. *Journal of College Student Personnel* **20**, 310–316.

Bloch, M. (1954). *The Historians Craft*, Manchester University Press; Manchester.

Bloom, B. S. (ed.) (1956). *The Taxonomy of Educational Objectives*, Vol. 1, *Cognitive Domain*, New York: Mackay.

Bloom, B. S. (1971). Learning for mastery. In B. S. Bloom, J. J. Hastings, and G. F. Madaus (eds), *Handbook of Formative and Summative Evaluation of Student Learning*, New York: McGraw-Hill.

Bloom, B. S. (1976). *Human Characteristics and School Learning*, New York: McGraw-Hill.

Blum, J. M., and F. Fitzpatrick (1965). *Critical Performance Requirements for Orthopaedic Surgery*, University of Illinois College of Medicine, Chicago.

Blyth, W. A. L., R. Dermiott, G. F. Elliott, H. M. Sumner, and A. Waplington (1973). *History, Geography and Social Science 8–13. An Interim Statement*, Schools Council Project, University of Liverpool.

Board, C., and D. R. Whitney (1972). The effect of selected poor item-writing practices on test difficulty, reliability and validity. *Journal of Educational Measurement*, **9**, (3), 225–33.

Bogen, J. E. and G. M. Bogen (1969). The other side of the brain. III The corpus callosum and creativity. *Bulletin Los Angeles Neurological Society* **34**, 191.

Bok, B. (1986). *Higher Learning*, Cambridge, Mass.: Harvard University Press.

Boli, J., H. Katchadourian, and S. Mahoney (1988). Analyzing academic records for informed administration: the Stanford curriculum study. *Journal of Higher Education* **59**, (1), 54–68.

Boud, D. (1986). *Implementing Student–Staff Assessment*, Higher Education Research and Development Society in Australasia, University of New South Wales.

Boud, D. J., and W. Harvey Holmes (1981). Self and Peer Marking in an Under-Graduate Engineering Course. *Institute of Electrical and Electronic Engineers Transactions*, **E-24**, (4), 267–74.

Boud, D. J., A. E. Churches, and E. M. Smith (1986). Student self assessment in an engineering design course: an evaluation. *International Journal of Applied Engineering Education*, **2**, (2), 83–90.

Boud, D., J. Dunn, and E. Hegarty-Hazel (1986). *Teaching in Laboratories*, Guildford: Society for Research into Higher Education.

Boyatzis, R. E. (1982). *The Competent Manager: A Model for Effective Performance*, New York: Wiley.

Boyd, H., and J. Cowan (1985). A case of self-assessment based on recent studies of student learning. *Assessment and Evaluation in Higher Education*, **10**, (3), 225–35.

Boyer, C. M., and A. Ahlgren (1987). Assessing undergraduates' patterns of credit distribution: amount and specialization. *Journal of Higher Education*, **58**, (4), 430–42.

Brandt, D. (1976). How to implement project orientation in science and engineering education by reason of portable video-recorders. Paper presented at the International Conference on Project Orientation in Higher Education, University of Bremen.

Branthwaite, E., M. Trueman, and T. Berrisford (1981). Unreliability of marking: further evidence and a possible explanation. *Educational Review*, **33**, (1), 41–6.

Braun, H. I. (1986). *Calibration of Essays. Final Report*, Princeton, NJ: Educational Testing Services.

Braxton, J. M. (1986). The normative structure of science: social control in the academic profession. In J. Smart (ed.), *Higher Education: Handbook of Theory and Research*, Vol. II, New York: Agathon Press.

Braxton, J. M., and R. C. Nordrall (1985). Selective liberal arts colleges. Higher quality as well as higher prestige? *Journal of Higher Education*, **56**, (5), 538–54.

Breland, H. M. (1983). *The Direct Assessment of Writing Skill*, New York: College Entrance Examination Board.

Brewer, I. M., and J. D. Tomlinson (1981). The use of learning profiles in assessment and in the evaluation of teaching. *Assessment and Evaluation in Higher Education*, **6**, (2), 120–64.

Briggs, K. C., and I. B. Myers (1976). *Myers–Briggs Type Indicator*, Palo Alto, CA: Consulting Psychologists Press.

Brockbank, P. (1968). Examining exams. *Times Literary Supplement*, No. 3465.

Brook, N., and A. Parry (1985). The influence of higher education on the assessment of students of physiotherapy. *Assessment and Evaluation in Higher Education*, **10**, (2), 131–46.

Brook, R. J., and P. J. Thomson (1982). The evolution of the Keller Plan Statistics Course. *Programmed Learning and Educational Technology*, **19**, (2), 135–8.

Brown, A. L. (1978). Knowing when, where and how to remember. A problem of metacognition. In R. Glazer (ed.), *Advances in Instructional Psychology*, Vol. 1, Hillsdale, NJ: Lawrence Erlbaum.

Brown, D. (1970). A scheme for measuring the output of higher education. In B. Lawrence, G. Weathersby, and V. W. Patterson (eds), *Outputs in Higher Education: their Identification, Measurement and Evaluation*, Boulder, Colorado: Western Interstate Commission for Higher Education.

Brown, G. A. (1975). *Microteaching: A Programme of Teaching Skills*, London: Methuen.

Brown, G. A., and J. M. Daines (1981). Can explaining be learnt? Some lecturers' views. *Higher Education*, **10**, (5), 573–80.

Brown, V. A., and H. Caton (1983). The theory of biology and the education of biologists: a case study. *Studies in Higher Education*, **8**, (1), 23–32.

Brown, W. F., and W. H. Holtzman (1966). *Manual of the Survey of Study Habits and Attitudes*, New York: Psychological Corporation.

Bruffee, K. (1985). *A Short Course in Writing*, 3rd edn, Boston, Mass.: Little, Brown.

Brumby, M. (1979). Problems in learning the concept of natural selection. *Journal of Biological Education*, **13**, (2), 119–22.

Bruner, J. S. (1986). *Actual Minds, Possible Worlds*, Cambridge, Mass.: Harvard University Press.

Bruner, J. S., J. J. Goodnow, and G. A. Austin (1956). *A Study of Thinking*, New York: Wiley.

Bryant, F. J. (1983). *Marking A-level Physics*, Manchester: Joint Matriculation Board.

Brynmor-Jones, Lord (1964). *Audio-Visual Aids in Higher Scientific Education*, Report of a Committee appointed by the University Grants Committee and the Department of Education, London: HMSO.

BTEC (BEC) (1980). *Notes for the Guidance on Examination of Modern Languages Options in BEC Higher National Award Courses.* (NB: BEC is now BTEC.)

Bunzl, M. (1978). Is development deviant? *Journal for the Theory of Social Behaviour*, **8**, (3), 333–9.

Butler, N. P. (1978). Job titles and job specifications of operating dental auxiliaries—an attempt at rationalization by means of a frequency distribution analysis. *Journal of the Irish Dental Association*, **24**, 3.

Butzin, D. W. *et al.* (1982). A study of the reliability of the grading process used in the American Board Pediatrics Oral examination. *Journal of Medical Education*, **57**, 944–6.

Bynner, J., and J. Henry (1984). Advanced project work in distance teaching. *Higher Education*, **13**, (4), 413–21.

Byrne, C. (1979). Tutor marked assignments at the Open University: a question of reliability. *Teaching at a Distance*, **15**, 34–43.

Call, P. E. (1982). Screening and placing basic skills students. *Improving College and University Teaching*, **30**, (4), 184–7.

Callas, D. (1985). Academic placement practices: an analysis and proposed model. *College Teaching*, **33**, (1), 27–33.

Cameron, L. A. (1984). Standardisation techniques in the aggregation of marks. *Studies in Education*, **2**, (2), 56–64.

Cameron, L. A., and J. Heywood (1985). Better testing: Give them the questions first. *College Teaching*, **33**, (2), 76–7.

Campbell, J. P., R. L. Daft, and C. L. Holin (1982). *What to Study. Generating and Developing Research Questions*, Beverly Hills, CA: Sage.

Canter, F. M., and M. Meisels (1971). Cognitive dissonance and course evaluation. *Improving College and University Teaching*, **19**, (2), 111–13.

Carpenter, N. (1975). Continuous assessment and student motivation in management studies. *International Journal of Electrical Engineering Education*, **12**, (1), 5.

Carpenter, N., and J. Heywood (1973). Undergraduate preparation for industry: a design for learning. *Proceedings of the Design Activity International Conference*, Design Research Society, London.

Carter, G., D. G. Armour, L. S. Lee, and R. Sharples (1980). Assessment of undergraduate electrical engineering laboratory studies. *Institution of Electrical Engineers Proceedings*, **127**, A(7), 460–74.

Carter, G., J. Heywood, and D. T. Kelly (1936). *A Case Study in Curriculum Assessment. GCE Engineering Science (Advanced)*, Manchester: Roundthorn Publishing.

Carter, G., and L. S. Lee (1974). University first year electrical engineering examinations. *International Journal of Electrical Engineering Education*, **11**, 149.

Carter, G., and L. S. Lee (1981). Project work in undergraduate studies. *Programmed Learning and Educational Technology*, **26**, 48.

Cavin, C. S., E. D. Cavin, and J. J. Lagowski (1981). The effect of computer-assisted instruction on the attitudes of college students toward computers in chemistry. *Journal of Research in Science Teaching*, **18**, (4), 329–33.

Centra, J. A. (1980). The how and why of evaluating teaching, *Engineering Education*, **71**, (3), 205–10.

Chalmers, R. A., and J. Stark (1968). Continuous assessment of practical work in the Scottish HNC course in chemistry. *Education in Chemistry*, **5**, 154.

Champagne, A. N., R. F. Gunstone, and L. E. Klopfer (1983). Naive knowledge and science learning. *Research in Science and Technology Education*, **1**, (2), 173–83.

Chansarkar, B. A. (1985). Assessing performance with a 'seen' component. *Assessment and Evaluation in Higher Education*, **10**, 3, 213–24.

Chaplen, E. F. (1970). Oral examination. *Examining Modern Languages*, London: CILT.

Chase, C. I. (1979). The impact of achievement expectations and handwriting quality on scoring essay test. *Journal of Educational Measurement*, **16**, (1), 39–42.

CHE (1973). *Carnegie Commission on Higher Education: Who pays? Who benefits? Who should pay?* New York: McGraw-Hill.

Cheatham, T. R., and W. J. Jordan (1979). Influence of poor evaluation on student attitudes and achievement. *Improving College and University Teaching*, **27**, (4), 174–7.

Chelvu, C. J., and L. R. B. Elton (1977). An item bank for multiple-choice questions. *Physics Education*, **12**, (4), 263–6.

Cho, C. (1982). Experiences with a work book for spatial data analysis. *Journal of Geography in Higher Education*, **6**, (2), 133–9.

Choppin, B. H. L. (1973). *The Prediction of Academic Success*, Slough: National Foundation for Educational Research.

Christenson, H. (1979). Test anxiety and academic achievement in high school students. *Perceptual and Motor Skills*, **49**, 648.

Church, C. H. (ed.) (1983). *Practice and Perspective in Validation*, Guildford: Society for Research into Higher Education.

Church, C. H. (1988). The qualities of validation. *Studies in Higher Education* **13**, (1), 27–44.

Cinquepalmi, R., M. T. Fogli-Muciaccia, and V. Picciarelli (1983). Piaget-type question-naire scores: a quantitative analysis and its implication in teaching science for freshmen. *European Journal of Science Education*, **5**, (1), 87–95.

Clanchy, J., and B. Ballard (1983). *How to write Essays*, Melbourne: Longman Cheshire.

Clark, C. R., T. R. Guskey, and J. S. Benninga (1983). The effectiveness of mastery learning strategies in undergraduate education courses. *Journal of Educational Research*, **76**, (4), 210.

Clark, J. (1974). Assessment of first year practical work by objective testing. In *Research into Tertiary Science Education*, Society for Research into Higher Education: Guildford.

Clark, M. J., and K. J. Gregory (1982). Physical geography techniques: a self-paced university course. *Journal of Geography in higher Education,* **6**, (2), 123–32.

Clarke, B. R. (1960). The cooling-out function of higher education. *American Journal of Sociology*, **65**, 569.

Clement, D. (1971). Learning and retention in student-led discussion groups. *Journal of Social Psychology*, **82**, (2), 279–86.

Clements, I., and I. F. Roberts (1980). Practitioner views of industrial needs and course unit content. In J. Heywood (ed.), *The New Technician Education*, Guildford: Society for Research into Higher Education.

CNAA (1979). *Developments in Partnership in Validation*, London: Council for National Academic Awards.

CNAA (1984). *Access to Higher Education: Non-standard Entry to CNAA First Degree and DIP HE Courses*, CNAA Development Services Publication, London: Council for National Academic Awards.

CNAA (1986). *The Credit Accumulation and Transfer Scheme*, London: Council for National Academic Awards.

Coffin, E. A. (1975). Preliminaries and preparation for examinations: examiner's report and evaluation. Paper presented at the Conference on the National Association for Self Instructional Language Programs, 19–20 September

Collier, K. G. (1969). Syndicate methods: further evidence and comment. *Universities Quarterly*, **23**, (4), 431–64.

Collier, K. G. (1982). Ideological influences in higher education. *Studies in Higher Education* **7**, (1), 13–20.

Collier K. G. (ed.) (1983). *The Management of Peer Group Learning: Syndicate Methods in Higher Education*, Guildford: Society for Research into Higher Education.

Collier, M. (1986). A specific investigation of relative performance of examination markers. *Assessment and Evaluation in Higher Education*, **11**, (2), 130–37.

Collingwood, V., and D. C. Hughes (1978). Effects of three types of university lecture notes on student achievement. *Journal of Educational Psychology*, **70**, (2), 175–9.

Colton, P., and O. N. Peterson (1967). An essay of medical students' abilities by oral examination. *Journal of Medical Education*, **42**, (11), 1005–14.

Cook, M. C. F. (1980). The role of the academic supervisor for undergraduate dissertations in science and science related subjects *Studies in Higher Education* **5**, (2), 148–156.

Corley, J. B. (1983a). Role playing simulations. In W. E. Fabb and J. R. Marshall, *The Assessment of Clinical Competence*, Lancaster: MTP Press.

Corley, J. B. (1983b). The forward evaluation of psychomotor skills. In W. E. Fabb and J. R. Marshall, *The Assessment of Clinical Competence*, Lancaster: MTP Press.

Corson, D. (1982). The Graeco-Latin lexical bar. *Hesperiam*, **5**, 49–59.

Cowan, J. (1983). How engineers understand: an experiment for author and reader. *Engineering Education*, **73**, (4), 301–3.

Cowell, M. D., and N. J. Entwistle (1971). Personality, study attitudes and academic performance in a technical college. *British Journal of Educational Psychology*, **41**, 85–9.

Cox, E. H. (1971). 15 + drop-outs, *Universities Quarterly*, **25**, (2), 169–76.

Cox. R. (1967). Examinations in higher education: a review of the literature. *Universities Quarterly*, **21**, (3), 292.

Cox, R. (1985). Higher education: assessment of students. In T. Husein and T. Neville Postelthwaite (eds), *International Encyclopedia of Education*, Oxford: Pergamon.

Cox, R. C., and J. S. Vargas (1966). A comparison of item selection techniques for norm referenced and criterion referenced techniques. Paper presented at the annual meeting of the National Council on Measurement in Education, Chicago.

Crane, D. (1970). The academic market place revisited: a study of faculty mobility using the Carter ratings. *American Journal of Sociology*, **75**, 953–64.

Cresswell, M. J. (1986a). Examination grades: how many should there be? *British Educational Research Journal*, **12**, (1), 37–54.

Cresswell, M. J. (1986b). A review of borderline reviewing, *Educational Studies*, **12**, (2), 175–90.

Cromwell, L. S. (ed.) (1986). *Teaching Critical Thinking in the Arts and Humanities*, Milwaukee: Alverno Productions.

Cronbach, L. T. (1946). Response sets and test validity. *Educational and Psychological Measurement*, **6**, 475–94.

Cronbach, L. J. (1951). Coefficient alpha and the internal structure of tests. *Psychometrika*, **16**, 297–334.

Cronbach, L. J. (1970). *Essentials of Psychological Testing*, 3rd edn, New York: Harper and Row.

Cronbach, L. J. and G. C. Gleser (1965). Interpretation of reliability and validity coefficients. Remarks on a paper by Lord in L. J. Cronbach, and G. C. Gleser (eds), *Psychological Tests and Personal Decisions*, Urbana: University of Illinois Press.

Cronbach, L. J., and R. E. Snow (1977). *Aptitudes and Instructional Methods*, New York: Irvington.

368

Cross, K. P. (1976). *Accent on Learning*, San Francisco, CA: Jossey-Bass.

Cross, K. P. (1986). A proposal to improve teaching or 'what taking teaching seriously' should mean. *AAHE Bulletin*, 9–14.

Crum, R. and A. Parikh (1983). Headmasters' reports, admissions and academic performance in Social Science. *Educational Studies*, **9**, (3) 169–84.

Cryer, P. (ed.) (1986). *Training Activities for Teachers in Higher Education*, Guildford: Society for Reseach into Higher Education, Staff Development Group.

Culver, R. S., and J. T. Hackos (1982). Perry's model of intellectual development. *Engineering Education*, **73**, (2), 221–6.

CVCP (1969). *The Assessment of Undergraduate Performance*, London: Committee of Vice-Chancellors and Principals.

Daniel, W. W., and N. McIntosh (1972). *The Right to Manage*, London: Allen and Unwin.

Daniels, A. (1980). Integrated sandwich courses in United Kingdom Universities. In K. B. Duncan (ed.), *Cooperative Education Today*, Windsor: NFER.

Dansegrau, D. F. *et al.* (1979). Evaluation of a learning strategy system. In H. F. O'Neil and C. D. Spielberger (eds), *Cognitive and Affective Learning Strategies*, New York: Academic Press.

Davies, G. K. (1986). The importance of being general: philosophy, politics, and institutional mission statements. In J. Smart (ed.), *Higher Education: Handbook of Theory and Research*, Vol. II, New York: Agathon Press.

Davies, G. K., and K. F. Slevin (1983). Babel or opportunity: recent reports on education. *College Board Review*, No. 130, 18–21.

Day, J. D. (1980). *Training Summarization Skills: A Comparison of Teaching Methods*, PhD dissertation, University of Illinois.

De Cecco, J. P., and W. R. Crawford (1974). *The Psychology of Learning and Instruction*, Englewood Cliffs, NJ: Prentice-Hall, pp. 287–93.

De Charms, R. (1968). *Personal Causation: The Internal Affective Determinants of Behaviour*, New York: Academic Press.

Dember, W. (1965). The new look in motivation. *American Scientist*, **53**, 409–27.

De Nevers, N. (1984). An engineering solution to grade inflation. *Engineering Education*, 661–3.

Derricott, R. (1985). *Curriculum Continuity, Primary to Secondary*, Windsor: NFER-Nelson.

DES (1987a). *Young People's Intention to Enter Higher Education*, Department of Education and Science, London: HMSO.

DES (1987b). *Access to Further and Higher Education: A Discussion Document*, Department of Education and Science, London: HMSO.

Devitt, S., and I. Czak (1981). Une experience d'apprentissage due russe par de futurs professeurs de langues vivantes, *Champs Educatifs* (Université de Paris VII), **3**, 12–26.

Devore, R., and M. McPeek (1985). Report of a study of the content of three GRE advanced tests. *GREB No. 78–4R*, Princeton, NJ: Educational Testing Service.

Dew-Hughes, D., J. Heywood, C. Mortimore, H. Montagu-Pollock, and F. Oldfield (1966). *A Group Study of Staff and Student Attitudes to the Distant Minor. A Report to the Leverhulme Foundation.* Department of Higher Education, The University of Lancaster.

De Winter Hebron, C. C. (1979). How lecturers see their teaching objectives. *Bulletin of Educational Research*, **17**, 24–31.

Diamond, J. J., and W. J. Evans (1972). An investigation of the cognitive-correlation of test wiseness. *Journal of Educational Measurement*, **9**, 145–50.

Diederich, P. B. (1960). *Short Cut Statistics for Teacher Made Tests*, Princeton, NJ: Educational Testing Services.

Diggins, P. (1979). *A Critical Incident Study of the Task of the Principal in Second Level Education in the Republic of Ireland as Perceived by Himself*, M.Ed. thesis, School of Education, University of Dublin.

Dinkelspiel, J. R. (1971). A teachable subject. *Journal of Higher Education*, **42**, (1), 42.

Dolly, J. P., and K. S. Williams (1983). *Teaching Testwiseness*, Paper presented at the annual meeting of the Northern Rocky Mountain Educational Research Association, Jackson, NY.

Dolly, J. P., and K. S. Williams (1986). Using test taking strategies to maximise multiple-choice test scores. *Educational and Psychological Measurement*, **46**, (3), 619–25.

Donald, J. G. (1982). Knowledge structure: methods for explaining course content. *Journal of Higher Education*, **54**, (1), 31–4.

Dorey, A. P., and B. R. Wilkins (1977). Teaching electronics using self-paced instruction. *International Journal of Electrical Engineering Education*, **14**, 197–209

Dressel, P. L. (1971). Values, cognitive and affective. *Journal of Higher Education*, **42**, (5), 400.

Dressel, P. L. (1976). *Handbook of Academic Evaluation*, San Francisco, CA: Jossey-Bass.

Dressel, P. L. (1980). *Improving Degree Programs*, San Francisco, CA: Jossey-Bass.

Dreyfus, A., and R. Lieberman (1981). Perceptions, expectations and interactions: the essential ingredients for genuine classroom discussion. *Journal of Biological Education*, **15**, (2), 152–7.

Duff, A., and S. Cotgrove (1982). Social values and the choice of careers in industry. *Journal of Occupational Psychology*, **55**, (5), 97–107.

Duguid, S. (1984). The humanities and higher education. *Canadian Journal of Higher Education*, **14**, (1), 41–57.

Duncan, O. D. (1975). *Introduction to Structural Equation Models*, New York: Academic Press.

Dwyer, F. M., and P. E. Parkhurst (1982). A multi-factor analysis of the instructional effectiveness of self-paced visualized instruction of different educational objectives. *Programmed Learning and Educational Technology*, **19**, (2), 108–19.

Ebel, R. L. (1958). Using examinations to promote learning. In Cooper, (ed.), *Two Ends of the Log*, Minneapolis: University of Minnesota Press.

Ebel, R. L. (1965). *Measuring Educational Achievement*, Englewood Cliffs, NJ: Prentice-Hall.

Eddy, J., M. Altekruse and G. Pitts (1981). *Counselling Methods: Developing Counsellors*, Lanham, MD: University Press of America.

Educational Evaluation: Concepts and Techniques for Evaluating Education Training Programs, San Francisco: Jossey-Bass.

Edwards, D. (1979). A study of the reliability of tutor-marked assignments at the Open University. *Assessment in Higher Education*, **5**, (1), 16–44.

Edwards, R. M. (1984). A case study in the examination of systems analysis. *Assessment and Evaluation in Higher Education*, **9**, (1), 31–9.

Eisner, E. W. (1979). *The Educational Imagination: On the Design and Evaluation of School Programmes*, New York: Macmillan.

Eisner, E. (1982). *Cognition and the Curriculum: a Basis for Deciding what to Teach*, New York: Longman.

Eizler, C. (1983). The meaning of college grades in three grading systems. *Educational Research Quarterly*, **8**, 12–30.

El-Khawas, E. (1986). *Campus Trends (1986)*, Higher Education Panel Reports, No. 73, August 1986, Washington, DC: American Council on Education.

Ellis, D. B. (1985). *Becoming a Master Student*, 5th edn, Rapid City, South Dakota: College Survival.

Elstein, A. S., S. A. Sprafka, and G. Bordage (1979). Problem solving: applications of research to undergraduate instruction and evaluation. *Programmed Learning and Educational Technology*, **16**, (4), 296–302.

Elton, L. R. B. (1984). Evaluating teaching and assessing teachers in universities, *Assessment and Evaluation in Higher Education*, **9**, (2), 97–115.

Elton, C. F., and H. A. Rose (1974). Students who leave engineering. *Engineering Education*, **62**, (1), 30–32.

Elton, L. R. B., and D. Lourillard (1979). Trends in research on student learning. *Studies in Higher Education*, **4**, 87–102.

Ennis, R. H. (1962). A concept of critical thinking: a proposed basis for research in the teaching and evaluation of critical thinking ability, *Harvard Educational Review*, **32**, 81–111.

Ennis, R. H. (1986). What is critical thinking? In J. B. Baron and R. H. Starnberg (eds), *Teaching, Thinking Skills: Theory and Practice*, New York: Freeman.

Ennis, R. H., and J. Millman (1971). *The Cornell Critical Thinking Test*, Urbana, Illinois: Critical Thinking Project.

Entwistle, N. J. (1981). *Styles of Learning and Teaching*, Chichester: Wiley.

Entwistle, N. J., and J. D. Wilson (1977). *Degrees of Excellence. The Academic Achievement Game*, London: Hodder and Stoughton.

Enyeart, M. A., D. Baker, and D. Vanharlingen (1980). Correlation of inductive and deductive logical reasoning to college physics achievement. *Journal of Research in Science Teaching*, **17**, (3) 263–7.

Epstein, H. (1970). *A Strategy for Education*, Oxford: Oxford University Press.

Ericksen, S. C. (1984). *The Essence of Good Teaching*, San Francisco, CA: Jossey-Bass.

Essex, D. L. (1976). A comparison of two item scoring procedures. *Journal of Medical Education*, **51**, 565–72.

ETS. Brief from ETS on the work of G. Conland and M. Fowles. *Test Development Manual for the Testing of Writing Ability*, Princeton, NJ: Educational Testing Service.

Evans, L. R., R. W. Ingersoll, and E. J. Smith (1966). The reliability and taxonomic structure of the oral examination. *Journal of Medical Education*, **41**, 651–7.

Evans, P., N. Mickelson, and N. C. Smith (1985). Computer-assisted instruction in college composition. *Alberta Journal of Educational Research*, **30**, 311–19.

Ewell, P. T. (1984). *The Self-rewarding Institution: Information for Excellence*, Boulder, Colorado: National Center for Higher Education Management System.

Ewell, P. T., and D. P. Jones (1986). The costs of assessment. In C. Adelman (ed.), *Assessment in Higher Education*. Washington, DC: US Department of Education.

Eysenck, H. J., and S. B. J. Eysenck (1964). *The Eysenck Personality Inventory Manual*, Sevenoaks: Hodder and Stoughton.

Fabb, W. E., and J. R. Marshall (1983). *The Assessment of Clinical Competence in General Family Practice*, Lancaster: MTP Press.

Fawthrop, T. (1968). *Education or Examination?* London: Radical Students Alliance.

Feldhusen, J. F. (1961). An evaluation of college students' reactions to open book examinations. *Educational and Psychological Measurement*, **21**, (3), 637–46.

Feldman, K. A. (1976). Grades and college students' evaluation of their courses and teachers. *Research in Higher Education*, **4**, 69–111.

Feletti, G. I. (1980). Reliability and validity studies on modified essay questions. *Journal of Medical Education*, **55**, 933–41.

Feletti, G. I., and R. L. B. Neame (1981). Curricular strategies for reducing examination anxiety. *Higher Education*, **10**, (6), 675–86.

Feletti, G. I. *et al.* (1982). Medical students' evaluation of tutors in a group learning curriculum. *Medical Education*, **16**, 319–25.

FESC (1981). *Profiling and Profile Reporting*, Coombe Lodge Report **14**, (13), 620–54, Blaydon, Bristol: Further Education Staff College.

FEU (1981). *How do I learn?* Further Education Unit, Department of Education and Science, London.

FEU (1984). *Profiles in Action,* Further Education Unit, Department of Education and Science, London.

Fincher, C (1985). Learning theory and research. In J. Smart (ed.), *Higher Education Theory and Research,* Vol. 1, New York: Agathon Press.

Fitzgibbon, A. (1987). Kolb's experiential learning model as a model for supervision of classroom teaching for student teachers in the press. *European Journal of Teacher Education,* **10**, (2), 163–178.

Fitzgibbon, A., and J. Heywood (1986). The recognition of conjunctive and identity needs in teacher development: their implications for the planning of in-service training. *European Journal of Teacher Education,* **9**, (3), 271–86.

Fitzgibbons, R. E. (1981). *Educational Decisions: An Introduction to the Philosophy of Education,* New York: Harcourt Brace Jovanovich.

Fischer, C. G., and G. E. Grant (1983). Intellectual levels in college classrooms. In C. L. Ellner and C. P. Barnes (eds), *Studies in College Teaching,* Lexington, Mass.: D. C. Heath.

Flanagan, J. C. (1949). A new approach to evaluating personnel. *Personnel,* **26**, 35–42.

Fleishman, E. A. (ed.) (1967). *Studies in Research and Industrial Psychology,* Homewood, Illinois: The Darsey Press.

Flood Page, C. (1967). Worrying about examinations. *Cambridge Institute of Education Bulletin,* **3**, (6), 2–7.

Flood Page, C. (1974). *Student Evaluation of Teaching: The American Experience,* Guildford: Society for Research into Higher Education.

Fong, B. (1987). The external examiner approach to assessment. Commissioned paper, AAHE Assessment Forum; Resource Packet, American Association for Higher Education, Washington, DC.

Ford, B. (1977). The dubious meaning of the first. *New Universities Quarterly,* **31**, (4), 396–421.

Ford, N. (1980). Teaching study skills to teachers: a reappraisal. *British Journal of Teacher Education,* **6**, 71–8.

Ford, N. (1981). Recent approaches to the study and teaching of effective learning. *Review of Education Research,* **51**, 345–77.

Fordyce, D. (1986). Engineering education: A total concept *Assessment and Evaluation in Higher Education,* **11**, (3), 240–56.

Forrest, G. M., and G. A. Smith (1972). *Standards in Subjects at the Ordinary Level of the GCE, June 1971.* Manchester: Joint Matriculation Board.

Forrest, G. M., G. A. Smith, and M. H. Brown (1970). *General Studies (Advanced) and Academic Aptitude,* Manchester: Joint Matriculation Board.

Forrest, G. M., and D. J. Shoesmith (1985). *A Second Review of GCE Comparability Studies,* GCE Examining Boards; Manchester: Joint Matriculation Board.

Foster, P. J. (1981). Clinical discussion groups: verbal participation and outcomes. *Journal of Medical Education,* **56**, 831–8.

Foster, P. J. (1983). Verbal participation in medical education: a study of third year clinical discussion groups. In C. L. Ellner and C. P. Barnes (eds), *Studies of College Teaching,* Lexington, Mass.: D. C. Heath.

Fox, E. (1985). International schools and the international baccalaureate. *Harvard Educational Review,* **55**, (1).

Fransonn, A. (1977). On qualitative differences in learning. IV Effects of motivation and test anxiety on process and outcome. *British Journal of Educational Psychology,* **47**, 244–57.

Fraser, W. J., and J. N. Gillam (1972). *The Principles of Objective Testing in Mathematics,* London: Heinemann.

Fredericksen, N. (1981). *Development of Methods for Selection and Evaluation in Undergraduate Medical Education*, Princeton, NJ: Education Testing Service.

Fredericksen, N., and W. C. Ward (1978). Measures for the study of creativity in scientific problem solving. *Applied Psychological Measurement*, **2**, (1), 1–24.

Freeman, J. (1984). Matters arising. *Family Practice*, **1**, (3), 191–6.

Freeman, J., J. G. M'Comisky, and D. Buttle (1968). Student selection. A comparative study of student entrants to architecture and economics *International Journal of Educational Science*, **3**, (3), 189–197.

Freeman, J., and P. Byrne (1976). *Assessment of Post-graduate Training in General Practice*, 2nd edn, Guildford: Society for Research into Higher Education.

Freeman, J., G. C. Carter, and T. A. Jordan (1978). Cognitive styles, personality factors, problem solving skills and teaching approach in electrical engineering. *Assessment in Higher Education*, **3**, (2).

Freeman, J., G. Keele, J. Roberts, and V. Hillier (1981). Clinical competence in general practice: correlation between techniques of assessment. Cyclostyled: Department of General Practice, University of Manchester.

Freeman, J., J. Roberts, D. Metcalfe, and V. Hillier (1982). *The Influence of Trainers on Trainees in General Practice*, Occasional Paper No. 21, London: Royal College of General Practitioners.

Friedman, T. and E. Belvin Williams (1982). Current use of tests for employment. In A. K. Wigdor and W. R. Garner (eds), *Ability Testing: Uses, Consequences and Controversies*, Part II, Washington, DC: National Academy Press, pp. 99–172.

Friedman, M., M. Mentkowski, M. Early, G. Loacker, and M. Diez (1980). *Validating Assessment Techniques in an Outcome-centered Liberal Arts Curriculum: Valuing and Communications Generic Instruments*, Milwaukee: Alverno Productions.

Frith, J. R. (1979). Testing the FSI testing kit. *ADFL Bulletin*, **11**, (2), November, 12 (4) (reported by Fong, 1987).

Furneaux, W. D. (1962). The psychologist and the university. *University Quarterly*, **17**, 33.

Furst, E. J. (1958). *Constructing Evaluation Instruments*, New York: Mackay.

Gabb, R. (1981). Playing the project game. *Assessment and Evaluation in Higher Education*, **6**, (1), 26–48.

Gagne, R. M. (1976). *The Conditions of Learning*, New York: Holt, Rinehart and Winston.

Gagne, R. M., and W. Dick (1983). Instructional psychology. In M. R. Rosenzweig and L. W. Porter (eds), *Annual Review of Psychology*, Palo Alto, CA: Annual Reviews.

Galassi, J. D., H. T. Frierson, and R. Sharer (1981). Behaviour of high, moderate and low test anxious students during an actual test situation. *Journal of Consulting and Clinical Psychology*, **49**, (1), 51–62.

Gale, J., and P. Narsden (1982). Clinical problem solving. The beginning of the process. *Medical Education*, **16**, 22–6.

Galyean, B. C. (1983). Guided imagery. *Educational Leadership*, **40**, (6), 54–8.

Ganzer, V. J. (1968). Effects of audience presence and test anxiety on learning and retentions in a serial learning situation. *Journal of Personality and Social Psychology*, **8**, 194–9.

Gardner, H. (1983). *Frames of Mind. The Theory of Multiple Intelligences*, New York: Basic Books.

Gardner, R. C., and S. Erdle (1986). Aggregating standard scores or raw scores. *Educational and Psychological Measurement*, **46**, (3), 533–6.

Garrick, C. E. (1978). Design of instructional illustrations in medicine. *Journal of Audio Visual Media in Medicine*, **1**, (4), 168–73.

Geisinger, K. F. (1980). Who are giving all those 'A's. *Journal of Teacher Education*, **31**, (2), 11–15.

Gerhardt, R. C. (1976). An alternative to grades. *Improving College and Teaching*, **24**, (2), 82–3, 86.

Gibbs, G. (1981). *Teaching Students to Learn: A Student Centred Approach*, Milton Keynes: Open University Press.

Gibbs, G. (ed.) (1986). *Alternations in Assessment 2. Objective Tests and Computer Applications*, Occasional Paper 21, Standing Conference on Educational Development Services in Polytechnics, Birmingham Polytechnic.

Gibbs, G., and A. Northedge (1979). Helping students to understand their own study methods. *British Journal of Guidance and Counselling*, **7**, (1), 92–100.

Gibbs, G., and M. Haigh (1984). *Designing Course Evaluation Questionnaires*, Educational Methods Unit, Oxford Polytechnic.

Gibbs, G., S. Habeshaw, and T. Habeshaw (1986). *53 Interesting Ways to Assess Your Students*, Bristol: Technical and Educational Services.

Gibbs, G., A. Morgan, and E. Taylor (1984). The world of the learner. In F. Marton, D. Hounsell, and N. Entwistle (eds), *The Experience of Learning*, Edinburgh: Scottish Academic Press.

Gibney, T., and W. Wiersma (1986). Using profile analysis for student teacher evaluation. *Journal of Teacher Education*, **37**, (3), 41–5.

Giencke-Holl, L., M. Methowski, N. Much, S. Mertens, and G. Rogers (1985). Evaluating college outcomes through alumnae studies: measuring post-college learning and abilities. Paper at Annual General Meeting of the American Educational Research Association, Chicago.

Gilbert, J. K., D. M. Watts, and R. J. Osborne (1982). Students' conception of ideas in mechanics. *Physical Education*, **17**, 42–6.

Glass, G. V., B. McGaw, and M. L. Smith (1981). *Meta-Analysis in Social Research*, Beverly Hills, CA: Sage.

Glutting, J. J., P. A. McDermott, and J. C. Stanley (1987). Resolving differences among methods of establishing confidence limits for text scores. *Educational and Psychological Measurement*, **47**, (3), 607–14.

Goldman, R. D., and B. N. Hewitt (1975). Adaption level as an explanation for differential standards in college grading. *Journal of Educational Measurement*, **12**, 149–61.

Goldman, R. D., and R. E. Slaughter (1976). Why college Grade Point Average is difficult to predict. *Journal of Educational Psychology*, **68**, 9–14.

Goldstein, H. (1986). On models for equating test scores and for studying the comparability of public examinations. In D. L. Nuttall (ed.), *Assessing Educational Achievement*, Lewes: Falmer Press.

Granzin, K. L., and J. J. Painter (1976). A second look at cognitive dissonance and course evaluation. *Improving College and University Teaching*, **24**, (2), 113–15.

Grasha, A. F. (1984). Learning styles: the journey from Greenwich Observatory (1976) to the college classroom (1984). *Improving College and University Teaching*, **32**, (1), 46–53.

Green, E. W., L. R. Evans, and R. W. Ingersoll (1967). The reaction of students in oral examination. *Journal of Medical Education*, **42**, 354.

Gregory, S. A. (ed.) (1972). *Creativity in Engineering*, London: Butterworths.

Gruber, H. (1973). Courage and cognitive growth in children and scientists. In M. Schuebel (ed.), *Piaget in the Classroom*, New York: Basic Books.

Guilford, J. P. (1954). A factor analytic study of creative thinking. *Reports from the Psychology Laboratory*, No. 1. Los Angeles, California.

Guilford, J. P. (1959). Three faces of intellect. *American Psychologist*, **14**, 469–79.

Guilford, J. P., and B. Fruchter (1973). *Fundamental Statistics in Psychology and Education*, New York: McGraw-Hill.

Gulliksen, H. (1950). *Theory of Mental Tests*, New York: Wiley.

Gur, R. C., and H. A. Sackheim (1979). Self-deception: a concept in search of a phenomenon. *Journal of Personality and Social Psychology*, **37**, 147–69.

Guthrie, R. D., J. D. Jenkins, and R. J. Quinn (1985). Organic chemistry by self-placed instruction. *Education in Chemistry*, **22**, (4), 112–13.

Haigh, M. J. (1986). The evaluation of an experiment in physical geography teaching. *Journal of Geography in Higher Education*, **10**, (2), 133–47.

Hake, R., and D. Andrich (1975). *The Ubiquitous Essay*, Chicago: Chicago University Press.

Hakstian, A. R., L. K. Woolsey, and M. L. Schroder (1986). Development and application of a quickly scored in-basket exercise in an organizational setting. *Educational and Psychological Measurement*, **46**, (2), 385–96.

Hale, Sir Edward (1964). *Report of the Committee on University Teaching Methods*, London: HMSO.

Hales, L. W., and E. Tokar (1975). The effect of quality of preceding responses on the grades assigned to subsequent responses to an essay question. *Journal of Educational Measurement*, **12**, (2), 115–17.

Hall, C. G. W., and N. D. Daglish (1982). Length and quality: an exploratory study of inter-marker reliability. *Assessment and Evaluation in Higher Education*, **7**, (2), 186–91.

Hall, G. G. (1982). Information and communication. *International Journal of Mathematical Education in Science and Technology*, **13**, (5), 559–63.

Halonen, J. S. (ed.) (1986). *Teaching Critical Thinking in Psychology*, Alverno productions: Milwaukee.

Hammersley, M. (1987). Some notes on the terms 'validity' and 'reliability', *British Educational Research Journal*, **13**, (1), 73–81.

Hargaden, F. (1982). From School to College: Testimony for National Commission on Excellence in Education, Chicago, 23 June.

Harris, C. W., M. C. Atkins, and W. J. Popham (eds) (1974). *Problems in Criterion Referenced Measurement*. Los Angeles: University College.

Harris, D. J. (1986). A comparison of two answer sheet formats. *Educational and Psychological Measurement*, **86**, (2), 475–478.

Harris, D. J., and M. J. Subkoviak (1986). Item analysis: a short cut statistic for mastery tests. *Educational and Psychological Measurement*, **46**, (3), 495–507.

Harris, J. (1986). Assessing outcomes in higher education. In C. Adelman (ed.), *Assessment in Higher Education*, Washington, DC: US Department of Education.

Harris, N. D. C., and K. Bullock (1981). What price projects? *Journal of Biological Education*, **15**, (2), 151–2.

Harris, N. D. C., and B. Smith (1982a). *CORE (Collected Original Researches in Education)*, **6**, (2), 7E10–1057.

Harris, N. D. C., and B. Smith (1982b). Undergraduate project work. *Assessment and Evaluation in Higher Education*, **8**, (3), 246–61.

Harrow, A. J. (1972). A taxonomy of the psychomotive domain. In *A Guide for Developing Behavioural Objectives*, New York: Mackay.

Hartle, T. W. (1986). The growing interest in measuring the educational achievement of college students. In C. Adelman (ed.), *Assessment in Higher Education*, Washington, DC: US Department of Education.

Hartley, J. (1986). Improving study-skills. *British Educational Research Journal*, **12**, (2), 111–23.

Hartley, J. and A. Branthwaite (1976). All this for two per cent: the contribution of course-work assessment to the final grade. *Durham Research Review*, **8**, 37, 14–20.

Hartog, P., and E. C. Rhodes (1935). *An Examination of Examinations*, London Macmillan.

Hartog, P., and E. C. Rhodes (1936). *The Marks of Examiners*, London: Macmillan.

Hawley, C. S. (1984). The thieves of academe: plagiarism in the university system

Improving College and University Teaching, **32**, (1), 35–9.

Haydn, D. C., and E. L. Holloway (1985). A longitudinal study of attrition among engineering students. *Engineering Education*, **75**, (7), 664–8.

Hazeltine, B. (1976). Student evaluation using lists of description statements. *Research in Higher Education*, **4**, 1–22.

HEA (1984). Symposium on the year of the reports: responses from the educational community. *Harvard Educational Review*, **54**, 1–31.

Hedges, L. V., and I. Olkin (1985). *Statistical methods for Meta-analysis*, Orlando: Academic Press. Review by V. L. Willson in *Education and Psychological Measurement*, **47**, (2), 535–6.

Helson, H. (1964). *Adaptation Level Theory*, New York: Harper and Row.

Henderson, E. S. (1980). The essay in continuous assessment. *Studies in Higher Education*, **5**, (2), 197–203.

Henry, J. (1977). The courses' tutor and project work. *Teaching at a Distance*, **9**, 1–12.

Hereford, S. (1979). The Keller Plan (PSI) within a conventional academic environment: an empirical 'meta-analytic study'. *The Journal of Engineering Education*, **70**, (3), 250–60.

Hesseling, P. (1966). *A Strategy for Evaluation Research*, Aassen: Van Gorcum.

Hewitt, E. A. (1967). *The Reliability of GCE 'O' level Examinations in English*, Manchester: Joint Matriculation Board.

Heywood, J. (1968). Technical education. In H. J. Butcher (ed.), *Educational Research in Britain*, Vol. 1, London: University of London Press.

Heywood, J. (1969). *An Evaluation of Certain Post-war Developments in Higher Technological Education*, Thesis, University of Lancaster.

Heywood, J. (1970). Qualities and their assessment in the education of technologists. *International Bulletin of Mechanical Engineering Education*, **9**, 15.

Heywood, J. (1971a). A report on student wastage. *Universities Quarterly*, **25**, (2), 189–237.

Heywood, J. (1971b). *Bibliography of British Technological Education and Training*, London: Hutchinson.

Heywood, J. (1973). Short courses in the development of originality. In S. A. Gregory (ed.), *Creativity and Innovation in Engineering*, London: Butterworths.

Heywood, J. (1974a). American and English influences on the development of a transdisciplinary course on the engineer and society. *Proceedings of Annual Conference (ERM Division) of the American Society for Engineering Education*.

Heywood, J. (1974b). *Assessment in History*, First Report of the Public Examination Evaluation Project, School of Education, University of Dublin.

Heywood, J (1974c). *New Patterns of Courses and New Degree Courses*, Strasbourg: Council of Europe.

Heywood, J. (1976). *Assessment in Mathematics (Twelve to Fifteen)*, A Report of the Public Examination Evaluation Project, School of Education, University of Dublin.

Heywood, J. (1977). *Examining in Second Level Education*, Dublin: Association of Secondary Teachers, Ireland.

Heywood, J. (1981a). The academic versus practical debate: a case study in screening. *Institution of Electrical Engineers Proceedings*, Part A, **128**, (7), 511–19.

Heywood, J. (1981b). Curricula, teaching and assessment. In R. Oxtoby (ed.), *Higher Education at the Crossroads*, Guildford: Society for Research into Higher Education.

Heywood, J. (1982). *Pitfalls and Planning in Student Teaching*, London: Kogan Page.

Heywood, J. (1983). In Church C. H. (ed.) (1983) *Practice and Perspective in Validation*, Guildford: Society for Research into Higher Education.

Heywood, J. (1984). *Considering the Curriculum During Student Teaching*, London: Kogan Page.

Heywood, J. (1989). *The Individual, Industry and Society*, Course book, St Mary's College of Education, Dublin. (In press). Paul Chapman Publishing: London.

376

Heywood, J., and L. A. Cameron (1985). Better testing: give them the questions first. *College Teaching*, **33**, (2), 76–7.

Heywood, J., and A. Fitzgibbon (1987). The evaluation of performance in management in education following in-service management training courses. Association of Teacher Education in Europe (ATEE) Conference, Berlin.

Heywood, J., C. Heward, and V. Mash (1968). Student reaction to undergraduate (Dip. Tech.) sandwich courses, *Bulletin of Mechanical Engineering Education*, **7**, 253–69.

Heywood, J., and D. T. Kelly (1973). The evaluation of coursework—a study of engineering science among schools in England and Wales. *Proceedings Third Annual Frontiers in Education Conferences (ASEE/IEEE)*, pp. 269–76.

Heywood, J., L. S. Lee, J. D. Monk, J. Moon, B. G. H. Rowley, B. T. Turner, and J. Vogler (1966). The education of professional engineers for design and manufacture (a model curriculum). *Lancaster Studies in Higher Education*, **1**, 4–153.

Heywood, J., S. McGuinness, and D. Murphy (1980). *Final Report of the Public Examination Evaluation Project to the Minister for Education*, School of Education, University of Dublin.

Heywood, J., and H. Montagu-Pollock (1976). *Science for Arts Students: A Case Study in Curriculum Development*, Guildford: Society for Research into Higher Education.

Heywood, J., and M. B. Youngman (1981). Pupils' reactions to multiple choice items in mathematics. *Educational Research*, **23**, (3), 228–9.

Higginson, G. (1988). Chairman of a Government Committee of Inquiry into the Advanced Level of the General Certificate of Education. Department of Education and Science, London. (Reviewed *Times Educational Supplement* 10th June).

Highhouse, S., and D. Doverspike (1987). The validity of the Learning Style Inventory 1985 as a predictor of cognitive style and occupational preference. *Educational and Psychological Measurement*, **47**, (3), 749–53.

Hilgard, E. R., and G. H. Bower (1981). *Theories of Learning*, Englewood Cliffs, NJ: Prentice-Hall.

Hill, M. M., S. R. Baker, L. J. Talley, and M. D. Hobday (1980). Language preferences of freshman chemistry students: an exploratory study. *Journal of Research in Science Teaching*, **17**, (6), 571–76.

Hilton, T. L. (1982). *Persistence in Higher Education*, New York: College Entrance Examination Board.

Hirsch, B. (1987). *Cultural Literacy*, Macmillan, New York.

Hoare, D. E., and M. M. Revans (1969). Measuring attainment of educational objectives in chemistry. *Education in Chemistry*, **6**, (3), 78.

Hodgkinson, H. L. (1971). *Institutions in Transition* (with commentary by Stanley J. Heywood), New York: McGraw-Hill.

Hodgson, V. (1984). Learning from lectures in F. Marton *et al.* (eds.) *The Experience of Learning*. Edinburgh: Scottish Academic Press.

Hoffman, B. (1982). *The Tyranny of Testing*, New York: Cromwell Collier Press.

Hogan, P. (1980). A critique of educational research, *Oxford Review of Education*, **6**, 141–55.

Holdsworth, R. (1981). Improving the selective interview. *Education and Training*, **23**, (2), 36–7.

Holland, J. L. (1978). *Manual for the Vocational Preference Inventory*, Palo Alto. CA: Consulting Psychologist Press.

Hollandsworth, J. G., R. C. Glazeski, K. Kirkland, G. E. Jones, and L. R. Van Norman (1979). An analysis of the nature and effects of test anxiety: cognitive, behavioural and physiological components. *Cognitive Therapy and Research*, **3** (2), 165–80.

Holloway, C. (1978). *Learning and Problem Solving* Part 1, Block 4 of Cognitive Psychology. Milton Keynes: Open University Press.

Holloway, P. J., J. L. Hardwick, J. Morris, and K. B. Start (1967). The validity of essay and viva-voce examining technique. *British Dental Journal*, **123**, (8), 227–32.

Holme, R. (1976). Towards the abolition of pre-testing. *Research in Assessment*, 77–85.

Holroyd, K. A., and M. A. Appel (1980). Test anxiety and physiological responding. In I. Sarason (ed.), *Test Anxiety: Therapy, Research and Application*. Hillsdale, NJ: Lawrence Erlbaum.

Hoste, R., and B. Bloomfield (1975). *Continuous assessment in the CSE: opinion and practice*, London: Evans/Methuen (Schools Council).

Hounsell, D. (1984a). Learning and essay writing. In F. Marton, D. Hounsell and N. J. Entwistle, *The Experience of Learning*, Edinburgh: Scottish Academic Press.

Hounsell, D. (1984b). Essay planning and essay writing. *Higher Education Research and Development*, **3**, (1), 13–30. (NB: Hounsell gives Saljob's meaning to the term 'conception'.)

Hounsell, D. (1985). Coursework: an agenda for research. *Evaluation Newsletter*, **9**, (1), 12–20.

Houston, W. R. (1980). The status of competency-based education: an American report. *Journal of Education for Teaching*, **7**, (1), 17–23.

Howard, R. W. (1987). *Concepts and Schemata: An Introduction*, London: Cassell.

Hudson, L. (1966). *Contrary Imaginations*, London: Methuen.

Hudson, L. (ed.) (1970). *The Ecology of Human Intelligence*, Harmondsworth: Penguin.

Humble, W. (1970). Classification was presented in Heywood, J., Qualities and their assessment in the education of technologists. *Bulletin of Mechanical Engineering Education*.

Iliffe, A. H. (1966). Objective tests. In J. Heywood and A. H. Iliffe (eds), *Some Aspects of Testing for Academic Performance*, Bulletin No. 1, Department of Higher Education, University of Lancaster.

Iliffe, A. H. (1969). Are sixth formers old enough for university? *The Times Educational Supplement*, **2**, 825, 13. Also internal report on the Foundation Year at the University of Keele (mimeo).

Imrie, B. W., T. M. Blithe, and L. C. Johnston (1980). A review of Keller principles with reference to mathematics covering in Australasia. *British Journal of Educational Technology*, **11**, (2), 105–21.

Isaacs, G., and B. W. Imrie (1980). A case for professional judgement when combining marks. *Assessment and Evaluation in Higher Education*, **6**, (1), 3–25.

Iyasere, M. M. (1984). Setting standards in multiple section courses. *Improving College and University Teaching*, **32**, (4), 173–9. (This issue includes two other articles on this topic.)

Jackson, I. (1985). On detecting aptitude effects in undergraduate academic achievement scores. *Assessment and Evaluation in Higher Education*, **10**, (1), 71–88.

Jahoda, M. (1964). *The Education of Technologists*, London: Tavistock.

James, C. (1977). The effect of 'paper error' on the reliability of examinations. *International Journal of Electrical Engineering Education*, **14**, 107–13.

James, C., and D. R. Hub (1983). The effect of question choice on the reliability of an examination. *International Journal of Electrical Engineering Education*, **20**, 375–84.

James, D. W., M. L. Johnson, and P. Venning (1956). Testing for learnt skill in observation and evaluation of evidence. *Lancet*, 25 August, 379–83.

Johnson, E. G. (1985). Analysis of assessment procedures used in an introductory course in psychology. *Assessment and Evaluation in Higher Education*, **10**, (1), 63–70.

Johnson Abercrombie, M. L. (1960). *The Anatomy of Judgement*, London: Methuen (subsequently Penguin).

Jones, E. S. (1933). *Comprehensive Examinations in American Colleges*, New York: Macmillan.

Jordan, T. A., and G. Carter (1986). The determination of attitudes of students to their undergraduate courses. *Assessment and Evaluation in Higher Education*, **11**, (1), 11–27.

Kalish, R. A. (1958). An experimental evaluation of the open-book examination. *Journal of Educational Psychology*, 200–4.

Kaplan, M. N. (1978). Aptitude–treatment interaction study of student choice and completion in a PSI course. *Journal of Engineering Education*, **69**, (3), 273–84.

Katz, J., and N. Sanford (1962). The curriculum in the perspective of the theory of personality development. In N. Sanford (ed.), *The American College*, New York: Wiley.

Kealy, M. J., and M. L. Rockel (1987). Student perceptions of college quality: the influence of college recruitment policies. *Journal of Higher Education*, **58**, (6), 683–703.

Keele, G. (1982). *The Assessment of Professional Competence in General Practice Using Rating Scales and Allied Techniques*. MD Thesis, Cambridge University.

Keller, F. S. (1968). Goodbye teacher. . . . *Journal of Applied Behavioural Analysis*, **1**, 78–9.

Kelly, J. A. (1982). Stress management training in a medical school. *Journal of Medical Education*, **57**, (2), 91–9.

Kelly, P. R., J. M. Matthews, and C. F. Schumacher (1971). Analysis of oral examinations of the American Board of Anesthesiology. *Journal of Medical Education*, **46**, 982.

Kempa, R. F. (1986). *Assessment in Science*, Cambridge: Cambridge University Press.

Kempa, R. F., and P. A. Ongley (1979). *Profile Assessment in Chemistry*, Department of Education, University of Keele, Stoke-on-Trent.

Kidson, M., and A. Hornblow (1982). Examination anxiety in medical students: experience with the visual analogue scale for anxiety. *Medical Education*, **16**, 247–50.

King, J. B. (1986). The three faces of thinking. *Journal of Higher Education*, **57**, (1).

Kingston, N. M. and N. J. Dorans (1982). The feasibility of using item response theory as a psychometric model for the GRE Aptitude test. *GRE Board 79–12 P*, Princeton, NJ: Educational Testing Service.

Kirk, S., and P. Eggen (1978). The effect of cue specificity and locus on learning from graphical material. *Journal of Educational Research*, **72**, (1), 39–44.

Klemp, G., and D. Connelly (1977). *Life History Exercise*, Boston, Mass.: McBer and Co.

Kloss, R. J. (1987). Coaching and playing right field: trying on metaphors for teaching. *College Teaching*, **35**, (4), 134–9.

Knefelkamp, L. L., and R. Slepitza (1976). A cognitive-developmental model of career development: an adaptation of the Perry scheme. *The Counselling Psychologist*, **6**, (3), 53–8.

Knox, J. D. E. (1975). *The Modified Essay Question*, ASME Booklet No. 5. Dundee: Association for the Study of Medical Education.

Knox, J. D. E. (1976). The modified essay question. In W. E. Fabb (ed.), *WONCA Examination Handbook*, Adelaide: WONCA.

Knudson, R. L. (1969). Involvement in video tape. *Audio Visual Instruction*, **14**, (10), 53.

Koen, B. (1985). The Keller Plan: a successful experiment in engineering education. *Engineering Education*, **75**, (5), 280–81.

Kohlberg, L., and E. Turiel (1971). Moral development and moral education. In G. Lesser (ed.), *Psychology and Educational Practice*, Chicago: Scott Freeman.

Kolb, D. A. (1976). *The Learning Style Inventory*, Boston, Mass.: McBer and Co.

Kolb, D. A. (1978). *The Adaptive Style Inventory*, Boston, Mass.: McBer and Co.

Kolb, D. A. (1984). *Experiential Learning: Experience as a Source of Learning*, Englewood Cliffs, NJ: Prentice-Hall.

Kolb, D. A., I. M. Rubin, and J. M. McIntyre (1984). *Organizational Psychology: an Experimental Approach*, 4th edn, Englewood Cliffs, NJ: Prentice-Hall.

Kozeki, B. (1984). Motives and motivational styles in education. In N. J. Entwistle (ed.), *New Directions in Educational Psychology: Learning and Teaching*, Lewes: Falmer Press.

Kozma, R. B. (1982). Instructional design in a chemistry laboratory course: the impact of structure and aptitudes on performance and attitudes. *Journal of Research in Science Teaching*, **18**, (3), 261–70.

Krathwohl, D. R. *et al.* (1964). *Taxonomy of Educational Objectives: The Classification of Educational Goals*. Volume 2, *Affective Domain*. New York: Mackay.

Kulik, J. A., C. L. C. Kulik, and P. A. Cohen (1979). A meta-analysis of outcome studies of Keller's Personalized Systems of Instruction. *American Psychologist*, **34**, 307–18.

Kulik, J. A., C. L. C. Kulik, and P. A. Cohen (1980). Effectiveness of computer based college teaching: a meta-analysis of findings. *Review of Educational Research*, **50**, 525–44.

Lake, G. (1983). Role playing careers in the technology policy area: some user's notes. *Bulletin of Educational Development and Research*, **25**, 16–17.

Lakoff, G., and M. Johnson (1980). *Metaphors We Live By*, Chicago: University of Chicago Press.

Lam, Y. L. J. (1978). Anxiety reduction correlates of adult learners: a longitudinal study. *Alberta Journal of Educational Research*, **24**, (2), 81–93.

Lane, D. S., K. S. Bull, D. K. Kundert, and D. L. Newman (1987). The effects of knowledge of item arrangement, gender and statistical and cognitive item difficulty on test performance. *Educational and Psychological Measurement*, **47**, (4), 865–880.

Larkin, J. H., and F. Reif (1979). Understanding and teaching problem-solving in physics. *European Journal of Science Education*, **1**, (2), 191–203.

Laurillard, D. M. (1979). The processes of student learning. *Higher Education*, **8**, 359–409.

Laurillard, D. (1984). Learning from problem solving. In F. Marton, D. Hounsell, and J. N. Entwistle (eds), *The Experience of Learning*, Edinburgh: Scottish Academic Press.

Law, B. (1984). *Uses and Abuses of Profiling*, London: Harper and Row.

Lawton, R. (1986). The role of the external examiner, *Journal of Geography in Higher Education*, **10**, (1), 41–51.

Leary, L. F., and N. J. Dorans (1982). *The Effect of Item Re-arrangement on Test Performance: A review of the literature*, Research Report 82–30, Princeton, NJ: Educational Testing Service.

Lee, J. A. (1986). The effects of past computer experience on computerized aptitude test performance. *Educational and Psychological Measurement*, **46**, (3), 727–33.

Lee, J. A., K. E. Moreno, and J. B. Sympson (1986). The effect of mode of test administration on test performance. *Educational and Psychological Measurement*, **46**, (2), 467–74.

Lee, L. S. (1969). *Towards a Classification of the Objectives of Undergraduate Practical Work in Mechanical Engineering*, M. Litt. Thesis, University of Lancaster.

Lee, L. S. (1970). Research report—projects or continuous assignments. *Further Education*, **1**, (3), 117–18.

Lee, W. L. (1982). An experiment to introduce conflicting human values to civil engineering undergraduates. *Engineering Education*, **73**, (3), 289–341.

Leeder, S. R., G. I. Feletti, and C. E. Engel (1979). Assessment—help or hurdle? *Programmed Learning and Educational Technology*, **16**, (4), 308–14.

Lefcourt, H. M. (1976). *Locus of Control. Current Trends in Theory and Research*, Hillsdale, NJ: Lawrence Erlbaum.

Leuba, R. J. (1986). Purposes, principles, and practices. Machine-scored testing, Part 1. *Engineering Education*, **77**, (2), 89–95.

Levine, H. G., and C. H. McGuire (1971). The use of role playing to evaluate affective skills in medicine. *Journal of Medical Education*, **45**, 700–5.

Levine, M. F., and P. L. Wright (1987). Testing transferability of a self-developed teaching effectiveness measure across colleges of business. *Journal of Higher Education*, **48**, (1), 85–100.

Lewin, K. (1936). *Principles of Topological Psychology*, McGraw-Hill, New York.

Lindenlaub, J. C., M. G. Groff and S. Nunke (1981). A hybrid lecture/self-study system for large engineering classes. *Engineering Education*, **72**, (3), 201–7.

Loacker, G. (1987). The power of performance in developing problem solving and self assessment abilities. Paper communicated to the author prior to publication.

Loacker, G., L. L. Cromwell, J. Fry, and D Rutherford (1984). *Analysis and Communication: an Approach to Critical Thinking*, Milwaukee: Alverno Publications.

Loacker, G., L. Cromwell, and K. O'Brien (1986). Assessment in higher education: to serve the learner. In C. Adelman (ed.), *Assessment in Higher Education*, Washington, DC: US Office of Education.

Locke, E. A. (1977). An experimental study of lecture note-taking among college students. *Journal of Educational Research*, **71**, (2), 93–9.

Lockheed, M. E., P. W. Holland, and W. P. Nenceff (1982). *Student Characteristics and the Use of SAT Test Disclosure Materials*, Princeton, NJ: Educational Testing Service.

Lomax, P. (1985). Evaluating for course improvement: a case study, *Assessment and Evaluation in Higher Education*, **10**, (3), 254–64.

Loevinger, J., and R. Wessler (1970). *Measuring Ego Development*, Vol. 1, San Francisco, CA: Jossey-Bass.

Lonergan, B. (1954). *Insight*, London: Darton, Longman and Todd.

Lonergan, B. (1971). *Method in Theology*, London: Darton, Longman and Todd.

Long, H. B. (1983). Academic performance, attitudes, and social relations in inter-generational college classes. *Educational Gerontology*, **9**, 471–81.

Long, S. (1976). Sociopolitical ideology as a determinant of students' perception of the university. *Higher Education*, **5**, (4), 423–35.

Lord, F. M., and M. R. Novick (1968). *Statistical Theories of Mental Test Scores*, Reading, Mass.: Addison-Wesley.

Lower, S. K. (1981). An audio-tutorial approach to the teaching of physical chemistry and electrochemistry. *Journal of Chemical Education*, **58**, (10), 773–6.

Lublin, J. R. (1980). Student assessment: a case study. *Assessment and Evaluation in Higher Education*, **5**, (3), 264–72.

Luchins, A. S. (1942). Mechanisation in problem-solving: the effect of 'Einstellung'. *Psychological monographs No. 248*.

Lumsden, J. (1977). Person reliability. *Applied Psychological Measurement*, 1, 477–82.

Lumsden, J. (1978). Tests are perfectly reliable. *British Journal of Mathematical and Statistical Psychology*, **31**, 19–26.

Lumsden, J. (1980). Variation on a theme by Thurstone. *Applied Psychological Measurement*, **4**, 1–7.

Lyons, N. P. (1983). Two perspectives: on self, relationships and morality. *Harvard Educational Review*, **53**, (2), 125–45.

McAshan, H. H. (1970). *Writing Behavioural Objectives: A New Approach*, New York: Harper and Row.

McBean, E. A., and C. Lennox (1982). Issues of teaching effectiveness as observed via course critiques. *Higher Education*, **11**, (6), 645–55.

McCauley, M. H., E. S. Godleski, C. F. Yokomoto, and E. D. Sloan (1983). Applications of psychological type in engineering education. *Engineering Education*, **73**, (5), 394–400.

McClelland, D. C. (1953). *The Achievement Motive*, New York: Appleton-Century-Crofts.

McClelland, D. C. (1980). Motive dispositions: the merits of operant and respondent measures. In L. Wheeler (ed.), *Review of Personality and Social Psychology*, Vol. 1, Beverly Hills, CA: Sage.

McClelland, D., J. Atkinson, R. Clark, and E. J. Lowell (1953). *The Achievement Motive*, New York: Appleton-Century-Crofts.

McClelland, D. C., and C. Dailey (1973). *Evaluating New Methods of Measuring the Qualities needed in Superior Foreign Service Information Officers*, Boston, Mass.: McBer and Co.

McConnell, D. M. (1983). Students' construction of a human biology degree course. *Journal of Biological Education*, **17**, (2), 143–8.

McConnell, T. R. (1962). *A General Pattern of American Higher Education*, New York: McGraw-Hill.

McCord, M. T. (1985). Methods and theories of instruction. In J. H. Smart (ed.), *Higher Education: Handbook of Theory and Research*, Vol. 1, New York: Agathon Press.

MacDonald, F. (1969). *Educational Psychology*, California: Wadsworth.

McDonald, R., and D. Sanson (1979). Use of assignment attachments in assessment. *Assessment in Higher Education*, **5**, (1), 45–55.

McDonald, R. J., and E. G. Taylor (1980). Student note-taking and lecture handouts in veterinary medical education. *Journal of Veterinary Medical Education*, **7**, (3), 157–61.

McElroy, A. R., and F. C. McNaughton (1979). A project based approach to the use of biological literature. *Journal of Biological Education*, **13**, (1), 52–7.

MacFarlane Smith, I. (1964). *Spatial Ability*, London: University of London Press.

MacFarlane Smith, I. (1979). Precis and discussion of a trilogy of papers by Dr J. E. Bogen entitled *The Other Side of the Brain*, Unpublished paper, Garnett College, London.

McGaghie, W. C., G. E. Miller, A. W. Sajid, and T. V. Telder (1978). *Competency-based curriculum development in medical education: An Introduction*, Geneva: World Health Organization.

McGaw, B. (1984). The changing secondary school: developing new arrangements and relationships with tertiary institutions. In J. E. Anwyl and G. S. Harman (eds), *Setting the Agenda for Australian Tertiary Education*, Centre for the study of Higher Education, University of Melbourne.

McGuire, C. H. (1980). Assessment of problem-solving skills. *Medical Teacher*, **2**, (2), 74–9.

McGuire, C. H., and I. M. Soloman (1971). *Clinical Simulation: Selected Problems in Patient Management*, New York: Appleton-Century-Crofts.

McKeachie, W. J. (1974). Instructional psychology. *Annual Review of Psychology*, **25**, 161–93.

McKeachie, W. J. (1983). Student anxiety, learning and achievement. *Engineering Education*, **73**, (7), 724–30.

MacMahon, J. (1988). Unpublished work for thesis, University of Dublin.

McMorris, R. F., J. A. Brown, G. W. Snyder, and R. M. Pruzek (1972). Effects of violating stem construction principles. *Journal of Educational Measurement*, **9**, (4), 287–95.

McPeck, J. (1981). *Critical Thinking and Education*, New York: St Martins Press.

McVey, P. J. (1975). The errors in marking examination scripts. *International Journal of Electrical Engineering Education*, **12**, (3), 203.

McVey, P. J. (1976a). Standard error of the mark for an examination paper in electronic engineering. *Proceedings Institution of Electrical Engineers*, **123**, (8), 843–44.

McVey, P. (1976b). The 'paper error' of two examinations in electronic engineering. *Physics Education*, **11**, 58–60.

Madaus, J., and J. MacNamara (1970). *Public Examinations*, Dublin: Government Publications.

Main, A. (1980). *Encouraging Effective Learning*, Edinburgh: Scottish Academic Press.

Malleson, N. (1965). *A Handbook of British Student Health Services*, London: Pitman.

Marchesse, T. (1985). Learning about assessment. *AAHE Bulletin*, September, 10–13.

Marinker, M. (1984). Matters arising. *Family Practice*, **1**, (3), 191–9.

Marlin, J. W. (1987). Student perception of end-of-course evaluations, *Journal of Higher Education*, **58**, (6), 704–716.

Marris, P. (1964). *The Experience of Higher Education*, London: Routledge and Kegan Paul.

Marsh, C. (1981). The assessment of skills in research methods. *Sociology*, **15**, (4), 519–25.

Marsh, H. W. (1982). Factors affecting students' evaluations of the same course taught by the same instructor on different occasions. *American Educational Research Journal*, **19**, (4), 485–97.

Marshall, J. C., and J. M. Powers (1969). Writing neatness, composition errors and essay grades. *Journal of Educational Measurement*, **6**, (2), 97–101.

Marshall, S. (1980). Cognitive-affective dissonance in the classroom. *Teaching Political Science*, **8**, (1), 111–17.

Marshall, T. H. (1963). Professionalism in relation to social structure policy. In *Sociology at the Crossroads*, London: Heinemann.

Marton, F. (1976). Study skills and learning. *Educational Development*, No. 1. Institute of Education, University of Goteborg.

Marton, F., D. Hounsell, and N. J. Entwistle (1984). *The Experience of Learning*, Edinburgh: Scottish Academic Press.

Marton, F., and R. Säljö (1976). On qualitative 1. outcomes and process 2. outcomes as a function of the learner's conception of the task. *British Journal of Educational Psychology*, **46**, 4–11, and **46**, 115–27.

Marton, F., and R. Säljö (1984). Approaches to learning. In F. Marton, D. Hounsell, and N. J. Entwistle (eds), *The Experience of Learning*, Edinburgh: Scottish Academic Press.

Masciantonio, R. (1977). Tangible benefits of the study of Latin: a review of research. *Foreign Language Annals*, **10**, (4).

Mathias, H., and D. Rutherford (1982). Lecturers as evaluators. The Birmingham experience. *Studies in Higher Education*, **7**, (1), 67–76.

Matthews, G. B. (1980). *Philosophy and the Young Child*, Chapter 6, Cambridge, Mass.: Harvard University Press.

Mayfield, E. C. (1964). The selection interview—a re-evaluation of published research. *Personal Psychology*, **17**, 239–60.

Meier, R. S., L. C. Perkowski, and C. S. Wynne (1982). A method for training simulated patients. *Journal of Medical Education*, **57**, (7), 535–40.

Melton, R. F. (1981). Individualized learning methods in perspective. *Higher Education*, **10**, (4), 403–23.

Mentkowski, M. (1988). Paths to integrity: educating for professional growth and performance in S. Sribastda (Ed) and assocs, *Executive Integrity. The Search for High Human Values in Organisational Life*. San Francisco: London.

Mentkowski, M., V. DeBack, J. M. Bishop, Z. Allen, and B. Blanton (1980). *Developing a Professional Competence Model for Nursing Education*, (NIE-G-77-0058), Milwaukee: Alverno Productions.

Mentkowski, M., and A. Doherty (1983). *Careering After College: Establishing the Validity of Abilities Learned in College for Later Careering and Professional Performance*, Final Report to the National Institute for Education, Milwaukee: Alverno Productions.

Mentkowski, M., N. Much, and L. Giencke-Holl (1983). *Careering After College: Perspective on Life Long Learning and Career Development*, NIE-G-77-0058, Milwaukee: Alverno Productions.

Mentkowski, M., and G. P. Rogers (1985). Longitudinal assessment of critical thinking in college: what measures assess curricular impact. Paper at the Mid-Western Educational Research Association, Chicago, October.

Mentkowski, M., M. J. Strait (1983). *A Longitudinal Study of Student Change in Cognitive Development, Learning Styles, and Generic Abilities in an Outcome-centered Liberal Arts Curriculum*, (NIE-G-77-0058), Milwaukee: Alverno Productions.

Messick, S., and Associates (1976). *Individuality in Learning: Implications of Cognitive Styles and Creativity for Human Development*, San Francisco, CA: Jossey-Bass.

Messick, S., A. Beaton, and F. Lord (1983). *A New Design for a New Era*, Princeton, NJ: Educational Testing Service.

Meuwese, W. (1968). Measurement of industrial engineering objectives. 16th International Congress of Applied Psychology, Amsterdam.

Meuwese, W. (1971). *Construction and Evaluation of a Course in Technical Mechanics*, Committee for Higher Education (ccc/ESR (71) 14), Council of Europe, Strasbourg.

Meyer, M. (1908). The grading of students. *Science*, **28**, (712), 243–50.

Michaels, S., and T. R. Kieran (1973). An investigation of open and closed book examinations in mathematics. *Alberta Journal of Educational Research*, **19**, (3), 202–7.

Mihkelson, A. (1985). Computer assisted instruction in remedial teaching in first year chemistry. *Education in Chemistry*, **22**, (4), 117–18.

Miller, R. I. (1979). *The Assessment of College Performance*, San Francisco, CA: Jossey-Bass.

Miller, S. (1983). A workshop that works: maths remediation. *Improving College and University Teaching*, **31**, (4), 172–5.

Miller, T. K., and J. S. Prince (1978). *The Future of Student Affairs: A Guide to Student Development for Tomorrow's Education*, San Francisco, CA: Jossey-Bass.

Milton, O., and J. W. Edgerley (1976). The testing and grading of students, *Change Magazine*, New Rochelle, New York.

Milton, O., H. R. Pollio, and J. A. Eison (1986). *Making Sense of College Grades*, San Francisco, CA: Jossey-Bass.

Mines, R. A. (1982). Student development assessment techniques. In G. R. Hanson (ed.), *New Directions in Student Services: Measuring Student Development*, No. 20, San Francisco, CA: Jossey-Bass.

Mitchell, J. V. (1986). Relationships between attitudes towards higher education and life values. *Assessment and Evaluation in Higher Education*, **11**, (2), 93–104.

Mitchell, K., and J. Anderson (1986). Reliability of holistic scoring for the MCAT essay. *Educational and Psychological Measurement*, **46**, (3), 771–5.

Mitchelmore, M. C. (1981). Reporting student achievement: how many grades? *British Journal of Educational Psychology*, **51**, (2), 218–27.

Monk, J. D. (1972). *An Investigation into the Role of the Design Function in the Education, Training and Course Patterns of Professional Engineers*, M. Litt. thesis, University of Lancaster.

Moodie, G. C. (ed.) (1986). *Standards and Criteria in Higher Education*, Guildford: Society for Research into Higher Education.

Moon, J. A. (1968). *The Ethical Attitudes of Chartered Mechanical Engineers and their Relationship to Formal Education*, M. Litt. thesis, Univeristy of Lancaster.

Moran, G. (1984). *Religious Education Development: Images for the Future*. Minneapolis: Winston Press.

Morante, E. A., and A. Ulesky (1984). Assessment of reasoning abilities. *Educational Leadership*, **42**, (1), 71–4.

384

Morasky, R. I. (1973). Evaluation in industrial programming systems. Paper presented at the 1973 International Symposium on Education Testing,. The Hague, Netherlands.

Morehouse, W., and P. Boyd-Bowman (1973). *Independent Study of Critical Languages in Undergraduate Colleges*, Washington, DC: Institute of International Studies.

Moreira, M. A. (1985). Concept mapping. An alternative strategy for evaluation. *Assessment and Evaluation in Higher Education*, **10**, (2), 159–68.

Morgan, A. W., and B. L. Mitchell (1985). The quest for excellence; underlying policy issues. In J. C. Smart (ed.), *Higher Education Handbook of Theory and Research*, New York: Agathon Press.

Morgan, S. V., and J. T. Puglisi (1982). Enhancing memory for lecture sentences; a depth processing perspective. *Psychological Reports*, **51**, 675–78.

Morris, L. W., and R. M. Liebert (1969). Effects of anxiety on timed and untimed tests: another look. *Journal of Consulting and Clinical Psychology*, **33**, 240–44.

Morris, L. W., and W. B. Engle (1981). Assessing various coping strategies and their effects on test performance and anxiety. *Journal of Clinical Psychology*, **37**, (1), 165–71.

Morrison, D. L. (1985). The effect of cognitive style and training on fault diagnosis performance. *Programmed Learning and Educational Technology*, **22**, (2), 132–9.

Morrison, R. B. (1974). Item analysis and question validation. In H. G. Macintosh (ed.), *Techniques and Problems of Assessment*, London: Edward Arnold.

Moses, I. (1985). *Supervising Post-graduates*. HERDSA, Green Guide No. 3, Kensington, New South Wales.

Mowbray, R. M., and B. M. Davies (1967). Short note and essay examinations. *British Journal of Medical Education*, **1**, 356–8.

Mrozik, C. (1984). Matters arising. *Family Practice*, **1**, (3), 191–6.

Much, N., and M. Mentkowski (1982). *Student Perspectives on Liberal Learning at Alverno College: Justifying Learning as Relevant to Performance in Personal and Professional Roles*, (NIE-G-77-0058), Milwaukee: Alverno Productions.

Murphy, D. E. (1974). In Heywood, J. *Assessment in History*, School of Education; University of Dublin.

Murphy, D. E. (1976). *Problems Associated with a New National System of Assessment*, M. Ed. thesis, University of Dublin.

Murphy, R. J. L. (1982). A further report of investigations into the reliability of marking of GCE examinations. *British Journal of Educational Psychology*, **52**, (1), 58–63.

Murray, H. G. (1984). The impact of formative and summative evaluation of teaching in North American universities. *Assessment and Evaluation in Higher Education*, **9**, (2), 117–32.

Murray Thomas, R. (1985). *Comparing Theories of Child Development*, California: Wadsworth.

Muscatine Committee (1968). (A committee of the University of California, Berkeley). *Education at Berkeley: Report of a Select Committee on Education*, Berkeley, CA: University of California Press.

Nadler, G., and A. Seirig (1982). Professional engineering education in the classroom. *Engineering Education*, **72**, (8), 781–6.

Nathenson, M. B., and E. S. Henderson (1981). *Using Student Feedback to Improve Learning Materials*, Beckenham: Croom Helm,

National Union of Students (1968). *Briefing on Wastage* and also (1967) *Executive Report on Examinations*, London: National Union of Students.

NCES (National Center for Education Statistics) (1985). *Indicators of Education Status and Trends*, Washington, DC: US Department of Education.

Nelson-Jones, R., and H. L. Toner (1977). *A Study of First Year University of Aston Students as Learners*, Department of Educational Enquiry, University of Aston, Birmingham.

Nelson-Jones, R., H. L. Toner, and P. Coxhead (1979). An exploration of students' sense of learning competence. *British Educational Research Journal*, **5**, (2), 175–83.

Nevo, B., and M. Spector (1979). Personal tempo in taking tests of the multiple choice type. *Journal of Educational Research*, **73**, (2), 75–8.

Nevo, B., and J. Sfez (1985). Examiners' feedback questionnaire. *Assessment and Evaluation in Higher Education*, **10**, (3), 236–49.

Newble, D. I. (1983). The critical incident technique: a new approach to critical performance. *Medical Education*.

Newble, D. I., J. Hoare, and P. F. Sheldrake (1980). The selection and training of examiners for clinical examinations. *Medical Education*, **14**, 345–9.

Newman, J. H. (1947 edition). *The Idea of a University*, London: Longman Green.

NGA (1986). *The Governors 1991 Report on Education*, National Governors' Association Centre for Policy Research and Analysis.

NIE (1984). *Involvement in Learning: Realizing the Potential of American Higher Education*, Study group on the conditions of excellence in American higher education, National Institute of Education, US Department of Education.

Nightingale, P. (1984). Examination of research theses. *Higher Education Research and Development*, **3**, (2), 137–50.

Nisbet, J. (1986). Staff and standards. In G. C. Moodie (ed.), *Standards and Criteria in Higher Education*, Guildford: Society for Research into Higher Education.

Norton, L. S. (1981). The effects of note-taking and subsequent use of long term recall. *Programmed Learning and Educational Technology*, **18**, (1), 16–22.

Novak, J. D., and D. B. Gowin (1984). *Learning How to Learn*, New York: Cambridge University Press.

Nuttall, D. L. (1986). Problems in the measurement of change. In D. L. Nuttall (ed.), *Assessing Educational Achievement*, Lewes: Falmer Press.

Nye, P. A. (1978). Student variables in relation to note-taking during a lecture. *Programmed Learning and Educational Technology*, **5**, (3), 196–200.

Nyberg, V. R., and A. M. Nyberg (1978). *Technical Report on the Alberta Essay Scales*, Edmonton, Alberta: Alberta Education.

Nyberg, V. R., and A. M. Nyberg (1980). Reliability of the Alberta essay scales, *Alberta Journal of Educational Research*, **26**, (1) 64–7.

Oakeshott, M. (1962). *Rationalism in Politics and Other Essays*, London: Methuen.

Obenshain, S., and A. G. Rezler (1987). Medical self assessment center at the University of New Mexico. Paper at AAHE Conference, Denver, American Association for Higher Education, Washington, DC.

Oltman, P. K. (1982). *Content Representativeness of the GRE advanced Tests in Chemistry, Computer Science and Education*, GREB 81–12p, Princeton, NJ: Educational Testing Services.

O'Neil, J. P. (1983). Examinations and quality control. In J. Warren (ed.), *Meeting the New Demands for Standards*, San Francisco, CA: Jossey-Bass.

Oosterhof, A. C., and P. K. Coats (1984). Comparison of difficulties and reliabilities of quantitative word problems in completion and multiple-choice item formats. *Applied Psychological Measurement*, **8**, 287–94.

Oppenheim, A. M., M. Jahoda, and R. L. James (1967). Assumptions underlying the use of university examinations. *Universities Quarterly*, **21**, (3), 241.

Orton, A. (1983). Students' understanding of integration. *Educational Studies in Mathematics*, **14**, (1), 1–18.

Owen, S. V., and R. D. Freeman (1987). What's wrong with three-option multiple choice items. *Educational and Psychological Measurement*, **47**, (2), 513–22.

Oxenham, J. (1984). *Education Versus Qualifications: A Study in Developing Countries of Relationships between Education, Selection for Employment and the Productivity of Labour*. London: Allen and Unwin.

386

Pace, C. R., and L. Baird (1966). Attainment patterns in the environmental press of college sub-cultures. In T. Newcomb and E. Wilson (eds), *College Peer Groups*, Chicago: Aldine.

Palmer, B. G. (1970). The use and efficiency of continuous assessment. In *Examining Modern Languages*, CILT Report No. 4, London: Centre for Information on Language Teaching.

Palmier, L. (1982). Occupations of Indonesian graduates, *Higher Education*, **11**, (6), 685–712.

Parlett, M., and D. Hamilton (1972). *Evaluation as Illumination: A New Approach to the Study of Innovatory Programmes*, Centre for Research in Education Sciences, Edinburgh University.

Pascarella, E. T. (1985). College environmental influences on learning and cognitive development. A critical review and synthesis. In J. C. Smart (ed.), *Higher Education: Handbook of Theory and Research*, Vol. 1, New York: Agathon Press, pp. 1–63.

Pascarella, E., and P. Terenzini (1982). Contextual analysis as a method for assessing residence group effects. *Journal of College Student Personnel*, **23**, 108–14.

Pask, G. (1977). *Learning Styles, Educational Strategies and Representations of Knowledge: Methods and Applications*, Progress Report No. 3, Social Science Research Council, Richmond, Surrey: Systems Resear ·

Paul, R. (1986). Dialogical thinking. Critical thought essential to the acquisition of rational knowledge and passions. In J. B. Baron and R. J. Sternberg (eds), *Teaching Thinking Skills: Theory and Practice*, New York: Freeman.

Pazdernik, T. L., and E. J. Walaszek (1983). A computer-assisted teaching system in pharmacology for health profession. *Journal of Medical Education*, **58**, (4), 341–8.

Pearson, M. (1983). Approaches to individualising instruction: a review. *Higher Education Research and Development*, **2**, (2), 155–81.

Pearson, M., and D. J. Carswell (1979). Student evaluation of Utopia. *Education in Chemistry*, **15**, (3), 84.

Pearson, M., P. McNeil, C. Magarey, and J. Powell (1977). *The Development of Film Material and Testing Procedures to Assess Students' Interpersonal Skills*, Tertiary Education Centre, University of New South Wales, Sydney.

Perry, W. G. (1970). *Intellectual and Ethical Development in College Years: A Scheme*, New York: Holt, Rinehart and Winston.

Persig, R. M. (1974). *Zen and the Art of Motorcycle Maintenance: An Inquiry into Values*, New York: William Morrow.

Petch, J. A. (1961). *GCE and Degreee—Part I* and *GCE and degree—Part II*, Manchester: Joint Matriculation Board.

Phillips, J. L. (1982). Do students think as we do? Progress with Piaget. *Improving College and University Teaching*, **30**, (4), 154–8.

Pinsky, S., and R. Weigel (1983). Engineering, a stress management plan for advisers. *Engineering Education*, **73**, (7), 742–5.

Piper, D. W. (1985). Enquiry into the role of external examiners. *Studies in Higher Education*, **10**, (3), 331–42.

Please, N. W. (1971). Estimation of the proportion of candidates who are wrongly graded. *British Journal of Mathematical and Statistical Psychology*, **24**, (2), 230–8.

Plovnick, M. A. (1971). *A Cognitive Ability Theory of Occupational Roles*, Sloan School of Management, Massachusetts Institute of Technology, Working paper, 524–571.

Pole, K. E. (1969). *A Study of Techniques for Measuring Creative Ability and the Development and Validation of Creativity Tests for Highly Intelligent Subjects*, B. Litt. thesis, University of Oxford.

Polya, G. (1957). *How to Solve it: A New Aspect of Mathematical Method*, Princeton, NJ: Princeton University Press.

Posner, G. (1977). The assessment of cognitive structure. *Curriculum Series Research Report No. 5*, Department of Education, Cornell University.

Powell, J. P. (1981). Helping and hindering learning. *Higher Education*, **10**, (1), 103–17.

Powers, D. E., and M. K. Enright (1987). Analytical reasoning skills in graduate study: perceptions of faculty in six fields, *Journal of Higher Education*, **58**, (6), 658–82.

Pradeep, B. and M. F. Rubenstein (1973). A systems approach to the design of an interdisciplinary course. *Journal of Engineering Education* **68**, 283.

Prescott, B. and B. Jarvis (1978). Continuous teaching and assessment: two stage assignments in a full credit course. *Teaching at a Distance*, **12**, 10–25.

Prosser, M. T. (1979). Tertiary science instructional materials: a cognitive analysis. *Research and Development in Higher Education*, **1**, 127–142.

Prosser, M. T., and D. Oliver (1983). Making the process and criteria of tertiary science project assessments more explicit. *Assessment and Evaluation in Higher Education*, **8**, (1), 29–41.

Pulich, M. A. (1983). Student grade appeals can be reduced. *Improving College and University Teaching*, **31**, (1), 9–12.

Purves, A. C. (1961). Literary criticism, testing and the English teacher. Quoted by Iliffe (1966).

Raaheim, K., and J. A. Wankowski (1981). *Helping Students to Learn at University*, Bergen: Sigma Forlag.

Ramsden, P. (1979). Student learning and perception of the academic environment. *Higher Education*, **8**, 411–28. (See also Chapter 9 of reference (63).)

Ramsden, P. (1984). The context of learning. In F. Morton, D. Hounsell, and N. Entwistle (eds), *The Experience of Learning*, Edinburgh: Scottish Academic Press.

Ramsden, P., and N. Entwistle (1981). Effects of academic departments on students' approaches to studying. *British Journal of Educational Psychology*, **51**, 368–83.

Ratzlaff, H. C. (1980). Upgrading grading practices. *Improving College and University Teaching*, **28**, (2), 81–4.

Rawls, J. A., O. Perry, and E. O. Timmons (1966). Study of conventional instruction and individual programmed instruction in the classroom. *Journal of Applied Psychology*, **50**, (5), 388–91.

Rees, L., and F. Reid (1977). *The Development and Evaluation of Study Skills Courses for Students in Higher Education*, Conference on Educational Development Services in Polytechnics, c/o PETRAS, Newcastle-upon-Tyne. Occasional Paper No. 4.

Renner, J., R. Fuller, J. Lockhead, J. Johns, C. Tomlinson-Keasey, and T. Campbell (1976). *Test of Cognitive Development*, Norman, Oklahoma: University of Oklahoma.

Renner, J. W. (1964). Learning, motivation and Piaget. *Engineering Education*, **64**, (6), 416.

Renner, J. W., and A. E. Lawson (1973). Piagetian theory and instruction and physics. *The Physics Teacher*, **11**, (3), 165.

Renner, R. R., G. Greenwood, and C. Schott (1986). Responsible behaviour as effective teaching: a new look at student rating of professors, *Assessment and Evaluation in Higher Education*, **11**, (2), 138–45.

Resnick, D., and M. Goulden (1987). Paper presented at the American Association for Higher Education Second National Conference on Assessment in Higher Education, Denver. An earlier edition is to be published in D. Halpern (ed.), *Student Outcomes Assessment. A Tool for Improving Teaching and Learning*, San Francisco, CA: Jossey-Bass.

Resnick, L. B., and D. P. Resnick (1982). *Standards, Curriculum and Performance: A Historical and Comparative Perspective*, A report to the National Commission on Excellence in Higher Education.

388

Riesman, D., and C. Jencks (1962). The viability of the American college. In N. Sanford (ed.), *The American College*, New York: Wiley.

Richmond, K. (1963). *Culture and General Education*, London: Methuen.

Ridd, T. (1983). *Marking A-level History, Syllabus A*, Manchester: Joint Matriculation Board.

Rist, R. C. (1987). Review of qualitative methodology and sociology. *Educational and Psychological Measurement*, **47**, (1), 279–81.

Robbins Lord (Chairman) (1963). *Higher Education*, Report of a Committee of the Privy Council, Cmnd 2165, London: HMSO. (*NB*: The research appendices are published in separate volumes.)

Robinson, F. P. (1946). *Effective Study*, New York: Harper.

Roderick, G., and T. Bilham (1982). The intake of mature students to undergraduate degree courses at British universities: trends (1974–80). *Studies in Higher Education*, **7**, (2), 119–31.

Rohlen, T. P. (1983). *Japan's High Schools*, Berkeley, CA: University of California Press.

Roizen, J., and M. Jepson (1985). *Degrees to Jobs: Employer Expectations of Higher Education*, Guildford: Society for Research into Higher Education.

Roller, D. R., R. Giardina, G. Herman, and G. Woditsch (1972). The first year of the first little college. *Journal of Higher Education*, **43**, (5), 337.

Rose, H. A., and C. F. Elton (1966). Another look at college drop out. *Journal of Counselling Psychology*, **17**, 56–62.

Rutsohn, J. (1978). Understanding personality types: does it matter? *Improving College and University Teaching*, **26**, (4), 249–54.

Ryle, A., and M. Lungi (1968). A psychometric study of academic difficulty and psychometric illness. *British Journal of Psychiatry*, **114**, 47.

Ryle, A. (1969). *Student Casualties*, London: Allen Lane.

Säljö, R. (1979). Learning about learning in higher education. *Higher Education*, **8**, (4), 443–451.

Samuelowicz, K. (1983). Assessment of project and laboratory work: a draft bibliography. *Labyrinth*, **12**, 1–8.

Sarason, I. G., and R. Stoops (1978). Test anxiety and the passage of time. *Journal of Consulting and Clinical Psychology*, **46**, 102–9.

Sarnacki, R. E. (1979). An examination of testwiseness in cognitive test domain. *Review of Educational Research*, **2**, 252–79.

Saul, B. (1987). At last. A hope of change for our students. *The Times*, 15 April,

Saupé, J. (1961). Learning. In P. Dressel (ed.), *Evaluation in Higher Education*, Boston, Mass.: Houghton Mifflin.

Scheffler, I. (1977). In praise of the cognition emotions. *Teachers' College Record*, **79**, (2), 171–86.

Schein, E. H. (1965). *Organisational Psychology*, Englewood Cliffs, NJ: Prentice-Hall.

Schenkat, R., and K. Tyser (1986). Are teachers ready to teach pupils to think? *Education Week*, 9 April, 24.

Schurr, K. T., A. S. Ellen, and V. E. Ruble (1987). Actual course difficulty as a factor accounting for the achievement and attrition of college students. *Educational and Psychological Measurement*, **47**, (4), 1049–1054.

Seneca, J. J., and M. K. Taussig (1987). Educational quality, access, and tuition policy at state universities. *Journal of Higher Education*, **58**, (1), 25–37.

Shaha, S. H. (1984). Matching tests: reduced anxiety and increased test-effectiveness. *Educational and Psychological Measurement*, **44**, (4), 469–481.

Shale, D., and D. Cowper (1982). A computer-based support system for mastery instruction. *Assessment and Evaluation in Higher Education*, **7**, (2), 167–80.

Shattock, M. L. (1986). The UGC and standards. In G. C. Moodie (ed.), *Standards and Criteria in Higher Education*, Guildford: Society for Research into Higher Education.

herman, T. M. (1980). *Instructional Decision Making: A Guide to Responsive Instruction*, Englewood Cliffs, NJ: Educational Technology Publications.

herman, T. M. (1984). *Proven Strategies for Effective Learning*, Columbus, Ohio: Bobbs-Merrill.

herman, T. M. (1985). Learning improvement programs: a review of controllable influences. *Journal of Higher Education*, **56**, (1), 85–100.

herman, T. M., L. P. Armistead, F. Fowler, M. A. Barksdale, and G. Reif (1987). The quest for excellence in university teaching. *Journal of Higher Education*, **48**, (1), 66–84.

herrin, D. C., and T. R. Long (1972). The educator's dilemma: what makes Clyde want to learn? *Journal of Engineering Education*, **63**, (3), 188.

hulman, L. S. (1970). Psychology and mathematics. In E. Begle (ed.), *Mathematics and Education*, 69th Year Book of the National Society of the Study of Education, Chicago: Chicago University Press.

HTA (1977). *Pupils in Profile*. For the Head Teachers Association of Scotland, Scottish Educational Research Association, London: Hodder and Stoughton.

igman, E., and P. K. Oltman (1976). *Field Dependence and the Role of Visual Framework in the Perception of Size*, Princeton, NJ: Educational Testing Service.

ilk, J., and S. Bowlby (1981). The use of project work in undergraduate teaching. *Journal of Geography in Higher Education*, **5**, (2), 155–62.

ims, R., J. G. Veres, P. Watson, and K. E. Buckner (1986). The reliability and classification stability of the learning style inventory, *Educational and Psychological Measurement*, **46**, (3), 753–60.

kager, R. (1982). On the use and importance of tests of ability in admission to post-secondary education. In A. K. Wigdor and W. R. Garner (eds), *Ability Testing: Uses, Consequences and Controversies*, Washington, DC: National Academy Press.

kinner, P., and J. Tafel (1986). Promoting excellence in undergraduate education in Ohio. *Journal of Higher Education*, **57**, (1) 93–105.

mart, J. (1986). College effects on occupational status attainment, *Research in Higher Education*, **24**, (1), 73–96.

mith, C. H. (1976). *Mode III. Examinations in the CSE and GCE. A Survey of Current Practice*, London: Evans/Methuen (School Council).

mith, J. K. (1982). Converging on correct answers: a peculiarity of multiple choice items. *Journal of Educational Measurement*, **3**, 211–20.

mith, R. M. (1986). Reason fit in the Rasch model. *Educational and Psychological Measurement*, **46**, 359–72.

mithers, A. G. (1976). *Sandwich Courses: An Integrated Education?* Windsor: National Foundation for Educational Research.

mithers, A. G., and A. Griffin (1986). *The Progress of Mature Students*, Manchester: Joint Matriculation Board.

peilberger, C. D. (ed.) (1966). *Anxiety and Behaviour*, New York: Academic Press.

peilberger, C. D., H. Gonzalez, P. Taylor, C. J. and W. D. Anton. Examination stress and anxiety. In C. D. Speilberger and I. G. Sarason (eds), *Stress and Anxiety*, Vol. 5, New York: Hemisphere/Wiley.

pivey, B. E. (1971). A technique to determine curriculum content. *Journal of Medical Education*, **46**, 269–74.

tancato, R. A., and C. F. Eizler (1983). When a 'C' is not a 'C'. The psychological meaning of grades in educational psychology. *Journal of Instructional Psychology*, **10**, 158–62.

tarch, D., and E. C. Elliott (1912). Reliability of grading high school work in English *School Review*, **20**, 442–57.

tarch, D., and E. C. Elliott (1913a). Reliability of grading work in mathematics *School Review*, **21**, 254–9.

Starch D., and E. C. Elliott (1913b). Reliability of grading work in history. *Sch* *Review*, **21**, 676–81.

Starr, J. M. (1968). Final examination versus cumulative assessment in a postgradu education course: a comparative study. *The Durham Research Review*, **5**, (2), 239–4

Steinaker, N., and M. R. Bell (1969). *An Experiential Taxonomy*, New York: Acaden Press.

Stephenson, B., and C. Hunt (1977). Intellectual and ethical development: a dualis curriculum intervention for college students. *Counselling Psychologist*, **6**, 39–42.

Sternberg, R. J. (1985). Beyond IQ. *A Triarchic Theory of Intelligence*, Cambrid Cambridge University Press.

Sternberg, R. J. (1984). How can we teach intelligence? *Educational Leadership*, **42**, 38–50.

Stevens, J., and J. Aleamoni (1986). The role of weighting in the use of aggregate scor *Educational and Psychological Measurement*, **44**, (3) 523–32.

Stewart, A. (1977a). *Analysis of Argument: An Empirically-derived Measure of Intell tual Flexibility*. Boston, Mass: McBer and Co.

Stewart, A. (1977b). Scoring manual for stages of psychological adaptation to t environment. Unpublished manuscript, Department of Psychology, Boston Univ sity.

Stewart, I. C. (1980). A modified version of the Keller plan in an advanced financ accounting course. *Accounting and Finance*, **20**, (2), 111–23.

Stice, J. E. (1979a). Grades and test scores, do they predict adult achieveme *Engineering Education*, **69**, (5), 390–93.

Stice, J. E. (1979b). PSI and Bloom's mastery model: a review and comparis *Engineering Education*, 175.

Strassman, H. D., A. Nies, and E. McDonald (1967). An attitudinal objective: measurement through the use of taxonomy. *Journal of Medical Education*, **42**, 20

Straton, R. G., and R. M. Catts (1980). A comparison of two-, three- and four-cho item tests given a fixed total number of choices. *Educational and Psychologi Measurement*, **40**, 357–65.

Strong, F., Dean of Freshmen of the California Institute of Technology in a letter to Milton. (Milton *et al.* (1986).)

Sutton, C. A. (1980). The learner's prior knowledge: a critical review of techniques probing its organisation. *European Journal of Science Education*, **20**, (2), 107–20.

Sutton, R. A. (1977). The interface between school and university. *Physics Educati* **12**, (5), 304–10.

Svinicki, M. D., and N. M. Dixon (1987). The Kolb model modified for classro activities, *College Teaching*, **35**, (4), 141–6.

Szafran, R. F. (1981). Question pool study guides. *Teaching Sociology*, **9**, (1) 31–43

Taba, H., and F. F. Freeman (1964). Teaching strategies and thought process *Teachers' College Record*, **65**, 524–34.

Taylor, H. (1977). Differences in grading systems among universities. *The Canad Journal of Higher Education*, **7**, (1), 47–54.

TDR (1976). *Computerised Item Banking System Handbook*, Test Development a Research Unit, University of Cambridge Local Examinations Syndicate.

Thomas, P. R., and J. D. Bain (1982). Consistency in learning strategies. *Hig Education*, **11**, (3), 249–59.

Thomas, R. (1980). Assigning grades more fairly. *Proceedings 1981 ASEE Ann Conference*, Vol. 2, pp. 705–15.

Thomas, R. (1984). Examination of a formula method for assigning letter grac *Engineering Education*, 673–5.

Thompson, D. (1969). *The Aims of History*, London: Thames and Hudson.

Thompson, D. J., and R. R. Rentz (1973). The large scale essay testing: implications test construction and evaluation. Mimeo, International Symposium on Educatio Testing, The Hague, Netherlands.

Thompson, P., and G. M. Borrello (1986). Construct validity of the Myers–Briggs type indicator, *Educational and Psychological Measurement*, **46**, (3), 745–52.

Thorndike, R. L., and E. R. Hagen (1977). *Measurement and Evaluation in Psychology and Education*, New York: Wiley.

Thornton, G. C., and W. C. Byham (1983). *Assessment Centres and Managerial Performance*, New York: Academic Press.

Thune, L. E., and S. L. Ericksen (1960). Studies in abstraction learning: IV. The transfer effects of conceptual versus rote instruction in a simulated classroom situation. *Office of Naval Research Technical Report No. 6*, Vanderbilt University, Nashville, Tennessee.

Threle, H. W. (1980). *Counselling Needs of University of Queensland External Students*, University of Queensland, Tertiary Education Institute, Brisbane.

Tinto, V. (1986). Theories of student departure revisited. In J. Smart (ed.), *Higher Education: Handbook of Research and Theory*, Vol. II, New York: Agathon Press.

Tollefson, N. (1987). A comparison of the item difficulty and item discrimination of multiple-choice items using the 'none of the above' and one correct response options. *Educational and Psychological Measurement*, **47**, (2), 377–83.

Topley, R. (1982). Lonergan and catechetics, *The Irish Catechist*, **6**, (3), 54–61.

Torrance, E. P. (1962). Non-test ways of identifying the creatively gifted. *Gifted Child Quarterly*, **6**, (3), 71–5.

Trabin, T. E., and D. J. Weiss (1983). The person response curve: fitness in individuals to item response theory models. In D. J. Weiss, *New Horizons in Testing*, New York: Academic Press.

Tracy, S., and E. Schuttenberg (1986). The desirable and the possible: four instructional models. *College Teaching*, **34**, (4), 155–60.

Trow, M. (1974). Problems in the transition from elite to mass higher education. In *Policies for Higher Education*, Paris: OECD.

Tussing, L. (1951). A consideration of the open book examination. *Educational and Psychological Measurement*, **11**, 597–602.

Tversky, A. (1964). On the number of alternatives of a choice point. *Journal of Mathematical Psychology*, **1**, 386–91.

Tyler, L. E. (1978). *Individuality: Human Possibilities and Personal Choice in the Psychological Development of Men and Women*, San Francisco, CA: Jossey-Bass.

Tyler, R. W. (1949). Achievement testing and curriculum construction. In E. G. Williamson (ed.), *Trends in Student Personnel Work*, Minneapolis: University of Minnesota.

US Office of Strategic Services (1948). *Assessment of Men*, New York: Rhinehart.

Vaughan, K. (1982). University first year general chemistry by the Keller plan (PSI). *Programmed Learning and Educational Technology*, **19**, (2), 125–34.

Vernon, P. (1965). *The Measurement of Human Abilities*, London: University of London Press.

Viertel, W. K. (1962). Letter in *Engineering Education*.

Vigotsky, L. S. (1962). *Thought and Language*, Cambridge, Mass.: MIT Press.

Wakeford, R. E., and S. Roberts (1984). Short answer questions in an undergraduate qualifying examination: a study of examiner variability. *Medical Education*, **18**, 168–73.

Walkden, F., and M. R. Scott (1980). Aspects of mathematical education. *International Journal of Mathematics Education for Science and Technology*, **11**, (1), 45–53.

Wallace, J. (1965). *Concept Growth and the Education of the Child*, Slough: National Foundation for Educational Research.

Walton, H. J. (1967). The measurement of medical student attitudes. *British Journal of Medical Education*, **1**, 225.

Wankowski, J. A. (1969). Some aspects of motivation in success and failure at university. *Report of the 1968 Annual Conference of SRHE*, Society for Research into Higher Education, London.

Wankowski, J. A. (1973). Disenchanted elite in motivation. *Report of the 1972 Annual Conference of SRHE*, Society for Research into Higher Education, London.

Warrington, E. K., M. James, and M. Hinsbourne (1966). Drawing disability in relation to laterality of cerebral lesion. *Brain*, **89**, 53–82.

Watkins, D. (1981). *Factors Influencing the Study Methods of Australian Tertiary Students*, Office for Research in Academic Methods, Australian National University, Canberra.

Watkins, D. (1982). Identifying the study process dimensions of Australian university students. *Australian Journal of Education*, **26**, (1), 76–85.

Watson, G., and E. Glaster (1964). *Critical Thinking Appraisal*, New York: Harcourt, Brace, Jovanovich.

Weiner, J. R. (1987). *National Directory. Assessment Progress and Projects (A Preliminary Prototype)*, American Association for Higher Education, Assessment Forum, Washington, DC.

Weinman, J. (1984). A modified essay question. Evaluation of pre-clinical teaching of communication skills. *Medical Education*, **18**, 164–7.

Weiss, D. J. (ed.) (1983). *New Horizons in Testing Latent Trait Theory and Computerized Adaptive Testing*, New York: Academic Press.

Weston, C., and Cranton, P. A. (1986). Selecting instructional strategies. *Journal of Higher Education*, **57**, (3), 259–88.

White, J. E. G. (1980). Trends in examinations and assessments in modern languages. *Assessment and Evaluation in Higher Education*, **6**, (1), 57–81.

White, M. (1985). *Teaching and Assessing Writing. Advances in Understanding, Evaluating and Improving Student Performance*, San Francisco: Jossey-Bass.

Whitehead, A. N. (1932). *The Aims of Education*, London: Benn.

Whitfield, P. R. (1975). *Creativity in Industry*, Harmondsworth: Penguin.

Whiting, J. (1982). Cognitive assessment and student attitude. *Assessment and Evaluation in Higher Education*, **7**, (1), 54–73.

Widick, C., L. Knefelkamp, and C. Parker (1975). The counselor as developmental instructor. *Counselor Education and Supervision*, **14**, 286–96.

Wieneke, C. (1979). *Attitude Change Among Minimun Time Graduates at the University of New South Wales*, Tertiary Education Research Centre, University of New South Wales, Australia.

Wigdor, A. K., and W. R. Garner (eds.) (1982). *Ability Testing: Uses, Consequences and Controversies*, Washington, DC: National Academic Press (two volumes).

Wigton, R. S. (1980). The effects of student personal characteristics on the evaluation of clinical performance. *Journal of Medical Education*, **55**, (5), 423–27.

Willingham, W. W. (1985). *Success in College: The Role of Personal Qualities and Academic Ability*, New York: College Entrance Examination Board.

Willmot, A. S., and D. E. Fowles (1974). *The Objective Interpretation of Test Performance*, Windsor: National Foundation for Educational Research.

Willmott, A. S., and D. L. Nuttall (1975). *The Reliability of Examinations at 16+*, Basingstoke: Macmillan.

Wilson, J. D. (1981). *Student Learning in Higher Education*, Beckenham: Croom Helm.

Wilson, J. M. (1981). The accuracy of A-Level predictions. *Assessment and Evaluation in Higher Education*, **6**, (1), 80–82.

Wilson, P. R. D. (1986). The forecasting of economics finals results—a case of *post hoc ergo propter hoc*. *Assessment and Evaluation in Higher Education*, **11**, (1) 28–42.

Wine, J. D. (1980). Cognitive attentional theory of test anxiety in I. G. Sarason (ed.) *Test Anxiety: Theory Research and Application*: Hillside, NJ: Lawrence Erlbaum.

Wine, J. D. (1982). Evaluation anxiety: A cognitive-attentional construct in H. W. Krohne and L. Laux (eds), *Achievement, Stress and Anxiety*, Washington: Hemisphere.

Winstead, P. C., and E. N. Hobson (1971). Institutional goals. Where to from here? *Journal of Higher Education*, **42**, (8).

Winter, D., D. McClelland, and A. Stewart (1981). *A New Case for Liberal Arts: Assessing Institutional Goals and Student Development*, San Francisco, CA: Jossey-Bass.

Winter, D., and D. McClelland (1987). Thematic analysis: an empirically derived measure of the effects of liberal arts education. *Journal of Educational Psychology*, **70**, 8–16.

Wiseman, S. (ed.) (1961). *Examinations and English Education*, Manchester: Manchester University Press.

Witkin, H. A. (1976). Cognitive styles in academic performance and in teacher–student relations. In S. Messick and Associates (eds), *Individuality in Learning*, San Francisco, CA: Jossey-Bass.

Witkin, H. A., C. A. Moore, P. K. Oltman, D. R. Goodenough, F. Friedman, and D. R. Owen (1977). *A Longitudinal Study of the Role of Cognitive Styles in Academic Evaluation in College Years*, GRE Research Report GREB 76–10 R, Princeton, NJ: Educational Testing Service.

Witkin, H. A., R. K. Oltman, E. Raskin, and S. A. Karp (1971). *A Manual for the Embedded Figures Tests*, Palo Alto, CA: Consulting Psychologists Press.

Witkin, H. A., and D. R. Goodenough (1981). *Cognitive Styles*, New York: International Universities Press.

Wittich, B. Von. (1972). The impact of pass-fail system upon the achievement of college students. *Journal of Higher Education*, **43**, 499.

Wolfe, L. M. (1985). Applications of causal models in higher education. In J. C. Smart (ed.), *Higher Education: Handbook of Theory and Research*, Vol. 1, New York: Agathon Press, pp. 381–413.

Wood, R. (1986). Agenda for educational measurement in Nuttall, D., (ed.) *Assessing Educational Achievement*, Lewes: Falmer.

Wood, R., and L. S. Skurnik (1969). *Item Banking*, Slough: National Foundation for Educational Research.

Wright, B. D., and M. H. Stone (1979). *Best Test Design: Rasch Measurement*, Chicago: Mesa.

Yang, J. (1985). An example of the application of a balanced incomplete block design. *Assessment and Evaluation in Higher Education*, **10**, (3), 250–53.

Youngman, M. B. (1980). A comparison of item-total point biserial correlation, Rasch and Alpha–beta item analysis procedures, *Educational and Psychological Measurement*, **40**.

Youngman, M. B., R. Oxtoby, J. D. Monk, and J. Heywood (1977). *Analysing Jobs*, Aldershot: Gower.

Zangwill, O. L. (1961). Asymmetry of cerebral hemisphere function. In H. Garland (ed.), *Scientific Aspects of Neurology*, London: E. and S. Livingstone.

Zoocolotti, P., and P. K. Oltman (1976). *Field Dependence and Lateralization of Verbal and Configurational Processing*, Princeton, NJ: Educational Testing Service.

Zuber-Skerritt, O. J., and N. Knight (1986). Problem definition and thesis writing: Workshops for postgraduate students. *Higher Education*, **15**, (1–2) 89–103.

Author Index

Subject Index

Ability, 347
Academic Appeals, 59
Accreditation, 13, 14, 347
Accrediting Agencies, 347
Achievement Test, 347
Admission (selection) to Higher Education,
    by estimates of general achievement, 59
    influence on school curricula, 7 ff, 38
    policies, 37 ff
Affective domain (*see* Moral development)
AH5 Intelligence test, 320
Aims (*see also* goals, objectives), 347
    failure to achieve in higher education, 118
    importance of, 106, 107
    of practical work in engineering science, 117
Alverno College, 19, 319
    competency based liberal education, 319 ff
    critical thinking project, 134 ff
    volunteer assessors, 73, 74
American Assembly of Collegiate Schools of Business, outcome measures project, 147, 148
American Association for Higher Education, 319, 345
American College Testing Program (ACT), 285
American Council on Education, 19
    Co-operative Institutional Research Program, 15
Anxiety (*see also* test anxiety), 76 ff
    and course structure, 81
    and curricular strategies, 90, 91
    and initial learning phase, 97
    and learning style, 81
    and need for clarity in objectives, 91
    and open-book examinations, 243

    and prior-notice examinations, 244, 245
    and relaxation, 97
    and training in coping skills, 81
    and transition from school to higher education, 98
    and *viva-voce* examinations, 255
Appraisal, 17, 347
Aptitude, 347
Aptitude Treatment Interaction, 319
Arithmetic Mean, 347
Assessment (*see also* examinations, objectives, performance, tests)
    and learning, 18, 21, 197, 317
    (*see also* learning and learning styles),
    and organizational structure, 319 ff
    as a resource, 224
    diagnostic interview (medicine), 252
    effect of overloaded syllabuses on, 235
    formative, 90
    in foreign language learning, 248
    meanings of, 2, 12 ff, 18
    objectives (of), 21, 235, 348
    of oral examinations, 250 ff
    of teachers by students, 16, 17
    philosophy (of), 332, 333
    student attitudes to, 15
    summative, 15, 90
    systems approach to design of, 20, 330, 331
    theory of, need for, 20
    threatening perceptions of, 235
    using in-basket techniques, 254
    using role playing, 252
    using simulations, 253
    value-added (as a measure of), 15
Assessment Center, 338, 339, 348
Assessment Center Technique, 147, 254
Assessment of Performance Unit (UK), 315

407

416

LIBRARY
ST. LOUIS COMMUNITY COLLEGE
AT FLORISSANT VALLEY